Things Worth Fighting For

ALSO BY MICHAEL KELLY

Martyrs' Day:
Chronicle of a Small War

Things Worth Fighting For

COLLECTED WRITINGS

◆ ◆ ◆

Michael Kelly

THE PENGUIN PRESS

NEW YORK

2004

THE PENGUIN PRESS
a member of
Penguin Group (USA) Inc.
375 Hudson Street,
New York, New York 10014

LIBRARY OF CONGRESS CATALOGING IN PUBLICATION DATA

Kelly, Michael, date.
Things worth fighting for : collected writings / Michael Kelly.
p.   cm.
Includes index.
ISBN 1-59420-012-2
I. Title
AC8.K375 2004
081—dc22   2003063204

This book is printed on acid-free paper. ∞

Printed in the United States of America
1   3   5   7   9   10   8   6   4   2

Designed by Stephanie Huntwork

For Tom and Jack
Beloved boys

Life goes on, and life is good.

MICHAEL KELLY, SEPTEMBER 20, 2001

CONTENTS

INTRODUCTION

I knew of, and admired, Michael Kelly long before I came to know him person-ally. Our first real meeting took place just before the start of the 2003 Iraq War, and for the next five weeks, as we covered that conflict, we enjoyed the chaste equivalent of a shipboard romance. We spent a lot of time together. In this kind of environment you can bond very quickly, and we did. Michael was a joy: funny, smart, and a wonderful companion.

By the standards of our everyday existence, life in the southern Iraqi desert was Spartan. We slept on the sand or in our vehicles. We tried to imagine buying a thousand dollars' worth of delicacies in some Kuwait City bazaar: food that would be portable and nonperishable in the heat. It gave us enormous, if some-what irrational, satisfaction to discover that the Meals Ready to Eat, issued to us by the military, were far better than anything we could have put together.

Michael and I laughed at similar things. When he was amused by something, which was often, he would emit something between a chuckle and a snort, as though he were simultaneously clearing his nose and his throat. Initially, it could be a little disconcerting, but it actually became rather endearing. If you told Michael a joke and it didn't elicit the snort, you soon came to understand that you had failed to meet an important standard. The punch line of a good joke, Michael felt, shouldn't broadcast its impending arrival. It should come as a sur-prise. In that sense, as Michael discovered and interpreted it, life was the perfect raconteur.

I have a photograph of Michael that was taken early one morning. He, jubilantly hoisting a folding chair to shoulder height, on his way to a discreet rendezvous behind a sand dune. Some creative infantryman had cut a toilet-size hole out of the seat and had lent the contraption to Michael. His rapture could not have been more complete.

Perhaps if we had known one another for five months or five years instead of merely five weeks, we would have argued or grown petulant over some trivial slight, as friends commonly do. We, though, were a couple of adrenaline addicts, rolling through the vast wilderness of the southern Iraqi desert, "embedded" with the command unit of the U.S. Army's Third Infantry Division. I was traveling with *Nightline*'s executive producer, Leroy Sievers; a camera crew; and an engineer. But Michael and I were the only two embedded reporters with the command unit, and as such we were granted extraordinary access and freedom of movement. We had free rein to listen in on the so-called commanders briefing early each morning or to linger, as Michael often did, through the night inside the command tent. He emerged, snorting with delight, from one such session. The intelligence officer, a lieutenant colonel, had refused to proceed with a briefing for Major General Buford Blount because Michael was present. General Blount told her to go ahead. That emboldened me to carry a video camera into the next session, with similar results. Michael and I couldn't get over it. We were at the center of the biggest story in the world, with total access and no competition.

Michael was gathering material for three extended pieces in the *Atlantic Monthly*. It would have required a minimal effort to convert those magazine pieces into a book. I, meanwhile, was broadcasting several times a day. We were in no competition with one another. We could trade tips and insights without concern. We liked each other a great deal. When we discovered that he was a Catholic married to a Jew and that I was a Jew married to a Catholic, it completed the symmetry of our relationship.

In Kuwait City the *Nightline* crew had rented a baby blue Land Rover (which they had repainted dun brown) and a puke yellow civilian Humvee. We drove our own vehicles into Iraq. Michael, meanwhile, traveled aboard one of the Third Infantry Division's Humvees, driven by a nineteen-year-old, whom Michael referred to only as Sergeant A. Sergeant A was, to Michael, the source of infinite wonder. The young infantryman could, and apparently did, talk for hours on end, and without repetition, about sex. He harbored bold, vivid, and imaginative sexual ambitions that he shared generously with his passenger. It was a lust, Michael reported, that did not extend to most of the female soldiers with whom

Sergeant A was, at that time, deployed in the Iraqi desert. These the sergeant dismissed contemptuously as unworthy of closer attention. The appropriateness of subject and language, as Michael appreciated, owes much to time, place, and context. The crudity of a young American soldier in combat tends to the extravagant. Michael, with an earthy sense of humor of his own, sometimes staggered under the weight of Sergeant A's obsessions of the flesh, but he also found them richly evocative, and some would almost certainly have found their way into his book.

This, as you certainly must know, is not that book. That book died with Michael on the outskirts of Baghdad. Some of what is left of that book is scrawled in pencil across the pages of several dozen writing tablets. These were so flimsily glued that the pages often came apart as soon as they were turned. But Michael had run out of decent notebooks before we even left Kuwait, and the tablets were the best he could find. He had reverted to using a pencil that he kept sharpened with a considerable hunting knife. The last of his ballpoint pens choked in the fine sand of the Kuwaiti desert. Michael had transcribed some of his notes onto a laptop, but he'd fallen badly behind. Anyway, the laptop remains buried under several feet of water in the mud of an irrigation canal, where Michael lost his life. Not that it would have made much of a difference. Michael kept fiendishly copious and illegible notes of whatever caught his attention at any given time of the day or night. Someone might have deciphered them, but they would then have needed to be cranked through Michael's memory, processed by his intelligence, and seasoned by his humor.

Good books can be an antidote to the banality of most war reporting and provide an irreplaceable context for even the best in daily journalism. Michael Herr's *Dispatches* was such a book for the war in Vietnam. Michael Kelly, whose *Martyrs' Day* played that role for the first Gulf War, would certainly have written another such book for the strange war that took U.S. forces into Baghdad with such brilliance and efficiency and subsequently metastasized into another war altogether. There had been a foreshadowing of that later crisis in some of the conversations that Michael and I had shared with senior military officers after we had made it through the Karbala Gap. We had asked about the nature and scope of postcombat planning. Both of us were left with the impression that the military was greatly frustrated by how little planning there had been.

Michael was planning to stay in Iraq to cover that phase of the story, at least into the summer. His wife, Max, had already made preliminary plans to take their two boys to their beach house and then to an August reunion at a safe location in the Middle East. The sacrifices that both Michael and I had imposed on our wives and children had been the subject of one long, late-night conversation in the desert. Many marriages in our profession don't survive the separations and the accumulated pressures of lengthy and dangerous assignments. We marveled at the enormous generosity and toughness of our wives and how fortunate we were in the freedom they had given us. There's never a truly equitable payback, but as we talked that night, I don't think it occurred to either of us that Michael might be denied even the opportunity to try.

I last saw Michael Kelly on the north bank of the Euphrates River. We had driven there together in the ABC Land Rover to get a last, quick briefing from General Blount before the division made its final drive on Baghdad. The objective, that night, was Saddam International Airport. Following our briefing, I dropped Michael at the encampment where we had spent the previous night. I drove off only to realize, about five miles up the road, that Michael had left his helmet on the front seat. I turned back, found Michael, told him what an absentminded asshole he was, and tossed him his helmet.

This book is a collection of some of Michael's best magazine pieces and newspaper columns. If you're unfamiliar with the work of Michael Kelly, it will introduce you to what you've missed. If you're an old fan, it will remind you of what we've lost.

Either way, if you pay attention, reading with your ears as well as your eyes, you will, at times, when the writer seems incapable of containing the mirth that bubbled up inside him, hear faint echoes of the snort.

TED KOPPEL

EDITOR'S FOREWORD

At the time of his tragic death, at age forty-six, Michael Kelly had already packed several lifetimes' worth of accomplishments and triumphs into a relatively short career. His membership in the fourth estate spanned two decades, but it was only during the last thirteen years of his life that he truly came into his own, producing a body of work that is remarkable for its diversity, incisiveness, wit, literary grace, and imperishability.

In the course of those thirteen years, Mike somehow managed to cover three wars and two presidential campaigns; to write laceratingly honest, state-of-the-art profiles of the seminal political figures of our time; to produce—as a reporter for the Washington bureau of the *New York Times,* as the sole staff writer of the *New York Times Magazine,* and then as the author of the prestigious "Letter from Washington" for the *New Yorker*—a string of penetrating campaign reports, compelling White House chronicles, and landmark cover stories that raised the level of political writing to literature; to author a wide-ranging, at times slashing, syndicated weekly column, first for the *New Republic* and then for the *Washington Post;* and at the same time, to be the editor of three successive magazines: the *New Republic, National Journal,* and most recently, the *Atlantic Monthly,* transforming that 147-year-old publication into a touchstone of vigorous, award-winning journalism. *All in thirteen years.* The articles and columns that appear in this book were written during that astonishing period of fecundity and journalistic adventurousness.

Mike's beat stretched from Capitol Hill to the concrete-and-sheet-metal headquarters of the Militia of Montana, from the battlefields of Iraq to the beaches of Cape May. Indeed, the sheer breadth of his reporting and writing became the guiding principle for this book's selections and organization. To capture Mike's expansive palette of subjects, genres, and styles, it seemed imperative to present not just the best and most memorable of his articles and columns but also the broadest possible mix. Thus the choice of pieces here, and their arrangement into five thematic sections, is intended to put on display not only Mike's wide spectrum of abiding interests and passions—politics, foreign affairs, war reporting, how we Americans live now, the adventures of his two young sons—but also the full panoply of his gifts: for physical description and scene-setting; for the satirical insight, the transformative detail, and the precise image.

He finds, for example, in Bill Clinton's ever-morphing smile a perfect symbol for the unsettling pliability of a president and his policies ("A Man Who Wants to Be Liked, and Is"). In the devastation of postwar Kuwait, he witnesses the U.S. Army Corps of Engineers' reinstalling gold bathroom fixtures in the looted palace of a Kuwaiti prince while people in the street go without food, water, and medicine—another observation elevated to powerful metaphor ("The Rape and Rescue of Kuwait City"). And he is there to capture the Keystone Kops scene—one that comically encapsulates the shaky rule of Yasir Arafat—when the Palestinian leader's security detail tries to emulate the American Secret Service ("Arafat Bombs on Opening Night"). "Mike had enviable eyes," Leon Wieseltier, the *New Republic*'s literary editor, has said. "He observed more in a glance than other reporters did in a week."

Voice is also a distinctive Kelly gift, another potent weapon in his literary arsenal. His prose can be softly lyrical, as in his columns chronicling family life (section V: Family Wealth), or it can be fiery, hectoring, even Old Testament wrathful, especially when it comes to the conduct of Bill Clinton (section III: The Age of Clinton). It can be gently ironic, as in an imaginary letter from Bush père to Bush fils over the selection of Dick Cheney as vice president ("But What About Dad?"), or it can be blisteringly caustic—turning "a Mencken-like blowtorch" (in the phrase of one *Boston Globe* reporter) on Washington insiders, knee-jerk liberals, the pseudo-hip, the pierced and tattooed, and sixties timewarp refugees. He can summon pure passion about the problems of black America ("A National Calamity") or, when the mood strikes, conjure a pitch-perfect parody that lays waste to the self-important (Robert Reich's book *Locked in the Cabinet,* in "The Reich Stuff") and the fake (Al Gore's dubious claims of an agrarian boyhood, in "Farmer Al"). Mike's voice was a musical instrument that he played in many different keys.

In retrospect, the magazine-profile form seems to have sparked the making of him as a writer. After a seven-year tour of duty as a newspaperman at the *Cincinnati Post* and the *Baltimore Sun,* he burst upon the national stage in the early 1990s, as a freelance writer for *GQ,* with profiles of two political mandarins, Ted Kennedy and Jesse Jackson (section II: The Game)—each of whom had been much written about over the years but never, it is safe to say, with such bold brushstrokes and unsparing intimacy. "Up close, the face is a shock," began Mike's unforgettably graphic word picture of Ted Kennedy's descent into alcohol, gluttony, and philandering ("Ted Kennedy on the Rocks"). "The skin has gone from red roses to gin blossoms. . . . The chiclet teeth are the color of old piano keys." Mike is equally sharp-edged in his assessment of Jackson, portrayed in "The Mid-life Crisis of Jesse Jackson" as a forlorn and increasingly irrelevant figure, consigned by his own voracious need for the camera and the reporter's notebook to the distant margins of real political power. In both these political icons, with their outsized gifts, ambitions, and flaws, Mike found early on one of his true subjects—a grand theme he would return to again and again for the remainder of his writing life: the complicated relationship between talent and character. In the feet of clay of Ted Kennedy and Jesse Jackson, Mike began to find his own literary footing.

The Persian Gulf War, in 1991, represented another key moment—perhaps even more crucial—in Mike's apotheosis as a writer. As prospects for war firmed, he managed to cadge assignments from several publications, most notably the *New Republic,* one of whose editors issued a challenge: "We'll use your stuff if you can be in Baghdad when the bombs drop." Mike hightailed it to the Middle East, borrowing $8,000 to cover travel costs, and, after securing an ordinary tourist visa in Jordan from the Iraqi embassy, arrived in Baghdad two weeks before the war started. At that point he was one of only a few Western journalists in the Iraqi capital. For those in the media, the Persian Gulf War was an altogether different experience from the Iraq War of 2003. In that earlier conflict, the Pentagon had clamped a hammerlock on firsthand reporting, barring all but a small number of pool reporters from access to the action. While most of his colleagues covered Operation Desert Storm from the safe remove of press briefing rooms in Saudi Arabia, Mike defied the Pentagon ban and went off on his own to report. "Doing a unilateral," the press corps called it.

Out of this act of journalistic independence came transcendence. Crisscrossing Iraq, Kuwait, and several other countries by rented and borrowed cars—once even hitching a ride on an Egyptian tank—Mike filed one electrifying dispatch after another (section IV: Wars and Peace), including "Before the Storm," in which he documents the hollow bravado of Iraqis waiting out the start of war in cafes, at the theater, and at the race track; "The Other Hell," a searing portrayal of the deplorable refugee camp in Iran where hordes of Kurds had been forced to flee after their abandonment by the Bush administration; and "Kiss of Victory," with its utterly bizarre, seriocomic scene, worthy of the movie *M*A*S*H,* in which ten Iraqi soldiers, retreating across the Kuwaiti desert, insisted on surrendering as prisoners of war to Mike and another reporter.

After Mike's death, while covering the 2003 Iraq War as an embedded reporter, a number of obituary writers saluted him for his "fearlessness." But although confident in his abilities to stay out of harm's way, he was very much in mind of, and concerned about, the inherent dangers. The quality that Mike aspired to was not fearlessness but bravery, which, as he told his sons, was doing the right thing in spite of your fears. In a 1997 column called "The Fear of Death" (section IV)—which paid homage to a small band of Bosnian resistance fighters and which now seems poignantly prophetic—Mike defined what was for him the quintessential test of character. "Accepting death is indispensable to defeating death," he wrote. "We [Americans] are a nation in which there are fewer and fewer people . . . who accept what every twelve-year-old [in Bosnia] knows: that there are things worth dying for."

Six years later, he elaborated on this theme in a radio interview he gave just before he died: "One of the things I found out [in the first Gulf War], which is quite interesting personally, is that people, at least men—I don't know about women—go to great lengths to not find out the answer to the question: how brave am I? War presents you with specific opportunities to find out the answer to that question—a question that is asked for you and answered for you, and in front of other people. It's interesting, because you see it in all the people around you and you see it in yourself. And that's knowledge that you have for the rest of your life."

Taken as a whole, the articles and columns in *Things Worth Fighting For* can be seen as both a portrait of our time and a self-portrait of its author. As the book's editor and as a longtime editor and friend of Mike's, I hope that many of the Michael Kelly qualities that have gone missing—the sparkling intellect, the irrepressible humor, the sixth sense for hypocrisy, the devotion to family and to fierce personal codes—will shine through, and live on, in these pages.

ROBERT VARE

I

◆ ◆ ◆

Visions
of America

King of Cool

◆ ◆ ◆

D o not blame it on the bossa nova. Nor on rock-and-roll nor soul nor jazz nor rhythm and blues. It wasn't Elvis or the Beatles or the Rolling Stones. It wasn't Washington or Hollywood or the Upper West Side. It wasn't Ted Kennedy and it wasn't Richard Nixon. It wasn't the Years of Rage or the Me Decade or the Decade of Greed. It wasn't the Commies or the Beats, or the hippies or the yippies, or the Panthers or the druggies, or the yuppies or the buppies, or the NIMBYs or the DINKs, or even the ACLU.

No, if you want to finger any one person, place, or thing for what went wrong with America, you need look no further than that accidental one man validation of the great-man theory of history, Francis Albert Sinatra, 1915–98. Yes—The Voice, the Chairman of the Board, Old Blue Eyes, the leader of the (rat) pack, the swinger in chief—he's the culprit. It's all Frankie's fault.

American popular culture—which is more and more the only culture America has, which is more and more the only culture everyone else in the world has (we live, as the gormless Al Gore keeps chirpily and horrifyingly reminding us, in a global village)—may be divided into two absolutely distinct ages: Before Frank and After Frank.

Sinatra, as every obit observed, was the first true modern pop idol, inspiring in the 1940s the sort of mass adulation that was to become a familiar phenomenon in the '50s and '60s. One man, strolling onto the set at precisely the right moment in the youth of the Entertainment Age, made himself the prototype of the age's essential figure: the iconic celebrity. The iconic celebrity is the result of the central confusion of the age, which is that people possessed of creative or artistic gifts are somehow teachers—role models—in matters of personal conduct. The iconic celebrity is idolized—and obsessively studied and massively imitated—not merely for the creation of art but for the creation of public self, for the confection of affect and biography that the artist projects onto the national screen.

And what Frank Sinatra projected was: cool. And here is where the damage was done. Frank invented cool, and everyone followed Frank, and everything has been going to hell ever since.

In America, B.F., there was no cool. There was smart (as in the smart set), and urbane, and sophisticated, and fast and hip; but these things were not the same as cool. The pre-Frank hip guy, the model of aesthetic and moral superiority to which men aspired, is the American male of the 1930s and 1940s. He is Humphrey Bogart in *The Big Sleep* or *Casablanca* or Archie Goodwin in Rex Stout's Nero Wolfe novels. He possesses an outward cynicism, but this is understood to be merely clothing; at his core, he is a square. He fights a lot, generally on the side of the underdog. He is willing to die for his beliefs, and his beliefs are, although he takes pains to hide it, old-fashioned. He believes in truth, justice, the American way, and love. He is on the side of the law, except when the law is crooked. He is not taken in by jingoism but he is himself a patriot; when there is a war, he goes to it. He is, after his fashion, a gentleman and, in a quite modern manner, a sexual egalitarian. He is forthright, contemptuous of dishonesty in all its forms, from posing to lying. He confronts his enemies openly and fairly, even if he might lose. He is honorable and virtuous, although he is properly suspicious of men who talk about honor and virtue. He may be world-weary, but he is not ironic.

The new cool man that Sinatra defined was a very different creature. Cool said the old values were for suckers. Cool was looking out for number one always. Cool didn't get mad; it got even. Cool didn't go to war: Saps went to war, and anyway, cool had no beliefs it was willing to die for. Cool never, ever, got in a fight it might lose; cool had friends who could take care of that sort of thing. Cool was a cad and boastful about it; in cool's philosophy, the lady was always a tramp, and to be treated accordingly. Cool was not on the side of the law; cool made its own laws. Cool was not knowing but still essentially idealistic; cool was nihilistic. Cool was not virtuous; it reveled in vice. Before cool, being good was still hip; after cool, only being bad was.

Quite a legacy. On the other hand, he sure could sing.

Girth of a Nation

◆ ◆ ◆

I have been for some days at the shore, in the company of many of my fellow middle-aged Americans who are wearing not a lot of clothes, and I have a report. My fellow middle-aged Americans, we are some kind of fat.

I don't mean we are getting a bit thick around the middle, or that we are pleasantly plump, or that we are zaftig, or Rubenesque (we are Reuben-esque), or settling into our bodies. I mean we are fat, fat, fat. It's true: As a people, we have never been this fat. Probably no people has ever been this fat. We are billowing immensities of avoirdupois, great, soft bins of finest quality lard, a nation of wide loads wallowing down the highway of life.

We have thighs that look like sacks of Parker House rolls. We have stomachs that can shelter entire kindergartens from the glare of the noonday sun. Our bottoms dwarf the seats of our poor suffering chairs as the mind of God dwarfs the mind of man. We do not walk; we shake, jiggle, and roll. We are Moby-Dick, the great white whale; we are Dumbo; we are countless refutations of the claim that no man is an island.

Also, we are some kind of ugly. We are men with Rudy Giuliani–quality hair who have convinced ourselves that the attractive solution to this is to drape the fourteen remaining strands on the left side of our domes over to the right side, while gathering the twenty-two remaining strands on the backside of our heads into the sort of ratty little ponytail once—ah, those were the days—favored only by aging record producers. We are men with lots of hair who have convinced ourselves that the ideal look is the mullet. The mullet is to a decent haircut as the leisure suit is to the suit; it renders the bearer not only ugly but somehow, stupid. It is impossible to look at a mullet head and think: There goes a sentient being.

We are pierced and we are tattooed to within an inch of all our available skin space, which is saying something (see paragraph two). We (men) walk around downtown with no shirts on, in the apparent bizarre belief that others enjoy viewing the mats of graying hair that cover our backs, necks, and watermelon-sized tum-tums. We (women) wear screaming pink Lycra stretch pants in sizes that run from one side of the boardwalk to the other: If you've got it, flaunt it; if you've got five times it, flaunt it in pink.

My fellow middle-aged Americans, let us admit a few salient truths. One: It is a nice thing to have an eighteen-year-old body and a nice thing for other people to be able to look at an eighteen-year-old body; so, when the owner of an eighteen-year-old body wears a minimum of clothing, this, too, is a nice thing. It adds to the general attractiveness of the world and the general happiness of humanity. But (and this is the critical point), we are no longer eighteen. With relatively few exceptions, we should ask ourselves if we might better serve our country by putting our clothes back on.

Two: Truly, nothing exceeds like excess. An earring—or two, or three— nicely complements the human form. Even a pierced navel, on the right body (again: eighteen) adds sex appeal. But oddly enough, adding on a staple through the tongue, a couple of ball studs in the upper lip and a troika of rings in the left nostril does not improve on this beginning. Similarly, with tattoos. A single but- terfly on a well-turned ankle is one thing; a torso-spanning butterfly garden is another. Remember, too, that in the due passage of time, things sag. Also, they wrinkle. Tattoos affixed to things that sag and wrinkle likewise sag and wrinkle. As the artist inks the image of your beloved across your back, stop and think that, years hence on the beach, you will resemble nothing so much as a man taking the picture of Dorian Gray for a walk.

And a few last reminders: A muffin the size of a softball is not breakfast. It is dessert; you are eating cake at eight A.M. Only wear a thong bathing suit if you can regard your nude self over your shoulder in a mirror and honestly say: The sight of my nearly fully exposed bottom is something most people would thank me for. Hawaiian shirts and Bermuda shorts are appropriate only in places where rum drinks are served in coconut shells. This does not include most churches.

Three Things I've Learned
Since Kindergarten

* * *

Share everything. Play fair. Don't hit people. Put things back where you found them. Clean up your own mess. Don't take things that aren't yours. Say you're sorry when you hurt somebody. Wash your hands before you eat. Flush.

—FROM *All I Really Need to Know I Learned in Kindergarten*
BY ROBERT FULGHUM

I am pretty sure Robert Fulghum and I went to different kindergartens. As most of us know, Mr. Fulghum is the author of several immensely popular how-to-live books: *Kindergarten* and a pair of sequels called *It Was on Fire When I Lay Down on It* and *Uh-Oh*. I did not actually read these books—that wouldn't be fair; they weren't built for that—but I did root through them, looking for the profound parts. It turned out there were no profound parts, but many silly ones.

Real books, at least the good ones, tell us what life is like. Often they are complicated and difficult, and usually they offer no solutions more magical than an injunction to do the best you can. The how-to-live books in vogue lately, by Fulghum, or John Bradshaw or M. Scott Peck, tell us what life should be like, or could be like, if we only tried harder, or paid more attention, or flew on gossamer wings in a buttermilk sky. The solutions they offer are as honest as a call girl's love. They are to real solutions as grilled cheese sandwiches and canned tomato soup are to real food: They are comfort philosophy.

But, of course, that is the very source of their charm. How satisfying to think, in a hideously complex world, that all our problems might be banished with just a dab more something or other—more love, or self-exploration, or vitamin C, or foot reflexology. Our streets may be full of thugs and our hospitals full of crack babies and our Congress full of crooks and ditherers, but we can still believe in the salving graces of pabulum.

Fulghum's basic idea is that the world is a special, special place. He reaches this through little parables that also demonstrate that he is a special, special person.

For instance, he tells us how he attached socks to himself with static electricity while he was doing the laundry. Bottled snow one winter and gave it to his neighbors the next Christmas. Saw a lady walk into a big spider's web and imagined it from the spider's point of view. Tasted Cheer detergent. (Fulghum usually doesn't bother with fussy old nouns and prepositions—he just starts sentences with verbs. Saves space. Makes his books shorter.)

Here is one of the things Fulghum writes: "Think what a better world it would be if we all—the whole world—had cookies and milk about three o'clock every afternoon and then lay down with our blankets for a nap."

And another: "Maybe we should develop a Crayola Bomb. And every time a crisis developed, we would launch one. . . . And people would smile and get a little funny look on their faces and cover the world with imagination."

It was after I read this last passage, and then noticed Saddam Hussein still staring at me from a nearby front page, that it struck me, pretty forcefully; that maybe it's about time Fulghum consider some stories with lessons for the post-kindergarten world. I myself have some that might be of relevance to him. He is welcome to use them in a new book, if he can think of a really cute title.

1. *Always be careful about what you say to a lady when you are naked.*

Once when I was naked, I nicely explained to the naked lady next to me that I thought it would be better if we did not see each other anymore. I talked to her for a long time. I said it was all my fault. I said I probably just did not know how to love. I said I was probably just real scared of commitment. Then I started to fall asleep, but suddenly my eyes opened and she was staring at me, really mean, like Nastassja Kinski in *Cat People*. I said, "What are you looking at me like that for?" She said, "I am waiting until you are sound asleep and then I am going to go to the kitchen and get the lighter fluid and set you on fire." I had to put my clothes on and go into the bathroom and lock the door and sleep in the tub.

This teaches us that sometimes in life, with some people, things just do not work out. And words will never, ever make them better.

2. *The answer to the question "Am I getting too fat?" is "No."*

I learned this from my older sister, Kate. She worried about her weight all the time when she was a teenager, even though she was not, in fact, overweight. But this was during the Twiggy era, so she asked me the fat question a lot. One time we were on a train between Providence, Rhode Island, and New York, and I answered yes. All of a sudden, Kate stood up in the aisle and started saying bad things about me in a very loud voice. She did this for a long time. I can still hear a lot of what she said, even after all these years, the way they say old soldiers feel their wounds when it's cold and damp.

This teaches us that mostly, no matter what they say, people do not want to hear the truth about themselves. Mostly what they want is to be made to feel better, and the truth doesn't always do that. What people want is something that only sounds like the truth.

3. *Never put a frozen glass eye in your socket.*

This is what my great-great-grandfather Richardson did. One cold winter night in New Orleans, after he had been out dancing, he plunked down his glass eye on a marble table beside his bed and by morning it had frozen, as much as a glass eye can freeze. He popped it in anyway. For some reason the coldness of the glass caused an infection. The infection spread from one socket to the other, and pretty soon my great-great-grandfather Richardson was blind in both eyes.

This teaches us that life is full of odd events from which one can learn nothing at all, and that some lessons—even beyond what you learn in kindergarten—aren't worth writing about.

Faux Commotion

◆ ◆ ◆

Here in weenie nation, we suffered through a terrible, frightening, awful, dangerous, very nearly deadly event last week: It snowed. Yes! Snowed! White stuff came down from the sky! Inches of it! It got all over everything! It was cold and wet and a person could slip and fall and hit his head and be knocked unconscious, and if his mouth fell open, as might very easily happen, it could fill up with snow and suffocate him before anyone noticed a thing! Flee! Flee!

And flee we did, to the grocery store for milk and bread and batteries and candles and toilet paper and diapers and family-size packages of potato chips and doughnuts; to the hardware store for rock salt and shovels, fire logs and more batteries; to the pharmacy for ibuprofen and cough syrup and a few final extra batteries.

Then we locked the doors, pulled shut the curtains and arranged ourselves under several layers of comforters, set our salt and sugar supplies close at hand, secreted our batteries in strategic caches throughout the house and watched the Weather Channel for three days straight. Miraculously, we did not die. We survived to flee again from whatever the next horror proves to be—rain, sleet, an unseasonably mild day with a breeze from the southeast.

We act as if weather were war. The boys and girls of the Weather Channel kept referring to the storm as "the Blitz," as in the Blitz of London, when the objects falling from the sky were incendiary bombs, not snowflakes. In New York, Mayor Rudy Giuliani hunkered down in what the Weather Channel people breathlessly called "The Bunker," as if he were Winston Churchill directing the desperate fight against the Nazis from his underground headquarters.

As a Washingtonian, I used to assume that weather hysteria was a peculiarity of the nation's capital, the result of living in a city overpopulated by people in the professional business of hysterical overreaction—politicians, tort lawyers, pundits, James Carville. But last year I moved to New England, and this winter I have been amazed to discover that the local response to snowfall here is the same as in Washington—flight, hoarding, and barricading. The local newscasts are filled with the same lunacy—the urgent bulletins from the Storm Center, the live interviews with bread-and-shovel buyers, the grim warnings: "The best advice we can give at this time is to stay in your homes. Don't go outside unless you absolutely have to."

Not to be rude about it, but why do we do this? When did we decide that the appropriate response to routine seasonal events of weather was sheer gibbering panic?

I guess the answer is that we decided to panic when panic became affordable. For most people, and for most of history, weather really was scary. If you lived in an uninsulated house heated only by a wood fire, and if you depended on your feet for transportation or, at best, on a horse and cart, and if what you had to eat was whatever was at hand, then a serious winter storm deserved your considerable respect. We live now with weather forecasting systems that are far more accurate than ever before, with central heat, with an SUV in every garage and nachos in every freezer. In this world, a storm is the occasion for a bit of shared faux excitement, as if we are all watching the same slasher flick, or the Super Bowl. It's not crisis that Storm Center 5 is showing, but the enjoyable shared ritual of pretend crisis.

Our other national weather, our politics, is also increasingly informed by the shared fun of pretend crisis. We are the fattest, safest people in the world. All of the aircraft supercarrier groups on earth belong to us. We have so much money that we are able to support a national chain of stores that sells coffee at prices approaching $5 per cup.

So we can afford the luxury of our crises: the Crisis of Our Schools, the Social Security Crisis, the Health Care Crisis, the Crisis of Our Children Smoking
Cigarettes, the Crisis of Urban Sprawl. We especially enjoy a nice Constitutional
Crisis; the past two years gave us two whoppers in that line—the impeachment
of a president, and the closest thing to a breakdown in the orderly transfer of
presidential power that has been seen in this century. We quite liked them both.
It's nice to have crises when you don't really have them. Gives us something to
talk about besides the weather.

Good Riddance
to the "New Man"
◆ ◆ ◆

But no event has so reorganized my priorities as the birth of our twin sons seven
months ago. . . . The rare moments they allow for reflection between feedings
and changing of diapers . . . are as close as I have yet come to an epiphany.

—"ABOUT MEN" COLUMN IN THE *New York Times Magazine,* NOVEMBER 6, 1983

I've been tinkering around the house ever since my father taught me to take
apart a window and make the pulleys work again—a sort of domestic epiphany.

—"ABOUT MEN," JULY 21, 1985

The score goes to 3–0, then to 5–0, then on to 8–0. . . . As the score piles up
in my friend Bruce's favor, I feel . . . the liberating flash of near-epiphany.

—"ABOUT MEN," MARCH 6, 1988

No one has ever called me "sir" on a basketball court before. . . . I experience
a minor epiphany.

—"ABOUT MEN," FEBRUARY 4, 1990

I sometimes imagine the ultimate "About Men" column, the widely read
Times feature that celebrates the New, or Sensitive, Man. It opens in a hospital room on an evening in April, the cruelest month. In a bed, limply, lies a man
who has collapsed on a busy street, struck by a fairly major epiphany.

He shows promise of a full recovery—until his father turns up. As the emotionally crippled older man stands by in mute despair, unable to verbalize his true feelings, the son suffers a second, more serious, epiphany.

Incredibly, he rallies again. But at this critical moment his son from his first marriage, whom he has not seen in the decade since the child's mother divorced him on grounds of irreconcilable similarities, arrives at his bedside. He looks at his son with misty eyes. Ditto, the son at him. "I love you, Dad," says the boy. "I lo—I, uh—I love . . ." he begins, then stops, unable to say it. As he realizes that he is, in the end, *the same man as his father*—the final, terminal epiphany racks his shuddering frame.

It has been seven years since the *New York Times* first foisted upon New Yorkers—and, via the *Times* syndicate, readers throughout the nation—the "About Men" column, its Jonathan-come-lately answer to all that stuff that happened about and between men and women in the 1970s that the paper of record missed because it was busy with the first rough draft of the sixties. That's seven years and a lot of epiphanies under the bridge.

The *Times* carefully keeps the New Man in his place, and a dismal place it is. While the Old, or Real, Man still lives in the news, sports, and business pages, "About Men" evokes the sneezy dustiness of the mausoleum, like saying "swinger" or "bra burner" or "white liberal." Reading it every other week is like finding yourself at a wake at which, for some insane reason, everyone is pretending that the fellow propped up in the open coffin, with a wineglass slipping from his hand, is not really quite dead.

What "About Men" is actually about is the business (and a lucrative business it has been) of fraud. Specifically, the fraud of the New Man, posturing in front of women as a sensitive-caring-feeling-person-in-touch-with-his-own-emotions. All frauds have their natural life span, and this particular one has been, as I say, dead for some time now, but it seems to be having a hard time getting buried. Consider this an obituary.

I remember catching the New Man fraud in a moment years ago, when it was young and fine, and thought, as all fine young frauds do, that it would one day grow up to be president. I was walking along Central Park South on a fine spring day, hustling along with lots of other pedestrians, including Phil Donahue and his wife, Marlo Thomas. Everyone else was looking fixedly ahead, the way New Yorkers do. Seeing all the people not seeing him, Mr. Donahue got a little frown on his face. A moue, I think the fellows at the *Times* would call it. Then, with a twinkle in his eye and a boyish smile on his face, he suddenly grabbed a handy signpost and twirled himself high up in the air. He clicked his heels. Gosh, to be alive! And all the people of course looked at him. And Ms. Thomas looked at

him, too. And as he came to earth, she rolled her eyes at the heavens in the manner of every woman who has ever felt the keen desire to strangle her jerk of a
man. I like to think the moment was a pretty good-sized epiphany for her.

As the moment with Mr. Donohue illustrates, the posture of the New Man
is a calculated thing, and not an attractive one. It is the half-cunning modern seducer's notion of what he thinks women really want to hear (but he is wrong). It
is the voice of faked emotion and false confession; the cheap and tinny sound of
a sinner crying out ersatz failings—not because he really thinks they *are* failings,
but because admission of wrongdoing is required for expiation.

Let us look again at "About Men," the country's greatest continuing forum
for the exposition of New Manisms. The *Times* has run more than three hundred
"About Men" essays since the column's inauguration in June 1983. Each column
is, as the premier one explained, devoted to "male-related topics of interest to
both sexes." What are male-related topics of interest to both sexes? Mostly, as it
turns out, they are topics that explore the general inferiority of men and the
willingness of the specific (male) author to admit that inferiority, making him superior after all.

The language of "About Men," like that of students in a Chinese reeducation
camp, is limited to the permissible, and the permissible covers just three wearily
self-conscious topics: (1) inadequacies—those of one's own, one's father, and
one's sex; (2) explorations of unmanly emotion; and (3) discoveries of a higher
self through admissions of one's baseness. In ninety-four columns, "About Men"
authors have had "feelings"; forty times, those feelings have reduced them to tears.
They are regularly "vulnerable" (eight mentions) and "weak" (nine). Their lives
are filled with tests of their "manhood" (twenty-three columns) and their "masculinity" (nine), which they mostly fail. Sometimes they rise above their failings
to know "intimacy" (twenty-four emotion-choked mentions), but more often
they are "awkward" with women and other men (thirteen) and lapse into "silence" (twenty-eight) of various kinds, including discreet, embarrassed, hostile,
virtual, thick, long, tense, and interminable.

And these are the good times. "About Men" men have many, many bad
times. They are preoccupied with occasions of "loss" (thirty-six) and "crisis"
(twelve) and "loneliness" (fifteen). Over all hangs the shadow of death, which
takes many forms, including the death of a father, of a son, of an army buddy in
Korea and another in Vietnam, of friends and total strangers, of John F. Kennedy,
and of sexual desire.

Beyond its obvious calculated effect, why is all this a fraud? (Some show
confessions are, after all, real.) There are two reasons to cry humbug, and they

are found in the two essential lies that form the foundation of all New Man thinking.

One: that men are about themselves, as women are about themselves—sensitive, emotional, and given to sudden, somewhat overwrought, reflection. We aren't, excepting poets. And real poets are rarer even than real New Men. The truth is, it takes an awful lot to force a moment of profound self-reflection through the mind of a man. Sometimes, but by no means always, marriage, birth, or death will do it. Most lesser events generate in the minds of most men something that may strike them as a nice little bit of thinking (especially if they've had a few drinks), but which is likely to strike everyone else as an old, familiar song. It is not that men don't feel things. We do. We are prone to despair, and loneliness and weakness and fear and all the rest of it. But those feelings are not triggered nearly so often, nor so conveniently, nor so casually, nor so movingly, as New Man writers pretend.

Epiphanies are extremely rare in the life of a man, and even when we get them, they're usually something that most women really wouldn't see what the big deal was about anyway. I remember my first epiphany. I was thirteen years old, walking my hard-on to school one day and ogling female passersby, when it struck me that *every single one of those females had a vagina.* All of them. Young, old, fat, skinny, black, white. Underneath their clothes every one of them had one. The thought literally stopped me in my tracks, and it remained lodged in a prominent place in my mind for about fifteen years.

Two: that having these deep thoughts about themselves, men yearn to share them with their fellow men. We don't. We are willing to do this with some women, sometimes, because we have learned that women seem to like this and reward us for doing it, sometimes even to the point of taking off their pants. When we're left to ourselves, about the only thing we would rather less do than share our deep emotions with another man is hear his.

A friend says that conversation in which one man shares with another man his deepest feelings is basically limited to variations on two thoughts: "That asshole" and "Fuckin' A."

For example:

FIRST MAN: I was thinking about my old man yesterday (brief pause to watch the first 200 miles of the Indianapolis 500 and drink five beers). That asshole.

SECOND MAN (after watching the next 200 miles of the Indy 500 and drinking three more beers): Fuckin' A.

FIRST MAN (having watched the final 100 miles and victory lap): Did you
    just call my father an asshole?

In the end, what is most extraordinary about New Manism is that everyone
knows it's a fraud. I don't know any New Men. I don't know any women who
know any New Men. I don't even know any women who *want* to know New
Men. The desire of women to understand the innermost workings of men is
mostly limited to the small degree of knowledge necessary to fathom one particular man and anyway it rarely rises above a need to confirm what was already suspected. This is why women's magazines are filled not with one damned thing
after another, but with the same damned thing over and over again.

So why are we still playing at this tired charade, embarrassing ourselves and
not fooling anybody? Beats me. Beats you, too? Fuckin' A.

The Road to Paranoia

◆ ◆ ◆

In a way, what has happened to the country is all about what has happened to
Bob Fletcher, and that seems odd when you meet him, because Fletcher is a
man of no obvious consequence at all. He is of intermediate size and age—a little below average height, a little above middle years. He has a roundish pink face,
brown hair that is beginning to go gray, and a small, pointed beard. He is faintly
but honorably seedy, in the way of a man who has been broke for a long time but
is still trying to keep up appearances. Wearing a dark blue suit that is shiny with
age and a light blue shirt that has become vaguely, permanently gray, he looks
like someone who occasionally dresses out of his car; the rear seat of his old
Volkswagen Beetle is filled with clothes.

Fletcher is a conspiracist. He is alive with conspiracies. They *whirr* in his mind
and welter in his heart, and they fill him so full of outrage and nervousness that
he cannot ever stay still. When he is on a roll—into the business of the New
World Order and the black helicopters and the Hong Kong police and the mi-
crochips that they put under your skin in the hospital and the secret program to
turn the weather into a weapon to kill us all—he gets so wound up he nearly
bounces off himself. Even when Fletcher is not up on his feet talking—even

when he is sitting—he is in motion, his legs jigging up and down, his knees bouncing in jittery counterpoise to each other, his little feet tap, tap, tapping on the floor, his soft, pale hand trembling in the violence of his agitation and the excitement of his nerves, as he holds out this piece of paper, and that one, and the next, and the next, and the next—the hodgepodge of documents and photographs that Fletcher believes are the proof that the government of the United States is part of a monstrous plot to destroy the United States, and Fletcher.

"Oh, they been planning this for years, for years," he was ranting one night a month ago in the bar at the Hereford Restaurant, near Noxon, Montana. "They built a bomb during the Gulf War that they are planning to use in a big way. The Wackenhut people—they own all the prisons in Australia—build seventy, eighty percent of the prisons in this country. They're *deep* into the New World Order, the sons of bitches. It's called a fuel-air bomb, and the way it works is you drop the thing and it explodes, sends out this spray of vapor—you know, tiny droplets in the air—and then, just a second or two after that, while the stuff is still in the air, a second bomb explodes: *boom!* And the thing is, if you have breathed in during those one or two seconds, well, when the second bomb explodes, it not only ignites the vapor in the air, it ignites the vapor in *you,* see, so you explode inside *and* out. *Boom!* Vaporized! You just freaking disappear! And that's what happened during the Gulf War, my intelligence sources told me, to two hundred thousand Iraqi soldiers. You remember those videos they showed every day? You saw all those Iraqi vehicles on the road? You never saw a damned body. Why? 'Cause they freaking vaporized them is why. Oh, just a little experiment, folks. Just George Bush's little New World Order experiment. Two hundred thousand. What the hell, they were only freaking Iraqis, right?"

Fletcher is a member of a small but showy political organization called the Militia of Montana. MOM, as it is commonly known, is a leader in the American militia movement, which has established groups in at least thirty-nine states. The leadership of MOM consists of a retired maker of snowmobile parts named John Trochmann; Trochmann's wife, Carolyn; his brother David; David's son, Randy; and Fletcher. In this little group, Fletcher's role is twofold: He is MOM's main "investigative researcher," and its frequent spokesman, particularly when it comes to television, because his unexceptional mien is less unnerving than the hairy, glaring, Old Testament face of John Trochmann. Being MOM's flack was a limited job until April 19 [1995], the day a 4,800-pound bomb, apparently made of ammonium nitrate and fuel oil, exploded at the Alfred P. Murrah Federal Building in Oklahoma City, killing 167 people. Investigators, after a brief false start in pursuit of the usual Middle Eastern suspects, arrested a former army enlisted man, Timothy J. McVeigh, and, three weeks later, McVeigh's friend Terry Lynn Nichols. The suspected terrorists were believed to be in philosophical accord with and perhaps inspired by the militia movement. The Militia of Montana became suddenly semifamous. And for a little while Bob Fletcher became what he had for a long time desperately wanted to be—a man to whom attention was paid.

I met Fletcher a week after the bombing, at the Landmark Café, on the main and nearly the only street in Noxon. By then, he had given more than forty interviews. He was sitting in the back corner booth and working over two young women—a television reporter from Missoula and her camera operator. He was running them through MOM's sacred text, "The Blue Book," which is also the name of the John Birch Society's 1958 classic of global-government conspiracism. The "Blue Book" theory, which was embraced by the Birchers and has now been adopted by MOM, is a variation on what might be regarded as the mother theory of conspiracism. According to this elaborate construct, whose genesis dates from the late eighteenth century, and which was most famously explained by the British writer and fascist Nesta Webster in a 1924 book, *Secret Societies and Subversive Movements,* the course of history has been shaped by a conspiracy, rooted in the occult religions of the pre-Christian era, which seeks to destroy the established Christian order of Western nations and to replace it with an atheistic, socialistic global government. In its most rococo version, the New World Order theory holds that the conspirators have been at it for more than two thousand years, perpetuating their plots through a succession of secret and semi-secret societies arcing across time and cultures from the early-Christian-era Gnostics and the Jewish Cabalists, and on to the Knights Templars of the twelfth century, the Rosicrucians of the fifteenth, the Bavarian Illuminati of the eighteenth, and from there, through the Freemasons, to the schemers of the twentieth—the Council of Foreign Relations, the Bilderbergers, and the Trilateral Commission. Along the way, step by step toward one-worldism, the plotters have caused everything from the French and Russian revolutions to the creation of the Federal Reserve, the United Nations, and the Gulf War.

The John Birch Society often gives away its "Blue Book"; MOM charges seventy-five dollars for its version and advertises it in the militia's own mail-order catalog, which goes out to tens of thousands of people around the country. The catalog boasts that "The Blue Book" contains "the enemy's own words" and "The Documentation," and promises, "When we take someone on a trip through 'The Blue Book' they cannot argue—*all they can do is say we are right or they just simply RUN AWAY!!!*"

In truth, the documentation is somewhat spotty. "The Blue Book" is an ordinary three-ring binder to which Randy Trochmann is always busily adding what he regards as further evidence of conspiracy, so that it bulges like an eccentric lawyer's briefcase with scraps of this and that, from here and there, which purport to show that the globalists' scheme—to subvert American sovereignty and reduce American citizens to vassalage—is in its final hours. The takeover will be executed by an occupation army, under United Nations command and composed of foreign troops, National Guard members, and inner-city gangs, which is hidden in national forests and is awaiting the order to spring forth. Exhibits in "The Blue Book" include a newspaper photograph of a depot yard in Mississippi full of old Soviet-bloc troop trucks; a 1994 United Nations development report replete with utopian blather about global government; a copy of a big color photograph that purports to show a Russian missile on its launcher in Texas; a similar photograph showing a U.S. Army helicopter that appears to be painted black; and, of all things, a photocopy of an illustrated map of America taken from the back of a 1993 Kix cereal box. The map shows the country divided into eleven regions, with Montana in the Mountain region, between the Pacific Coast and the Heartland. This, MOM maintains, is a representation of the New World Order plan for dividing the United States into regional departments after the invaders emerge to take over the country, which is scheduled to happen any day now. Why the conspirators have chosen to publicize their intentions on the back of a cereal box is not clear.

Fletcher is originally from New Jersey, and when he is working hard at the difficult job of selling the threat of the imminent conquest of America he tends to sound like a Secaucus saloon debater. "Russian missiles! Russian trucks! Russian armored personnel carriers! On American soil!" he whooped at the carefully blank-faced TV newswomen. "What's wrong with *that* picture? Huh? What in the freaking hell is *that* all about? Meanwhile, they're dumping three thousand U.S. tanks into the ocean so we can't defend ourselves. What kind of sense does *that* make, sports fans?"

Fletcher harangued the women for an hour, and by the time he slammed "The Blue Book" shut they were sitting silent and still, apparently stunned, as if each had been blackjacked lightly upside the head. This is a common response to a Fletcher performance, and it fills Fletcher with a craftsman's pride, as I found when I followed him outside the Landmark Café and introduced myself. "You see those girls?" he said to me. "Hah! I destroyed them. *Destroyed* them! I *Fletcher-ized* them! After I got through with them, they had to look at their drivers' licenses to see who the hell they were!"

We were standing on the concrete porch in front of the Landmark, Fletcher smoking and talking, doing both things in the same hyper, jangly way, in the bright, cool, late-morning sun. I asked Fletcher how he had ended up in Noxon, a tiny town in the northwestern corner of the state, and also how he had ended up a believer in "The Blue Book."

"Basically, I'm the same as everybody else in this country," he said. "I got into this because I got screwed, big time, by my government. It's a long story."

I said I'd like to hear it, and that seemed to please Fletcher. He drew on his cigarette in fast, sharp little puffs, then stepped closer to me, so that his nose was only a few inches from mine.

"Listen, I'm gonna tell you something," he said. "I got a story I haven't given to any of the other reporters, but you might be interested. The story of my whole life, the amazing story of how I came to be involved in all this. It's an amazing goddam freaking story, I'm not bullshitting you. I haven't even finished my autobiography—it's seven hundred and fifty-eight pages, or something like that, long already—and already I been asked by the Disney people about it. They want to make a movie of my life. Well, I can't blame them. When you hear my story you will be amazed. *Amazed*. It's an amazing story. To put it as simply as I can, let me just say this: There probably isn't a single major thing that has happened in the last ten years that I haven't been right in the middle of: Iran-Contra, Ollie North, October Surprise—all of it, all of it. Christ, the bullshit I've seen! Curl your freaking hair."

I. US VERSUS THEM

The reason the story of Bob Fletcher's life is of interest to others besides students of the fringe begins with the fact that Fletcher is not all that unusual. He is a stranger *of* a strange land, warped not against his culture but by it, and the curve of his warp follows the curve of the culture; it is only steeper and continues further, off the edge of the graph. What Fletcher believes is nothing but an extreme manifestation of views that have long been shared by both the far Right and the far Left, and that in recent years have come together, in a weird meeting of the minds, to become one, and to permeate the mainstream of American politics and popular culture. You could call it fusion paranoia.

Although fusion paranoia draws from, and plays to, the Left and the Right, it rejects that bipolar model for a more primal polarity: Us versus Them. In this construct, the Us are the American people and the Them are the people who control the people—an elite comprising the forces of the state, the money-political-legal class, and the producers of news and entertainment in the mass media. From this fundamental assumption, fusion paranoia builds to an array of related beliefs: that the governing elite tells lies as a matter of course; that it is controlled by people acting in concert against the common good and at the bidding of powerful interests working behind the scenes; and that it routinely commits acts of appalling treachery.

What the historian Richard Hofstadter called "the paranoid style" has always been strong in American culture. But what is happening now is, in a large way, new. To understand why, it helps to define more particularly the American model of political paranoia. The American model, in contrast to its European antecedents, has never been primarily about conspiracies of race or religion or class but rather, about the betrayal of the central faith and promise of America—the ideal of democracy. What American political paranoia posits is that sinister, antidemocratic forces have wormed their way into the inner workings of the government and have subverted it to serve not the interests of the nation but those of a powerful few—have turned the instrument of the people against the people. This fearful idea has animated American political movements ranging in diversity from the Antimasons, organized in the 1820s in opposition to a presumed Freemason conspiracy, and the anti-Catholic, anti-immigrant Know-Nothings of the mid-nineteenth century, to the Populists of the late nineteenth century, the American Communist Party of the 1920s and '30s, and the anti-Communist McCarthyism of the early 1950s.

But the conspiracist appeal was always limited. Apart from the Populists, whose radical democratic ideas outlived the party, the other movements came to little. The Antimasons were born into this world in 1826 and had passed from it by the late 1830s. The Know-Nothings lasted only a decade, and enjoyed just three or four years of real popularity. Huey Long's Share-the-Wealth movement and Father Coughlin's National Union for Social Justice were serious forces for less than five years during the Great Depression. When Hofstadter wrote, in 1964, he could accurately say that in this country (as opposed to Fascist Germany or Communist Russia) "the paranoid style is the preferred style only of *minority* movements."

Since then, however, the paranoid style has been (to extend Hofstadter's psychological interpretation) internalized. In its extreme form, paranoia is still the province of minority movements, but the ethos of minority movements—anti-establishmentarian protest, the politics of rage—has become so deeply ingrained in the larger political culture that the paranoid style has become the cohering idea of a broad coalition plurality that draws adherents from every point on the political spectrum: a coalition of fusion paranoia. For one reason or another, and to one degree or another, the paranoid view of government and of government's allies has become received wisdom for many millions of Americans.

At its broadest level, fusion paranoia is entirely rational. There is a governing elite. Its interests and values are often radically different from those of the ordinary citizens, and this elite does indeed work to advance those interests and values in antidemocratic fashion. Four years ago, the Kettering Foundation, which studies government and public policy, explored the reasons that Americans had become disgusted with politics. It would be hard to quarrel with the realistic vision of politics articulated by the voters interviewed. "People talk as though our political system had been taken over by alien beings," Kettering's president, David Mathews, wrote. "Many Americans do not believe they are living in a democracy now! . . . They don't believe that the average citizen even influences, much less rules. . . . They point their fingers at politicians, at powerful lobbyists, and—this came as a surprise—at people in the media. They see these three groups as a political class, the rulers of an oligarchy that has replaced democracy."

This widespread perception is the source of the bipartisan rejection of the governing class that has been the hallmark of the politics of the 1990s. Its apotheosis was the 1994 elections, which saw the repudiation of a national Democratic power structure that had been in place for generations and the rise of a popular movement toward smaller, weaker central government. What distinguishes this legitimate view of reality from the surrealism of Fletcher's New World Order is only a matter of degree. Where the realists see tacit collusion among members of the governing elite, the radicals see flagrant, treasonous plots. But the root of the paranoia—the belief that government isn't working in the interests of the people—is the same, and it is on that common ground that populism and conspiracism, healthy mistrust and crackpotism, meet. You can hear this distant echo of sanity in the voice of one small madman of the people, as Fletcher lectures an audience of one, his soliloquy loud and tinny against the strong silence of Noxon on a Sunday afternoon.

"They call us radicals," Fletcher said. "How come they don't call Bill Clinton a freaking radical for passing an executive order to steal twenty-one billion dollars from the American people, telling their Senate and Congress to go to hell, and sending it to his Mexican banking friends? . . . We don't want to hear about Left and Right, conservative and liberal, all these bullshit labels. Let's get back to the idea of good guys and bad guys, righteous government—the honest, fair, proper, American government that all of us have been fooled into believing was being maintained."

Fletcher's conviction that the Right and the Left must converge to fight their common enemy—the governing elite—is the guiding philosophy of the rapidly growing alternative media that traffic in conspiracism. Here, the conspiracists put aside their ideological differences and meet in paranoia.

Literally, they meet in *Paranoia,* the magazine. They also meet in such publications as *Flatland, Spotlight, The New Federalist, NEWSPEAK, KattaZzzine, Steamshovel Press, Nexus, Crash Collusion, Behind the Barricades, Conspiracy Update, The Probe, The Eye, Incite Information, Extraphile, Flashpoint, Trajectories;* in publishing houses such as IllumiNet Press, III Publishing, Victoria House, S.P.I. Books, Aries Rising Press, Feral House; in the bookstores-by-mail of America West, Flatland Books, and the Ruling Class/Conspiracy Research Resource Center; in computer databases such as CIABASE and NameBase; on the Internet in the news-groups alt.CIA and alt.conspiracy.

Some of these entities are old and established, and represent an identifiable ideological point of view; some of them are on the extreme edge of paranoia, while others are more or less sober in content and tone. But most of them are only a few years old—upstarts of the information highway—and the most interesting of them are radical and explicitly fusion-oriented, rejecting the Right-Left dichotomy. Three on the cutting edge—and a strange place that is—are *Paranoia, Flatland,* and *Steamshovel Press.* These magazines are essentially of the Left, but they publish and advertise much of what the Right has to offer, too, as long as it is conspiracist, radical, and antigovernment. They present the world according to Noam Chomsky and Jerry Rubin and Timothy Leary and Oliver Stone and William Burroughs and Ramsey Clark and Allen Ginsberg. They also present the world according to the John Birch Society and Lyndon LaRouche and Nesta Webster and the Holocaust revisionist Eustace Mullins and retired Lieutenant Colonel James (Bo) Gritz, the far-right conspiracist-populist-survivalist of Almost Heaven, Idaho.

In this world of pure fusion paranoia, the Jonestown massacre is linked to the murder of Martin Luther King Jr., Woodstock never happened (it was faked by the media); J. Edgar Hoover set up Teddy Kennedy at Chappaquiddick; government agents are brainwashing Americans through drugs and mesmeric techniques; Dan Rather's "Kenneth, what's the frequency?" mugging is traced back to the CBS News anchor's "extremely curious behavior in Dallas, Texas, on November 22, 1963"; Newt Gingrich is a secret Rockefeller Republican; AIDS is a government plot to kill off blacks and homosexuals; and the environmental movement masks a plot by the Rothschilds to gain control over all the land on the planet.

There is no Left and no Right here, only unanimity of belief in the boundless, cabalistic evil of the government and its allies. In a characteristic *Paranoia* article, the writer Mark Westion argues a New World Order theory quite similar to that of the rightist militia movement—a "shadow government" operating behind the scenes, George Bush and Bill Clinton as puppet presidents, the Gulf War as a vast scam to enrich the Bush family—except that Westion is coming at the subject from the vantage point of hippie nostalgia, an attitude not ordinarily associated with the militias. In Westion's theory, the government not only intentionally killed the Branch Davidians and shot up the family of the white supremacist Randy Weaver in Idaho but it also orchestrated the 1970 Kent State shootings, built up the Latin-American cocaine cartels, and introduced disco—all for the purpose of ending the Age of Aquarius.

Chip Berlet, a writer for Political Research Associates, in Cambridge, Massachusetts, has extensively researched what he calls the "ideological cross-fertilization" among groups and activists on the far Right and the far Left. Berlet's work, published in a monograph and several articles, has portrayed a complex and growing network of alliances between right-wing and left-wing activists and groups, who border on respectability and attract media attention. Among the connections: The left-leaning conspiracist and attorney Mark Lane has represented the extreme-right Liberty Lobby; the rightist LaRouche operation participated in a leftist demonstration against the Gulf War.

Consider also the two most sharply opposed camps on environmental issues. On one edge of the divide, most visibly represented by the antigovernment "Wise Use" movement, anger over environmental policies that limit land use has hardened into full-blown paranoia. The Sahara Club USA, an anti-environmentalist group based in Baja California, represents the epitome of this view. The club's philosophy, reflected in its newsletter, begins with the premise that government officials, paid-off politicians, and the national press are involved in a conspiracy comprising "New Age nuts, militant vegetarians, anti-gun pukes, animal rights goofballs, tree worshippers, new world order pushers, human haters, pro-socialists, doom-sayers, homosexual rights activists, radical eco-Nazis, slobbering political correctness advocates, militant feminists and land closure fascists." According to the Sahara Club, all the elements of this conspiracy—including the government officials—should be treated as "the enemy."

On the other edge, radical environmentalists see the same corrupt conspiracy as the Wise Users, but in a mirror image. For them, the governing elite (even the governing elite of environmentalism) exists to serve the interests of the land-raping corporations that support the major political parties. "Once revered and feared as the most effective public interest movement in America, the environmental movement is now accurately perceived as just another well-financed—and cynical—special interest group, its rancid infrastructure supported by Democratic Party operatives, and millions in grants from corporate foundations," writes the environmentalist Jeffrey St. Clair in a recent *Earth First!* article.

II. OUT OF THE MARGINS

Converging from the far reaches of the ideological spectrum, fusion paranoia is not only obliterating many distinctions between the Left and Right but is also seeping into the political mainstream. Even moderate conservatives see an implicit conspiracy among liberals in government, the academy, the press, and Hollywood. And liberals see a conspiracy among conservatives in government, corporate interests, and the forces of bigotry. In feminist theology, the idea that half the population conspires against the interests of the other half is not uncommon. Among African Americans, paranoia seems to have become something close to a defining attitude. According to a 1990 poll, 60 percent of blacks do not reject the idea that the government intentionally spreads narcotics into black communities; another survey found that a third believe that HIV was produced by scientists and disseminated through black neighborhoods for the purpose of genocide.

One way to put in context the degree to which political paranoia has worked its way into the culture at large is to consider the kinds of allegations that have been almost casually made against a figure at the heart of American politics and government—the president. The current holder of that office, Bill Clinton, has been accused in books, videotapes, publications, and speeches of complicity in (a) a drug smuggling and gunrunning conspiracy directed by the CIA out of an airport in Mena, Arkansas; (b) the murder of his close friend Vincent Foster; (c) the murder or beatings of people who threatened to expose his many illegal and improper activities as governor of Arkansas; (d) the Bank of Commerce and Credit International financial scandal; and (e) a plot to keep in office an incompetent Arkansas medical examiner because the official had covered up a death caused by Clinton's late mother, Virginia Kelley, in her job as a nurse-anesthetist.

The man who held the presidency before Clinton, George Bush, has been publicly accused of (a) playing a key role in a 1980 conspiracy between the Reagan-Bush campaign and the government of Iran to keep American hostages in Teheran imprisoned until after the election, in order to prevent a so-called October Sur-

prise benefitting the Democratic incumbent; (b) sending 500,000 American soldiers into war in the Middle East to protect Bush-family oil investments; (c) joining Clinton in the Mena conspiracy, and participating in other cocaine-smuggling
schemes to finance the Reagan administration's anti-Communist campaigns in
Central America; and (d) approving, when he was director of the Central Intelligence Agency, the drug-smuggling operation run by the Panamanian strong-
man Manuel Noriega.

Among those who have no problem believing that two U.S. presidents were
involved in plots of murder and drug dealing is Bob Fletcher. "I don't want to
break anyone's balloon out there," Fletcher said. "But yes—there's too much documentation to doubt it."

It is not remarkable that accusations of abuse of power should be leveled
against presidents—particularly in light of Vietnam, Watergate, and Iran-Contra.
But now, in the age of fusion paranoia, there is no longer any distinction made
between credible charges and utterly unfounded slanders. Any suggestion of conspiratorial evil against a prominent politician, no matter how extreme the charge
or how scanty the evidence, glides from the margins of politics to the center, on
a sort of media conveyor belt that carries it from the rantings of the fringe groups
of the Right and the Left into the respectable zone of public discourse. Political
partisans and ideologues push such charges along for reasons of self-interest, and
the mainstream media, which used to demand at least a modest level of proof,
now requires only that the accusation be slightly laundered, by way of the
tabloids or the ideological press. Thus, the stories from Arkansas accusing former
Governor Clinton of complicity in criminal enterprises appear in the Right
Reverend Jerry Falwell's "Clinton Chronicles" and in the pages of the right-
wing *American Spectator*—and also in the left-wing *Nation,* in the *New York Post,*
and in the proto-establishment *Times* of London. Similarly, the charge that Bush
took part in a conspiracy to keep Americans held as prisoners in Iran in order to
ensure Republican electoral victory in 1980 vaulted without evidence from the
mouths of proven fantasts and liars to the national press, and from two books put
out by major publishers to congressional investigations happily carried out by
Democrats.

In 1992, conspiracism made a dramatic entrance onto the national political
stage in the person of Ross Perot, the first fusion-paranoia candidate for the presidency. Perot was himself an example of the melding of populism and paranoid
style, of legitimate critic and crackpot, of giving voice to valid grievances and
hysterical fears. He believed that the North Vietnamese had engaged the Black
Panthers to kill his family, and, during the 1992 presidential race, charged that

the Republicans had threatened to sabotage his daughter's wedding with the release of phony dirty pictures. Perot was an enthusiastic dabbler in conspiracy theories, ranging from the Right's belief that the government was covering up evidence of American servicemen still being held captive in Vietnam to the Left's fantasy about a "secret team" of ex-military men and CIA officials seeking control of the government. He got nearly 20 percent of the vote.

But Perot was only a harbinger. In the 1996 race, paranoia already has its first truly out-of-the-closet candidate, in the pugnacious form of Pat Buchanan. Over the past year, Buchanan has more and more openly embraced the idea that America is being undermined by a New World Order conspiracy, manifested by globalist free-trade initiatives like the GATT accord and the NAFTA agreement. Declaring his candidacy in his syndicated column, Buchanan wrote: "The giant explosive protests against NAFTA, GATT and the peso bailout have shown how far the U.S. establishment is detached from Middle America. No one wants their New World Order. Americans want their country's sovereignty restored and her independence reasserted." He warned that "America's culture is under attack from within." At other times, Buchanan has spoken of the "Manhattan Money Power, the one power to which neither party is any longer able to say 'No!,'" has charged that "the GOP is acting less like a great party than the Political Action Committee of Goldman, Sachs," and has described the Republican primary contest as "a battle between the hired men of the Money Power who long ago abandoned as quaint but useless old ideas of nationhood—and populists, patriots and nationalists who want no part of Robert Rubin's world."

Buchanan understands that the voters he needs to reach in order to have any impact on the Republican primaries are the same people who made Pat Robertson's book *The New World Order* a *Times* best seller. This constituency knows exactly what Buchanan means when he writes of the Manhattan Money Power and the political influence of people with names like Rubin and Goldman and Sachs. It knows that the question "Who owns America?" is not meant to be merely rhetorical. The voters whom Buchanan is seeking are clued in to both his text and his subtext. They understand when they hear him that he is confirming his solidarity with those who believe that the international bankers and the Wall Street moneymen and the bought-up pols of Washington are conspiring to destroy America and usher its citizens into the New World Order of the Antichrist.

◆ ◆ ◆

Bob Fletcher, in his own inconsequential fashion, represents the confluence of all this. He embodies both the reality-based outrage of populism and the hysteria of conspiracism. Like many of his fellow citizens, he has his reasons for thinking that the elite Them of America are conspiring against him. Some of his reasons are entirely personal. Some are imaginary, conjured up out of the vaporings of his agitated mind. But others are rational and real.

"A thought I have in my mind is that all of my heroes have died," Fletcher said, apropos of no question or preceding remark. "We Americans are brought up to love our country and our leaders. We believed in them, and they have lied, cheated, stolen from us; they have done atomic tests on us like guinea pigs. They have lied and lied. Look at that McNamara coming forward now with his brand-new book, telling us that the patriot movement of thirty years ago was absolutely right, and that the war was a lying, fraudulent, disgusting thing."

Although the outrage that drives Fletcher is shared by millions of Americans, not many will go as far as he has to express it. They may support a Buchanan or Perot, fight for term limits, and vote for the legislative dismemberment of the federal government, but they will stop far short of even thinking about taking up arms. People like Fletcher, though, are different. They are literalists. They grow up taking at face value the lessons of the civics books and the church. They are fundamentalists. They need an order to things, an explanation of the world that is both logically and morally absolute.

The realizations that for most people are simply part of the gradual disillusioning process by which adulthood is reached—people cheat, love is fickle, governments lie, power corrupts—are for them shattering events. They overreact, wildly. They are determined to reimpose order on life, but they are also determined not to be fooled again. They question everything, and believe nothing but what is proven to their own satisfaction, until they have refigured the world. In this way, truth lies. Unfortunately, so does madness. The difference between the two is not that great. Eternal questioning leads one man to write *The Social Contract* and another to believe in the threat of the New World Order. In the end, people like Fletcher are undone by an excess of expectation and a dearth of imagination, by the failure of their country to live up to itself, and by their own failure to explain how this can have happened. They are driven to distraction, and to organizations like MOM.

III. FLETCHER'S ODYSSEY

Fletcher sat on the edge of the bed that was closer to the door in my room at the Noxon Motel, and I sat on the other bed. He lit a cigarette and took a sip from a can of Coke and started talking fast. After a short time, I got edgy watching him squirm and bounce, and asked him if he wouldn't prefer to lie back on the bed—and, to my surprise, he did. From then on, he spoke from a nearly reclining position, propped up slightly by a pillow against the backboard. Being more or less prone seemed to calm him a little; at least, his legs stopped moving.

"In 1985, I was in Marietta, Georgia, and I was running a little company which manufactured small puppets," he began. "We were doing rather well. The projections for that year were real high. I would have made at least a half a million dollars with my little company in '85, and it was my intention to expand, go on television. I would have become wealthy with it. There's no question about it."

That year, in an effort to expand, Fletcher said, he merged his business with a holding company known as Vista Joint Ventures. Vista was owned by a man named Gary Best and his wife, Patricia. Fletcher said that he learned over time that Best's company was a front for a covert arms-smuggling operation dealing with Latin American and African markets. According to Fletcher, Best was connected, in some way, to the U.S. intelligence community, and his arms operation was part of a network of fund-raising groups and front companies associated with a then unknown National Security Council staffer named Oliver North.

Fletcher said that he became unhappy about his involvement in what he increasingly came to regard as an illegal and dangerous business, and that in early 1986 he told Best he wanted out. "Basically what happened then was we had a blowup," Fletcher told me. "Best said, 'If you say anything you will be killed.' So I decided, obviously, I was going to get out of this crap. I called somebody in the FBI, and also attempted to call the Central Intelligence Agency." As Fletcher recalled it, none of the federal agencies was much interested in pursuing the matter, so he began his own investigation. "I contacted my lawyer, a lady friend of mine, and we started doing some snooping, flipping over rocks, and one thing led to another, and I began to realize that this was directly connected to the highest levels of government."

I have no way of knowing how much of what Fletcher says about Gary Best and the ill-fated toy company is true. Best, who is reportedly the president of a company that is prospecting for oil in the former Soviet republic of Azerbaijan, has in the past denied Fletcher's accusations. But Fletcher, who filed Freedom of Information Act requests for the government files pertaining to him, received a 1987 memorandum from the FBI that he believes supports his story (although in the circular world of intelligence gathering, Fletcher himself may have been the source for the information in the FBI memo). "The office of independent counsel has developed information that Gary L. Best . . . has the modus operandi of purchasing small business operations and using the small businesses as a front to hide his real operation of purchase, sale and distribution of weapons possibly to Central American, other foreign nations, and/or unknown groups," the FBI memo says. "Several small businesses have been victimized by Best. One was a toy company originally owned by Robert B. Fletcher . . . who currently resides in Orlando."

Whatever the ultimate truth is, there is no doubt that Fletcher is sincere in his views about Gary Best and the loss of the toy company, and that these views started him on the journey of radicalization which would take him eventually to paranoia. "Who is Gary Best?" Fletcher raves in his unfinished memoirs. "Who is the character that took over the Toy Company and used it for the CIA Weapons Programs? The character that had raped my company and stole my company for the CIA operations, threw me into the last few years of speaking engagements, investigations and the need to write this book!"

In his search for answers, Fletcher began in 1986 what he calls "my inquiries," which he likes to suggest were of vital importance to the nation. As Fletcher tells it, he became an important independent investigator, supplying information to Senator John Kerry's office, the Iran-Contra congressional investigating committee, and the office of Iran-Contra independent counsel, Lawrence Walsh. Fletcher established what he describes as his own "network of intelligence persons worldwide," becoming a one-man clearing house for a slew of congressional investigations.

In Fletcher's world, all roads led to Fletcher. When Senator Kerry's office was investigating allegations of drug smuggling in Mena, Arkansas, "a Kerry staff member referred someone to Bob Fletcher, because I was the guy that would have all the information that she would need to get started on," Fletcher recalled, with the satisfaction of a man who has made enough of a mark on history to be justified in referring to himself in the third person. When Representative Henry Gonzalez, chairman of the House Banking Committee, needed to get to the bottom of the BCCI banking scandal, to whom, according to Fletcher, did he turn? Fletcher, naturally. And when House Democrats were investigating the October Surprise case—yes, of course, Fletcher. "I was very much into that one," Fletcher told me. "I was specifically involved with that in terms of supplying investigative research. I had more than one hundred and seventy-five documents."

In truth, Fletcher was never a congressional investigator, and, as far as I can determine, never an important asset in any investigation. Staff investigators for the Iran-Contra committee interviewed him but did not follow up on his story, and Fletcher's involvement with other congressional investigations didn't really amount to anything more than kibbitzing. Yet Fletcher found the environment of Washington in the latter half of the 1980s curiously welcoming. There have always been a lot of people like Fletcher hanging around Washington—amateur detectives pursuing stories and rumors of malfeasance and skulduggery in high places. They are the national capital's equivalent of the types who loiter in the halls of every county courthouse—people with time on their hands, who have made a hobby out of knowing why the So-and-So rape case is never going to trial, and who the important drunks are, and who is doing what to whom behind closed doors. Those whose professional business it is to know the score—politicians and lawyers and reporters—pay attention to these amateurs, even the ones who are obviously a little cracked, because they never know when somebody will stumble onto one of those incredible tales that turn out to be true.

The Iran-Contra affair, which broke open shortly after Fletcher began his career in conspiracism, was perhaps the greatest example in American history of such a tale—one in which the national security adviser to the president of the United States had actually given a birthday cake shaped like a key to Ayatollah Khomeini. The unfolding revelations of Iran-Contra gave a great and lasting boost to conspiratorial thinking everywhere in America: If this impossible scenario was true, then nothing was beyond credibility. Iran-Contra turned the nation's capital into a bazaar of fantastical stories and wild plots.

In this fun-house milieu Fletcher found an odd solace. The shock of losing his company had, I think, destroyed in him an assumption fundamental to a comfortable life—the false but necessary conviction that this is an ordered, sane, rational world. There was nothing Fletcher could do to restore his faith in the old order of things. But in the conspiracist world of Washington after Iran-Contra he found a new order—an understanding of why bad things happened to good people like Fletcher.

"I was listening to a radio talk show," Fletcher recalled, "and there was a guy talking about some of these same people who were in and out of my toy factory and linking them to international activities, and that blew my mind a bit. So I turned the radio up, and it was this fellow named Danny Sheehan, who was then in the process of filing this gigantic legal action against people connected with Oliver North and other persons. I contacted him, and I said, 'Gee, I heard you on the radio, and I have all these names and dates and people and places, and I don't know if they fit in or not.' What happens next is he falls off his seat. He says to me, basically, 'You're, like, right in the middle of it.'"

Sheehan, a leftist lawyer and champion of radical causes, ran an operation called the Christic Institute out of a warren of small, crowded offices in a self-consciously shabby row house on North Capitol Street. The mission of the

Christic Institute was to effect social change through litigation, and in 1986 Sheehan was riding the crest of his biggest case ever—a lawsuit against a large collection
of former U.S. intelligence and military officers who Sheehan said constituted a
"secret team" operating a vast drug-smuggling and arms-running enterprise that
had been directly involved in many of the unhappy events of American history
since the fifties. Eventually, Sheehan's case was thrown out of court, and the
Christic Institute would be fined more than a million dollars for filing what the
judge called an action based on "unsubstantiated rumor and speculation." To
Fletcher, though, the "secret team" theory offered the restitution of rationality,
and he embraced it with the relieved enthusiasm of a religious convert.

From Danny Sheehan and the Christic Institute, Fletcher moved deeper into
his newly ordered world. There were, he discovered, other people in Washington
who were trying to find the truth, who took seriously the story of what had happened to Fletcher. One truth seeker he encountered was an ex-CIA man named
David MacMichael, who ran the Association of National Security Alumni, an
anti-CIA watchdog group. MacMichael is also a member of the Covert Operations Working Group, a small band of conspiracists, aging sixties radicals and representatives of the religious left, which meets every three weeks or so in a sunny
front room in an old mansion across the street from the Supreme Court to discuss what evils the U.S. government—especially the CIA—has been up to lately.
At these meetings, Louis Wolf, the director of research for *CovertAction Quarterly,*
is a regular, and so are MacMichael and Ralph McGehee, another former CIA
employee turned whistle-blower and watchdog. A guiding spirit of the Covert
Operations Working Group is Pat Tatum, who is by profession a cabdriver.
Tatum chairs the meetings, and maintains the group's mailing list, working in the
early mornings and at night in the house where he rents a basement room cheap
from a friend. I asked Tatum once what the group meant to him, and he answered, in a soft, somewhat shy, voice, "Oh, I guess there's no question that it's
the most important thing in my life. It gives a certain amount of meaning and
purpose to my life I wouldn't otherwise have."

At Tatum's invitation, I sat in on one meeting of the group. There were fourteen people, which was about par, I was told. The meeting ran for nearly three
hours and most of the talk was earnest, dull stuff about American perfidy in Haiti
and other such subjects. Still, there was a strong undercurrent of paranoia in
the room, and it bubbled up now and then—most notably when it was Ralph
McGehee's time to speak.

McGehee retired in 1977 after a career of twenty-five years in the CIA, and
he has devoted himself ever since to the task of exposing the sins of his old em-

ployer. McGehee's great work, on which he has been laboring for twelve years, is CIABASE, an indexed encyclopedia of usual and unusual information about the CIA. McGehee works on CIABASE at least five days a week, at least four or five hours a day, in the basement office of his home, in the suburban Virginia community of Herndon.

"Whew, this is a subject I am not happy to talk about," McGehee said when his turn came to speak, late in the meeting. "I have been sort of one who's pooh-poohed dozens of conspiracy theories—you know, people who say they've got a transmitter in their tooth, they're being controlled by Langley, that sort of thing. Now, all of a sudden, I find myself in the middle of one of these things, and I feel very unusual about it." In fact, McGehee said, he had been reluctant to admit the truth to himself—that the CIA was conducting a campaign to spy on him, and to turn the people of Herndon against him. "Probably the sign that was most indicative of the fact that it wasn't my imagination occurred when I went to the movies one time with a friend, and a line of people were going up to buy tickets, and I got in the line, and there was a line of people after me," McGehee said. "In front of me, all the people bought tickets, but when I got to the window the guy says, 'We're closed. We're closed.' I thought I hadn't heard him right, so I put out some money, and finally he did sell me a ticket but it was quite obvious that the staff had been prepared for me. Things after that began to accumulate. When I would go biking on the bike trail in Herndon, there would be a bicyclist or a man in a suit just standing there, with a walkie-talkie, obviously announcing my position as I went by."

After McGehee finished talking, Lou Wolf spoke. "Let me just say, Ralph, and I hope I'm speaking for all of us, that I don't by any stretch think you're paranoid," he said. "If you're paranoid, I'm made of cheese. And we all want to welcome you to the world of those who *do* believe in conspiracies."

"Thank you, thank you very much," McGehee said. "That's what I was hoping you would say."

Little organizations like the Covert Operations Working Group and the Association of National Security Alumni are hardly noticed in Washington, and most people would not take them seriously. Fletcher, however, found in this microworld of conspiracies the great gift of resurrected importance. "You know, David MacMichael, he thought my case was probably one of the most interesting of all he'd seen," Fletcher told me proudly. "I became part of that organization of his, and he wrote me up in the association newsletter probably—shit—seven times, something like that."

A revitalized Fletcher decided to give the mainstream, and the political system, one more chance. In 1990, four years after moving to Orlando, Florida, and taking a job selling recreational vehicles, he entered public life.

"I became a candidate for the United States Congress," Fletcher told me modestly.

"You ran for Congress?" I asked, surprised.

"That's correct," Fletcher said.

"As an independent?"

"Oh, no. I ran as a Democrat, the candidate for the Democratic Party."

"You were the candidate of the *Democratic Party*? Backed by the party?"

"Oh, yes. Of course, they did not give me *much* backing."

It is a remarkable fact that Bob Fletcher was the Democratic candidate against Representative Bill McCollum of Florida in 1990. He ran as a liberal, and on a platform that was pretty much limited to the story of his victimization by the North conspiracy. By and large, the press treated the story, and Fletcher, with sympathetic respect. Still, there wasn't much of a positive reason to vote for Fletcher, and he lost to McCollum by a margin of 20 percent. But even if Fletcher had succeeded in his brief career as a Democratic office seeker, it is unlikely that he would have stayed in Orlando very long. By 1989, he had become convinced that the conspiracy against him was being played out on a new and more troubling level: The shadow government, he believed, was trying to kill him.

"Yes, in 1988, when I was in the middle of my inquiries, there were two attempts to murder me," Fletcher said. "The first was, this fellow drove through my wall in Orlando, Florida. Came in, carefully selected my office, and drove through the wall and almost killed me."

The second attempt followed immediately. "The fellow who had driven the car through my wall then proceeded with Operation Part Two on Bob Fletcher," Fletcher recalled. "He came right up to me, in an apologetic manner. Well, while he was doing it, he was excessively *manhandling* me. He shook my hand several times, touched me on the back of the neck, and grabbed my shoulder and my arm. That did not mean too much to me until approximately eighteen hours later, when I had a major heart attack. I was put into intensive care, and they ran extensive tests, and they found out that my blood had been chemically altered, and that fact is in my blood test. So I had a chemically induced cardiac by this son of a bitch."

"Your blood had been chemically altered how?" I asked.

"With a dust that is utilized in the intelligence community as an assassination chemical. It's absorbed through your pores. So that's why the funny stuff, physical manhandling, took place."

In the fall of 1991, Fletcher moved to a place far away from Washington, a place where it would be harder for the shadow government to get to him.

IV. VIEW FROM THE HILLS

The headquarters of the Militia of Montana consists of five small, cluttered, and mildly dirty rooms in a sternly utilitarian building of sheet metal and concrete, which David Trochmann built in 1984. The building is on the edge of Noxon, which is, in turn, on the edge of America. It is high in the glorious mountains of northwestern Montana, on the far side of the Clark Fork River, which is gin clear in some lights and a pellucid bottle green in others, and is lively with trout and muskrats. Noxon is approachable by road only over a one-lane bridge, and is surrounded by conifer forests climbing to snowy peaks and hills and descending into ravines full of elk and bighorn sheep and deer and mountain lions and black bears and hunters. It is a natural terminus to a long journey, a fine place for a final stand.

John Trochmann is a sort of natural terminus himself. Perhaps Fletcher, in his long search for order and meaning and defense against the dangers of the world, always had someone like Trochmann in some part of his mind. Trochmann is fifty-one years old, but a full, thick white beard and gray bristling eyebrows make him seem older. He has a strong, firm mouth, and brown eyes that frequently glare. He looks remarkably like the Avenging Angel of Harpers Ferry, John Brown.

Trochmann has been a conspiracist nearly all his life; indeed, he is a second-generation conspiracist. When we met—in the Landmark Café, while Fletcher was Fletcherizing the television newswomen—I asked MOM's leader when it was that he first began to think there was something drastically wrong with America. I thought he would say, "When Nixon resigned," or "When Saigon fell," or something like that.

"Well, I believe I was nine years old when I first took note of something being wrong, and that was when my dad refused to be part of the Lutheran Church anymore, because they had joined the National Council of Churches, or the World Council of Churches, whatever it was," Trochmann said. "It raised a question in my mind. Why should a little country church be part of a big international system? I was a questioning child."

In 1960, at the age of seventeen, Trochmann dropped out of high school and joined the navy "to see the world—they didn't tell me I'd be seeing it from a porthole." On trips to Iceland and Puerto Rico, he was shocked to discover how the world saw him. "When I went to foreign countries and found out how they felt about America, I had a very, very rude awakening. They would say to me, 'Look what America has done to my country. They brought democracy here and destroyed my way of life.' . . . I began to ask bigger questions, have less trust. I started seriously studying, reading about things like the comments the Founding Fathers made when they said the government that governs best governs least."

In twenty years in the family business building race-car engines and snowmobile parts, Trochmann continued asking questions, and over time he became a full-fledged convert to New World Order conspiracism. In 1987, following his brother David, he moved to Montana, where the environment was, if not always sympathetic, at least tolerant of views like his. From the mid-1980s on, the tristate region of northwestern Montana, the Idaho panhandle, and eastern Washington attracted a whole range of antigovernment and white-supremacist movements: the Church of Aryan Nations, the White Aryan Resistance, the Freemen movement, the County movement, Posse Comitatus, Christian Identity, the Tax Protest movement, and the Constitutionalists. Trochmann flirted with at least one of the groups. He was a speaker at a 1990 Aryan Nations congress but he says he never joined the Aryan Nations, and he did not become prominently identified with any of the others. He needed an organization—and a vision—he could call his own.

In August 1992, there occurred an event that provided Trochmann with what he needed, the answer to the question of where it was all, finally, heading. Fifty miles from Noxon, outside the tiny town of Naples, Idaho, federal agents set out to arrest a forty-four-year-old survivalist and white supremacist named Randall Weaver. As the federal agents moved in, Weaver holed up in his small cabin on top of a steep, narrow hill called Ruby Ridge. On a path leading from the cabin, Weaver's fourteen-year-old son, Sam, who was armed, encountered armed federal officers. The ensuing exchange of gunfire killed a deputy marshal—and Sam. The federal agents surrounded the cabin. The next day, an FBI sharpshooter killed Weaver's wife, Vicki, who had been standing in the doorway with her infant daughter in her arms. For the next eight days, Weaver and his three surviving children stayed barricaded in the cabin with Vicki Weaver's decomposing body a few feet away. At the foot of Ruby Ridge, an angry crowd of neighbors and protesters stood vigil. Trochmann was among them. "We witnessed the tyranny of government," Trochmann said. "It was a devastating event for me."

A second event, even more devastating to Trochmann, occurred on April 19, 1993, when a standoff in Waco, Texas, between the FBI and the followers of an apocalyptic Christian preacher ended in the death of seventy-two people, among them twenty-four children. Waco confirmed Trochmann's most dire fears. He began organizing in earnest, taking what to him was the last logical step—the establishment of an armed militia to do battle with the forces of the shadow government. In January of 1994, the Trochmann family founded the Militia of Montana.

Fletcher, who was living in the town of Livingston, Montana, several hundred miles from Noxon, met Trochmann that month, at a Patriot meeting in Billings, where both men were speakers. Trochmann invited Fletcher for a visit to Noxon. "I went up there and spent some time with the Trochmanns," Fletcher recalled, "and I was very impressed with their humanitarian caring for each other. And not only for each other but for the rest of the country. It was a kind of intense caring that is unusual in the modern day, a genuine concern for people I had found lacking elsewhere in the country."

The idea of becoming part of MOM's family must have had particular appeal to Fletcher at the time. The year before, he and his wife of twenty-five years had separated over his conspiracist activities. "My wife wanted me to stop pursuing the bad guys, and I just felt it was too important," Fletcher explained. Fletcher returned to Livingston, but he stayed in touch with the Trochmanns. "They needed me," Fletcher said. "They would call me because of my contacts in Washington, and they would ask me to check out this or that, and I would do it."

Last August, Fletcher decided to go home to MOM. "I said to them that it was goofy to work apart, since I was doing so much for them, and why didn't I come live in Noxon, and we'd do this together," Fletcher recalled. "It was the right time for me to do that, because I no longer had any of those miscellaneous things that would normally bind you—my wife being gone. I was alone in this big house I didn't need."

Fletcher's new home had a conspicuously end-of-the-line feeling to it. From its inception, the Militia of Montana was different from like-minded groups in one critical regard. While the others kept to themselves, MOM was, as Trochmann puts it, "very outspoken, very high profile" in its campaign to spread the militia movement across the country, primarily by means of an aggressive mail-order program. From the beginning, MOM's literature was open in its view that the point of a militia is to prepare for war against various enemies, including the government. "The security of a free state is not found in the citizens having guns in the closet," MOM's manual for forming a militia noted. "It is found in the citizenry being trained, prepared, organized, equipped and led properly so that if the government uses its force against the citizens, the people can respond with a superior amount of arms, and appropriately defend their rights." The MOM newsletter, which has become a leading periodical of the militia movement, is called *Taking Aim*. MOM's mail-order catalog features on its cover a pen-and-ink drawing of a backwoods sniper drawing a bead on some unseen soul, and offers budding militiamen everything from biochemical-protection suits to U.S. military publications on the art of war (no. 424: "Sniper Training & Employment"; no. 428: "Booby Traps"; no. 433: "Small Arms Defense Against Air Attack"; no. 435: "Incendiaries").

Since MOM's first week in business, there has been a steady demand for its goods. The morning I visited its offices, there were four large boxes stuffed with packages ready to go out. David Trochmann, who runs the mail-order operation and takes a cheerful pride in it, says he often fills hundreds of requests for merchandise and information per week. "I've carried as many as sixteen boxes down the hill in one day, all filled with this stuff," he said, waving his hand around at the shelves filled with books, pamphlets, and videotapes which line the walls. "Our shipping costs generally run to two hundred bucks per day, and we've had it go as high as twelve hundred bucks."

There are some who suspect that MOM is in it mostly for the money, but John Trochmann talks as if he is following a course that will end in death for somebody. He says he has no doubt of the coming attack from the government he believes is illegitimate. "I am concerned about it, like anybody else who speaks out against evils in government," he said. "I mean, these people don't want to give up the reins of the total control of their drug running, of their slave labor, of their child molesting and child murder. They don't want to give this up, and people like me get in the way, by exposing what they are doing."

It will happen soon; in paranoia, the moment of reckoning is always close at hand. "Oh, this is the final stage, there's no doubt about that," Trochmann rambled on. "When the troops come in, they'll come in such force it will be incredible! In forty-eight hours, they can have one hundred million troops here. They'll come out of the ground! They'll come from submarines! They'll come from air drops! They'll come from everywhere!"

When the great and bloody day comes, Trochmann says, he intends to fight, and others will fight with him. "We've had meetings about it. We've picked out strategic points, obviously," he said. "We're here to defend our community, not just ourselves, but the whole community. These hills out here, my county has about five thousand hunters, and every hunter is a sniper. And the enemy that would come in here to destroy our way of life knows that. Because I've been so outspoken for so many years, our lives aren't worth a plugged nickel anyway, so if it comes to it, why not give it all we've got? I'm not willing to die, but I'm willing to make the other bastard die. If they come after me, I'll do my best to put them in the ground."

Trochmann, looking very much indeed like God's wrathful servant, said all this one afternoon as he was driving down a logging road in the woods near Noxon in his battered white Impala. The Impala was missing a passenger-side window from a recent encounter with the law. Plastic sheeting that had been put in its place whistled and thumped in the sideslip, and the heavy car banged up and down in the ruts of the road. On his belt Trochmann had clipped two magazines of ammunition for his Colt .45 semiautomatic, which was not in sight, but which, he said, was in the car. In his shirt pocket he carried a small two-way radio. "Many, many people—I won't say how many, but a lot—have these radios," Trochmann said, "and we stay tuned to a certain frequency, a certain channel, and our radios are always on, so if there was an armed attack—an entry of armed people that come up here to do us dirt, like they did to Waco, well, we're not going to let that happen. When these agents go off the deep end, they are our flat enemy. They deserve to be treated kind for kind. If they come in shooting people, what do you expect us to do?"

It isn't clear how much of an army there really is out there in the Montana hills, waiting for Trochmann's call to arms. The state, in reaction to its growing population of extremist groups, has passed a law forbidding paramilitary training, so a visitor to Noxon is not likely to be treated to the sight of middle-aged men playing soldiers in the woods. Still, there is no question that Trochmann has adherents: He draws upward of three or four hundred people at his speeches. And he has already come close to a shooting incident—an encounter that cost his Impala its window.

According to newspaper accounts and the Montana attorney general's office, on a Friday afternoon in March, two members of the Montana Freemen movement, Dale Jacobi and Frank Ellena, were arrested in Roundup, Montana, after sheriff's deputies discovered that both were carrying concealed handguns. Deputies also discovered a number of other weapons in Jacobi's pickup truck, including several Chinese-made SKS semiautomatic rifles with bayonets attached. A few hours later, three men believed to be affiliated with the Militia of Montana—Paul Stramer, Cajun James, and Amando Gerry Lopez—walked into the jail and accosted the deputies. One of them had a handgun under his jacket; all three were arrested. In the parking lot, deputies found Trochmann and another man locked in Trochmann's car. They smashed in the passenger window and arrested them. Charges of criminal syndicalism were filed against all seven men, but the charges (which were disputed by Trochmann and the others) were later dropped, after the Montana attorney general's office determined that the case was probably too weak to go to trial. Perhaps the prosecutors did not want to bring the matter to court. Nobody is really that eager for Armageddon.

Just before I left Noxon, I dropped by MOM's headquarters to say good-bye. Trochmann was on his way out, heading for a meeting with the FBI. The feds like to keep tabs on Trochmann, but they are gentlemanly about it, considering that they are the servants of the shadow government. A special agent drives all the way over from Missoula—a trip of three hours—and he and Trochmann have coffee together. "Oh, he's a very nice fellow," Trochmann said. "We get along fine."

There was a photographer at the headquarters, from the *Missoulian,* to take some pictures. Trochmann said he would stand still for a few shots before he left. He headed outside, and we all trailed him—the photographer, Fletcher, and I. The photographer picked out the spot he wanted—a rail fence with some grass in front of it and some trees and mountains in back—and he said, "Why don't you go stand against that and sort of lean over it, and we'll only be a minute." Trochmann, rather impatiently, moved. "No, I mean both of you," the photographer said. "I need Bob Fletcher, too."

Fletcher hurried over to join Trochmann at the fence. He leaned against the top rail, like Trochmann, and hitched up one foot, cowboy style, on the lowest rung of the fence, like Trochmann. "Okay, that's great," the photographer said. "Looking good. Smile. Keep it up. Just a few more. Great! Great! Almost done. I may not be good but I'm fast. At least, that's what my wife said." The remark struck me as a little off-color for God-fearing men, but Fletcher and Trochmann both laughed loudly, and when I left I thought that Fletcher looked about as happy and as much at home as he ever could hope to be.

Imitation Activism

◆ ◆ ◆

The weather in Washington was dismal on Monday, raw and chilly with a driving rain under skies that never brightened beyond slate. Ah, it did my heart good. Thinking, in the comfort of my office, of how miserable—how wet, how cold, how thoroughly, splendidly wretched—must be the tens of thousands of magenta-haired nose ringers who, in their great crusade to stop the world's finance ministers from doing lunch, had taken a hard-pressed police department away from its long, losing battle to protect the city's poor from the city's predators, I felt toasty and happy and at one with a just world.

Children—you over there dropping your Gap trousers in front of the Gap store to protest Gap labor policies, and you, protest organizer Mary Bull with the plastic-foam tree on your head—may I mention a few things? (1) Imitation is not the sincerest form of flattery; it is the sincerest form of imitation. (2) That whole thing your parents did back then—you know, the revolution in the streets, the trashing of the dean's office, the purposely shocking sartorial and tonsorial styles, the stoned grooving to bad pretentious music, the nakedness and the love-ins— well, it was pretty stupid the first time around. An awful lot of it was just about getting wasted and getting together with young women with perfect noses and ironed blond hair; the rest was about getting even with Daddy and Mommy, for his crime of making money and her sin of keeping house. (3) Your dad at least had a compelling reason for, like, trashing The System, man; he was trying to do his bit to stop the war in Vietnam before his second college deferment ran out and the government, like, hauled him out of Yale and sent him off to Vietnam to get himself all shot up, as if he were the son of a plumber or something. In terms of antagonizing large policemen with clubs, this, boys and girls, was a cause on an order of magnitude different from saving sea turtles.

Actually, kids, not to be rude about it, but it must by now have occurred to the swifter among you that you don't possess anything that can coherently be called a cause. I quote from an admirably restrained Associated Press dispatch concerning the arrest on Monday of some five hundred to six hundred demonstrators "by police obliging their wish to be taken into custody."

"The demonstrators blame the global lenders for problems from environ-mental damage to sweatshop labor. But they came for causes ranging far beyond those complaints: for animal rights, against nuclear weapons, for District of Co-lumbia statehood, against sending Elián Gonzalez back to Cuba, for more AIDS research. . . . What they wanted seemed to depend on who was chanting loudest.

" 'What do we want?' a young woman called. 'Justice,' the crowd replied. A few minutes later, the street crowd was singing the anthem of the civil rights movement, 'We Shall Overcome.' Then a debt forgiveness chant."

"Then a debt forgiveness chant." On August 28, 1963, when I was six years old, I stood with my mother and my sister Kate on the sidewalk in front of my parents' house at 404 Constitution Avenue on Capitol Hill, and we watched a quarter of a million people walk by on their way to hear the Rev. Martin Luther King Jr., in his oddly soft roar, speak the words that would break Jim Crow. It was a boiling day, and the marchers, who were formally dressed, the men in suits and, often, hats, and the women in dresses and, often, gloves, suffered. Our mother had made great amounts of lemonade, and we stood on the sidewalk and ladled out cups of the stuff from a big metal pot in which floated a big block of ice, to the men and women who walked solemnly and magnificently by, singing "We Shall Overcome," which they did not follow with a chant on debt forgiveness.

As an adolescent during the Vietnam War years, I came to admiringly see my-self as passionately antiwar (although I couldn't have told you what the war was about). But even as I demonstrated, and tried to get myself a little bit tear-gassed and mildly arrested, I vaguely knew there was something awful in the presump-tion of we young white privileged things, who filled the Mall in the years after King's marchers had gone, that we occupied anything like the same moral plane.

How much more awful is this, now, a generational imitation of a generational imitation of a form of politics that was once reserved for matters of life and death—and is now reserved for that space between spring break and summer va-cation, and between the last body piercing and the first IPO.

Oh, Those Heartwarming
Communists

◆ ◆ ◆

In the study of contemporary culture, nothing is more rewarding of attention than newspaper human interest stories. This is because the point of such stories is to evoke a common emotional response, and so they rest on assumptions of shared values. The writer takes it for granted that pretty much everyone will find it naturally good that the granny surprised the mugger with the Detective Special in her purse and that the kid from the projects won the city science fair.

Thus, to read the human interest stories in any community's newspaper is to know not only what that community thinks is news, but also what it thinks about what is admirable and what is amusing and what is moral and what is inarguably true. The assumptions of human interest stories describe a community's values, its culture.

The community served by the *New York Times* is of particular interest in this regard, for it is the community of America's elites. What the writers and editors of the *Times* assume their readers will find funny or heartwarming or uplifting or cute is a nearly pure reflection of the values of what *New Yorker* writer Richard Rovere called the Establishment.

These values, at least as reflected in the *Times,* increasingly seem disconnected not only from those of most other Americans, but even from reality. On April 6, the *Times* ran a front-page human interest story of a standard sort, in the subgenre of Those Wonderful Wacky Old Folks. Every paper in America runs this sort of story: Harry and Bob and Joe and Mabel and Edith may be nearly fossilized, but there's life in the old coots yet, as witnessed by their passion for baseball/ballroom dancing/gardening/dabbling in the stock market.

So *Times* reporter Sara Rimer went out to Los Angeles and found, in a place called Sunset Hall, a lovable bunch of senior citizens who are kept young at heart by their passion for . . . Communist totalitarianism.

Yes, Communist totalitarianism. Yes, Marx and Lenin and Mao. Yes, the Soviet Union and the People's Republic of China. Yes, the greatest experiment in government through mass murder in history: between 45 million and 72 million victims of the state in China, 20 million in the Soviet Union, 2.3 million in Pol Pot's Cambodia, 2 million in North Korea, 1 million in Eastern Europe, 1 million in Vietnam, 1.7 million in Africa, and so on. As reckoned by the leftist French scholar Stéphane Courtois in his recently published *Black Book of Communism,* the butcher's bill for Marx and Lenin's big idea adds up to somewhere between 85 million and 100 million dead on four continents. Yes, for every blessed one of those necessarily broken eggs.

Yes, fascism, the Gulag, the Cultural Revolution, the jailing and the torturing and the expelling of Jews and Christians and intellectuals and democrats. Yes, the Moscow spy machine that ran the American Communist Party as an espionage center, that nearly destroyed the American labor movement and that corrupted and crippled American liberalism not once but twice. Yes to all that, say the cute old folks in the *Times.* And about all that, the *Times* speaks nary a word.

At Sunset Hall, writes Ms. Rimer, "the library has an extensive collection of books on Marxism, Trotsky, Mao and the Rosenberg trial, as well as the complete works of Shakespeare. There is a framed certificate from the American Civil Liberties Union honoring Sunset Hall's 'tradition of activism' on one wall, a picture of Paul Robeson on another and, on a shelf, a bust of Lenin. At 101, Jacob Darnov, a rabbi's son from Russia, who was a messenger in the Bolshevik army, is unwavering in his admiration for Lenin. 'He's the greatest politician we ever had in this world,' said Mr. Darnov, whose other hero is Leo Tolstoy." And then there is Glady Foreman, ninety, who, writes Rimer, "proudly recalls how, at the age of 8, she was proclaimed 'a little Socialist' by her father" and who predicts "Socialism, crushed to the earth, will rise again."

If a *Times* reporter found a brave little band of aging Nazis, who kept a bust of Hitler in the living room and who declared that fascism would rise again, and wrote this up cute—well, this simply could never happen. But a *Times* reporter writes Darnov and Foreman and company up cute—and the editors say: That *is* cute. Put it on A-1.

Why did they do this extraordinary thing? They did it because to them it is not extraordinary. They did it because they think it really is heartwarming that the Sunset Hall folks are sustained by their old faith, and they assume that it will be heartwarming to their readers as well. And the awful thing is, they are probably right.

The Systematic Corruption
of the Catholic Church

◆ ◆ ◆

BOSTON—A few weeks ago, Cardinal Bernard F. Law met with an annual convocation of the Archdiocese of Boston's pastors and leading laity. By all reports,
many among the laity harshly criticized Law for his decades-long and now-
exposed efforts to hide and protect sex-predator priests under his supervision.

A few days later, the priest in the church I attend spoke of this event in his
Sunday sermon. He seemed shaken by what he had seen and heard at the convocation—by the openly expressed threat to the authority of the Catholic Church
and even to the faith that the church serves. He pleaded with the parishioners to
continue attending church, to continue believing. He admitted that the church,
in its handling of cases of sexual abuse by the clergy, had been guilty of "what
could be called a crime of silence."

Then he said: Yes, it was a crime of silence. But it was not only the church
that was guilty of this crime. No, he said, there was blame to go around. Lots of
people had kept silent their knowledge or suspicions of priestly abuse: other
priests, leading members of parishes, the parents of victims—why, the victims
themselves had contributed to the silence.

Yes, those little boys who suffered the vile and evil gropings of Father John J.
Geoghan and his fellow sexual criminals in collars—they, too, shared in the crime
of silence. As a child sitting through a long Sunday Mass, I frequently wished I
could walk out. But that was a matter merely of boredom. This was the first time
I ever wanted to get up and leave a church out of disgust.

What has been revealed about the Catholic Church in recent years, and overwhelmingly in recent months, is clear. Over the course of at least decades, a large
number of priests used their offices, and used the exceptional trust manifested in
the title accorded them—"Father"—to sexually prey upon (mostly) adolescent
boys who had been taught to look up to them as, literally, father figures.

This pattern of criminal abuse was not limited to a few priests or a few
parishes, but involved the Catholic Church in America as a whole and as an in-

stitution. As many as two thousand priests have by now been formally accused. Cases of serial molestation involving multiple victims have been reliably documented in dioceses ranging from Boston to Los Angeles to Cincinnati to Dallas to St. Louis to Bridgeport to Palm Beach, and on and on.

In case after well-documented case, the same pattern can be seen: First there are suspicions that a priest is "fooling around" with the altar boys, then complaints, then more complaints, then more complaints. Diocesan superiors take notice; so do diocesan lawyers. The complainers are urged to keep quiet, for the good of the church and the faith. No one tells the parishioners, no one tells the police, no one tells the children. The lawyers (good Catholics) stonewall and hardball; the church's doctors (good Catholics, too) pronounce the priest cured, or cured enough; the bishop orders a quiet transfer to another parish; the whole thing repeats its terrible self. When necessary, the church pays out hush money, buying some more crimes of silence. Finally, after many lives have been crippled: exposure, scandal, a grudging apology.

This pattern is not accidental but obviously a matter of policy. The Catholic Church leadership, it has been overwhelmingly proved, knew—again, at least for decades—of widespread crimes of sexual abuse by its priests and systematically worked to conceal these crimes. Thus, the church—again, at least for decades, and, again, not in one or two dioceses but across the country—functioned to allow predator-priests to continue in positions where they might continue to prey. Leading prelates of the American church—Law in Boston and Cardinal Edward Egan in New York among them—stand implicated in this fashion, and so does the church hierarchy as a whole.

Let us be clear: Ultimately, this is not about individual criminal acts or individual failures in leadership. This is about the systematic corruption of an institution. This is about the church as a hierarchy and a whole betraying the faith and the faithful in the most serious fashion imaginable. It is about a massively powerful institution using its power to conceal and effectively perpetuate—knowingly perpetuate—crimes (and sins) of the most evil nature against the most innocent and vulnerable of the souls who trusted the church.

Betsy Conway, a sister of St. Joseph in the Archdiocese of Boston, was quoted in the *Boston Globe* the other day: "This is our church, all of us, and we need to take it back." Yes.

Getting Hip to Squareness

◆ ◆ ◆

C an we be square again? We were last square half a century ago. Then we were, more or less successively, hep, hip, cool, wild, beat, alienated, mod, groovy, radical, turned on, dropped out, camp, self-actualizing, meaningful, punk, greedy, ironic, Clintonian, and, finally, postmodern, which is to say exhausted—and who can blame us? In all these states we were, first and above all, not square. Everything was a variation on that; to be seen as clever and even profound you had to be not much more than not square.

Now we are supposed to be square again. No one puts it that bluntly, because square remains the condition that dare not speak its name. Even country music gave up on square, Merle Haggard's 1969 great anthem of square, "Okie From Muskogee," being more on the order of a last defiant gasp than a call to arms. Nevertheless, post–September 11 we are, the surveys say, patriotic, prayerful, serious, and determined. We love our country. We support our president and our armed forces. Our heroes are police officers and firefighters. Our first official war hero was a CIA agent. Well, beat me, Daddy, eight to the bar, as Mamie Eisenhower used to say, this is squaresville.

But is it sustainable? Returning to square seems like revirginizing. The problem is knowingness. All anti-square postures stand on a base of superior knowingness: Suburban life may look wholesome and sweet, but it is really one vast snake pit tarted up as a gunite swimming pool. George Washington may look like the star of Founding Father Knows Best, but really he was a false-toothed real-estate speculator. Woody Guthrie carries a nice tune, but this land is not your land, unless you are a Trump or a Tisch.

Knowingness, of course, is not knowledge—indeed, is the rebuttal of knowledge. Knowledge was what squares had, or thought they had, and they thought that it was the secret of life. Knowingness is a celebration of the conceit that what the squares knew, or thought they knew, was worthless. In *The Graduate,* the career advice ("plastics") of a family friend, Mr. McGuire, to Benjamin Braddock, played by Dustin Hoffman, is classic square knowledge. Benjamin's mute disdain toward that advice—and his elaborately played out disdain for all that McGuire and the Robinsons represent—is classic anti-square knowingness.

You can see in this example the problem that a return to square poses: Anti-square is so much easier and more fun. Knowledge, even on McGuire's level, is notoriously difficult to acquire. Sixteen years of hard, slogging schoolwork, and what do you know? Not enough to carry on ten minutes of intelligent conversation on any subject in the world with any person who actually knows something about the subject. Knowingness, though—a child can master that. (Can and does: There is an obvious inverse relationship between age and knowingness; the absolute life peak of knowingness generally arrives between the ages of twelve and sixteen for females, fourteen and eighteen for males—whereas, as these cohorts can attest, grown-ups don't know anything.)

This is why Benjamin Braddock had to ignore, with prejudice, Mr. McGuire. McGuire may have been a fool, but he was, in the limited area of business and economic trends, probably a knowledgeable fool. Had Benjamin been obliged to respond to McGuire's advice in terms of knowledge, he would have been utterly lost—he would have been the one exposed as a fool. But for Ben—and more to the point, for the movie's audience—knowingness offered a lovely way to not only counter McGuire's knowledge but also trump it. Ben didn't have to know anything about McGuire to show himself intellectually (and aesthetically, and even morally) superior to McGuire. He only had to know that what McGuire thought he knew was a joke and McGuire was a joke because—because the McGuires of the world are definitionally jokes, and if you don't understand that, I can't explain it to you, because you are a McGuire. That's knowingness, and for no-sweat self-satisfaction you can't beat it.

The hard-easy dynamic that obtains with knowledge and knowingness covers other aspects of square and anti-square. Square: virtuous, chaste, modest, honest, brave, industrious, tough, kind to children and waiters. Anti-square: vice-tolerant, promiscuous, boastful, honest when it suits, don't-get-mad-get-even, sharp, retains a tough attorney, kind to Kennedy children and waitresses who look like supermodels. Square: proper dress required, also proper manners, proper morals, and proper language. Anti-square: Jack Kerouac. Square is not overly concerned with comfort. My father, who is seventy-eight, will sartorially relax to the point of allowing, on occasion, corduroy trousers and a tweed jacket instead of a suit, but he doesn't venture much beyond that. His father's idea of unbending was to appear on his front stoop of a Saturday without coat and tie and stiff detachable collar, and with the sleeves of his washed, bleached, starched,

ironed white shirt rolled up nearly to his elbows. And this, mind, was the relatively relaxed standard of the working classes.

When America was square, even being anti-square was hard. Take, for example, the issue of courage. A man could be manifestly courageous or not, but if he
was not courageous, he was well advised to hide that fact. In square America
other men and even women made life hard for men who clearly failed the minimal (and, it should be noted, they always were minimal) requirements of man-
liness. Likewise with other social conventions. In square America you could
choose to be a seducer of women, a drunk, a gambler, a layabout, a sartorial disgrace. But this would not be a respectable life; indeed, it would be, to a degree
now hard to imagine, a harried life. The Beats were the first figures to rebel
openly against the social conventions of post–World War II America pretty much
across the board. Reading what they wrote in the late 1950s and early 1960s, you
are struck (apart from the generally third-rate quality of their thoughts and
words) by the rigor it took to lead the anti-square life then.

After all that went away, we ended up with a culture in which the anti-square
values achieved their natural status as the default positions of life. Not terribly inclined to painful honesty? Not to worry: Learn from Seinfeld that honesty is for
people who live in Duluth. Inclined to sharp practices in your business dealings?
Relax: Nobody pays retail anymore, why should you? Not terribly brave? Oh,
well, who truly is?

It is some distance from this territory to Mayberry, RFD. But you never could
get there from here anyway. The idea of America described in *The Andy Griffith
Show* and other programs of the fifties and sixties that have come to stand for the
collective cultural sense of square was never intended to be taken as real. These
shows were a camp take on a cartoon fantasy of American life and values, and
they amounted to a running inside (and fairly cynical) joke on the part of the un-
square people who made and marketed television. Their America never did exist, and that America is not what returning to square means.

What did exist, and what perhaps could be returned to, is the modern, hip
urban America of the thirties and the forties. This is the America fictionalized
and idealized in Hollywood from Humphrey Bogart to Stephen E. Ambrose's
Band of Brothers, but it was not at root a fiction. It was real, and it was a time and
a place that no one could ever mistake for square. Indeed, this was the America
that defined American style so absolutely that every evocation of cool since has
been in imitation of it or in reaction to it.

Yet the values of this America were values that came to be associated with
square: courage, bravery, strength, honesty, love of country, sense of duty. Then,

though, these values were not seen as square. Nor were they seen as square's political analog, conservative. There was then no necessary disjunction between cool and patriotic, or cool and strong, or cool and conservative, and no understood conjunction between square and patriotic or strong and liberal. (See Bogart in *Casablanca* for the ultimate expression of all of this.) This seems to me a cultural state that might again, finally, be attainable. And I think people might like it, too—especially if we get to wear fedoras again.

The Nice Column

◆ ◆ ◆

The other day a fellow suggested that some people regard this column as not nice—given to ad hominem insults and uncharitable impulses and that sort of thing.

Well, it stung, of course, and after brooding on it, I have decided to mend my ways, at least once a year. Here, then, the first annual Mike's Nice Column.

Lizzie Grubman, I read in the New York tabs the other day that you are now expressing heartfelt remorse as you approach trial for that sad mishap last summer in which you allegedly plowed your Daddy's big old SUV into all those people (although, as you allegedly and no doubt rightly pointed out, some of them were trash anyway). Ms. Grubman, I have suggested that you were less than a fully conscientious and caring person. I can see now that this was wrong, and that any debt you may or may not owe society has been more than paid by your own suffering. Here's hoping you walk, Ms. Grubman—or better, drive. Take my car, it's an Escalante.

Allen Iverson, I have written unkindly about you, too, suggesting that you were a dangerous thug. Mr. Iverson, you are a fine man and a role model to our nation's youth, and you have every right to allegedly threaten people with guns if you need to find out where your wife is. Or for any reason at all, sir.

I see that WorldCom has just won (so far) the bankruptcy sweeps, its $107 billion Chapter 11 filing easily eclipsing the $50 billion collapse of Enron, whose bankruptcy last December held the title of largest in U.S. history for only seven months. I'd like to take this opportunity to extend the hand of friendship to Bernard J. Ebbers of WorldCom, Kenneth L. Lay of Enron, and all the good senior management folks at Global Crossing, Qwest, Adelphia Communications, Arthur Andersen, and AOL Time Warner. When I wrote that our captains of industry were "the greediest bunch of no-talent morons the world has seen since the Harding administration," I was talking through my hat. You guys are awesome. You made a few mistakes—but look, am I so perfect? On behalf of our nation's investors, pensioners, widows, and orphans, and also on behalf of your many, many thousands of grateful former employees, I would like to thank you all for your years of hard slogging as stewards of our great corporations. You deserve every penny you got your sticky mitts on, and I, for one, am happy to be left holding the bag. I would invest my little all with you again, if I still had a little all.

My fellow Americans, I have repeatedly suggested that when the poet said that nature pleased in all her prospects and only man was vile, he was talking about you. I have criticized your habits, appearances, manners, and tastes. Let me recant. You are lovely in every way. You are paragons of style and grace. Your popular culture daily reaches new heights in refinement, and I don't just mean cable, but the networks, too. And there is nothing more aesthetically gratifying than a seventeen-year-old skinny boy with multiple tattoos and piercings and no shirt and his pants around midbottom, except for a fifty-year-old fat man with a three-day beard and a ponytail and no shirt and his pants around midbottom.

John Walker Lindh, your father says that you are "a really good kid" who "loves America." Right-o, all is forgiven; sorry. John Henry Williams, don't listen to the critics. There is nothing shabby about freezing your dad and selling off his DNA.

Simple filial piety, in my opinion.

Mr. Disgraced and Impeached Former President—there I go again; I mean, simply and respectfully, Mr. President—I got a fund-raising letter from you last week in which you said that you were proud of what you had done for the country. Let me second that. Proud is exactly the word that comes to mind when I think of you. Also, honest, sincere, selfless, modest, mature, and classy. Especially classy.

Finally, Jack, you were quite right to dump the ten gallons of birdseed on the driveway and to say, "That's okay, Daddy, you can clean it up." Tom, on reflection, I agree that you should stay up as late as you want every single night. Both of you are entirely correct in your theory that ice cream sandwiches are the ideal breakfast food, and so it shall be from now on.

By God, I feel good!

II

• • •

The Game

Master of the Game

• • •

On November 9, 1960, the day after John F. Kennedy defeated Richard M. Nixon to become the thirty-fifth president of the United States, a reporter for the *Washington Daily News* and a reporter for the Associated Press dropped by Nixon's house in Washington, looking for an interview with the loser. The vice president answered the door himself, and standing on the front stoop, the three men settled into a polite routine of questions and answers. Suddenly, Pat Nixon appeared. She was angry and, it was clear, not in control of her emotions. She damned the reporters and their colleagues for favoritism toward Kennedy that she said cost her husband the election. Nixon calmed her and led her away. When he returned, he said nothing about his wife's outburst, and the reporters resumed their inquiry as if nothing unusual had occurred. Neither reporter ever wrote about Mrs. Nixon's behavior; it wasn't news.

This small, oddly dignified scene, remembered by one of the reporters, belongs to a world that has vanished utterly. A journalist interviewing the losing candidate on the day after the 1992 election would have done so as a member of a large pack, covering a set piece of political theater—a media event, as it is called. The event would have been scripted down to the level of minor jokes, in an effort to ensure that the candidate committed no gaffes before the cameras. The reporters, hoping to shake things off-script, and aware of their own video presence, would have shouted self-consciously aggressive questions. Had the defeated candidate's wife interrupted to scold the press, this would have been regarded by his handlers as a calamity (unless they had secretly arranged it) and by the reporters as the news of the day.

The story of this vast change is the story of how the idea of image became the faith of Washington, and how the president became the central figure of that faith, the architect and ultimately the victim of the world's most elaborate personality cult.

In this new faith, it has come to be held that what sort of person a politician actually is and what he actually does are not really important. What is important is the perceived image of what he is and what he does. Politics is not about objective reality, but virtual reality. What happens in the political world is divorced from the real world. It exists for only the fleeting historical moment, in a magical movie of sorts, a never-ending and infinitely revisable docudrama. Strangely, the faithful understand that the movie is not true—yet also maintain that it is the only truth that really matters.

By the time Bill Clinton was elected the forty-second president of the United States, the culture of Washington (and therefore of governance and politics) had become dominated by people professionally involved in creating the public images of elected officials. They hold various jobs—they are pollsters, news-media consultants, campaign strategists, advertising producers, political scientists, reporters, columnists, commentators—but the making of the movie is their shared concern. They are parts of a product-based cultural whole, just like the citizens of Beverly Hills. Some are actors, some are directors, some are scriptwriters, and some are critics, but they are all in the same line of work and life. They go to the same parties, send their children to the same schools, live in the same neighborhoods. They interview each other, argue with each other, sleep with each other, marry each other, live and die by each other's judgment. They joust and josh on television together, and get rich together explaining Washington to conventions of doctors and lawyers and corporate executives.

Not surprisingly, they tend to believe the same things at the same time. They believe in polls. They believe in television; they believe in talk; they believe, most profoundly, in talk television. They believe in irony. They believe that nothing a politician does in public can be taken at face value, but that everything he does is a metaphor for something he is hiding. They believe in the extraordinary! disastrous! magnificent! scandalous! truth of whatever it is they believe in at the moment. Above all, they believe in the power of what they have created, in the subjectivity of reality and the reality of perceptions, in image.

The growth of the faith in image has had a gradual but cumulatively momentous effect. It has made the old distinctions of profession and ideology that had defined the culture of Washington seem outdated and naive, like the blush-ingly remembered fervors of adolescence. If the reality of an action is defined by the public presentation of the action, then what is a television reporter but an ac-tor? What is a newspaper writer but a theater critic? If the truth of an idea is de-fined by its advertising campaign, who but a mug can seriously believe in one set of ideas or another? If perception is reality, what is the point of any differences at all—between Republicans and Democrats, between journalists and govern-ment officials, between ideologues and copywriters, between the chatterers of television and the thinkers of the academy, between Washington and Holly-wood?

Indeed, the differences have become harder and harder to see. Yesterday's re-porter is today's White House spokesman is tomorrow's pundit. On the Sunday talk shows, the celebrity host and the celebrity reporter and the celebrity politi-cal strategist sit side by side, and the distinctions between them are not apparent to the naked eye. In effect, they are one, members of the faith, the stars of a cul-ture they themselves have created. Indeed, they have acknowledged their one-ness. They have given themselves a name, the Insiders, and a language.

The language reveals, as all languages do, a great deal about how its speakers see themselves and the world. It is self-referential, self-important, self-mocking, and very nearly (if subconsciously) self-loathing. It is deeply cynical. It portrays a society where to be knowing is to admit the fraud of one's functions in the act of performing them.

This is how the Insiders describe the passage of a day:

The day is composed, not of hours or minutes, but of *news cycles*. In each cy-cle, *senior White House officials* speaking *on background* define *the line of the day*. The line is echoed and amplified *outside the Beltway* to *real people*, who live *out there*, by the president's *surrogates*, whose appearances create *actualities* (on radio) and *talking heads* (on television). During the *rollout* of a new policy, the president, coached by his *handlers* and working from *talking points* and *briefing books* churned out by *war room* aides, may permit his own head to talk. There are various ways in which he might do this, ranging from the simplest *photo op* to a *one on one* with a media *big-foot*, to the more elaborately orchestrated *media hit* (perhaps an im-promptu with real people) to the full-fledged spectacle of a *town hall*.

The line, a subunit of the administration's thematic *message*, is reinforced by *leaks* and *plants* and *massaged* through *the care and feeding* of the press. It is adjusted by *spin patrol* and corrected through *damage control* when *mistakes are made* or *gaffes are committed* that take attention *off message* and can create a dreaded *feeding frenzy*. Reaction to the line is an important part of the cycle, and it comes primarily from congressional leaders of both parties, the strange-sounding *biparts,* whose staff-written utterances are often delivered directly to *media outlets* via *fax attacks.* The result of all this activity passes through the *media filter,* where it is cut into tiny, easily digestible *sound bites* and fed to already overstuffed *pundits,* who deliver the ultimate product of the entire process, a new piece of *conventional wisdom.*

◆　◆　◆

Every species produces its perfect flower and every culture its perfect moment. In the late spring of 1993, the perfect flower of the Insider species and the perfect moment of the image culture met in the presidential appointment of David R. Gergen, Washington's circular man.

The career of David Gergen represents the triumph of image. The character of David Gergen represents the apotheosis of the insider. The two are rolled up in him together, in a shining, seamless roundness whose mirrored surface reveals nothing but the political scene rolling by. In himself, Gergen has conflated all the old distinctions. Over the course of twenty-two years, he has traveled from White House to White House, from government to journalism to punditry and now back to government (and soon enough, you may bet on it, back to journalism again), from the Democratic camp to the Republican to the Independent to the Democratic again. So perfectly is he of his time and place and class that he is himself part of the tribal language. To be Gergenized is to be spun by the velveteen hum of this soothing man's smoothing voice into a state of such vertigo that the sense of what is real disappears into a blur. Nothing is more Gergenized than Gergen himself. The blur is the man. He is his own magic movie, forever revising the reality of himself.

On May 29, David Gergen was appointed counselor to the new president, a Democrat. The move surprised many who had known Gergen as a servant of three Republican presidents, including one—Ronald Reagan—whom the new president had charged with ruining America. Actually, Gergen hastened to say with bland audacity: "I'm not a Republican. I've always been a registered Independent."

On June 7, standing at the podium in the White House press room where he had often spoken on behalf of Republican presidents, Gergen was asked to define his politics more fully. His answer was marvelous for its accidental revelation of the heart of the man. When he first went to work for Richard Nixon in 1971, he had been a registered Democrat. Later, under Nixon, Gerald Ford, and Ronald Reagan, he had voted Republican, worked in Republican political campaigns and served as the public defender of Republican policies. But he characterized this as a matter more sartorial than ideological: "wearing Republican cloth." Leaving the Reagan White House in 1984 to begin a career at the more rarefied levels of journalism (a fellowship at the John F. Kennedy School of Government, a stint as editor and later as columnist for *U.S. News & World Report,* and a regular spot as a commentator on *The MacNeil/Lehrer Newshour*), he had "thought it was important" that he "not be seen as a, quote, 'Republican.'" And so he had "evolved" into "an independent voice" that was "moderately right of center."

In most places, this sort of performance could win one a reputation for opportunism. It does that in Washington, too, but here the tag is meant as a compliment. Possessing a large degree of what the Washington columnist and talk-television star Michael Kinsley has called "intellectual, uh, flexibility" is no sin here. Wrong lies in the opposite direction, in the gaucherie of displaying passionately held convictions. (Stage passion is fine, but it is crucial to know the difference. The real anger displayed by the Republican strategist Mary Matalin during the 1992 presidential campaign was considered such a breach of manners that her boss, the deep-insider George Bush, forced her to apologize. Meanwhile, the faux tantrums of Matalin's boyfriend, the Democratic strategist James Carville, won him admiring fame.) A man like Gergen, unafraid to admit that his loyalties and convictions are no more than outerwear, is always welcome at the table.

The moment that proved this true—the perfect flower's perfect moment— occurred on the evening of June 4, and of course on television. The scene was the set of *The MacNeil/Lehrer Newshour,* the insider's evening news, where reasonable men and women meet to mostly agree and occasionally agree to disagree (in the mildest possible manner). Until his latest presidential appointment, Gergen had been a weekly guest on the show, playing (barely) conservative to the columnist Mark Shields's (barely) liberal, a relationship whose evident amiability was never once threatened by even a hint of strong disagreement.

This evening's program focused on two related presidential events of the past week: the public relations disaster of Lani Guinier's abandoned appointment to head of the Justice Department's civil rights division and the hiring of the public relations impresario David Gergen.

Who did *MacNeil/Lehrer* invite to assess the impact of Guinier and Gergen? Who but, as host Robert MacNeil put it, a man who was until recently "a weekly analyst here on the *Newshour* . . . here tonight in his new role . . . David Gergen, news maker."

After interviewing Gergen on Guinier and Gergen on Gergen (he was modest and judicious on both subjects), MacNeil bade the news maker good-bye and introduced the show's political panel, which appeared minus the regular guest . . . David Gergen.

Once the panel host, Roger Mudd, had finished a bland discussion of the Guinier mess, he then turned to a subject of more intimate concern, the White House appointment of . . . David Gergen.

"Well, I wish David Gergen hadn't done it," said the conservative commentator Linda Chavez. "Because he's a friend of mine. Who would wish this job on anybody?"

The liberal commentator Eddie Williams chimed in: "I dropped him a note saying I congratulated him on what I felt was a fantastic match, my words, the match between Gergen and Clinton."

Added Shields: "Let me tell you what David Gergen brings, I think, to Bill Clinton. . . . He has that ability to come in and speak the truth."

At which point, Mudd turned to face the table to Shields's right, and reintroduced . . . David Gergen.

"Did you realize he's been sitting, listening to us the whole time?" Mudd asked, as the director switched cameras to show Gergen there at the table, laughing, grinning slyly, from under his long, pale blond eyelashes, as if to say: Aren't we naughty? And everyone else, Williams and Chavez and Shields and Mudd, was smiling and laughing, too. The joke was, really, delightful. The whole time they had been discussing Gergen, acting as if they were trying to give an honest appraisal of the man—why, he had been right there sitting among his pals. How delicious (*how perfect*) to admit that it was all just a great big shucks, that it didn't matter where Gergen sat or whom he worked for at the moment, that he and they were in on it together and that only those saps out there, outside the Beltway, were dumb enough to think it was for real.

Oddly enough, no one knows better what is wrong with all this than David Gergen. It is a dislocating experience to hear him—this former Nixon speechwriter, this former Reagan director of communications, this man who has spent the larger part of his adult life building the images of presidents and of himself, this insider so dedicated to the insider's art of leaking that old colleagues call him the Sieve—as he disdains and regrets his life's work.

"So often now, presidents are being judged, politicians are being judged by the quality of their performances: How well do they play the game?" Gergen says. "Did they give a good speech? Or did they do something interesting today? It's all the same. The horse-race nature of the campaign, which gets covered ad nauseam, now also dominates the presidency. And I think in some ways that the people who are in the business of government and the people in the punditry business are almost co-conspirators. They are feeding off each other. The people in the press are judging you on that basis and the people inside are responding to that. Instead of saying, 'How do we change things in people's lives?,' it has become: 'How do we put the packaging together? How do we put the bright ribbons on it that will make people think it is important, or interesting or different? How do we make the pundits say, "Gee, that was impressive"?' And this has no bearing on what happens underneath, and it creates a deepening cynicism."

What he's criticizing, it is suggested, "Is stuff I've done. I admit that. I've done a lot of it. But you realize . . ." Here he pauses for a long moment. "Look, I plead guilty to having played the game and inventing some forms of the game that I thought eventually went beyond what was intended. . . . It gave way over time to—and this is what I regret—a selling for the sake of selling. It had nothing to do with ideas. It had nothing to do with anything that was real. Eventually, it became selling the sizzle without the steak. There was nothing connected to it. It was all cellophane. It was all packaging. And I feel I contributed to that. There's no question about that. I'd been aggressive in my early years trying to get some of that set up. I did that in part because I thought that was the only way you could govern. I think now, as I get older, that the steak is very important, too. Yes, the selling has to continue, but it's not sufficient in and of itself. That becomes, over time, just an empty exercise."

◆ ◆ ◆

What happened to the presidency and to Washington was, Gergen argues, inevitable. "We have an inherently weak institution in the presidency," he says. "It was intentionally set up that way by the founders. There is a reason why the presidency is Article II of the Constitution, not Article I. The Congress was always intended to be the leading body, with the presidency set up as a somewhat weaker body. And it was the weaker body for most of our history."

But modern presidents and the news media both tend to exaggerate the powers of the office, says Gergen, voicing a theory most prominently advanced by the historian Richard Neustadt. This exaggeration, the theory goes, has magnified the gulf between what the president can accomplish and what the public expects of him.

"Given this, and given the increasing power of the press, and the inability of contemporary presidents to master the press enough to master the message, there has been a lot more effort on the part of the White Houses to manage the message, to orchestrate," Gergen says. "And that, in turn, increases the cynicism on the other side."

There is obvious truth in this vicious-circle theory, but the cloak of inevitability obscures the more complicated, larger story—and the role of David Gergen in it. The empty exercise Gergen now deplores is not simply the product of historical forces nor merely the result of the irresistible rise of news-media power. It is also the conscious design of a small group of smart, purposeful men—advertising executives and scriptwriters and pollsters and strategists—who worked over a period of two decades to invent a new type of presidency, one that would be primarily defined by the television screen. Gergen occupies a curious position in the group. He invented none of the big ideas or foundation techniques of the image-age presidency. But he had the good fortune to find himself on the inside more or less at the beginning of the change (he has a great knack for being in the right place at the right time), and he had the skills to prosper.

He was intelligent and hard-working and he had a complex charm. A big man who underplayed his presence, he was solicitous of the opinions of others and expressed his own unthreatening thoughts in a soft, friendly voice that gave way easily to laughter. He was not a brilliant student of history or politics, but he was a dedicated one. He tended naturally to the accepted view and to the middle ground. And he had one more important talent. He was gifted at manipulating the appearances of all sorts of realities, including the reality of David Gergen.

From Nixon to Ford to Reagan to Clinton, Gergen carried the faith of image and the image of himself, polishing and adapting and expanding both. As the years passed, his predecessors and peers fell by the wayside, the victims of changing tastes and times. But Gergen changed apace, and quietly, almost inconspicuously, grew toward the great role to which he now aspires—wise man of the age of image.

◆ ◆ ◆

On the day Pat Nixon told off the reporters on her doorstep, the age and Gergen were both bright and young. Kennedy's 1960 campaign had redefined politics. While other politicians had dipped into the waters of the new age—Eisenhower had starred in both the first televised presidential news conference and the first prime-time visit to the White House—Kennedy was *of* the age. He had a generational grasp of what screen presence was about, and he ran for president essentially on qualifications of image: beauty, grace, youth, courage, wit, charm. The public JFK, shaped with a lapidary precision by the patriarch Joseph P. Kennedy, was a World War II hero, a Pulitzer Prize–winning author, the pride of an ideal family and a devoted husband to a loving wife. That these achievements were in considerable part the creation of professional mythmakers was overlooked by a press corps that was (as Mrs. Nixon pointed out) largely pro-Kennedy and also ignorant of the extent to which it was being conned. In office, Kennedy was similarly attentive to image, and similarly successful. His administration shone with a gloss that maximized such minor accomplishments as inviting Pablo Casals to dinner and minimized such major disasters as the invasion of Cuba.

Kennedy's achievement made a powerful impression on Nixon and his advisers, who had to overcome one of the worst images in political history. On November 28, 1967, the speechwriter Ray Price, who would later become Gergen's boss and mentor in the Nixon White House, wrote a memorandum to his campaign colleagues explaining how the lessons of Kennedy could be applied to the problems of Nixon, who was planning a second campaign for president the following year.

Nixon's woes, Price wrote, stemmed from "the fact that for years Nixon was one of those men it was fashionable to hate," a reaction to Nixon's style—what Price called his "cutting edge." To change this political reality, Price said, it was not necessary to change the objective reality of Nixon. Voter approval for a presidential candidate, Price argued, is not about reality but is "a product of the particular chemistry between the voter and the image of the candidate." He continued: "*We have to be very clear on this point: that the response is to the image, not to the man, since 99 percent of the voters have no contact with the man. It's not what's there that counts, it's what's projected—and . . . it's not what he projects but rather what the voter receives. It's not the man we have to change, but rather the received impression.*"

Price's insight, translated into a campaign plan of action by the advertising executive Frank Shakespeare and the television producer Roger Ailes, was revolutionary. The Democrats had never really advanced past the press-agentry techniques of inflating accomplishments and hiding flaws—maintaining a tenuous connection to reality. Price postulated that a new political reality need not correspond at all to objective reality, that a new image could override both the known facts and the previous image of a candidate to become the only reality that mattered.

By Election Day 1968, Nixon had been so thoroughly repackaged that he became, in a sense, the first president to win the office by suicide. The man sworn in on January 20, 1969, was someone the press called the New Nixon.

There was, of course, nothing really new at all. "You see in history a number of references to 'the New Nixon,'" recalls Herb Klein, Nixon's director of communications. "What that really meant was that he came on with a slightly different television technique. But he was the same man, had the same hostility to the press, the same values."

In 1971, two years after the New Nixon took office, the twenty-nine-year-old Dave Gergen—a navy veteran, a graduate of Yale and Harvard Law School—went to work for the president. The Nixon White House was Gergen's true university, and it was an extraordinary school. Here, a public-relations-obsessed president and his staff would create the prototype of the image-age presidency. This model, which remains in use today, assumes that the powerful, chronically hostile news media work steadfastly against a president's interests, and that this must be countered by a systematic program of propaganda. What a president (or presidential candidate) says or does must always be calculated for its effect on his image, plotted as points along the arc of his ideal persona, a construct largely determined by what the pollsters say the people regard as ideal at the moment. Since the news media will trumpet the slightest deviation from the ideal as evidence of a flawed presidency, the marketing of the president and his policies must be the primary concern of a White House, and campaigning must be a permanent feature of governance.

Gergen remembers the selling of the Nixon image as a central fact of life in his first White House. "The great cynicism had already begun when Nixon took office," he says. "It came with Vietnam when a generation of reporters concluded that their government was lying to them. Nixon arrived on the back end of that, and he came carrying this great personal animosity, a lack of trust in the press.

"And Nixon understood that unless you mastered television, your presidency would be ripped apart. And so he developed, the Nixon White House developed, a whole series of ideas about how one talks to the press and communicates through the press. A sort of rules for the road for how a White House acts."

The Nixonian rules, Gergen says, "have been handed down from one presidency to the next and have had enormous influence. In many ways, I think almost everything we do now has come from those years."

Gergen's contention is borne out by the archival records of the Nixon White House. In their first several years in office, the new president's men, guided by an unending flow of orders from Nixon and supervised by a former advertising executive, the chief of staff, H. R. Haldeman, invented virtually all the practices of public relations and press handling that would become standard in later White Houses.

Among the innovations were the coordination of an administrationwide "line of the day" that was in turn part of an overall thematic "message"; the orchestrated use of surrogates and White House-connected "grass-roots" organizations to build support, plant stories, and attack enemies; a continuing effort to nullify the Washington press corps through an ongoing "outreach" program to the generally more friendly and malleable regional press; the carrot-and-stick technique of rewarding reporters and news organizations whose coverage was positive and attacking those who were critical.

The ideas behind these techniques were not new. What Nixon's men did was to systematize the tricks of puffery and calumny that had long been used in campaigns and incorporate them into the routine operation of the White House. A critical advancement in the corruption of the Washington culture, this not only created new and expanded forms of such tactics, but also legitimized them. Future White Houses would embrace them as essential elements of "how the game is played," as Gergen puts it.

"It was much more than just 'line of the day,'" Gergen remembers. "This was total orchestration. It was much more sophisticated than anything that had come before. There was a desire to control the entire environment, and a feeling that if you didn't control it, they would control it—they, the great outside they."

In their everlasting search for control, Nixon and Haldeman set up four separate press and propaganda operations. The traditional office of the press secretary remained, but with its power diminished by the exclusion of the person who held that position, Ron Ziegler, from a great deal of information, thus increasing White House control and providing the administration with a mechanism for denying statements that later proved inconvenient. In addition to the press office, there were two inventions that would also shape the way future White Houses worked: the Office of Communications, directed by Herb Klein, and the Office of Public Liaison, directed by Charles W. Colson.

Klein created two devices of lasting import, the pan-governmental coordination of the White House line and the establishment of a press operation to feed local, regional, and specialty news organizations outside the Washington press corps.

"My concept was that the problem with government was that everybody went off on their own way and there was no coordination," Klein recalls. "We set up weekly meetings with the people assigned to public affairs in each department of the government, so the same song was singing through each department. At the same time, we built up coverage from the regional press—a Cabinet officer speaking in Los Angeles or Minneapolis is going to make a lot more news than that same person speaking in Washington."

The fourth division of the Nixon operation was Dave Gergen's home, the speech-writing office headed by Ray Price. Charged with producing not only presidential speeches and talking points but also most of the endless stream of speeches needed for Klein and Colson's surrogate operations, the shop employed as many as fifty people during the peak period of the 1972 campaign. Price hired Gergen in 1971 as a staff assistant, and in 1972 made him his deputy, which entailed keeping track of writers' assignments and helping Price edit copy. By the beginning of Nixon's second term in 1973, the continuing crisis of Watergate had forced some officials senior to Gergen out of the White House and left those who remained exhausted and distracted. Price quit the speech-writing department to deal with Watergate full time, and Gergen took over the shop until Nixon's resignation on August 9, 1974.

◆ ◆ ◆

Until Watergate, the overarching task of the entire press and public relations operation was the perpetuation of the New Nixon image. The obsession with this is illuminated in an unsigned "background memorandum" of December 1970. Kennedy, the memo noted caustically but accurately, had compiled a record in foreign policy of "utter disaster," but "his 'charm' saved the day for him." Eisenhower had been "distant and all business" with his staff, but had succeeded in projecting a "mythology" that he was really a "warm, kindly, fair man."

The memo prescribed a series of steps to "build" a public President Nixon who would embody "those fundamental decencies and virtues which the great majority of Americans like—hard work, warmth, kindness, consideration for others, willingness to take the heat and not pass the buck."

By the time Gergen came to work in 1971, the makeover effort had been organized into something that vaguely resembled a giant earth-moving job. Convinced that, in the awesome task of rebuilding Nixon, God lay somewhere in the details, White House "anecdotalists" dug and dug for "warm items" and "human-type incidents" about the president. The effort reached its sublimely silly peak in the RN Human Interest Story Program, ordered up in a 1971 memo from Haldeman to Price.

A speech-department staff member culled dozens of anecdotes about Nixon from intimates and aides in a lengthy report, with each anecdote indexed according to the character trait it was meant to advertise: Repartee, Courage, Kindness, Strength in Adversity. What is most painfully obvious about these undertakings is how little the anecdotalists had to work with. Exemplifying the president's talent for Repartee was an account of Nixon silencing a New York businessman who had upbraided him over the Vietnam War by telling the man not to "give me any crap." Illustrating the president's Strength in Adversity was a bald little story of how the young Congressman Nixon, falling on an icy sidewalk, still managed to keep his two-year-old daughter, Tricia, safe in his arms.

In this perfectionist and paranoid atmosphere, Gergen learned the bones of his craft.

He learned the importance of saying the same thing, over and over and over: "Nixon taught us about the art of repetition. He used to tell me, 'About the time you are writing a line that you have written it so often that you want to throw up, that is the first time the American people will hear it.'"

He learned about the gimmicks of phrasing calculated to catch the public ear: "Haldeman used to say that the vast majority of words that issue under a president's name are just eminently forgettable. What you need to focus on is what's the line that is going to have a little grab to it."

He learned the theory of controlled access. If you gave the press only a smidgen of presidential sight and sound on a given day, reporters would be forced to make their stories out of that smidgen: "Nixon used to go into the press room with a statement that was only one hundred words long because he did not want them editing him. He knew if he gave them more than one hundred words, they'd pick and choose what to use."

He learned the endless discipline required to protect the image, which was as evanescent as morning mist: "It went into everything—the speeches, the talking points, the appearances. Haldeman had a rule on appearances: If you wanted to put in a scheduling request for anything the president was going to do in public, your request had to fulfill what we called HPL—Headline, Picture, Lead. You had to say, in writing, what the headline out of the event was going to be, what the lead was going to be and what the picture was going to be."

The young Gergen also learned lessons he does not volunteer to talk about. These came under the tutelage of Chuck Colson, who managed the effort to shape perception of the president through a variety of hidden-hand means.

"In 1969, Colson was brought in, and his big job was to rally national organizations of various stripes to support the president, and to set up new organizations to do this," recalls Lyn Nofziger, a longtime political operative who joined the White House staff that year. "Colson was tougher than hell, smarter than hell, meaner than hell. He built himself an empire there, twenty-five people working for him, and their whole job was to build up Dick Nixon and tear down his enemies."

Colson adapted to governance the campaign strategy of using carefully controlled surrogates and grass-roots groups, using them not only to generate statements of ostensibly spontaneous support for the president and his policies, but also to attack political enemies from behind cover. In White House parlance, such surrogates were said to be "programmed" for attack, and were regarded as something akin to useful idiots. "Let's let columnists and Congressmen do that kind of work for us," sniffed a Haldeman aide, Jeb Stuart Magruder, in a 1970 memorandum urging a White House–staged offensive against the recently retired Supreme Court Justice Earl Warren.

The speech-writing department was charged with scripting such attacks, and Gergen, in his administrative role, became increasingly responsible for assuring that Colson's orders were carried out. The critical period of Gergen's involvement—and education—came in the 1972 presidential race between Nixon and the liberal Democratic candidate, George McGovern. In this campaign, Colson established a new standard in negative campaigning, using surrogates and the "line of the day" to put together one of the most effective, sustained, and brutal political assaults in American history. Today's campaigns, dominated by systematic, tightly planned, character-based attacks, are the direct descendants of the 1972 Colson operation.

The operation was directed through a daily 9:15 A.M. "attack meeting," led by Colson and famous still among old Nixon hands. Gergen attended the meetings as a representative of the speech-writing department.

"These were real hardball meetings where we used to figure out, day by day, how we were going to tear McGovern's hide off, and it was Gergen's job to see to it that the necessary speeches were written to carry out each day's attack," recalls David Keene, a political consultant who attended the meetings in his role as an aide to Vice President Agnew. "The group charted, about a week in advance, what the attack message was going to be every day, what we were going to hit McGovern with that day and how to mobilize the entire resources of the campaign and even the administration to focus on that single message and dominate the news."

Some of Gergen's neat, handwritten notes of these meetings can be found in the White House records from that time. Each entry describes a specific attack to be carried out against McGovern. On September 26, for example, Gergen wrote: "What do we have on Hill to embarrass McG for voting absences? Try to have Dole hit." And on that same day Gergen noted Colson's order that the campaign find "an incensed POW wife to strike out at [the former attorney general, McGovern supporter and antiwar activist Ramsey] Clark. Get Sybil from Conn. Also get labor leader—building trades."

In typed memoranda, Gergen gave status reports on the actions ordered at the

9:15 meetings. "[Nixon supporter and future pundit John] McLaughlin on *Today* show," he wrote in one typical memo. "I spoke with him yesterday and fed him Ray [Price's] line asking how well George would sleep the night our boys came home and the N. Viets were slaughtering the S. Viets."

◆ ◆ ◆

Gergen's last lesson at the Nixon White House was the most important—how to survive in Washington.

By mid-1973, Watergate had reduced relations with the press to a state of war. "I have never seen anything like it since," Gergen says. "Every question was seen as a dagger pointed at the president."

It was during this time that Gergen began to win an enduring reputation, both inside the White House and among reporters, as (depending on your point of view) a major leak or an excellent source. Toward the end, while most Nixon officials were refusing to deal with the press, Gergen was talking to investigative reporters who would write the history of Watergate. In one scene from *The Final Days,* Bob Woodward and Carl Bernstein's sensational account of the last months of the Nixon White House, Gergen admits to angry chief of staff, Alexander Haig Jr., that he was one of the ones leaking to the press. Pointing to a *Washington Post* article that had particularly incensed Haig with its portrait of a White House in wild disarray, Gergen confessed that he was the source of two damaging paragraphs quoting "one presidential aide." (Today Gergen acknowledges that he did leak to Woodward, a fellow Yale graduate he had known for years, but only as "a designated leaker," acting "with Nixon's blessing.")

Two points about this scene illustrate the basic relationship between Gergen and the press. One, it shows Gergen in a flattering light. (He may have leaked, but he did it for good reason, and he manfully admitted it.) Two, this flattering light was provided by David Gergen. Unless the authors resorted to fiction, Gergen had to have been at least one of the sources for the scene because his private (blameless) thoughts are described in detail. This is not an isolated happenstance. Gergen appears throughout *The Final Days*—and always sympathetically. In scene after scene, he comes across as a moral, sometimes anguished, man, who insists on doing the right thing while being lied to repeatedly by his president.

This characterization is probably true. Gergen's recollection today of himself as "tortured" by Watergate is confirmed by several associates. But it also seems likely that Gergen has always known how the history he helped make in *The Final Days* made him look. Recalling Watergate twenty years later, Gergen volunteers that he has always "tried to maintain a standard of honesty," and twice suggests a rereading of *The Final Days* as proof. "You go back and read that, and you'll find I was trying to present a government that was legitimate," he says.

Having learned that history belongs to those who create it, Gergen developed a talent in the post–Watergate years for reshaping the historical perception of himself, exaggerating his role in some instances and minimizing it in others. In *The Power Game,* Hedrick Smith's best-selling 1988 account of how Washington works, Gergen is cited as the person "put in charge of scripting the ['72] Republican convention." In political circles, this is an important credit, because that convention was the first to be fully stage-directed for television, now a standard procedure. The account Gergen gives in *The Power Game* of how the operation worked is fascinating and wonderfully candid—except that Gergen was not at all in charge of scripting that convention.

Ron Walker, who was chief of advance for the White House in 1972, says that he and a number of Nixon aides, including Dwight Chapin and Bill Timmons, were the chief scriptwriters of the Republican convention that year. "Gergen wasn't involved much," Walker says. "I can remember him sitting in meetings with us, and as a speechwriter. I'm sure he participated in some of those meetings, but that's all I remember of him there."

But Gergen has quietly played down other activities of his early career. "He tried to forget he was ever part of the nine-fifteen meeting," David Keene recalls. "I remember Colson gave all of us who had been in it these cufflinks that were engraved with nine-fifteen. Years later, I ran into Gergen at a dinner, and he saw I was wearing those cufflinks, and he was horrified. He said: 'You actually wear those? Are you crazy? Someone might see them.'"

After Nixon flew away in the summer of 1974, Gergen went to work writing speeches for William E. Simon, then secretary of the treasury. Simon, a Wall Street financier whose investing acumen made him one of the world's richest men after he returned to private life in 1977, was at the time considered presidential material. He was also a deeply committed conservative, to the right of Nixon and well to the right of Gergen.

Gergen made the ideological adjustment with seeming effortlessness. "I had a point of view and he understood it," Simon recalls. "He caught on real quick."

Bill Schulz, a Washington editor who later worked with Simon on two books, remembers Simon's marveling at Gergen's adaptability. "Bill told me that Gergen was the hardest hard-line speechwriter that he ever had," Schulz says. "He knew Gergen didn't believe in any of it. But when he wrote for Bill Simon, he wrote what Bill Simon wanted."

In 1975, Gergen went to work for president Ford, in his first big-title White

House job, director of communications. After Jimmy Carter took the White House in 1977, Gergen made his first forays into political journalism, writing freelance articles and, in March 1978, becoming the first managing editor of *Public Opinion,* a new magazine published by the American Enterprise Institute, a conservative think tank.

On the side, Gergen the journalist remained Gergen the political operator, writing speeches in 1977 and 1978 for Ronald Reagan and Simon, as they explored their presidential chances. But it was clear that Simon's appeal to nonplutocratic voters was limited, and Gergen began looking for a candidate in the 1980 race. He settled, very lightly, on George Bush, the slim reed upon whom Republican moderates rested their hopes of stopping Reagan from taking over the party.

"He became Bush's unofficial issues guy," recalls David Keene, who was then Bush's national political director, "putting together gatherings of economists in Kennebunkport and writing speeches." But at the time Bush attracted so little support in the polls that news accounts called him the "asterisk" candidate. Gergen kept a low profile, citing a busy schedule as the reason for turning down an offer by Bush and his campaign manager, James Baker, who had also worked with Ford, to join the campaign formally as issues director.

Then, on January 21, 1980, Bush unexpectedly won the Iowa Republican caucus and became the instant front-runner. "The very next day, Gergen called up Baker and said, miracle of miracles, he had managed to clear his schedule and would be able to take the job after all," Keene says. "When Baker said the job was filled, Gergen came in as a volunteer speechwriter." In the month between the Iowa caucus and the New Hampshire primary, when Bush was the leading Republican candidate, Gergen, according to Keene, "was very visible."

But on February 26, Bush lost the New Hampshire primary to a resurgent Ronald Reagan. "And Gergen just disappeared completely, I mean right away," recalls Peter Teeley, Bush's press secretary at the time. "We never heard from him again until he turned up with Reagan at the Republican convention."

Even the Reaganites, who benefited from Gergen's leap, were appalled by the speed of it. "He came to us as soon as it began to seem Bush was going to lose, definitely before Bush pulled out, and quite frankly this made us very suspicious of him," recalls a former Reagan campaign official. "I mean, there's jumping ship and there's *jumping ship.* This guy was elbowing the women and children aside to get overboard."

Gergen strongly denies that he showed any undue haste in switching allegiances. "It is not true that I disappeared in the campaign," he says. "I continued to advise Bush much in the same way I had up to the point he was nominated vice president."

After the Republican convention, the Reagan campaign hired Baker as an adviser, and Gergen was assigned, along with fellow Bush alumnus Frank Hodsoll, to the task of preparing the candidate's briefing books for the presidential debates. He thus became party to the most infamous episode of the 1980 campaign—the appropriation by members of the Reagan camp of the briefing papers prepared by President Jimmy Carter's staff for the campaign's first and only debate.

Gergen says today that he has "a vague memory" of receiving the Carter material, which he remembers giving to Hodsoll. But he claims that the material consisted of "a summary of what Carter had said publicly and public documents." He says he "was not aware that the material was stolen; it could have been leaked by some disgruntled person in the Carter camp." And anyway, he says, "We didn't really use the stuff."

But a 2,413-page report of the House Subcommittee on Human Resources, which investigated the "Debategate" affair in 1984, contradicts Gergen. The report concluded that the Reagan campaign had "obtained foreign policy and national defense briefing papers prepared to assist president Carter," that the papers were the "property of the Federal Government . . . likely taken from the offices of the National Security Council" and that the materials obtained "were not publicly available." It also found that the Carter papers "were used . . . to enhance Governor Reagan's performance in the debates. The persons using these papers were aware that they were using Carter debate briefing materials."

◆ ◆ ◆

Also a matter of sharply differing memories is Gergen's role in the 1980–81 presidential transition. It was during this period that the Reagan team produced a document that would become famous in political circles as "the 100 days memo," a blueprint for the successful postinaugural program to sell the nation on Reaganomics. Gergen has routinely claimed authorship, or coauthorship, of the plan; as recently as June 7 of this year [1993], he recalled it as something "I wrote." And this credit was one reason Clinton strategists sought out his advice during the 1992–93 transition.

Richard Wirthlin, Reagan's chief pollster at the time and widely acknowledged to be the primary author of the memo, remembers Gergen's contributions in more modest terms—a recollection corroborated by other former Reagan aides. "I brought together a small team—myself, Roger Porter, who later came to the White House as a domestic policy adviser, and Richard Beal, who'd worked on issues in the campaign," Wirthlin says. "We were the unit that produced the paper. Gergen contributed in a minor way—an eight-to-ten-page historical overview of other presidential beginnings—and a suggested first-month schedule."

Gergen joined the Reagan White House in January 1981 as a staff director, and became communications director toward the end of the first one hundred days, following the shooting of James Brady, the press secretary. "Up to this point, our guys had never really understood how to work a story," recalls Ed Rollins, who was hired as deputy to Lyn Nofziger, the first director of the White House political affairs office. "But Gergen really understood sound bites. He understood how to pick a story, how to get a story that somebody was working on and change it, how to get the reporters to call the people you wanted them to call and make the story come out how you wanted. He understood that you had to be proactive about it, as opposed to just letting you guys do your job and us just reading about it in the paper the next day."

The Reagan White House set up a structure closely modeled on the Nixon operation, with a coordinated program for disseminating the administration line through government and party surrogates and a sophisticated system of news-media manipulation. "It isn't hard to do," says Joe Canzeri, then a White House advance man. "You get all your team together ahead of time and you say 'Gentlemen, this week we will be selling tacos, not nachos.' Whether they really are tacos doesn't matter. If we tell you guys they are tacos enough times, you'll believe they're tacos."

The news-media operation was principally directed by a group that included Michael Deaver (the deputy chief of staff and the president's chief imagist), Gergen, Richard Darman, Kenneth Duberstein, and Canzeri. Deaver directed the meetings, which took place every Friday afternoon at Blair House, the White House's guest residence.

"We tried to plan and manage hour by hour what Reagan was going to do, to keep the focus on the theme," Deaver remembers. "We would go through the president's schedule day by day and hour by hour, and figure out what we wanted the story to be at the end of each day and at the end of the week. And that worked about ninety percent of the time."

To Gergen fell the crucial task of spinning and leaking. "Baker decided early on that there were only two constituencies that mattered—the national media and Congress—and he devoted a great deal of time and energy to wooing the media," Rollins recalls. "Larry Speakes"—the White House spokesman—"wasn't allowed in the key decision-making meetings, so he really couldn't tell the press anything but the canned lines. Anybody who wanted to find out anything beyond that had to go somewhere else. And in that White House, pretty much the only place they could go was to Baker and Gergen.

"Gergen was Baker's man, and reporters had to go to him to get to Baker," Rollins continues. "Every major news organization had an hour a week with Baker, every week. When he was chief of staff, Baker spent thirty-five hours a week talking to journalists. He gave an hour a day to the three networks, to the *New York Times,* the *Washington Post,* the *Los Angeles Times* and the *Wall Street Journal.* Gergen had to fill in all the blanks. Baker would give the big overview to the press at the end of the week—this is what we're going to do next week, et cetera—and then Gergen would, day by day, hour by hour, deal with things that came up."

As the chief daily leaker, Gergen became an essential figure for reporters, someone with whom it paid to speak as often as possible. This gave him access to valuable information in return—the daily knowledge of what the White House press corps was working on. Then, completing the circle, he was in a position to spin the reporters, so that the final stories would reflect, at least in part, the White House point of view.

"Dave was compulsive in his leaks," recalls one former White House official. "When he would leave a meeting in a hurry, people would joke that he was rushing to meet his deadline. People called him the assistant to the president for the *New York Times.*"

Gergen's work in shaping the image of Ronald Reagan allowed him to shape another image—that of David Gergen. "He was not discerning about how his leaks made the president appear," says the former Reagan official. "There was a very strong feeling that he was motivated more by a desire to ingratiate himself with reporters than by any desire to help the president."

Eventually, according to several former administration officials, including Vic Gold, a Bush biographer and speechwriter, Baker called Gergen in for a discussion of the leaks. This led to Gergen's resignation in 1983.

"There is no question Gergen's leaking had something to do with his departure," says another official. "He did not leave by his own choice. He was strongly encouraged to move on by Baker."

Gergen recalls today that Baker did indeed call him in for a meeting and told him that there were "many daggers" aimed at him, including one wielded by the well-manicured hand of Nancy Reagan. And, according to Gergen, when he told Baker he had decided to leave the White House, Baker replied, "I think that's a wise decision." But Gergen maintains the decision was strictly his own: "I was not pushed."

It is the autumn of 1993, and Bill Clinton, who is as surely of the apex of the image age as John F. Kennedy was of its dawn, looms over the video landscape, cordless microphone in hand, forever talking, listening, empathizing. At times, it seems his is the presidency as public-access television; everyone gets on the air with him sooner or later. He talks with Larry King and Tabitha Soren and Katie Couric and Dan Rather and Arsenio Hall and Don Imus—and with mall shoppers and redwood loggers and hardhats and soldiers and sailors and teachers and children and folks eating lunch.

In the selling of the administration's health plan, politics, policy, advertising, and journalism have become, finally, a single organism. Speaking before Congress to introduce the health plan on September 22, the president holds aloft a red, white, and blue card of gleaming Visa-like plastic, on the back of which is printed, in the language of a late-night-television insurance pitch, a promise of such largesse as to give God pause: "This health security card guarantees you a comprehensive package of benefits that can never be taken away."

In the surrounding hoopla: Hillary Rodham Clinton makes five televised congressional appearances and sits for interviews with Tom Brokaw, Dan Rather, Paula Zahn, Katie Couric, and Joan Lunden. . . . The president answers questions from the citizenry for two and a half hours on *Nightline,* is the host of a televised "town meeting" in California and conducts an Oprah Winfrey–style show at a Queens diner, where people chosen by the White House to illustrate inadequate health insurance tell of their suffering. . . . The Democratic National Committee kicks off a direct-mail-and-telephone drive featuring letters, which are Robo-signed by the president and resemble in tone Ed McMahon's missives on behalf of Publishers' Clearinghouse. ("The winner of this campaign would not be a politician, but every American family.") . . . The Clintons hold what Gergen calls "a very dignified lunch" for two dozen big-foot journalists, including R. W. Apple Jr. of the *New York Times,* David Broder of the *Washington Post,* Jack Germond of the *Baltimore Sun,* Michael Kinsley of the *New Republic,* Jack Nelson of the *Los Angeles Times* and Albert Hunt of the *Wall Street Journal.* . . . Meanwhile, fifty-five radio talk-show hosts broadcast live from tables set up on the front lawn of the White House, as administration spinners shuttle and weave among them.

By contrast, Franklin Delano Roosevelt introduced the Social Security Act in 1935 with a modest, brief message to Congress that was read by clerks; during the ensuing legislative process, he spoke publicly about it only twice: once in a short press conference and once in a radio address.

But the president in 1993 seems to have lost the option of exercising dignity or restraint in support of his policies. The conversation of politics now is carried on in the vernacular of advertising now. The big sell, the television sell, appears to be the only way to sell. Increasingly, and especially in Washington, how well one does on television has come to determine how well one does in life.

The attorney general presides over a disastrous commando raid on a religious cult in Texas that leaves at least eighty people dead—and is hailed as a new American hero for performing well on *Nightline.* The vice president appears on *Late Show with David Letterman,* where guests are expected to mock themselves, and wins applause by doing so with gusto; he says his Secret Service code name is Buttafuoco and performs the Stupid Vice President Trick of breaking a glass ashtray with a hammer. Ross Perot, a rich man who made his fortune on government contracts to computerize the welfare state, becomes a political force playing the made-for-television character of a feisty, folksy, six-gunning outsider. Washington writers work overtime crafting clever bits for turns on the talk shows; a Sunday on *Meet the Press* does more to reaffirm a print reporter's standing than all the work he might do in that week.

Washington has become a strange and debased place, the true heart of a national culture in which the distinction between reality and fantasy has been lost, a culture that has produced Oliver Stone as a historian, Joe McGinniss as a biographer, Geraldo Rivera as a journalist, Leonard Jeffries as a geneticist, and Barbra Streisand as an authority on national policy. The standards and boundaries that have been eroding for years have at last faded almost completely away. The rare governmental privilege of speaking under the cloak of anonymity, traditionally granted only to presidents, secretaries of state and generals in time of war, has become an accepted practice for midlevel White House aides explaining routine policy matters to large roomfuls of reporters. Movie stars show up with their press agents and their bodyguards to "testify" before Congress. Politicians and reporters make cameo appearances as movie stars, playing themselves in fictional scenes about politics and reporting.

Political operatives call themselves journalists and journalists behave like political operatives, giving private advice to their politician friends—and this practice is so widely accepted as to be uncommented on. In early 1992, the advisers to presidential candidate Clinton included the journalist Gergen. In February, on the darkest day of the campaign, when the story broke of the candidate's famous 1969 letter on his Vietnam War draft status, Gergen says he "had a serious talk" with Clinton, "all about where he was going, what he was going through." "I walked through with him what the essence of the charge against him was," Gergen says, "and the essence of his response . . . and I told him what particular point in his response had made the best impression on me."

Journalists have also joined politicians in the business of selling the pleasure of their company to special-interest groups. Not long ago, only someone in position actually to create objective reality—a lawmaker, for instance—could hope to receive an "honorarium" of thousands of dollars for spending an hour or so chatting up a roomful of lobbyists. Now the marketplace recognizes that those who create the perception of reality are equally worthy of honor in the form of cash. At a convention of the American Medical Association last year in Atlanta, according to an AMA spokesman, the paid speakers included Tom Brokaw, Michael Kinsley, Jeff Levine (the CNN health issues reporter), and Marshall Loeb (the managing editor of *Fortune* magazine). In his last year and a half as a journalist, before joining the White House, Gergen earned almost $700,000 from speaking engagements.

The press pack has become both obese and incestuous. There are 1,700 accredited White House reporters, and most of them keep in promiscuous electronic touch—through Nexis and the Federal News Service and the Associated Press and Reuters and CNN and PBS and C-Span—with one another's work and with the vast bloviation of words and pictures that Washington produces every day. Overwhelmed by size and undermined by excessive intimacy, the pack has lost its howling way. It has become as faddish as a teenager, vacillating in its attitudes toward the powers that be, going from bubbling enthusiasm to hysterical anger, from cheering all that the president says to denouncing all that the president does. It is so thoroughly conformist that it celebrates group-think as (conventional) wisdom.

Obsessed with the appearances of things, the pack is perpetually susceptible to the machinations of the image makers. It rewards, with glowing praise, triumphs of form over content: medium-well-turned phrases, smart photo ops, effective PR stunts. But it is also unhappily aware of its vulnerability, and exacts a perverse revenge by seizing on the slightest misstep, the smallest deviation from the perfect image, as an example of what Gergen calls "a naked moment in politics," a metaphoric event that presumes to cut through the theater to show the true man. A single such event—Clinton and the haircut, Quayle and the potato(e), Carter and the killer rabbit, Bush at the checkout counter—its significance heightened with every retelling, can permanently scar a public figure, and several in a row can be fatal. Every year, a new species of misdemeanor is defined as a high crime. This year, inattention to the tax laws regarding babysitters and house cleaners became the hanging offense.

Unhappily aware that much of what government officials say and do in public is a charade, unknowing of much that occurs behind closed doors and unwilling to admit ignorance, reporters fashion reality out of perceptions. A *New York Times* article in February reports that the president's advisers are worried about "the perception thus wrought" by his rocky beginning, and says the administration is working "to refocus its image as a government of broad, middle-class interests." A *Times* report in May finds "a perception that the president," who won office as a political centrist, "has come to look very much like the same old—liberal—thing."

These bits of fatuousness are unexceptional in contemporary Washington journalism; they stand out in my mind only because I wrote them myself.

◆ ◆ ◆

A lot of people, even in Washington, look upon all this with regret and even horror, but for David Gergen the reaction is more painfully personal. After twenty years of helping make the game of Washington what it is, he is now stirred, he says, by feelings of sadness and guilt.

"This is a hard thing to discuss," he says. "It's very close to the bone. But in our public affairs, including the presidency, there's a certain amount of propaganda that goes on, a certain amount of overselling, and I plead guilty to doing a lot of it in the past. . . . I feel a measure of guilt about accelerating the game, and making it bigger in years past. I felt at the time it was important . . . and I contributed to it, participated in it, I believed in it, I thought it was the right thing. And I think what I did helped lead to the changes in the way the game is played today, where it has been taken beyond where we were then. It had some consequences we didn't foresee. The game has become more and more the thing; there is an overselling in politics now that was not there to this degree twelve years ago, fourteen years ago. . . . It has become structural.

"But my larger sense of guilt, to the degree that I share in this responsibility, is not about the PR game that has developed, but about what's happening to the people of this country because of it. I don't think government over the last twenty years has been anywhere near as responsive as it should have been with some very real problems. And I realize now that the measure of success ought not to be, you know, presidential rhetoric—although that's an important element of measured success—but actions that really make a difference in terms of how we affect people's lives. And in this sense, I think government and the people in Washington have been derelict over the last twenty years."

He defends his return to the White House as an act not of opportunism but of expiation for the sins of his work in administrations past. "I guess I feel I pay my debt back to society by seeing changes made that would affect our lives in a way that would match our public rhetoric," he says.

In two long conversations, Gergen returns again and again to this theme. "What I've become cynical about is that a lot of what happens in Washington now is not about things that have connection to people's lives outside this city. It's all the ball game now. It's not about whether an idea makes sense in terms of changing the country. And through all these games over the years, the country has been going down the tubes."

He says he would like to leave the game behind. "I know that some of it is necessary. I know that it is part of the way that the game is played, but I just don't find it personally as alluring as I once did. . . . I've evolved. I used to spend a lot of time worrying about how do we shape the next day's headline? How do we shape that nice picture? Maybe it's a question of age, or maybe just that I've been there, but I'm not the person who thinks about that sort of thing every day now."

The Sieve leaks only on occasion now, and only at the highest levels. At fifty-one, he says, he sees Washington—and himself—differently from the days when he was young and "very ambitious and very much going after the brass ring." When he speaks of the men he admires, he speaks of the legends of the city, the political players who became insiders' insiders and finally reached the apogee of success, the special status known as wise man. The names roll off his tongue— Robert Strauss, the consummate deal maker; Bryce Harlow, the lawyer-lobbyist who worked for two Republican administrations, and, of course, Clark Clifford, adviser to Democratic presidents since Truman—the city's eminence grise until, Gergen contends, "he was smeared" in the BCCI scandal.

Gergen does not claim the wise man title for himself yet, but already he is talking like one. When he speaks of counseling the forty-seven-year-old Clinton, he sounds a bit like a proud teacher noting the progress of a promising student.

"He's evolving," Gergen says of the president. "I think he's got a much better grasp of the job." When Gergen first came to the White House in May, he says Clinton "had been buffeted so heavily in the early months that I felt he had lost his footing and wasn't as sure of what it is he wanted to be as I had seen in the past. And it seemed to me over the course of the summer, he was gaining it back."

There are still problems, Gergen says: "He needs more time to think. We need to build more time into his schedule so he can think. . . . He's at his best when he's decided what he really thinks. He's not comfortable otherwise. I've seen this just again and again. On gays in the military—he wasn't comfortable until he had a chance to really work his own way through it. He wasn't comfortable with Lani Guinier until he'd worked his way through it. He wasn't comfortable in Somalia until he had worked his way through it."

In this ongoing process, Gergen sees his own role as "not to say, 'Here's what you must do in the next three days on this issue,' but to say: 'Here are your options. Let's talk about them and sort through what the consequences are. Let's think it through. Let's ask some hard questions. Let's look down around the corner. When the thing blows up in our faces, as it may, where do you want to be, and how are you going to feel about that?'"

But even more important, Gergen says, the Bill Clinton of today, "has developed—and I've talked about this with him a fair amount—a different view of the presidency and what leadership is about, and how to lead."

Interestingly enough, this different view of leadership harks back to the presidency of yesterday, the presidency in a time before people like Gergen went to work on it. "There have been so many lies told in the past, so many things oversold in the past," Gergen says. The president, he argues, must abandon the role of "commentator in chief," appearing on television every night to pronounce on whatever needs to be sold that day or whatever the press wants reaction to. "People don't need to see him out there with a comment on whatever it is." Instead, Gergen says, the president must "set this larger vision and be working toward that, and set goals for the nation, and try to inspire people toward those goals. And I think he's gotten much better at that."

The selling of the president, Gergen says, has got to calm down, to return to a closer connection with reality. "We have been subjected to so much hype and fluff, that a bit more modesty could pay dividends," he says. "The resources you have to deal with are so limited and the changes you can make are mostly so incremental, that it is important not to oversell. If you do, the bs factor is so high on both sides that people see it immediately as over the top."

It would be nice to think that this modest proposal isn't merely Gergen's ultimate spin—the spinner renouncing his past spinning, as he spins again. It would be nicer yet to think that Gergen's words might become reality, that the game might end or at least slow down, that the faith of image and insiderism that defines Washington might finally lose its appeal. But not even David Gergen, the budding wise man, really thinks that is going to happen anytime soon.

"The other day, as I was leaving the White House," he says, "I counted the cameras on the lawn for the evening standups. There were twenty-four of them. Twenty-four! What do you do about that? What do you do about the line of interview requests as long as your arm. If the president says to hell with them, then he's inaccessible. If he does the interviews, he's overselling again.

"So much of what we do has become a necessary part of the game. It's almost impossible to change the rules in the middle."

He sounds almost wistful. "To think that you can turn off the government's information machine and still run the government is—why, it's hard to imagine it. It requires an enormous leap into a wholly different approach, and one that would probably bring about some unforeseen consequences to the whole system. You know, the presidency probably would just become dysfunctional."

Wonk New World

◆ ◆ ◆

I am an old man, and I sit on my porch watching the world go by. Watching the world go by became a major pastime again after the enactment in 2020 of the Communications Sweetness and Light Act, which built upon the Communications Decency Act of 1996, the Communications Wholesomeness Act of 2000 and the Communications Purity of Spirit Act of 2008, and which pretty much finished off what there was worth watching on the tube.

I smoke my pipe. Well, not "smoke" exactly, and not "pipe," really. It's shaped like a pipe, but it's made of solid recycled farm-raised maple. It has no bowl, no hollow stem. Real pipes have been illegal since the first year of the first Rodham administration. The pipes were the last of the regulated Nicotine Delivery Systems to be phased out; cigarettes of course were the first, banned by Surgeon General Brazelton in 2002, followed by cigars in 2005 and smokeless tobacco in 2006.

A lot of people still illicitly smoke, of course; and you can score snuff on any inner-city corner, and there are kits you can buy to convert a solid pipe into a fully hollow one. But since the passage of the "three puffs and you're out" bill, I haven't really wanted to take any chances with the law.

I watch my grandson M (they shortened all names to initials in '07, part of President Gore's Fourth Reduction in Paperwork Act) pedaling his bike up the sidewalk. He's coming home from his volunteer work at the recycling center. He volunteers for something every day. Well, you have to, of course. In the first year after passage of the Restoration of the American Community Act, they tried voluntary volunteerism, but it didn't work at all. It turned out the only people who wanted to volunteer were already volunteering for a lot of things, and didn't want to do any more, except for ex-President Carter. Lord, he was busy that year. Anyway, after a year, Volunteerism Czar Etzioni instituted the all-draft volunteer force, and after that everything went pretty smoothly, except for the expected problems with draft-dodgers—people trying to duck their duties by signing up with the army and that sort of thing.

M is fourteen now, and next year the mandatory training wheels can come off his bike. I can see that he is getting bored riding (with the governors they put on the new bikes, you can't go much faster than one of those old pre–Info Wars modems), and I call him over to chat. As he walks up the path, it's clear that he is itching to take off his helmet, but he doesn't. The regulations say you have to keep the helmet on for a full minute after disembarking from your bicycle, and he's a good boy. Besides, a helmet is required for any form of locomotion at any speed exceeding that determined to be safe by the Recreational Safety and Health Administration (RSHA) according to the age, weight, and health of the locomotor, surface upon which the locomotor is locomoting, adjoining surfaces, incline or decline if any, and weather conditions. It's all very complicated, and most people just figure it's easier to wear the helmets any time they are moving at all, to be on the safe side.

M walks up the differently abled access ramp to the porch. He used to enjoy using the stairs, but they banned stairs last year; people just wouldn't stop using them, even though they knew it was against the law to flaunt their abledness. They tried prosecuting stair climbers, but the ACLU challenged the law, arguing that, under First Amendment rights, stair climbing was, in certain circum-stances—including but not limited to climbing the stairs of a public building and using a Stairmaster—a form of protected speech. After the Estrich Court ruled for the ACLU in a split decision, the Justice Department backed down for a while, but Attorney General Reno, in her famous "end it, don't mend it," speech, proposed outlawing stairs entirely. The measure was immediately passed by a focus group of six representatives and three senators (under the terms of the 2011 Morris-Luntz Government Flexibility Act, legislation could be passed by focus groups convened by licensed pollsters, thus doing away with the unwieldy and time-consuming process of actual head-count voting, and allowing the rep-resentatives of the people to spend more time in their districts). So that was that for stairs.

M sits down on the hammock (it turned out chairs were really tough on your back, and, as Food and Drug Administration Director Michael Jacobson pointed out in his seminal testimony on the matter, the costs incurred by chair sitters with all their chiropractic sessions and massage therapies were passed on to all of us in the form of higher premiums for Medicare, Part E; so that was that for chairs). He turns to me.

"M," he says to me (we share the same initial; according to the Fifth Reduction in Paperwork Act, all same-sex members of a family unit may "employ no more than 1.5 initials," and no one knows what .5 of an initial is). Our house signer draws the letter in the air: a big fancy "M." Under the bipartisan Kennedy, Kennedy, Kennedy & Thurmond Act of 2012, which combined the Fourth Amendment to the Americans with Disabilities Act to the Sixth Amendment to the Personal Responsibility and Work Opportunity Act, the government mandated signing for the hearing challenged in any conversation involving two or more persons conducted in any setting defined as public, semipublic, or quasi-private; and then it put everybody still on welfare to work training everybody else as signers. So we are all signers now. To be honest, a lot of people don't take it very seriously. You see a lot of bad grammar and slang out there. Then, of course, there have been the usual identity problems to sort out. The furor over House Majority Whip Maxine Waters's proposal to mandate Ebonics signers for any conversation taking place in an area where it might infringe upon the space of a hearing-challenged African American was deeply troubling. God knows what would have happened if Senator Biden had not defused the issue with his proposal for a $225 million program to study the whole issue, under the auspices of a recognized leader in the Ebonics field, the Maxine Waters School of Government.

"Yes, my boy," I say. The signer looks askance, and I know I've made some sort of mistake again.

"It's the 'my boy,'" says M, helpfully. "That's genderism, grandperson."

"Oh, yes," I say. "Well, what is it, my young one?" Again no movement from the signer.

"Ageism, grandperson."

"Right. Well then, how about it, my person in his or her own right?" The signer beams approvingly, and makes a flurry of motions.

"Grandperson," says M, "tell me again about the time when the era of big government ended."

A Plea for Diversity

• • •

Around here, we have been talking lately about whom President Clinton should pick as his new secretary of state, and, by and large, the conversation has been conducted on a pretty elevated plane. Until now. By the time this is read, Clinton may have made his choice, but I would still like to take this opportunity to get on the record with a low, ad hominem assault against two fine men. I'm violently opposed to the idea of Richard Holbrooke as secretary of state and only slightly less set against George Mitchell, and it is entirely personal. I don't care if they're qualified. They represent that which makes life in Washington hell. They are archetypes of the Washington Male. The Washington Male is the reason so many Washington females have that drawn, pained expression all the time. It comes from having dinner with Washington Males. I grew up here, and I have been going with mounting reluctance to Washington dinner parties more or less all my life, and at every table I have ever sat at there has been either a Holbrooke or a Mitchell. One is louder than the other, but they're both unbearable. There is nothing that arises in This Town on which they do not have an opinion. And it is going to be an informed opinion. And it is going to be an informed opinion that they have recently shared with the president, or Ted Koppel, or Bill Safire. And it is going to be an informed opinion expressed in ringing, plonking tones. And it is very likely going to be a fatuous informed opinion recently shared, ringingly expressed. But there is not going to be any gainsaying it, not unless you are prepared to spend the next two hours arguing the finer points of Pamela Harriman's subtle influence on our policy toward Nagorno-Karabakh. There's no kidding about it, either; the Washington Male has absolutely and profoundly no sense of humor.

And greater love hath no man than this: that of the Washington Male for the Washington Male. A really pure Washington Male can be wrong about everything he does and says for decades without harboring a single twinge of self-doubt. (Robert McNamara was probably the platonic ideal here. You would think that a man who had given the world the Edsel, flexible response, and the war in Vietnam would stop to consider whether he was really cut out for executive work. But no, on to the World Bank and to building the debt crisis.) Earlier this year, the playwright Anna Deavere Smith spent a couple of months in Washington observing the locals. The thing that above all amazed her, she told me, was her discovery of the habit the Washington Male has, when reaching for a particularly bon mot, of literally quoting himself. "You will be seated next to some man at a dinner party—a reporter, usually—and he will turn to you, and say, 'As I said on Brinkley yesterday,' and then he will, honestly, repeat word for word what he did say on Brinkley yesterday," she marveled. "It's the most astonishing thing." There are women in Washington who have been listening to this sort of stuff every night for thirty years. It's a miracle the homicide rate is as low as it is.

Holbrooke is, in a very obvious way, the perfect Washington Male. You couldn't make him up. I spent some time last summer trailing him around Washington and Croatia for a story in the *New Yorker* about his efforts to negotiate a peace in Bosnia. Generally, the problem in this kind of reporting is getting access to the person you are writing about: People involved in sensitive diplomatic missions tend to be wary about talking to the press. With Holbrooke, the problem was limiting the access. I would spend two or three hours taping, say, Holbrooke on Milosevic, walk back to my hotel room and barely get my shoes off before the phone rang with a call from the State Department operator patching through Holbrooke on Karadzic. He once called me in the middle of the night to announce that he had made space for me on his jet for a flight early the next morning from Belgrade to Sarajevo. But, I said weakly, I was not in Belgrade. I was in Washington, in bed. He was appalled. Well, he said, the flight leaves in seven hours. Could I get to Belgrade by then? Eventually, exhaustedly, I wrote a modest story that I thought was mostly positive; it gave Holbrooke the credit he deserved for the Dayton peace plan, such as it was. I don't think Holbrooke liked it very much. A year later he found a better biographer: himself. He wrote up his own story and the *New Yorker* published it, at about the time the Nobel Committee was deciding who should get the peace prize this year. A few days after the magazine went on the stands, the *New Yorker*'s publicity department got a telephone call from Holbrooke's office. The ambassador's office wanted to know if the *New Yorker* had sent a copy of the issue to every member of Congress.

Mitchell is a less obvious Washington Male than Holbrooke. He is a lot quieter, for one thing. But he is alike in the essentials. Where Holbrooke has ostentatiously clawed and grappled his way up the greasy pole, Mitchell has more gently floated ever higher, borne on the uplifting vapors of mediocrity rising to its natural level. As Senate majority leader, he managed to be both relentlessly partisan and relentlessly ineffective. He did at least as much as Newt Gingrich to cost the Democrats Congress, and he was even more sanctimonious about it. Actually, in a contest between Holbrooke and Mitchell, Holbrooke comes out ahead. He is at least skilled at what he does (that is to say, he is skilled at bullying people, which is how he got the boys to sign in Dayton, and he is skilled at leaking and spinning to the press, which is how he made Dayton look like Appomattox). And he is naked in his hungers, and there is something perversely appealing about that. Mitchell manages, like McNamara, to augment a nearly total lack of competence with a nearly total conviction that he is perfectly competent for anything. Holbrooke is Kissinger without the wit; Mitchell is Christopher without the suits. Holbrooke as secretary would mean that the *New York Times* would run every day a story detailing how, in the words of an unnamed senior administration official, everyone in the administration except Secretary Holbrooke was an utter buffoon. Mitchell as secretary would mean that the *Times* would run every day a story explaining how, in the words of an unnamed senior administration official, we could do business with the Serbs, but not with the Republicans.

So what is called for is diversity. Give the job to the candidate from the other gender. Madeleine Albright has a lot of things going for her. She is smart, she is not averse to the use of force, she has been tough and right at the United Nations, she can't abide Boutros Boutros-Ghali, and at times she is even funny. It is true that she is a friend of Barbra Streisand, but it's only a matter of time before Richard Holbrooke and George Mitchell are friends of Barbra Streisand, too.

The Midlife Crisis
of Jesse Jackson

◆ ◆ ◆

When Jesse Jackson hears the news, thrilled in his ear in the elevator at the Democratic National Committee headquarters, that his friend Mitch Snyder has hanged himself with electrical cord, he is, of course, stunned, but it takes him just twenty seconds to see the silver lining of opportunity peeping from the cloud on this fetid summer day. Let's get over there, he says, and nine minutes later his Lincoln Town Car pulls up to the shelter where homeless-rights militant Snyder lived and died. A scene, as is so often the case in the venues of Jackson's triumphs, of chaos and anger and despair.

Hundreds of street people wander about, some talking to the cameras, a few wailing, others merely looking crazy. Fat, hot raindrops splatter off the bodies of the unwashed, and the air steams with sweat and urine. Jackson's arrival is a pandemoniac event. Bag ladies shriek "Jesse! Jesse!" Reporters throng. Cameramen curse and jockey for fresh positions. Stepping lightly in his black tasseled loafers, Jackson sails through, up to the yellow police ribbon that bars the shelter door. The cops usher him in; Jackson's presence at a newsworthy tragedy has become part of the script in the Age of Talk, like the microwave trucks and the lawyers seeking the rights to the story.

When Jackson comes out, an hour later, he has a triumph in his pocket. He had taken Snyder's girlfriend, shelter administrator Carol Fennelly, upstairs, and together they planned Mitch's long good-bye: a televised memorial service and a televised funeral, complete with Hollywood stars, followed by a televised protest march to city hall. And the ringmaster of the whole shebang, the star of every luscious, brightly lighted moment, will be Jesse. Another stunner by the grand master of media. Who but Jesse Jackson would have dared this?

Who but Jesse Jackson could have succeeded?

Except . . . here we are on burial day and something is wrong. It isn't the featured player. On the steps of Washington, D.C.'s District Building, facing the cameras and shouting that attention must be paid, Jackson is turning in his standard fine performance. It's not the props; he's come bearing a dead man, and you can't beat that. It isn't the cast; the cameramen are here, and the reporters, and hundreds of grieving protesters. It is the audience.

Where is it? Where are the people who aren't paid to be here or aren't part of the protest? Where are the multitudes at the feet of Jesse?

A small and sweat-drenched rabble is all there is. Jackson faces them and shouts his great call of self: "I *am* somebody!" All his life, he has been yelling this at the world. "I am somebody," giggles a young black man who is wearing nothing but a pair of nylon running shorts and who has pranced all the way to city hall as a drum major of the mind, throwing an imaginary baton high in the air and catching it every time. "Respect me!" Jackson yells. "Respect me," says a man with a sign that reads WHO KILLED MITCH SNYDER? ("The CIA killed him, of course," confides the man. "He was always trouble for the government.") "Protect me!" shouts Jackson. "Protect me," says Louis Farrakhan's legal adviser George X Cure, beaming at Jackson's side. "Never neglect me!" Jackson thunders. "Never neglect me," says perpetually angry ex-comedian Dick Gregory. "I *am* somebody!" Jackson crows again. "I *am* somebody!" yell the handful of semi-pro protesters who will soon get themselves arrested trying to harass city-council members who, unfortunately, have already departed.

Jackson looks out over the mini-mob. "This is the real Rainbow Coalition," he says. He means this as a happy thought, but it is not.

◆ ◆ ◆

Jesse Louis Jackson is forty-nine years old and suffering from a midlife crisis. It is not the usual sort, not a tremor of waning libido or of looming mortality. It is a crisis of relevance. Relevance is the base of all that Jackson has. His extraordinary career rests on the strength of his great talent for seizing the moment, for being in the right place at the right time and shouting the right thing. This skill has made him America's foremost political celebrity. More than 80 percent of his countrymen know who he is, and when he walks down the street, passersby call his name and rush to touch him. He is as ubiquitous as television itself, the pièce de scenes of resistance all over America: union picket lines and college protests, rallies and marches, boycotts and farm foreclosures. He demands meetings with cabinet ministers and senators, and they comply. He jets around the world as secretary of his own state of mind, taking meetings with kings and rebels. He has twice run for president and thus has won a prominent place both in politics and in history. He has become a major force within the Democratic Party, dominating its national conventions in 1984 and 1988. He even has his own television program, *Jesse Jackson*.

And yet, all of a sudden, there is an awkward feeling in the air. A scent of So What.

A strong whiff of Who Cares.

All of a sudden, people are dismissing Jackson, or joking about him, or, worst of all, ignoring him. For any politician, this is the 4 A.M. cold-sweat nightmare. For Jackson, it is a refutation of a life that has been one ceaseless, driving demand: Attention must be paid. Really, it *must* be. When you see Jackson beam with honest delight after what must be his ten thousandth standing ovation, you know he wants to be loved; and when you hear him recount forty-year-old insults from whites as if they happened yesterday, you know he relishes hatred, too. But inattention is intolerable. One morning recently, Jackson and I were talking on the phone. He was holding forth on a favorite theme, the lousy way America treats black people. White America's ultimate weapon, Jackson said, is not to hate blacks but to ignore them. Since Jackson is America's most prominent black person, this isn't an abstract concept. He is talking about himself, about his life, about his greatest fear. "The opposite of love isn't hate, you know. It's indifference," he said. "Indifference is worse than hate." This isn't true, of course. The opposite of love *is* hate. And indifference may be terrible in its effects, but hatred kills more and kills faster. Still, these words are true to Jackson. In his two presidential runs, he received hundreds of death threats; they waited for him like nightmarish welcome mats everywhere he went. But he stayed in the races. Better the danger of death than the threat of irrelevance. The threat that faces him now.

◆ ◆ ◆

The summer of 1990 was when it became obvious America was turning away. In June, after Nelson Mandela had been released from jail, Jackson worked himself so persistently into the hero's American tour that you could hardly take a picture of one man without the other. Photo editors cropped Jackson out. In July, he declared his campaign to make Washington, D.C., a state to be "the most important civil-rights issue of our time." Fewer than two hundred friends and allies, all called last minute by hustling aides, attended the free lunch and speech. In August, Jackson demanded the government give minorities first crack at assets salvaged from failed savings and loans. Only one reporter showed up for that announcement, and he wrote a mocking story for the *Wall Street Journal* that began "Suppose Jesse Jackson gave a news conference and nobody came."

The worst came just before Labor Day, when Jackson went to Iraq and returned home accompanying a planeload of Western hostages. When the plane landed in London, Jackson stepped out carrying five-year-old Stuart Lockwood, the boy Saddam Hussein had failed to charm in his video agitprop campaign. In 1984, when Jackson returned from the Mideast with his first celebrity hostage, navy pilot Robert Goodman Jr., the press had lionized him. This time, the reaction was brief and shallow and mostly hostile. The *London Evening Standard* said young Stuart had won an unenviable distinction: "He has been cuddled by two world-class demagogues in the space of two weeks."

Politically, things are no better than they are theatrically. This past summer, Jackson's Chicago-based Operation PUSH launched its first big boycott in years, against the Nike shoe company; the boycott is faltering in the face of corporate hostility and black indifference. Jackson's Washington-based National Rainbow Coalition has utterly failed to meet left-wing hopes that it would rise to become a serious force. "It has no professionalism, no budget, no planning . . . no field staff, no state political director, no legislative staff, no fund-raising staff," says recently resigned general counsel Jamin Raskin. "It's not an organization."

When Jackson moved to Washington in 1989, many of his advisers told him to run for mayor, for what may be his last chance to shut up the critics who say he's never done anything but talk. But Jackson decided to run instead for a job that is literally all talk: a seat as a "shadow senator," an elected lobbyist for Washington in the effort to persuade Congress to make the capital a state. "After traveling this country in two presidential campaigns and getting seven million votes," he declared in an astonishing burst of super-rampant ego, "I have *earned* the right to be part of the national governing body." But the only way you can really earn the right to be part of the national governing body is to be elected to it, and Congress isn't at all interested in making D.C. a state and Jesse Jackson a senator.

Over at the Democratic National Committee, his friends don't want him around much anymore. They have quietly rescinded some of the 1988 deals that would've made it easier for him to capture convention delegates, and they are considering cutting future conventions from four to three nights, eliminating the time for Jackson to give a prime time speech. Party chairman Ronald Brown, who was Jackson's convention manager in 1988, has urged Democrats to unite early behind a candidate who can beat Bush. Jackson, he says flatly, is not that candidate: "I think the political landscape of America would have to change significantly for that to be the case. We are going to need a candidate able to generate broad-based appeal."

Even Jackson's own wise men no longer talk of him as a growing force. John White, the former Democratic national chairman who was one of Jackson's top advisers in 1988, says Jackson blew his career by not running for mayor of Washington. "If he ever wanted to be the nominee of the party, here was his chance to prove himself," White says. "[But] this diversion throws everything out the window." Gerald Austin, Jackson's '88 campaign manager, says Jackson will run in '92 but will do no better than in 1988. "That will be his last viable hurrah," says Austin. Bert Lance, another 1988 adviser, says the only good thing Jackson can do for his party in '92 is support someone more electable; otherwise, says Lance, "not only will we not win in '92, we won't win in '96 either."

Jackson busies himself by sending out mixed signals to keep alive '92 speculation. He takes two waters-testing trips to Iowa and later says, "If I ran, I would get 10,000,000-plus votes, and that's enough to win [the nomination]." But he also says, when pushed, that he is not inclined to run.

The problem is, no one seems to care either way. The fickle fancy of the pundits has turned to a new generation of leaders—politicians who happen to be black, they are called, to differentiate them from men like Jackson, who are black politicians. The newcomers—Virginia Governor Douglas Wilder, Mississippi

Congressman Mike Espy, North Carolina's Harvey Gantt—run with the party, not against it, and build power on a coalition of white and black votes. They are the future, and, as one prominent black political strategist puts it, "Jackson is history."

Ron Brown offers me a nice little eulogy for his old boss: "It's a human tragedy more than anything else. Here is a guy who is brilliant, got great political instincts, been right on most of the issues . . . but as happens so often, not only in politics but in life, he just might not be the right message carrier."

Perhaps. But Jesse Jackson is not planning to go gently into anybody's good night. He has defined today's Democratic Party more than it cares to admit, and he is not finished with it. Jackson is the most spectacular political orator of his generation, but he has prospered not just because he knows all the tricks of the pulpit (the plummy metaphors and the witty parallelisms, the cadence of poetry trapped in prose, the sotto voce confession that soars to thundered peroration) but because he has the gift that marks the important populists and demagogues—a sense of the desire of the people and a grasp of how to exploit it.

Jackson sees something now. He sees that this is a time of identity crisis not only for himself but for the Democrats and for black America. In all three cases, the matter centers on fundamental questions of direction: moderation or militancy? Pluralism or separatism? Unity or polarization?

And in each of the three cases, the crux is the relationship, and the differences, between blacks and whites, the most emotionally charged issue in American politics still, and forever. Race has become the great subtheme in the national discourse, roiling just below the surface in debates that are ostensibly about the economy or crime or personal liberties. Old wounds are opening up.

Eyeing that storm, Jackson has spotted what he hopes is the path out of the valley of irrelevance. His choice is rooted not only in his politics but in his life. Almost everyone who knows Jackson has been struck by the sharply conflicting nature of his parts, bone-deep and unconcealable. The contradictions bubble endlessly to the surface. Jackson is a defender of egalitarianism and a champion of the workingman, but his employees know him as a dictatorial boss who can be "extremely imperious and highhanded and rude," as one former staffer puts it; the kind of man who "has a tendency to treat everyone around him like servants." He is the nation's leading scourge of bigotry, but his career has been stained by remarks of seeming prejudice against Jews, and his private conversation is notable still, says the ex-aide, for "insensitive" and "disturbing" remarks about Jews, Asians, and other nonblack minorities.

One day at a rally in Iowa, I watched Jackson comfort the widow of a farm-organization leader whose husband had been killed by lightning the year before. As I watched him hug the widow, enfolding her slight build in his big, strong arms, he seemed as good and decent a man as you could imagine in public life.

The next day, at another farm rally, I watched a grandfather come up to Jackson as he was trying to push his way to his car. "Jesse," said the old man, pushing two small boys forward, "these boys helped set this up. I hope you will shake their hands." Jackson swooped up the smaller of the two boys in his arms. He looked down at the other boy, a plump, awkward kid with a kick-me smile. "Can't pick you up," Jackson said with a laugh. "You got too much jelly." The boy's face folded in on itself. The grandfather tried to help. "Oh, he's strong. He carried bricks today." Jackson pointed at the kid's stomach and laughed again. "He carries a brick every day," he said. "Maybe two." He walked off laughing.

The difference between the one side of Jackson and the other is profound enough to disturb those who see it.

The night before Mitch Snyder's funeral, the bad Jesse shocked his naive young press secretary, Unnia Pettus, with his sneering assessment of the event the good Jesse would be attending the next day. "It really tripped me out," Pettus recalls. "He was making fun of Mitch Snyder, saying he didn't even agree with a lot of the stuff Mitch was doing, and making jokes about the funeral. . . . He said this thing is basically just a photo opportunity for him."

◆ ◆ ◆

There are at least three obvious Jesses, all of them oversized and contradictory. One is a self-anointed king/god, who sees himself in terms both imperial and messianic, as a historically great leader engaged in a lifelong mission. This is the Jesse who compares himself to Jesus Christ, Moses, and Martin Luther King Jr. and who routinely speaks in the royal *we*. This is also the Jesse who has become a powerful national voice of moral authority, a minister who has inspired generations of black youths with his stirring message of self-reliance and hope and who has become America's most important voice on behalf of, as he says, "the dispossessed, the disenfranchised and the dislocated." The second Jesse is the Huey Long of the television age, a demagogic and cynical manipulator of the press and the public who owes allegiance to no one and stoops to anything to advance himself. The third, and the best hidden, is a quasi-revolutionary, an angry boy grown into an angry man in unending conflict with a nation he sees as immoral and unjust. I spent five weeks this past summer with all three Jesses, running around in limousines and jets from speech to speech and camera to camera on the sixteen-hour-a-day campaign-without-end that is Jackson's life.

It was a confusing time. The three Jesses kept interrupting one another. One minute, I would be humbled before His Majesty, watching him flick peanut shells on the floor of his stretch limo for the driver to clean up later, as he dismissed impertinent questions like Queen Victoria addressing a footman who had strangely forgotten his place. A minute later, I would be dazzled by the Redeemer, the godly voice of higher good: "I believe leaders must go to where they are tested; not just sit on committees but go to the point of challenge where some workers are fighting for their dignity, farmers at some auction, people in some emergency room trying to get medical care," he says in a tone rich with compassion. "It is not my position in the Kingdom that matters; it is that I am in a position to help."

But then, swooping in from the wings would descend the Kingfish, snatching greedily at every bright bit of grandeur and angling for each grain of gain, such as when he dropped hints to appalled Democratic leaders that as a shadow senator he expected to be treated "as a peer" and invited to speak on the Senate floor.

Later, I would hear the hard, bitter voice of the core Jackson, the kid from Jim Crow country who will never forget and never forgive an America that did him wrong: "I had to go to the back of the bus or go to jail. It was not very subtle. I had to walk past [the] school where I couldn't go because of race. I couldn't just wander down to Simpson's or J.C. Penney's [to shop] because of race. I couldn't use the bathroom downtown because of race," he says, his voice rising as he jumps from his hotel-room bed to pace the floor in agitation. "I saw my father hang his head because he could not vote. Was a veteran of World War Two and could not vote! Mowed the lawn for some German people he had fought in the war—they could vote, he could not!

"I saw the men in my neighborhood picked up by the white police, who called them vagrants if they decided the men didn't have enough money in their pockets—didn't have eleven dollars—and took them off to jail! And then brought them back in chain gangs, to the same streets where they lived. Brought them back in chain gangs, wearing those striped suits, bundled up in chains! And made them clean the gutters of the streets where they lived—in front of their wives and children. While the *white* man sat there with his shotgun."

This chilling story illustrates the inevitability of the Jackson of 1990. Jackson has spent most of his adult life as a race warrior, fighting the enemy of his youth, paying back the old hurts. During his long years as a civil-rights activist, his style and message were about conflict. In 1987 and '88, in pursuit of white votes, he abandoned the theme of racial discord. The new Jesse Jackson preached a message of political harmonic convergence. It worked, but only to a limited degree;

he got about 12 percent of the white vote and finished second in a crowded Democratic field.

Now, desperate under the goad of political and personal imperative in fast-changing times, Jackson has returned to the beliefs of his heart and the ways of his early success. The route he has chosen to escape irrelevancy is old, not new. It represents the ascendancy of the latter two Jesses over the Redeemer. It is the way of polarization, of race against race and class against class.

There are several things wrong with his solution: It is an exploitation of prejudice, anger, and fear. It almost certainly won't work. And if it does work, it will further cripple the Democratic Party as a force in presidential politics for the foreseeable future and ultimately destroy Jackson himself. But those are more long-term problems. In the here and now, there are three things right with Jackson's approach, at least from his point of view: It will probably allow him to retain considerable power within the Democratic Party for at least one more presidential cycle. It reflects, as we shall see, his true beliefs. And it couldn't be more relevant. Meet the Reverend Jackson, the preacher of apocalypse now.

◆   ◆   ◆

July. Washington, D.C., is in trouble and on edge. The levels of murder, illegitimate births, crack addiction, infant deaths, and high-school dropouts are staggeringly high. Almost all of the people represented by these indexes of wretchedness are black and poorer than ever. Former Mayor-for-Life Marion Barry, once the symbol of black political pride here, is in the middle of a perjury-and-drug trial that stars His Honor on videotape, cursing and smoking crack. The mayor, seizing on what will turn out to be a successful defense tactic (the judge declared a mistrial on the most serious charges; Barry was convicted of one misdemeanor possession count), feeds angry talk among Washington's majority black population that he is the victim of a racist plot to return the city to white rule. Nation of Islam leader Louis Farrakhan packs the huge Washington Convention Center two nights running with tens of thousands of middle-class blacks who cheer his saying that "there is no better example of crucifixion in the modern era than Marion Barry." That it's time to elect politicians "who are more afraid of you than they are of the white Americans and Jewish Americans." That black politicians who "sell us out should be killed." That the white man "is guilty of the worst crimes of humanity." And that "all white America could be asked to die to equal the score."

Washington is a part of the whole. Across the country, urban crime is skyrocketing, the desperate poor are more desperate, the middle class is more nervous. The peddlers of bigotry—Al Sharpton and Sonny Carson in New York City, Gus Savage in Chicago, David Duke in Baton Rouge—run rampant. In short, it's a time of ugliness and danger, flush with haters. The country needs to hear the voice of a peacemaker. Ideally, a black peacemaker—for it is the blacks who seem angriest—but one who can reach at least some whites. Who could be better than a minister of God trained by Martin Luther King Jr., a believer in rainbow-colored harmony?

◆ ◆ ◆

At first, when Jackson takes the podium this July morning at the Saint Benedict the Moor Church, in Northeast Washington, it sounds as if he is going to spread sweetness and light. "A city divided by fears, unfounded fears, must be unified by hope and by necessity," he says in tones of cherry wood and honey, as the black men and women of his audience nod in agreement and the television cameras roll. But suddenly, he is roaring in anger. Suddenly, the real message: Black Washingtonians, African Americans, your fears are not unfounded at all. The whites are out to destroy you.

Black Washington, Jackson yells, is a city under "oppression and occupation," its people "locked out by law and pushed out by money," ruled by a "mean-spirited" Congress determined to "insult" them. He recites a litany of congressional abuse. Texas Senator Phil Gramm has proposed legislation to mandate jail terms for first-time criminal offenders in Washington. The government has made it, according to Jackson, "illegal even to lobby the federal government" for statehood. He compares the situation to the South African system of apartheid.

There's worse. The president "is using race-conscious code words to polarize the country." Jackson says Bush, in his objection to the 1990 civil-rights bill over the issue of racial hiring quotas, has made "a calculated choice of words to galvanize [whites] by fear." In nominating David Souter to the Supreme Court, Bush secretly moved to "undercut those who fought for school desegregation by law."

And still worse. Jackson's voice sinks to a deep and bitter sadness. "Last week, I had an awful experience," he says. He tells the crowd he went to the Senate and watched the debate on the 1990 civil-rights bill. "I stood there in the gallery of the U.S. Senate, denied the right to take part in the discussion. It was an awful and agonizing feeling. I stood there and watched a hundred senators debate our civil rights." And now he is shouting again. "I saw people like Hatch from Utah and Dole from Kansas—I saw them pull off their gloves and start screaming at the top of their voices 'You are attacking white males! You are attacking white males!'"

The members of the audience gasp and murmur in understandable shock. "Unrestrained, rabid race signals from the highest places in government!" Jackson shouts.

Jackson then warns that "history has a way of recycling." He tells the audience America is going into a period analogous to the post-Reconstruction years that saw the destruction of black freedoms gained by the Civil War. "Now that things are sinking economically, people are looking for scapegoats on matters of race, sex and religion!" he yells. "We must fight for our share!"

This is not an isolated speech. The persecution of blacks by the white ruling class has this year become a dominant theme in Jackson's speeches and interviews, in marked change to the tone he adopted in his last presidential campaign. In a radio interview, Jackson says government officials plotted their "setup" of Marion Barry to desecrate the memory of black America's most sacred figure: "They had actually planned to do it on January 15, the date of Doctor King's birthday. They meant to make the occasion of Doctor King's birthday a date of national ugliness and disgrace." He further charges the Justice Department and Bush with making an "insidious and ugly" effort to mock the anniversary of King's assassination by releasing on that date the department's recommendation to veto the 1990 civil-rights bill. He offers no evidence for this charge.

Over and over now, Jackson accuses the white-run federal government of seeking to destroy all politically powerful black men, as it supposedly tried to destroy King and Barry. "As blacks grow prominently in power, those who oppose them, if they have the judicial power, they try to undercut their power in that way," he says on CNN's *Larry King Show.* "What we see is a pattern across this country . . . of basically white judicial leadership attacking black political leadership. . . . As blacks rise in power prominently, they are moved on by the IRS, the FBI, and all of the above."

Yet often still, and especially with white audiences, Jackson movingly calls for racial unity. It is fair to say that such rhetoric represents a real side of Jackson, but it is also fair to point out that even much of Jackson's brotherhood talk masks another polarizing message. The only difference is that the division Jackson is seeking is along class lines, not racial ones. To poor white farmers in Iowa, for instance, Jackson is eloquent in urging black-white, urban-rural unity. "We can't let them play us off, black against white, and urban and rural, and women against men. We must rise above the division!" he thunders. But the unity is not for its own sake. It is to fight a class enemy—the rich. "We have foxhole options," he tells the white farmers, using the language of war. "We are in the same hole and the bullets coming our way do not judge us on color or race or religion," he says. "The enemy is shooting at us."

As he does with his black audiences, Jackson tells the poor and angry farmers of Iowa that their fears and angers are all too true. He tells them "government by the few, the rich, and the greedy" is trying to turn the rest of the country against farmers. "They tell us in Chicago, 'Have no mercy on the farmers! They got all that subsidy! Urban America, don't worry about the farmers!'"

The dividing line between populism and demagoguery has to do with the admittedly shaky area of relative truth telling. Jackson has crossed that line. Building on the larger reality of racism and class struggle in America, he has constructed an edifice of specific untruths, half-truths and exaggerations. Senator Phil Gramm's legislative proposals would mandate jail sentences only for those convicted of certain drug and armed-weapon offenses, not for all criminal offenders in Washington. Congress has not made it illegal to lobby for statehood. And nobody on the Senate floor screamed "You are attacking white males!" or, as Jackson claimed in another speech, "You can't do this to white males!" Orrin Hatch at one point calmly said, "If you vote for the Kennedy amendment, you will be voting, in effect, for disproportionately stripping white males of their day in court, a right they currently have according to a Supreme Court decree."

In 1987 and 1988, after a media bruising over his companionship with Farrakhan, Jackson was careful to distance himself from Nation of Islam leaders and other antiwhite blacks. Now Jackson is reaching out again to the race demagogues. In announcing his candidacy for shadow senator, Jackson invited to the podium former Catholic priest George Augustus Stallings, who had recently quit the church, charging racism in the face of allegations that he had sexually molested youths in his care and had misused church funds. Stallings is a leading proponent of the white-plot theory of prosecution of black politicians. Jackson also extended a public welcome to Farrakhan's chief spokesman, Abdul Alim Muhammad, and Nation of Islam adviser George X Cure.

Jackson is talking so divisively for reasons that are personal and political and intertwined, like the parts of himself. All the reasons stem from the imperative of his life: Attention really *must* be paid.

Jackson and I talked about his life and views in six or seven hours of interviews. At one point, Jackson said he hadn't been asked such questions in years and he hoped I understood him. I don't believe he will think I did, and in a sense he is right; he is a hard man to fully understand. But I think I did get down some of what Jesse Jackson sees when he looks out on the world, and what he sees is right in line with his race-against-race, class-against-class rhetoric. This is the personal part of Jackson's rationale for embracing the politics of polarization. He talks like this because this is what he believes. It is what he has learned from life.

♦ ♦ ♦

We are in a hotel in Chicago. By the time we arrived, Jackson had already been talking to me for an hour and a half and he was so tired he seemed punch-drunk, shoulders slumping as he dragged himself to his room. Now he is talking fast and hotly. "America," he lectures, paraphrasing Isaiah, "was founded in sin and brought forth in iniquity." This may sound like just a bit of Bible thumping, but how many men who want to be president would say something like that?

Jackson's universe is one of unending struggle, in which whites oppress people of color, the rich oppress the poor and the first world oppresses the third. The first dynamic of this universe is racial conflict; the second dynamic is class conflict. Jackson's America is a mixture of hope and hopelessness; a country that is profoundly flawed, unjust, racist, and immoral, that only in recent years has started down a long path of expiation to possible redemption. Everything America does and is, and everything in Jackson's life, fits into this view, a unified field theory of race and class politics.

The formation of Jackson's outlook began with his birth, on October 8, 1941, in the small, segregated city of Greenville, South Carolina. He was born to an unwed mother, and to this day he tells audiences that when he was young, "people called me a bastard and rejected me."

But Jackson's mother married when he was an infant, and he grew up in a stable and love-filled environment. Jackson says that what has driven him all his life is not anger over illegitimacy in the narrow sense but in the societal and racial sense. "We had to overcome the attempt to take away our legitimacy as human beings. Racism is always trying to make us illegitimate," he says. "So I see it in terms much broader than my own circumstances."

Jackson never forgets the way the America of his youth treated him. Standing on the tarmac at a tiny airport in eastern Illinois, he has just finished a speech before 1,200 cheering young white terra-hippies. The sun glints off the shine on his soft, fine shoes and the diamonds on his gold Rolex Oyster. In a minute he will board a private jet for Iowa, where thousands more cheering white people wait. His traveling aide is busy checking on the reverend's food and drink; the pilot and copilot hover in deference. At this moment, Jackson speaks. "You know, I remember when I was a student legislator and we went to a convention, the white students could stay in the Hotel Carolina and we had to stay with families and in cars," he says, and his voice tightens and his mouth purses shut and the bile is still there, twenty years later.

Jackson cannot forget the injustices of his life because the pain of poverty and prejudice, and the quasi-religious vision of himself as one overcoming that pain to triumph over the hostile white world, defines him. "I have no anger about my background, because it has served to make me strong," he says. "[This background] was a weapon to protect myself. . . . You learn to incorporate the pain and the concerns of other people."

In conversation, Jackson harps on the ceaseless efforts of whites to hurt him. No amount of accolades from whites touches this core. In Iowa, the white reporters fell all over Jackson. One Associated Press political reporter actually hugged him, and another reporter, an ex–farm boy with a face so open you could walk through it, prefaced his first question by telling Jackson, "This is going to be tough to do, sir. I've admired you since high school." Yet, just before flying out of the state, Jackson launched into a thirty-minute harangue on the bigotry of the white press, as evidenced by perceived slights and insults to himself, some of them fifteen years in the past. Attention comes so easy for white guys. But not for me, not for me.

Jackson's critics look at his career and see a master media manipulator who has exploited white guilt and black pride for twenty years of soft and heavy coverage. Jackson looks at it and sees a bunch of white guys gunning for him every step of the way. "You're a reporter. Your job is to report what I say. Period," he says in a flash of anger. It isn't fair. "This stuff about my lack of experience," he says, "the fact is, my experience is vastly greater than most officeholders'. They talk about governing. U.S. senators do not govern. They have their staffs, paid for by our government. They sit on committees. They conduct hearings. They handle legislation the staff writes for them. They're not governing any more than what I do."

Jackson sees an unbroken string of triumphs so great they demand the royal we: "We brought in the most new Democrats. We restored the Senate to the Democrats. . . . We raised the critical issues of the day. And the guy who helped us manage our campaign is now party chairman. . . . Now if any other person had done that, Michael, the party would relate to him differently."

But the endlessly gunning whites are all around. Flying over America, Jackson looks out the jet's round little window and sees racism everywhere; some places, it's just hidden better than in others. "All those liberals up North, they like to be against those southern bigots," he says. He mimics the voice of a white liberal Bostonian: "I'm against those terrible bigots, oh, my, yes!" And then, in tones of deep scorn, he says, "But meanwhile, at Harvard, they say they can't find one black woman in America qualified to teach [at the law school]." It is a lesson Jackson learned as a child: "There were white people who were better than others, and from them we learned that not all white people were evil," he says. "But all white people were part of the evil system."

◆ ◆ ◆

Jackson's America was not born of a revolution that delivered the widest expansion of political and human rights in the history of the world. His America began with a denial of those rights. "Look at what our society has been built upon," he says. "Denying rights to women—sexism; denying full humanity to African Americans—racism; denying some whites, non-landowners, the right to vote—classism; denying American Indians the right to live. That's our foundation."

His reading of history is thematic; in viewing any event, any period, Jackson sees the nation's behavior in the worst light and ascribes to the white establishment the worst motives. The Civil War, in Jackson's view, was "an economic conflict" that had very little to do with ending slavery. Lincoln "wasn't worried about morality. No, no, no, no," he says heatedly. Again, in looking at the civil-rights era, Jackson rejects the idea that whites were driven even in part by moral motives in the enactment of civil-rights laws. "You had these pictures of females being dragged off to jail and dogs biting people and so on. That shit was a disgrace," he says, biting off his words in bitter little snips. "It was not the conscience of whites; it was the death of blacks—and the embarrassment caused by that." When pushed, Jackson rejects not only white altruism but even white guilt. "Most whites have no sense of guilt or pain about being in the lineage of slave masters," he says.

Given these views, Jackson naturally gives white society little credit for the remedies it has undertaken to try to redress past racial injustices. Jackson wants reparations, actual monetary payments, for black Americans, to compensate for past suffering. "Affirmative action is a very conservative approach for a remedy," he argues. "You must have a government program to recognize those who have been damaged by law, a recognition of the damage done and commitment to repair that damage." He defines reparations as "a plan for aid, trade, loan, markets, and development," similar to that offered by the United States to foreign nations.

America's economy, in Jackson's view, is designed to benefit the rich at the expense of everyone else, through ceaseless conflict between the "haves and have-nots," and is rooted in "capitalistic exploitation" driven by "a racist ideology."

In such a country, Jackson argues, it is not possible for a black to be racist, because in a white-dominated society, only whites have such power. When blacks don't like whites, that's not racism; that's just learned wisdom: "One must not call a deep distrust based upon bad experiences 'racism.'"

"If I say to you, 'You cannot trust black people; they lie,' that is a racist remark, isn't it?" I ask Jackson.

"It is a stereotype," Jackson says. "It is inaccurate, therefore it is a racist remark."

"And if a black person says to me, 'You can't trust white people; they lie,' is that not also a racist remark?" I ask.

Jackson leans back in his airplane seat. He taps the ends of his fingers together and reflects. "Well, a lot of black people, their experience has been that," he says. "They see white people lying in the courts, lying about [blacks'] not being qualified for a job, not qualified to go to school."

The other public Jesse, the Redeemer, the voice of moral authority, is still around but seems almost weirdly unaware that Jackson the race/class warrior is preaching a message that feeds animosity among men. Flying into Iowa, Jackson looks out over endless cornfields and muses, "This is a wonderful country. So bountiful. So much for all. It takes an awful lot to turn us against each other." But it doesn't really. We Americans have always been disposed to squabbling among ourselves; all we need is a bit of encouragement. Jackson knows this. But he cannot afford just now to let the better angels of his nature tell him what to do. He has always done and said whatever he has to do and say to ensure continued attention—even at the expense of the causes and groups he holds dear.

He had been attempting to move away from race politics, but as Jamin Raskin, former counsel for the Rainbow Coalition, points out, "There is growing militantism in the black community, and, at the same time, certain leaders, like Wilder, are positioning themselves in the other direction. Jesse has to walk a tightrope."

"What you are seeing today is the growth of black radicalization," says Eric Easter, a former Jackson press secretary. "A lot of the angry young kids already see Jesse as someone who compromises too much for their tastes. And he cannot write off that age group."

Jackson's perspective on white society, views that he honestly holds but that he downplayed in 1988, may be unacceptable to a majority of white voters, but they are completely in sync with the opinions of a majority of black voters. Polls clearly show that blacks see their nation as less fair, less decent, less caring than do whites, a sense that grew during the Reaganite 1980s.

But Jackson faces a tremendous, and probably impossible, dilemma. The growing militancy among poor blacks, academics, and radical-chic white college students is at least balanced by a rapidly growing black middle class that is in-

evitably adopting middle-class values. The same polls that show a great gulf between black and white perceptions also indicate great, and increasing, similarities.
The polls also show real increases in social integration—measured by the willingness of whites and blacks to live together, send their children to school together and call one another friends.

The contradiction seen in the polls is reflected in life. I was in New York during the Bensonhurst racial-murder trial and in Washington during the Barry trial.
In both cities, I was struck by the difference in tone between the screams of the
hatemongers and the rational, understanding voices of the black (and white)
people I interviewed on the street. Al Sharpton, working in a city with 3 million
blacks, generally draws 200 or 300 people to his rallies and is blamed equally by
whites *and* blacks in polls in New York City as the single leading cause of racial
tension. Marion Barry, in a city that is more than 70 percent black, drew no more
than 1,000 people to any one of his rallies. In the Democratic mayoral primary
that followed Barry's trial, the winner in a crowded field was a black business executive and political newcomer, Sharon Pratt Dixon, the only candidate who
openly attacked Barry for his disgraceful behavior and who promised to clean out
Barry's inept, corrupt city hall. Dixon's victory was a harbinger of the next phase
in black politics, when the successful will be judged on individual competence
rather than on racial credentials.

Still, those who dismiss Jesse Jackson are, for the short term, making a mistake. Jackson should be able to hold on to a core of angry voters, mostly, though
not entirely, black. This will give him, for at least one more presidential cycle
(whether he chooses to run in 1992 or not), sway over a group that amounts to
at least 20 percent of the party, and possibly more.

And Jackson's short-term strength in the Democratic Party is boosted by his
shrewd and aggressive packaging of himself as a class warrior on behalf of working-
class whites. His brand of strident economic populism is the coming thing in
Democratic national politics, encouraged by disgruntled Republican pundit
Kevin Phillips in his provocative new book, *The Politics of Rich and Poor.*

But the appropriation of Jackson's message by white liberals will not allow
Jackson to become what he truly wishes to be, a national leader (in moral terms,
if not electoral ones), respected by whites as well as by blacks. Jackson can never
escape his own paradox. Given his personal and political imperatives, the only
path to power open to him within the party lies in the continued embrace of
militantism. But that power is wholly destructive. America, a centrist, pluralistic
nation at heart, has never accepted a truly radical national leader or party. It is not
about to now. All the great populists/demagogues before Jackson—William Jen-

nings Bryan, Huey Long, George Wallace—foundered on this. Jackson will founder, too, and so probably, for reasons directly connected to him, will the Democrats' newfound populism.

The pity is that America could use the good Jesse. It's a beautiful summer evening in Creston, Iowa. Jackson is on a little stage in the town park, the sun setting behind him, a couple hundred farm-community families sitting on the grass. He is telling a parable. He is the only politician in America who can get away with parables. This one is the story of a poor black woman who works in a chicken slaughterhouse. Telling the story, Jackson drops into the old lady's dialect, hunches his shoulders and crooks his back so his big, heavy athlete's body becomes the twisted wreck of a crone:

"'Reverend,' she said to me, 'I really don't want to be on welfare. I got a lot of pride. Three children, no husband. I works in a chicken plantation. And I be pluckin' them wings. I be pluckin' them wings—up to sixty wings a minute—and sometimes they speeds the machine up on us. And then you get that carpal syndrome. And you cannot bend the wrist or the elbow. I be workin' real hard, and they get stiff on me, my shoulder gets stiff. And then we cain't afford no insurance, and then they fire us. And then we cain't redress our grievances, 'cause we ain't got no union. And we cain't get another job, 'cause we's crippled. And we cain't get on Social Security, 'cause we ain't old enough. And then we put on welfare. And they call us lazy bitch.'"

You could cry listening to this. We are not a nation that worries a great deal about the chicken pluckers among us. Somebody has to speak for them, and Jesse Jackson does, with beauty and with strength. In a country where most of the well-fed white men who run both parties have made a corrupt peace with the abandonment of the poor, with the devastation of entire cities, with the decimation of generations of black families, it is desperately important that there be a voice demanding that attention must be paid. The good Jesse does this better than anyone else.

But that isn't enough. In the end Jackson will fail to become a true national leader not because he is black (in fact, his legacy may be that he has single-handedly made the notion of a black president plausible) but because he is partially blind. You can't lead a country you can't see, and Jackson cannot really see the America that has much good in it. It is not that Jesse's America doesn't exist. It does. The American Revolution *was,* at first, a victory only for landed white guys. Our industrial growth and foreign expansion *did* depend greatly on race and class exploitation. But that is less than half the story of the nation. As much as the history of America is about subjugation, it is even more about liberation. Our history has been consumed in sometimes messy, sometimes ugly, but mostly successful fights to make true the promises of equality and justice that were given 214 years ago.

Moral leadership lies in seeing both Americas. On that score, Ronald Reagan was a failure. Most of the time, he saw only the better America, and a rose-tinted colorized version of that. Jesse Jackson is the mirror image of Reagan, one who sees mostly an America defined, forever and ever, by the lessons of his childhood. Once, I asked Jackson why, in almost every speech to black audiences, he listed a litany of white sins—lynchings and murders and Jim Crow laws—from a quarter century ago. I understand this is important, I said, but is it necessary to talk about it all the time? Doesn't it just keep old wounds open and breed hate? He was sitting next to me in a limousine, but when I said that, he looked at me from a very great distance. "Only people who are brain-dead forget the past," he said. Jackson will never forget the past. Which is why it owns him.

Banality and Evil

◆ ◆ ◆

Louis Farrakhan is so far out of his gourd that at times he appears almost literally beside himself, but nuts is not the same as stupid. The leader of the Nation of Islam is a smart man, and he knows a good deal about the world in which he wishes to play a conspicuous part. He knows that politicians are greedy for any support they can get. He knows that journalists are easy to gull and to bully. He knows that many white people regard black people with fear and guilt, and will go to great lengths to avoid conflict with them. He knows that many white people also regard black people as their mental inferiors, and are therefore willing to be impressed by an intellectual performance from a black person that they would not find impressive from a white person. And he knows that, in an era of resegregation, most whites don't want to be around blacks, and most blacks don't want to be around whites.

Knowing all this, Farrakhan believes that the moment is arriving at which he will win recognition as the legitimate leader of black America. This would be an extraordinary achievement—Farrakhan is about as radical a figure as American politics is capable of producing—but he is right that the tenor of the times gives him reason for hope. The values of the left have been so thoroughly internalized and institutionalized in America that Farrakhan's radicalism is coming to seem quite conventional. With Malcolm X replacing Martin Luther King Jr. as the indispensable man among younger blacks, with the NAACP transforming itself from a force for integration to a force for racial Balkanization, with a black intellectual and popular culture that is overwhelmingly and openly hostile to whites, Farrakhan may convincingly pose as a figure of the mainstream. The values of the left have been adopted by whites, too, and this also helps Farrakhan. The once-radical idea of America as a sick society and American government as a corrupt oppressor is now a banality, the informing truism of Hollywood tripe and doctoral theses alike. The man and the times are coming together.

Farrakhan's Million Man March in October 1995 was the first officially segregated demonstration in Washington, and the first open expression of racialist political power, since the Ku Klux Klan marched on the Capitol in 1925. But, by adopting the minor cover of also stressing themes of economic self-help and spiritual revival (interestingly enough, also themes prominently sounded by speakers at the KKK march), Farrakhan was able to trick a complacent press into reporting the day's events as uplifting and even encouraging racial news.

In the time since then, the minister has made further strides. He has been able to fool some Jews in search of brotherhood, such as Mike Wallace and Edgar Bronfman, into brief flirtations. More significantly, he has made some progress in attracting Republicans, who are eager for any black votes they can get and attracted by the doctrine of black self-help (not to mention the doctrine of separate but equal). Most famously, Jack Kemp, under the influence of the noted loony Jude Wanniski, spoke well of Farrakhan, but then realized the unwisdom of this and shut up. Wanniski recently found a new convert in the person of the cable television reactionary Robert Novak.

On April 14, Farrakhan won a coveted role as, of all things, a racial mediator. Mayor Edward Rendell of Philadelphia, seeking to calm the black anger that arose after a group of white men beat a black woman and two black men in the Irish-Catholic Gray's Ferry neighborhood (in the same neighborhood, shortly thereafter, blacks murdered a sixteen-year-old white during a robbery, but this was, predictably, deemed to be not racially motivated), invited Farrakhan to join him at a "racial unity" rally. While five hundred blacks marched through Gray's Ferry, some of them yelling "white trash" at the residents, Farrakhan delivered an eighty-five-minute diatribe on the "half-slave and half-free" nation of America.

All of this is why the April 13 edition of *Meet the Press* was such an important event. In a masterful interview, Tim Russert used Farrakhan's own words, and the teachings of the Nation of Islam, to lead the minister into the territory he works so hard to avoid: the territory of his beliefs.

Farrakhan had said a few years ago that the ultimate answer to America's race problems was segregation. Did he still believe that? Why, yes: "it appears that way." Elijah Muhammad, founder of the Nation of Islam, has written that whites were created by a mad black scientist named Yakub, and that whites will ultimately perish at the hands of a spaceship that will rain death upon them. Did Farrakhan believe that? "I subscribe to every word that the Honorable Elijah Muhammad taught us."

Russert quoted a Nation of Islam essay recently posted on the Internet on the subject of "the Jews' awesome control over American society and government: All presidents since Franklin Roosevelt, 1932, are controlled by Jews." Did Farrakhan believe that? "I believe that, for the small numbers of Jewish people in the United States, they exercise a tremendous amount of influence in the affairs of government."

Russert quoted Farrakhan to Farrakhan: "Who controls black art? Who controls black sports figures? Who controls black intellectuals, black politicians? When I talk to the Jews, I'm talking to a segment of that quorum that holds my people in their grip." Farrakhan replied: "And that is true. Who controls the movement of the NAACP? The Urban League? Who controls black politicians?" The Jews, he ranted on, "exercise extraordinary control, and black people will never be free in this country until they are free of that kind of control. And I do intend by the help of God to break up that control."

The ugliest and most revealing moment of all came when Russert played a videotape of Farrakhan speaking, on March 19, 1995, on the subject of the Holocaust. "German Jews financed Hitler right here in America: Loeb and Kuhn and Jacob Schiff," Farrakhan yelled, his face contorted with hatred. "International bankers financed Hitler, and poor Jews died while big Jews were at the root of what you call the Holocaust. . . . Little Jews died while big Jews made money. Little Jews being turned into soap while big Jews washed themselves with it. Jews playing violin. Jews playing music while other Jews marching into the gas chambers."

When the clip was over, Farrakhan smiled a creepy smile of mock beatification. "The question is: Is it truth?" he said. "If it is truth, then it is not anti-Semitic."

It would be immoral even to deal with this. It is immoral to deal with Farrakhan at all, except to fight him. The man is a bigot and a hater. He hates whites and he hates Catholics and he hates Jews. If he were in a position to do serious harm to the people he hates, he would. As it is, he does what harm he can. And so do his willing dupes.

A National Calamity

◆ ◆ ◆

So now we are four, as along comes Jack, 8 pounds, 4 ounces, to join Tom, who for the record welcomes this development; and now I know what my job will be for the remainder of my days. I will be the man sitting behind the driver's wheel saying: Boys, listen to your mother.

This is a good job, and one of the better things about it is the nice clarity it lends to life. Fathers (and mothers) relearn that the world is a simple enough place. They discover that their essential ambitions, which once seemed so many, have been winnowed down to a minimalist few: to raise their children reasonably well and to live long enough to see them turn out reasonably okay. This doesn't seem like a great deal to ask for until you find out that it is everything to you. Because, it turns out, you are everything to them.

We know this not just emotionally but empirically. We know—even Murphy Brown says so—that both fathers and mothers are essential to the well-being of children. Successive studies have found that children growing up in single-parent homes are five times as likely to be poor, compared with children who have both parents at home. They are twice as likely (if male, three times as likely) to commit a crime leading to imprisonment. They are more likely to fail at school, fail at work, fail in society.

What, then, would we say about a society in which the overwhelming majority of children were born into homes without fathers and who grew up, in significant measure, without fathers? We would say that this society was in a state of disaster, heading toward disintegration. We would say that here we had a calamity on a par with serious war or famine. And, if that society were our own, we would, presumably, treat this as we would war or famine, with an immediate and massive mobilization of all of our resources.

Of course, this society is our own. Of black children born in 1996, 70 percent were born to unmarried mothers. At least 80 percent of all black children today can expect that a significant part of their childhood will be spent apart from their fathers.

Millions of America's children live in a state of multiplied fatherlessness—that is, in homes without fathers and in neighborhoods where a majority of the other homes are likewise without fathers. In 1990, 3 million children were living in fatherless homes located in predominantly fatherless neighborhoods—neighborhoods in which a majority of the families were headed by single mothers. Overwhelmingly, those children were black.

These figures, and most of the others that follow, come from a report, "Turning the Corner on Father Absence in Black America," released to no evident great concern this week by the Morehouse Research Institute and the Institute for American Values.

As the report notes, things were not always thus. In 1960, when black Americans lived with systemic oppression, 78 percent of black babies were born to married mothers, an almost mirror reversal of today's reality. In the 1950s, a black child would spend on average about four years living in a one-parent home. An estimated comparable figure for black children born in the early 1980s is eleven years. According to the research center Child Trends, the proportion of black children living in two-parent families fell by 23 percentage points between 1970 and 1997, going from 58 percent to 35 percent.

The disaster of black fatherlessness in America is part of a larger crisis. In every major demographic group, fatherlessness has been growing for years. Among whites, 25 percent of children do not live in two-parent homes, up from 10 percent in 1970. Overall, on any given night, four out of ten children in America are sleeping in homes without fathers. (True, in the past few years, the number of out-of-wedlock births has begun to fall, but that trend is too nascent and too modest to much affect the situation.)

Some people think all of this matters. One is David Blankenhorn, a liberal organizer who learned realities as a Vista volunteer and who eleven years ago founded the Institute for American Values, coauthor of this week's report. It is Blankenhorn's modest suggestion that fathers are necessary to children, that their abdication on a large scale is calamitous to the nation and that the people who run the nation should do something serious about this.

The man who currently runs it is not a factor here; he does not do serious. What about the men who would run it? Al Gore says nothing; he is too busy fighting the loss of green spaces in Chevy Chase. Bill Bradley preaches about racism but is silent about the ruination of a race. George W. Bush is full of compassionate conservatism, but he won't say quite what that is. And so on. History will wonder why America's leaders abandoned America's children, and why America let them do so.

Mass Sentimentality

♦ ♦ ♦

The deaths of John Kennedy Jr., his wife, Carolyn, and her sister Lauren Bessette are sad enough. Three attractive and accomplished and relatively young people, with promising lives ahead of them, die in terror and violence; their families are shattered in grief. Why is sad enough not enough? Why do we lard up the sorrow with this great and gross festival of national media blah-blah about Camelot and royalty and The Kennedy Curse and Jack and Jackie and all the rest of it?

In recent weeks, as in all weeks, the *Washington Post* has carried many stories about death. Two struck me particularly.

One was a feature about a woman named Carol Ross Joynt, whose husband contracted pneumonia. When it became apparent that he would die soon, Joynt told the couple's five-year-old son that his father would not be coming home from the hospital. She took the boy to say good-bye, and she listened, outside the screen, as the son sang to his dying father: "You are my sunshine, my only sunshine . . ."

The other story was about the killing of Joshua Tyler Deen, 5, smashed by a car gone out of control as he was walking with his mother into a grocery store, where they had stopped to buy a cold drink for the boy. As a store employee labored vainly to resuscitate her only child, Helen Deen screamed, "My son, my son, my son."

Are either of those deaths (pages C1 and B1, respectively) less tragic, less crushing, than the deaths of the three in the Piper that appear day after day on A1? No, an editor might say, but the C1 and B1 deaths are quotidian tragedies, part of the endless stream of deaths that flows around us every day, and that does not really affect us unless death strikes one of our own. But some deaths, the editor might add, are in a real sense more tragic than others; they affect the nation or the people as a whole, and they deserve exceptional attention, exceptional grief.

Of course, this is true. The assassination of Lincoln was immensely more sad than any other death in America on April 15, 1865, because Lincoln had done great good and might have been expected to do further good. A death such as Lincoln's is properly treated as a death in the national family, and an occasion of national mourning. We have had other such deaths, a notable one being the assassination of John F. Kennedy Jr.'s father.

Important differences exist between the death of president Lincoln and the death of president Kennedy. In the latter's case, greatness was to some degree assumed, largely on the basis of Kennedy's huge personal attraction (his beauty, wit, grace), but its promise was still mostly unfulfilled (and its flaws still hidden) at his death. Still, many millions saw in Kennedy a wonderful hope for a better country and world, and his death caused a deep national sense of loss.

But is that what we have here, in the death of Kennedy's namesake? Not quite. We have—in the case of the nation, not the Kennedy family—something else entirely, the death of a symbol. The media effusion is not about what Kennedy did with his life, or indeed in any real sense who he was. It is about the death of someone whom the celebrity-media culture deems to stand for mass sentiments. That is a type of death that has become familiar, its most striking recent occurrence before Kennedy being the demise of Princess Diana.

This gets fairly odd. Diana was a symbol of the horror of being a symbol. John Kennedy Jr. was not just a symbol but a symbol of a symbol; in fact, a symbol of a symbol of a symbol. There never was a Camelot; that in itself was a symbol, a conscious (postmortem) confection that was intended to evoke the sentiments of a musical based on a myth based on symbol.

This also gets fairly cynical. It is doubtful that very many people actually feel the death of John Kennedy in the manner that his uncle, Edward Kennedy, described: "unspeakable grief." Indeed, the absence of true grief is what makes it possible to wallow in vicarious grief. The media understand and exploit this. People are product. The more symbolic the person, the greater value of the product. (This is why Hillary Clinton on the cover guarantees newsstand sales; she is almost pure symbol.) Everything that happens to symbolic people is product. Especially death; nothing sells like symbolic death.

Richard Daley Jr.
Gets the Last Laugh

◆ ◆ ◆

On this sunny summer day, Richard Michael Daley is following—still, after all these years—in his father's footsteps. Buttoned up in a suit, but
toned down in a collar, his hair combed as neat as an altar boy's, the mayor of
Chicago is leading the annual Feast of the Assumption parade of Saint Jerome's
Church through Bridgeport, the South Chicago neighborhood where his family
has lived and ruled for fifty years. His father, Richard I, the great Boss Daley, led
this same parade down these same streets more times than anyone remembers,
which everyone remembers. The parade is a political event (in Bridgeport, life is
a political event), and its form never varies. The marchers represent the partners
in Chicago's open marriage of church and state: God, crime and politics, a mé-
nage à trois so old and cozy that everyone wears socks to bed and calls one another "Dear." Daley, of course, embodies politics, leading a troop of currently
unindicted public servants. The pols march ahead of crime, as represented by the
spiffed-up cops of the American Legion's Chicago Police Department Chapter,
and God, in the form of the old ladies in black of the Saint Mary Isle of Cherso
Benevolent Society. The mayor and his fellows huff along; like Lewis Carroll's
oysters, some of them are out of breath and all of them are fat. The cops trudge
flat-footedly, hammering and tootling on drums and bugles. The aging belles of
Saint Mary's shuffle and pray to the Virgin in dead but not forgotten Latin:
"Santa Maria, ora pro nobis . . ."

The mayor seems a bit shy, and he walks along in stilted discomfort, now and
then waving a stiff arm to the cheering people on the sidewalks, who are his
neighbors, folks he has known all his life, friends of his father's. When Virginia
Vulich shoves her three-year-old son, Frank, in the great man's path, Daley smiles
briefly and beautifully and it is like a glimpse of winter sun. But his joy fades
faster than an undertaker's grief and is replaced by his habitual public expression:
a tight little frown, like that of a man trying hard to remember what it is he
wasn't supposed to forget.

Well, that's okay. All everybody around here asks is that Young Richie, as some call him still, play his part in this ritual of his life and theirs, not that he excel. A large, ruddy-faced bystander named Petey beams as the mayor passes, and says, "This is a beautiful day for Bridgeport, and it's a great thing that he is here, like his father was before him. I am fifty-nine years old, and I can remember the Blessed Mary being celebrated on this holy day of obligation, the Feast of the Assumption of the Blessed Mother, every one of those fifty-nine years on August the fifteenth, I don't give a shit it falls on a Friday or a Monday."

Amen.

◆ ◆ ◆

The Life of Richard M. Daley is a classic with a twist. For the first two reels, it's *Oedipus Boss,* an Irish American docudrama about a not conspicuously talented but determined son struggling to live up to a father of gigantic stature. In the socko finish, it switches to *The New Hurrah,* for a surprise and happy ending. There are three stars in this story: the father, the son and the city itself.

The father: Richard Joseph Daley was the last and the greatest of America's great political bosses. For twenty-one years, 1955 to 1976, he ruled Chicago, his well-lubed machine turning votes into jobs and jobs into votes in a cycle of such seamless perfection as would bring tears to the eyes of every politician who ever lived. He shaped America's then-second-largest city to his steel desire, building skyscrapers in the Loop and miles of housing projects for the blacks, and freeways so that the whites could get to the one without going through the other. He was a figure of such power that most Chicagoans referred (and many still refer) to him simply by his title: Duh Mare. To the truly loyal, in the Irish bars and the Slavic social clubs, he was Duh Greatest Mare Chicago Ever Had.

The son: Richard Michael Daley is the boy who was born to inherit Chicago. Learning at his father's knee, crawling in his father's shadow, he was slated for his father's job from the moment he opened his eyes—never mind that he seemed to have as much natural grace for politics as a pig has for modern dance.

The city: Chicago is to politics what Paris is to love. This city defined modern urban politics and in turn was defined by it. Its pols pioneered such classic tactics as voting the dead and employing bands of roving repeat-voting vagrants (Hobo Floto Voto, this ploy was called). The essential point of politics is the control and exercise of power, and while that fact may be glossed over in more genteel places, in Chicago it has always been a matter of civic pride. The town's official motto is *"Urbs in Horto,"* which means "City in a Garden," but most people here prefer the motto cited by columnist Mike Royko: *"Ubi Est Mea"*—"Where's Mine?"

Back in 1977, when Young Richie's destiny did not seem so manifest, a reporter asked if he dreamed about holding the job his famous father had owned for a generation. "You have dreams," answered the son. "When your father has been the mayor that long, you have dreams about it. It's something that you think about, dream about, but they're dreams."

Sitting today in his city-hall office—the cherubic son under a portrait of the jowly father—he says, in his nervous, fumbling way, that yes, it is, uh, true; he has always dreamed of this. "Everybody has dreams about what they'd like to do. Especially if you're excited about what your father did, uh, you know, in a profession that you think he did very well in . . ." His voice trails off in embarrassment. Richard J. beams encouragingly down from the wall, but Richard is not smiling. He has been compared to his father every second of his life, and naturally he doesn't like it even a little bit. Perched on the edge of his armchair, twisting his hands around a coffee cup, he is as defensive as a man with lipstick on his collar. The more he feels attacked, the more disjointed his speech becomes, a collection of fits and starts punctuated by an idiosyncratic use of the word "fine." Daley says "Fine!" to suggest that the matter under discussion is not fine. To suggest "Fuck you." When I ask him if he knew all his life that he would be measured against his father, he goes off in a fine bluster of "Fine!"'s: "I knew people . . . were saying 'Well, you're not as good as your father, he did this'—you know. Fine! But if you let that bother you, I would never have entered politics or government, and, uh, it was a challenge. I said, 'Fine! I'll challenge that attitude! I'll show you what I can do!' And it's a great standard to follow. Can I be better than my father? . . ."

Daley's life has been one long fight to answer that question in the affirmative—and in the face of much doubt. Like Richard Nixon, he has been molded by one of the great emotions: an ardor to show the bastards. The desire and the hurt come bubbling up in conversation still. "People used to say, in all my campaigns: 'If your name wasn't Daley, I'd be someplace else,'" he says, his mouth tightening. "They *all* said that. This has been going on since—I don't know." His voice rises as he mimics his accusers: "'I couldn't play on this team! I couldn't do this!'" He breaks off again.

Did it make him angry when they treated him like that?

"Well, you know what happens. You say 'Fine! You don't like my name, fine! I'm not going to change it for you. 'Cause, you know, you're doing this for your own personal advancement. . . . Fine! I'm going to go out and do what I have to do and not worry about my name.'"

Easier said than done. It is good to be king. It is less good to be crown prince.

By the time Rich Daley was born, in 1942, his father was already King of
Bridgeport and on his way to becoming Emperor of the World and Sovereign of
the Universe, which is how Chicagoans regard their mayor. Quiet, cautious,
tough, and smart, Dick Daley had risen through the ranks to become a powerful
state senator and the committeeman of the Eleventh Ward Democratic Organization, the biggest by far of the city's fifty Democratic ward operations and the
linchpin of the great machine. In any ward, the Democratic committeeman was
a mighty figure, the conduit for city jobs, the arbiter of political fights and the
dispenser of charity in a pre-welfare-state society. In Bridgeport, he was a giant.
Priest–writer Andrew Greeley, a lifelong Chicagoan and a chronicler of the city's
Celtic tribalism, calls Bridgeport the city's royal borough. Other working-class
boys grew up to labor in the big city; Bridgeport boys grew up to run the big
city. Bridgeport has produced five mayors since 1933, and the mightiest of them
all was Young Richie's dad, elected to the first of six consecutive terms just before the boy's thirteenth birthday.

◆ ◆ ◆

From early on, Rich showed a desire to emulate his father. "He always had [an
interest in politics]," says brother and confidant Bill Daley. "Whether he felt pressure to do it or whether he really, truly, wanted to do it, I don't know. Maybe
some shrink would be able to tell us that." Maybe the motives can be discerned
without therapy. They are not subtle. "All the sons worshiped their father and beyond that had an extraordinary affection for him," says Greeley. "If you admire
your father and like him as well, there is a strong inclination to follow him, and
his sons did. All four of them are in politics, in one way or another."

Rich faced a special responsibility. "I think probably the firstborn son in an
Irish family is immediately taken under the wing of the father, who sets his eyes
and puts the goals of the family name on the eldest," says retired judge Richard
J. Fitzgerald, a long-time Daley-family friend. Rich, he says, idolized his father
and "to be like him was probably a goal he set very early on. And to be like his
father meant that you get into politics and that you ultimately climb to the top
of the ladder." Others who have watched Daley at close quarters agree with that
assessment. "I think that privately, all his life, he has wanted to be mayor," says
Thomas Donovan, Dick Daley's former chief aide. "Because his father saw that
as the highest calling a man could have, so did he. Not governor. Not senator.
Not president. Mayor. Mayor of the city of Chicago."

By the accounts of the Daley brothers and friends of the family, the elder Daleys went to considerable lengths to provide their children with a life approxi-

mating normalcy. The family lived in a brick row house on South Lowe Avenue that was only a little grander than its neighbors. Dad took the kids to the bakery on Halsted Street and to Comiskey Park to see the White Sox play. The children shared bedrooms and were not allowed to use the family's one telephone in the evening. They were expected do their homework and chores and to obey. On Sundays, the young Daleys knelt knee to knee with everyone else at Nativity of Our Lord, the parish church a few blocks from their home where Christ on the cross had the yellow hair and big blue eyes of a pinup girl and bled scarlet paint from open wounds.

But the other kids in the pews were the sons and daughters of cops and firemen. The other kids did not go to the White House or meet the queen of England. And the other kids' dads worked for the Daley kids' dad. Rich noticed the difference. "We were like the First Family, something like that," he once said. "My father protected—I think very well—our lives. . . . He was very careful of people using us for their personal gains or public gains. [We were] very careful where we went, who we were with."

The pride the Irish feel when one of their own makes good is equaled only by the delight they feel when he proves to be bad after all, and the Daley kids felt the scrutiny. "We all thought about it, and we knew we were constantly watched," says the next-to-youngest son, John P. Daley. "You knew people who might be waiting for you to stumble." Rich, keeper of the name, was the most carefully observed. "I think he had to prove himself as being Richard J. Daley," John recalls. "People were watching him more in everything he did, as the eldest son of the mayor. . . . [P]eople would say, 'Okay, he's the oldest son, let's see if he's going to produce.'"

Unfortunately, the boy seemed wildly unsuited for the part he was scripted to play. Politicking requires, if nothing else, an acceptance of public attention, and Young Richie not only shrank from the spotlight, he didn't even want to hang around in the wings. "He basically has *always* been a shy person," says Bill Daley. "He was not the guy who would walk into the room and yuk it up . . ."

Shy and maybe not too smart was the common suspicion. Daley was no scholar (he needed three shots to pass the state bar exam) and was a poor speaker. Many observers concluded he was not awfully bright. "There was a theory that the father—who was, in his own way, a political genius—spawned three parts of himself in the boys," says Brian Kelly, a former Chicago political reporter. "Bill got the political savvy. Michael got the business smarts. And Richie got the charisma, such as it was."

Fine! Rich kept his thoughts to himself, his face set in sullen defiance, and chased the milestones of his father's life as if they were predictors of success. He followed the Boss's path through Nativity of Our Lord and De La Salle High School (where he listed in his yearbook his ambition "to become a great lawyer and politician" and where his nickname was Mayor), and DePaul University, Chicago's traditional finishing school for politicians and his father's alma mater. Dick Daley smoothed the path before his son like a red carpet down the center aisle. When Rich needed a summer job while in law school, the old man got him one: crier for a federal judge, $425 a month for yelling "Hear ye, hear ye" when His Honor walked into the courtroom. (The Boss believed in helping his own. Once, when he was criticized for steering a million dollars' worth of city insurance business to his insurance-agent son, John, the mayor explained his philosophy: "If a man can't put his arms around his son, then what kind of world are we living in? If I can't help my sons, [my critics] should kiss my ass.")

Rich graduated from DePaul law school in 1968, the year his father ordered Chicago police to "shoot to cripple or maim" blacks rioting in the wake of Martin Luther King Jr.'s assassination, the year Chicago's cops staged what the Walker Commission called "a police riot" during the Democratic National Convention, yelling "Kill, kill, kill!" as they rampaged through the longhairs in Lincoln Park. A lot of young men and women looked at the system as represented by Rich's dad and decided it was time for a radical change. Not Rich. While others of his generation took to the ramparts, he joined his father's Eleventh Ward Democratic Organization and became a precinct captain in the dear old machine. In 1969, with his father's backing, the twenty-seven-year-old Daley ran for delegate to the Illinois Constitutional Convention. He pulled in more votes than any other delegate. A newspaper called it his "first hurrah."

In 1972, the Boss persuaded State Senator Ed Nihill, an old party man and city employee from Bridgeport, to step down from his seat, the same seat the Boss himself had once held. Rich won the office in a landslide victory, the only conceivable result.

◆ ◆ ◆

As a freshman state senator, Rich was, in the opinion of a lot of fellow Democrats, nothing but his daddy's errand boy and the machine's hatchet man, a bad legislator with no redeeming social graces. In his first few years, he offered no important bills and spoke rarely except to criticize the "good-government" reformers who were his father's natural enemies. Appointed chairman of the powerful judiciary committee in 1975, he fought the "goo-goos" on his father's behalf, scuttling reform bills and boasting of his ability to punish the "phony liberals." Five years after he assumed office, *Chicago* magazine named him one of the state's worst legislators for his "arrogance, for sharklike qualities, for living off his father's name, and for pulling puppet strings attached to some of the worst members of the Senate."

"I think most of his philosophy and his learning and his operation down in Springfield were pretty much dominated by his father on a day-to-day basis," says Judge Fitzgerald. "His father pretty much told him what to do and how to do it." He adds, "And Daley had so many friends down there that if Rich ever got out-of-bounds, the word would get back to the old man."

Not surprisingly, Rich was not popular. "He was just an absolute little prick during most of his senate time," recalls liberal political strategist and Daley critic Don Rose. "One of the worst-case personalities of 'My father is going to shit on you if you don't behave. I am great because my father is great.'" Senator Dawn Clark Netsch, then the leader of the good-government clique, says of the man she called Dirty Little Richie, "It was almost as if there was a glass wall around him. Part of it was shyness, but part of it was reflected power." He was regarded, she says, "with awe and fear."

Today, Daley is still angry about those who said he was just following the Boss's commands. "Fine! I didn't care," he says. "I didn't go back and tell my father. I didn't ask him what I should do. Fine!" He admits that he killed "seventy-five percent, eighty percent" of the reform legislation submitted to the judiciary committee but says he was motivated not by machine politics but by a conviction that the bills were ill conceived or poorly drafted. However, even brother Bill acknowledges that Rich had the reputation of being someone who would "screw people just to screw them."

A son who idolizes a larger-than-life father eventually faces three options: He can remain an acolyte forever, he can reject his father, or he can put the old man respectfully aside and get on with his life. The first two choices are crippling, the third is liberating. Daley's first important step toward liberation came on December 20, 1976, when his father did the only thing that could ever allow Young Richie to grow up: He died. Daley's words on his father's death are surprisingly revealing. "Before my father died, I had to be very careful about what I did and what I said because everything I did ended up as 'Mayor Daley's son this and Mayor Daley's son that,'" he said in a 1980 interview. "After he died, I knew I had to seek not my own identity, maybe, but the things I wanted to take on personally. I had to seek my own goals and decide what I wanted to do in the legislature and in politics."

Bill Daley says his father's death "freed [Rich] in the sense that he then had to

grow on his own," a process he says was not completed until 1989, when the eldest son took over the father's job. "There is no doubt that the tremendous, all-
encompassing being that my dad was . . . to try and play in that shadow was
impossible," he says.

Daley went to work right away on his new persona. In 1977, he recruited
Frank Kruesi, a twenty-seven-year-old intellectual from the University of Chicago, and began crafting a reputation as—of all things—a reform-minded legislator. Dawn Clark Netsch had proposed a comprehensive reform of the state's
mental-health system. To handle the huge issue, she suggested the establishment
of a special joint House-Senate committee. To her shock, Daley asked to be the
chairman. She agreed, with apprehension. "But he really worked hard on it and
we developed a very good relationship and we produced a very good package of
mental-health bills," she says now. "He enjoyed it immensely, and he really dug
in. I think he liked it so much simply because it was the first time he had ever
really worked on anything of his own." The mental-health package was enacted
in 1978, and Daley followed it with leadership work on other major reform bills.
Today, Netsch speaks of him with respect and says, "I think he really had grown
up enormously, and it sounds cruel to say it, but the major factor was his father's
death. He came out from the glass cage and got a chance to grow on his own."

The timing of Daley's assumably sincere conversion was politically fortuitous,
gaining him vital allies among Chicago's lakefront liberals at a time when he desperately needed their help for his second great period of testing and growth: a series of battles with Mayor Jane Byrne, a former Boss Daley protégée who had
been elected mayor in 1979. "When Byrne won, we became the enemy," says
Bill Daley. "And we knew this from day one because we had people on the inside telling us she was being fed this: 'You got to kill Richie, you got to end
Richie, he's your enemy.' And she bought into it."

In doing so, she did Daley the favor of giving him the first real fight of his
life. In the face of opposition by Byrne and his father's old organization, Daley
ran for Cook County state's attorney in 1980. He won—in great part, says Bill
Daley, because of his new stature as a champion of reform legislation. Almost
everyone expected Daley to fail in his new office. He had never tried a case and
had never conducted a criminal investigation. But Daley surprised his critics,
most of whom came to see him as a good administrator, if not much in the
courtroom. He instituted some smart programs for streamlining the legal process
and helping victims and hired smart prosecutors without regard to their politics.
He also zeroed in on the area most likely to win voter support, vastly increasing
the number of drug cases prosecuted. His predecessor had tried 900 such cases

and had won 78 percent of them in his last year in office; in 1984 Daley tried 4,500 and won 82 percent. Today, Daley sounds like Nixon recounting one of his Six Crises—through-hard-work-I-persevered victories—as he remembers his triumphs over the doubters: "Everybody thought when I became state's attorney I was going to turn it over to politics; the precinct captains were going to run it. [But] I just made it a very good professional office. Kept people. Hired people from the federal government, private practice. . . . I worked very hard at it."

In 1983, Daley felt secure enough to finally go for his father's former job. He was forty-one, twelve years younger than his father had been when he became mayor, and he was not, as it turned out, ready yet. Going up against Byrne and Representative Harold Washington, the city's leading black politician, in an ugly, brawling primary campaign that focused entirely on race, Daley proved a poor candidate. Former *Chicago Sun-Times* columnist Roger Simon recalls Daley's performance in the first candidates' debate: "If he had five minutes to answer a question, he'd still do it in thirty seconds and then just sit there, hanging out. It was difficult to watch him." On election day, Daley prayed at his father's grave, but Washington won anyway, taking nearly all of the heavy black vote and 10 percent of the white. The hated Byrne came in second. Daley was a miserable third. It was, he says now, the low point of his political life.

An even lower personal point had come two years earlier, with the death of his two-year-old son, Kevin, who had been ill since birth with a crippling spinal condition. During the child's long illness, Daley spent many nights in hospital wards, and friends say he learned compassion through the tragedy. "You reassess what is important in life," says Daley himself. "It says a lot about life when you see a two-and-a-half-year old struggling to live."

Daley took both losses well, at least publicly. In 1984 he ran for reelection as state's attorney and won; in 1988 he won again. Meanwhile, Chicago's government had gone to hell. Washington's first term was a nightmare of fighting between the black and white members of the city council, winning Chicago the nickname Beirut on the Lake. Washington had won the council wars by the end of the term and was moving forward when he was reelected in 1987. But he died shortly after the election, sparking a fierce council fight over the choice of an interim mayor until a special election could be held, in 1989, to fill out the unexpired years of Washington's term. The white choice, easygoing Alderman Eugene Sawyer, became the acting mayor, which outraged Washington supporters, who saw Sawyer as a pawn and so threw their weight behind Alderman Timothy C. Evans in 1989.

Daley moved in, ran a smooth, race-free campaign that pledged to make things work again and pulled off a reverse of Washington's triumph, winning virtually all of the white vote (including the liberal vote) and close to 10 percent of the black to beat Sawyer in the Democratic primary and Evans in the general election.

Not long after the second Daley became Chicago's forty-fifth mayor, a friend dropped by to see him in the big office on the fifth floor of city hall. "He's like a little fucking kid," the friend recalls. "He's sitting with his feet up on his old man's desk and he's got a cigar stuck in his mouth just like his old man and he's got this shit-eating grin on his face. He's happy as a puppy 'cause he's finally in the big chair. He says to me, 'Can you believe this?' I say, 'You must be pretty happy.' He says, 'This is the most relaxed I've ever been in my whole life.' It's like he's allowing himself a moment of contentment because he's finally gotten out from the shadow of his father. But the moment passes. He takes his feet down and he starts waving the cigar and he starts talking about all the problems of the city. He points at the windows and he says, 'Can you believe it? They haven't even cleaned the windows since my father died? I asked the guy why not, and he said 'cause no one told him to. So I told him to!'"

He did a lot more than clean his father's windows. He had a lot to prove, a lifetime's worth. "I think, finally, the thing that drives him is the thing he has heard from the day he entered politics, which is that he was only there because of his name and that he wasn't particularly bright," says David Axelrod, the mayor's media adviser. "More than anything else, Rich Daley is a guy who wanted to make a reputation, a positive reputation, in his own right."

He has done that. It is now more than a year since the day the windows were cleaned. Daley is a runaway success. He is a sure thing for reelection. The polls show he has an approval rating of more than 75 percent among white voters and—astonishingly—more than 40 percent among blacks. His enemies, Jane Byrne in particular, are vanquished. Daley faces a new election in 1991, and there isn't a soul in Chicago who doubts he will win it. Two months shy of Daley's first anniversary and 366 days before election day, the *Chicago Tribune* predicted "The winner, by a lot, of the Democratic nomination and as such the inevitable mayoral election victor, will be Richard M. Daley."

How did a man known only a year ago as "Dumb-Dumb" Daley come to find such success?

By being just what he has been all his life: his father's son.

In the old days, there were two kinds of big-city mayors. There were the song-and-dance artists, such as New York's Gentleman Jimmy Walker, who wore Broadway as a boutonniere, and Boston's James Michael Curley, who served a term in office and a term in jail simultaneously. And there were the engineers—tough, dull men with all the charm of a blister on the heel, who spent their days in the boiler room of city hall, tinkering and oiling and keeping the machine humming smoothly along.

Dick Daley was the greatest engineer-mayor who ever lived. He did not invent the Chicago machine, but he perfected its design. It was a massive thing, with so many moving parts that only a wizard of an engineer could keep them all from crashing into one another—50 ward aldermen, 50 ward committeemen, 2,911 precinct captains, and 30,000 city patronage jobs. The machine picked candidates for every office and ensured victory for the chosen with a cushion of 100,000 votes from 11 machine-controlled wards. The machine lived on after the Boss died, but it was ailing from declining immigration, antipatronage court rulings and its own irrelevancy. The election of 1983, which showed that the organization could no longer deliver black votes or white, proved the old behemoth had finally clanked to a halt.

In the years of chaos that followed Daley's death, the engineer-mayor vanished in Chicago. In other cities, too, the late 1970s and the 1980s saw the triumph of a new and selfish kind of song-and-dance mayor, born of the low spirit of the times, the politics of group greed. These new mayors played to select audiences of people like themselves, and they played on racial, ethnic, and class fears at the expense of the city they governed. In New York, Ed Koch pirouetted his portly form down the sidewalks and sang "How'm I Doin'?" to whites while the city machinery he neglected was looted and racial hatred swelled. In Washington, D.C., Marion Barry chased skirts, swigged cognac and (it is most convincingly alleged) stuffed his head with cocaine, telling black supporters he was the victim of a racist plot to return the city to white rule—while the city machinery he neglected crumbled into chaos.

We are seeing now, in backlash, a new generation of mayors come to power who have rejected racial song and dance-ism in favor of actually governing. Atlanta's Andy Young and Baltimore's Kurt Schmoke were the first such black mayors of the new era, and New York's David Dinkins may prove to be the most prominent. Rich Daley is the first important white mayor of the new school. What Dinkins is trying to do in New York, Daley has already accomplished in reverse in Chicago: He has become a self-sustaining crossover success, reaching out from an essentially conservative white ethnic base to attract serious support among blacks, Hispanics, and white liberals—enough support to govern a tough city well and to ensure continued election.

Everything in Chicago politics is about race. "Race has replaced party identification in the city," wrote Chicago political scientist Milton Rakove after the 1983 election. "People don't identify as Democrats or Republicans very much anymore. They identify now as blacks or whites in Chicago." The city's population is about 40 percent white, 40 percent black and 20 percent Hispanic. No black mayor can succeed without at least a small measure of white and Hispanic support, as no white mayor can make it without at least a small measure of black and Hispanic support.

What has happened in Chicago—and this is why the Daley model is important beyond the city—is true only to a slightly lesser degree in the rest of the country. This is, to appropriate a concept, the age of zero-sum politics, in which interest group battles interest group and regards any gain for a rival as an intolerable loss for itself. We define our political interests in terms of our group: black or white or Hispanic or Asian or homosexual or feminist or American Indian or handicapped, and so on. As Theodore H. White predicted, this has created a fragmented society. Governing has always meant dividing finite resources among competing groups; what makes today's climate different is the great increase in petitioners who claim a legal and moral right to the spoils of victory.

For a leader, the conundrum of zero-sum politics is that you must give something to everyone who asks (or face the lethal charge of discrimination), but there is only so much to give. You must give just enough so that each group feels it has gotten perhaps not the double portion it wanted but at least a reasonable share of the pie.

It is the great achievement of Rich Daley that, rare among Democrats (but, increasingly, not among Republicans) these days, he understands the alchemy of this. And the funny thing, the thing that makes his whole life come together so well, is that if you look closely, you can see that what he is doing is just exactly what his dad did so well. Boss Daley is dead, but Young Richie is his true heir after all, the evolved but genetically coded master engineer, a new look that is really just a spin-off of the old. If he were a building, he would have a broken pediment in the middle of his forehead, America's first postmodern mayor.

"Politics," his father always said, "is a game of addition, not subtraction." Dick Daley was perhaps a bigot but he was a master of zero-sum. The five wards controlled by black alderman William Dawson were crucial to Daley's organization (it was their padded vote totals that gave Illinois and the presidency to John F. Kennedy), and he took pains to see they were not ignored. "His attitude toward blacks was 'If you can't beat 'em, join 'em—or at least placate 'em,'" says Daley's old friend Fitzgerald. Don Rose, a former aide to Martin Luther King Jr., says it another way: "He was the master of co-option. He always made just enough concessions, hired just enough blacks here and there to have a few symbols around. He offered the kind of soft resistance that made it very, very difficult to organize around."

Rose makes a crucial point. Daley never let King or any other black leader gain any real headway in integrating Chicago, which remains one of the most rigidly segregated cities in the country. Milton Rakove wrote "Daley gave the blacks what he thought they wanted and needed: jobs, welfare and public services. And he gave the whites what he thought they needed and wanted: segregation. And if he gave the whites segregation, they didn't care if he gave the blacks jobs, welfare and public services. If he gave the blacks jobs, welfare and public services, they didn't care a great deal whether he integrated the city. This arrangement began to come apart only in Daley's last year in office."

Now another Daley is in office, and he has renewed the arrangement, with a few postmodern touches, and it is working.

◆ ◆ ◆

It is a hot, humid noon at Daley Plaza, the square next to city hall named after Richard I. The new Mayor Daley is up on a shadeless stage under the broiling sun. He is sweating; his red, round face is bursting from his tight collar like a beefsteak tomato ready to drop from the vine. He looks out of place. He looks, in fact, just like what he is: a very pink man in a too-tight suit surrounded by a couple dozen dark brown men in African tribal gowns. He is here to make a statement that practically no one believes he believes: I am one with my black brothers. The vehicle for this statement is the announcement of a sister-city pact between Chicago and Accra, the capital of Ghana. The ceremony lasts for a very long, very hot time. Daley sits stolidly through three dances, eight speeches, and three anthems. Five times he unsticks himself from his metal folding chair and walks to the podium to speak or to shake hands or to exchange proclamations or to accept gifts. He receives a carved wooden stool and a brightly colored scarf. He watches with fixed attention during what is presented as the traditional Ghanaian ceremony of "libation," in which a man wearing no socks takes a pint of gin from his back pocket, drinks some, gives some to a friend, then pours some on the stage and dances around the puddle. Throughout the whole, Daley's face remains set in his Mayoral Serious Occasion Look.

In his first official act as mayor, Daley reauthorized a Harold Washington–instituted program that set aside a percentage of city contracts for firms owned by minorities or women. He appointed eleven blacks to cabinet positions, retained the black police superintendent, put blacks on the new interim school board, hired a black press secretary, and picked a black machine pol to fill his vacated seat as state's attorney. And as his father did, Daley makes frequent public appearances with blacks, before black audiences and in black wards.

Importantly, though, Daley remembers the other half of the lesson. He gives to the blacks only what he can politically afford to take from the whites, and he never forgets his core group. He keeps a campaign-style schedule of public appearances, and while a lot of them are in black or Hispanic neighborhoods, at least as many are in white wards. When the more militant, or more power-hungry, black politicos push him, he pushes back, publicly, where white voters can see him—and he wins. This past May, black activists tried to force Daley to select nine blacks, from a list of forty-five candidates, for appointment to the city's new fifteen-member school board. Daley nominated seven for the board but left eight seats open, after rejecting thirty-eight of the nominees. Seeing a chance to pull together opposition to the mayor, the black activists launched a series of protests— which failed to catch on.

A *Chicago Tribune* reporter covering one of the city-hall protests caught perfectly, in the voice of one black alderman, the sound of power changing hands: "I look at this stuff and I think, Am I that old? Am I that dated? These are the same tactics we used against the real Daley in the sixties, and I've got to wonder, has time passed us by?"

Daley avoids all rhetoric that even hints at "liberal" attitudes and will not be drawn into any discussion of racial politics. In his frequent speeches (delivered in such an amateurish fashion that they are perversely effective), Daley sounds like a Republican, or, more to the point, like an old-fashioned Democrat. Like, in fact, his father. He talks of law and order, of building a better city, of getting the streets clean and the crime rate down and the drugs out of the schools. This is the kind of Democrat whom working-class whites used to vote for. It's the kind they are voting for in Chicago again. And it may be the kind of Democrat working-class blacks will vote for, too.

◆ ◆ ◆

"Good government is good politics," his father always said. The race-balancing act gets the audience into the tent, but substance, in the long run, is what counts. Daley's first year was a blur of accomplishments, all designed to show the doubters that the new mayor was a man in charge. He mothballed his armor-plated limousine, saying he didn't want to be the last one alive in a nuclear attack. He cut the fleet of city cars in half and the number of city car phones by 80 percent. He ordered the illegally parked cars of aldermen and city workers towed from in front of city hall. He contracted with a private company to rid the streets of abandoned cars—and got the company to pay $25 a car for the privilege. He bought twenty-five new street sweepers, doubling the city's force. He taxed cigarettes to fund a $1-million-a-year homeless shelter program. He cut $40 million from the city budget, and gave the voters a $25-million property tax cut. He persuaded the state legislature to increase by $85 million 1989's allotment of state funds for the city and to pump an additional $70 million into the school system. He appointed an interim school board that negotiated a new contract with public-school teachers early enough to start the academic year promptly for the first time in years. He dogged the city's airport concessionaires for back rent. He started a "greening of Chicago" program that aims to plant 500,000 trees in five years.

"And good politics," his father always added, turning it around, "is good government." To build something big and lasting, a man needs a machine: Daley can't rebuild the old Twentieth Century Limited his father drove; that one depended on jobs, and Chicago's mayor nowadays can hire and fire freely only in about 1,000 of the city's 40,000 jobs. But Daley can—and is—building his own Little Engine That Could. It rests on essential links to the past, a core of advisers and key department heads who are joined to the mayor by bonds of family, history, and neighborhood, and an outer network of politicians, bureaucrats, city workers, legislators, and judges with whom he has old and strong ties. Frank Kruesi, Daley's chief of programs and policy, says the mayor has secret, reliable sources in every city department, a lot of them people who worked for his father. "A large number of people who were put in there ten years ago, twenty years ago, are still there, in midmanagement positions," says Tom Donovan, Dick Daley's old master of patronage. Rich Daley, he says, "by virtue of being his father's son, is able to use these people."

According to Donovan, Fitzgerald, and Bill Daley, the regular Democratic organization still quietly dominates in nine or ten wards, which gives Daley an initial advantage in any election of 200,000 to 250,000 votes out of Chicago's 1.5 million. The automatic victories of the old days are gone, Donovan says, but "the organization can still be the balance of power in a close election." Especially with a Daley back in office, he says: "I think it will get better and better with Rich as mayor. People want to be considered part of the team again. It isn't a quid-pro-quo thing anymore. You can't go to a precinct captain and say 'I'll give you a job if you deliver.' It's more like a sense that the mayor will help if he can, that he is someone you can talk to and that he has your best interests at heart."

"Where are *their* programs? What have *they* done? Who are *they* to criticize?" his father always said. In the end, nothing matters if you aren't tough enough. A boss has to be able to strike fear. He has to be ruthless. God knows Dick Daley was. His greatest weapon was his what-have-*they*-done roar, his answer to any criticism, any critics. The roar grew with age. In his early days, when he was just Mayor Daley, not Boss Daley, he was willing to listen sometimes and even to compromise. But the years of power hardened his attitude along with his arteries, so that by the end he could not brook even the littlest challenge. That's the Daley the world remembers, not the freshman mayor too shy (as one biographer recounts) to handle a maître d' at a posh restaurant but the aged Boss, the law-and-order caricature of shoot-to-kill and the purple-faced screamer raging at his critics on the floor of the '68 convention.

Toward the end of our talk in his office, I asked the new freshman Mayor Daley about some of his own critics, the ones who said he wasn't smart enough to be mayor, the ones who said he was just living off his old man's name. Rich leaned forward in his chair and his face reddened and his voice revved and thickened and out came—a little softer yet, a little muted still, but there—the Boss's roar. "I don't listen to them. They're sitting out there. I'm in here. *Fine!* Let them question what they want! . . . Why aren't *they* making decisions? You know, where are *they?*"

Then he smiled the brief, beautiful smile, like a glimpse of winter sun: contented at last, at least for the moment. Sitting under his father's portrait, his father's funeral-mass card on his father's old desk, his father's old briefcase in the corner, his father's job in his pocket, he has finally become just like the man who married dear old Ma.

Texas-Size Failure

◆ ◆ ◆

In the beginning, and also in the end, the promise and the problem with the campaign of Ross Perot was Ross Perot.

It was not ideology, or party affiliation, or political experience that gave rise to the odd quasi-candidacy of a short tycoon from Texas. It was himself; the appeal of a President Perot was simply Perot. This was true for the millions of people who rushed to support him, and it was true for Perot, too.

When he announced his willingness to serve, on the cable television program

Larry King Live, five months ago, that was all he offered to voters—himself—in a take-it-or-leave-it shot: "If voters in all fifty states put me on the ballot—not forty-eight or forty-nine states, but all 50—I will agree to run."

And no matter the immediate cause of his angry, abrupt good-bye on Thursday, the root reasons of Perot's epic failure are not things politics did to Perot, but things Perot brought to politics.

On its most basic level, what proved disastrous about Perot as a candidate was precisely the same thing that made him initially so attractive to so many. He had, and displayed, utter contempt for the political process, which he liked to dismiss as "irrelevant to selecting a good candidate."

But the process cannot be irrelevant to selecting a candidate, for the inescapable fact that it produces that candidate. This is something neither Perot nor his top advisers ever grasped.

In an interview yesterday, Thomas D. Barr, one of New York's most prominent lawyers and one of Perot's closest aides, summed up what he and Perot had learned over the last five months. It was not that they had mishandled anything, but that the process had mishandled them.

"The great lesson of this was that a person of quality—and Ross Perot is certainly that—who could have given a great deal to the country has been seriously discouraged and disinterested in doing so," he said. "There is just so much of the process that is wretched and onerous and appalling, and what happens is that this causes an exclusionary effect, a sort of natural selection process, so that there are only a very few people—Bill Clinton, for example—who are prepared to go through this."

Perot's unwillingness to put up with the wretched, the onerous, and the appalling may have stemmed in part, Barr suggested, from the fact that he began his unorthodox drive for the presidency without any real seriousness of intent. "I think he said what he said on the Larry King show because he believed that this would bring to an end the talk of 'Run, Ross, Run.' When it went the other way, he was stunned. This wasn't something he really wanted to do."

What Perot hated most about the process was being criticized by the press, or attacked by the other side.

"He expected rock throwing," Barr said. "But I think he was not prepared to be ridiculed."

Perot showed no qualms about gutter fighting. He was for months nearly ubiquitous on television news and talk shows, responding to criticism and offering criticism of his own in some of the most colorful and harshest political language heard in years.

Reporters who asked questions or raised accusations he did not like were "whining" about "schoolgirl" stuff, were "lying," and were subject to "flights of fantasy."

Perot openly and repeatedly questioned President Bush's masculinity, saying, in connection with Bush's decision to wage war over the Iraqi invasion of Kuwait, "I don't have to prove my manhood by sending anyone to war." He once referred to Bush's Texas campaign coordinator, Jim Oberwetter, as "Jim Bedwetter."

But Perot's style of fighting proved ineffective and, to many, increasingly unattractive. What had once been seen in benign terms—as forthright, feisty candor—metastasized into a more malign image, that of a bully.

A professional politician with such a serious image problem, and suffering as well from the sort of self-perpetuating negative press that is nearly invariably fatal, would probably have countered with an immediate, professionally managed media campaign. This is what the Democratic presidential nominee, Governor Bill Clinton of Arkansas, has done to overcome image problems far more serious than any Perot faced.

But Perot's disdain for the political process included the professionals of that process, and he made it clear he wanted to do no business with them. "What you see is what you get," he said in an interview with the *New York Times* in March. "I'm not going to be one of those people who hires handlers and image makers."

When Perot finally did hire political professionals—Edward J. Rollins, a Republican, and Hamilton Jordan, a Democrat, along with a dozen lesser lights, he resisted their strong advice to mount an image-building advertising campaign. He dismissed Hal Riney & Partners, an advertising firm that had shot a number of elaborately filmed interviews with Perot volunteers. It was this refusal by Perot to follow his counsel that led to Rollins's quitting the campaign the day before Perot pulled the plug completely.

"The whole method of selling a candidate in a political campaign is something I can't accept very easily as being honest or appropriate, and I think Ross had real problems with it, too," Barr said. "And he didn't like the idea of spending money to send people junk mail they would just throw in the wastebasket, or spending money on the kind of television commercial he wouldn't watch himself."

In *Perot: An Unauthorized Biography,* Todd Mason describes Perot's disregard of professionals as an article of abiding faith. Perot's world, in Mason's descriptions, is divided into two camps: "professionals," who are stupid, lazy, or unimaginative, and Perot, who, along with a small band of loyal lieutenants, alone sees the true path.

The religion of antiprofessionalism surfaces repeatedly in the story of Perot's life. To cite one example, there is the case of Perot's 1971 takeover of the huge Wall Street brokerage firm du Pont Flore Gorgan & Company. He derided the brokers of the firm as incompetent, and instituted sweeping changes in work rules that encouraged great numbers of them to quit. He lost more than $60 million before bailing out.

Beyond his problem with the process and the professionals, Perot had a problem with the hard currency of politics: ideas. He did not seem to like them, did not want to talk about them, and apparently did not think they were of any concern to voters. His favorite phrase to reporters pushing for any sort of details on just what he thought about the nation's concerns was eloquent in its utter dismissal. "See," he would say, "it's simple."

It was his frequent claim that only journalists cared about such things. After much pressing, he said in May that he would arrive at a set of policy positions in sixty days (he never did), but even then, he sneered at the notion that it was really necessary. All the people really needed, or wanted, he seemed to believe, was Ross Perot, himself.

In a *Time* magazine interview in May, he offered this typical observation: "The phone banks are going crazy with working folks saying 'Why are you wasting your time on this? We're not interested in your damn positions, Perot. We're interested in your principles.'"

By July, even volunteers in the Perot headquarters in Dallas were telling reporters that they needed to hear some specifics from their candidate.

With no core of ideology to guide him, Perot was peculiarly vulnerable to the pitfalls of political dialogue. Nuances seemed beyond him; a few televised remarks concerning homosexuals landed him in a mess he clearly did not expect or fully understand, and it took months of negotiations with gay groups to work his way out. No sooner had he done that, than he was back in trouble again, with remarks before a convention of the National Association for the Advancement of Colored People that struck many in his audience as patronizing and insensitive.

He concluded his political adventure in a way that, like his abundant belief in himself and his disdain for professionals, is part of the long pattern of his life. When events went not to his liking, he had, all his adult life, quit things: the navy, the search for missing American servicemen in Vietnam, Wall Street, General Motors. On Thursday, with his name having been placed on the ballot by thousands of volunteers in nearly half of the fifty states, he quit one more time.

But What About Dad?

♦ ♦ ♦

Dear Junior,
Just a quick note to say I think your veep choice is fine. Fine, fine. Dick Cheney—fine. Fine choice. Said that already. Perfectly fine. Splendid fellow. Sterling character. Heart of gold. Sinews of steel, thews of iron, abdomen like one of those old-time washing boards the cleaning gals used to use before Bar bought them a machine back in '73. Sorry, got carried away there. Never think about Dick's abdomen. Or thews. Especially thews. Don't even know what thews are. Connected to thighs? (Ask Noonan) Point is: excellent choice. Our kind.

But, hey, wild thought, another idea. Still time to think again, say it was just a misunderstanding, press got it wrong—make a joke, don't dare criticize the press. No, not ever. They don't ever forget that, vicious never-in-the-arena-carpers-and-mewlers. Whoops, carried away again. Point is, just a little joke. Point is: Dick is a fine man, but what about Dad? Dear old Dad. George the first. (Joke again, plenty of Georges before us. I remember you telling me just the other day about that disciple of our Lord named George. News to me. Surprising you don't hear more about that. Matthew, Mark, Luke, John, and George. Also, of course, one of the Beatles, I don't remember which one. George, I guess.) Anyway, point is, how about D.O.D. for vice president?

Pluses and minuses. Minuses first. Not a lot here. Age thing, not a problem. You're as young as the last time you jumped out of an airplane. (Related parenthetical plus: flip-side, age-wise—gravitas. No need to linger here, dwell-wise.) Constitutional? Not there. Baker looked the thing over, amendments etc. Nothing at all. Elected a much-deserved second time by a properly Desert Storm–grateful nation in '92, instead of being hosed by a media-warped minority of the voting-age public who to their everlasting sorrow gave a once-undefiled Oval Office to Monsieur Hot Pants from Hot Springs? Well, then, might have been an issue, now. But spilled milk under the bridge.

What else? Father and son thing? Psychology, now. Bear with me, not easy for either one of us. Point is, been there, done that. I'm recalling the time you were crocked off your—well, the time we went mano a mano. We sang that song. You don't need to mano me again, and I don't need to mano you. No mano either way, man.

Which brings me to the primo of the pluses. Mano-wise, I'm ultra-comfortable-wise being number two. Not a wimp-factor thing at all. Just comfortable. Fact is, made for number two. Who better, trained and groomed (I mean, besides El Gore-o). Fact is, I liked number two. Never was keen on number one. Your mother's idea. I liked the other house, liked the other plane (not so showy, more lived-in, less right-money), liked the job. Liked the whole thing—the lunches with Ron, the funerals, the bread-and-butter notes. Especially the bread-and-butter notes. Son, I'm your father so I can tell you, you've always been a disgrace at bread-and-butter notes. Something to think about.

Other pluses: re the traditional weekly number one–number two lunch. One thing that always drove me nuts—and, son, this is between you and me and the focus group you rode in on—was lunch with Mr. Potatoe, not to name names. Not his fault, the fault of the darned liberal media that made him feel so darned, well, vulnerable (sorry, psychology again). But every week it seemed he was more determined than the week before to talk big thoughts. He used to bring that darned Paul Johnson book to the darned table and read out loud from it! Sorry, I get so darned mad just remembering. Point is, you know and I know there wouldn't be any of that between us. Just a nice lunch, a few jokes, a little soup, an el grande combination plate, call it a day. No big thoughts. Darn it, no thoughts at all. Another something to think about.

More pluses: This one is a little tricky to follow, so bear with me again, G-II (Not W. They never get anything right). There you are. In the Oval Office. Behind the big desk. The phone rings. It's me. Full of advice. Chatter, chatter, chatter. Natter, natter, natter. Helpful suggestions, blah, blah, blah. Been there, done that, you should be there, do that, too. Gonna happen, no matter what. But hey—wouldn't it be less aggravating if it were official business? If it were part of the old job description and not just the old familias obligation to the old pater? Just one last something to think about.

Yours, etc.,

Ted Kennedy on the Rocks

◆ ◆ ◆

Edward Moore Kennedy works harder than most people think, and this morning he is working very hard at a simple but crucial task. He is trying to face the day. It is 9:30 A.M., September 26, and Kennedy is in Room 138 of the Dirksen Senate Office Building to introduce a bill to lure new and better teachers. This kind of thing is ice cream and cake for any practiced politician, a simple piece of business that will provoke few tough questions and at least a few approving editorials. But for Kennedy it seems a great challenge, and no fun at all. He hastens tonelessly through his prepared statement like a court stenographer reading back testimony to the judge. He passes off most of the perfunctory and easy questions to the other politicians and education-establishment figures joining him, and he stares into space as the other men do the job. When he goes to the podium to introduce his fellow speakers, he walks with a nervous, cautious shuffle, like Steve McQueen after he's been let out of solitary in *Papillon*. When he holds out the piece of white paper to read the introductions of men he's known for decades, it flutters and shakes in the still air.

Up close, the face is a shock. The skin has gone from red roses to gin blossoms. The tracery of burst capillaries shines faintly through the scaly scarlet patches that cover the bloated, mottled cheeks. The nose that was once straight and narrow is now swollen and bulbous, with open pores and a bump of what looks like scar tissue near the tip. Deep corrugations crease the forehead and angle from the nostrils and the downturned corners of the mouth. The Chiclet teeth are the color of old piano keys. The eyes have yellowed, too, and they are so bloodshot, it looks as if he's been weeping.

Edward Kennedy was once the handsomest of the handsome Kennedy boys, with a proudly jutting chin, a Nelson Eddy jaw and Cupid's-bow lips under a thatch of chestnut hair. When he is dieting and on the wagon, there is a glimpse of that still, which makes it all the harder to see him as he more often is. There is a great desire to remember him as we remember his brothers. The Dorian Grays of Hyannis Port, John and Robert, have perpetual youth and beauty and style, and their faces are mirrors of all that is better and classier and richer than us. Ted is the reality, the fifty-seven-year-old living picture of a man who has feasted on too much for too long with too little restraint, the visible proof that nothing exceeds like excess.

◆ ◆ ◆

After the press conference, as reporters hustle around Kennedy for follow-up questions, it becomes clear that something is especially wrong today with his left eye, which he has been poking and rubbing. He has lost a contact lens. Motioning for room, he slowly searches the floor. A reporter spots the lens and scoops it up with a forefinger. Kennedy takes out a contacts case and screws it open so the reporter can drop in the lens. But there is a problem. The senator's right hand is shaking so violently that he cannot hold the case steady. The reporter hovers his finger over the case, trying to coordinate the path of the lens with that of the case, but the case is all over the map, jiggling up, down, left, right. For a second, Kennedy gets it steady and the reporter swoops in—but there goes the hand again, and the case is off, jogging to the right and the left for another few agonizing seconds before Kennedy stills his hand and the reporter drops the lens home, safe. The senator slowly screws the top back on, to the evident relief of a young aide who stands at his elbow, clutching the boss's bottle of Visine.

I grew up on Capitol Hill, the son of Kennedy Democrats and the child of an age shaped by Kennedy myths, and I remember playing on the Capitol grounds one fall day, watching the young Senator Kennedy stride importantly by. He seemed a great man: tall, broad-shouldered, with a big, deep chest that stuck out like the prow of a ship as he rushed forward. The man in front of me now seems, as the writer Henry Fairlie described him a few years ago, a "husk," dried up and hollowed out.

But as I watch, a startling thing happens. With a heave of the chest, a deep-lunged breath, a squaring of the shoulders, Kennedy abruptly pulls himself together, becoming suddenly full of himself once more. As reporters press, he expounds on his bill with knowledge and enthusiasm. The Excellence in Teaching Act of 1989 would establish a new National Teacher Corps, like the old LBJ model Reagan killed in 1981, by giving scholarships to students who sign on for four- or five-year teaching hitches. Kennedy has spent his political career pushing the religion of the Great Society and he remains devout, even if it often seems these days that he's no longer preaching to masses of the converted but to two old ladies there for vespers and a guy looting the poor box.

"By God, this is exciting," Kennedy says, talking fast and sure, jabbing his finger at a reporter. "What we can do with this bill, we can go into inner-city neighborhoods, we can go into places where there is very little hope, and we can say to the young people 'Become a teacher! Here is an option for your life! Here is a mission for you!' "

In his autumn years, Senator Edward M. Kennedy is a man of parts. Sometimes, especially in the mornings, he seems as weak and fluttery as a butterfly. Sometimes, especially in the evenings, he seems a Senator Bedfellow figure, an aging Irish boyo clutching a bottle and diddling a blonde. But he is also a man who can rise above that caricature to stature: the leading voice of what is left of the Left in American politics, a lawmaker of great and probably increasing power, the self-appointed tribune of the disenfranchised, the patriarch of America's most famous political family and the world's most conspicuous Democrat. He is in obvious ways tragic. His three brothers and one of his sisters died violently, two by public murder. His cruel marriage ended in divorce, with his wife a recovering alcoholic. He suffers still from a back broken in a near-fatal airplane crash. His elder son lost a leg and almost his life to cancer.

The parts of his life collide with each other like bumper cars, the Teddy of the tabloids giving a boozy shove to the senior senator from the Commonwealth of Massachusetts, the sordid tragedies of his unprivate private life darkening the face of the public man.

◆ ◆ ◆

The Kennedy brothers always perpetuated their own glorious images, but over the years the last brother has built an image—not glorious at all—of his very own. For his hard public drinking, his obsessive public womanizing and his frequent boorishness, he has become a late-century legend, Teddy the Terrible, the Kennedy Untrammeled.

In Washington, it sometimes seems as if *everyone* knows someone who has slept with Kennedy, been invited to sleep with Kennedy, seen Kennedy drunk, been insulted by Kennedy. At Desirée, a private Georgetown club where well-heeled fat men mingle with society brats and party girls, Kennedy is known as a thrice-a-month habitué and remembered by at least one fellow customer for the time he made a scene with his overenthusiasm for a runway model during a club fashion show. In a downtown office, a former congressional page tells of her surprise meeting with Kennedy three years ago. She was sixteen then. It was evening and she and another sixteen-year-old page, an attractive blonde, were walking down the Capitol steps on their way home from work when Kennedy's limo pulled up and the senator opened the door. In the backseat stood a bottle of wine on ice. Leaning his graying head out the door, the senator popped the question: Would one of the girls care to join him for dinner? No? How about the other? The girls said no thanks and the senator zoomed off. Kennedy, the former page said, made no overt sexual overtures and was "very careful to make it seem like nothing out of the ordinary." It is possible that Kennedy did not know that the girls were underage or that they were pages and, as such, were under the protection of Congress, which serves in loco parentis. Nevertheless, the former page said she did find Kennedy's invitation surprising. "He didn't even know me," she says. "I knew this kind of stuff happened, but I didn't expect it to happen to me."

A former midlevel Kennedy staffer, bitterly disillusioned, recalls with disgust one (now ex-) high-ranking aide as "a pimp . . . whose real position was to procure women for Kennedy." The fellow did have a legitimate job, she says, but also openly bragged of his prowess at getting attractive and beddable dates for his boss. The former staffer also recalls attending a party at Kennedy's McLean, Virginia, mansion and finding it "sleazy and weird" to see that the senator had apparently established as his live-in girlfriend a young woman known to the staff as the T-shirt Girl, a New Englander who had previously sold tees at a beach resort and who had reportedly met the senator through his son Teddy junior. A waiter at La Colline, a French restaurant near the senator's office, remembers a drunken Kennedy and a fellow senator recently staging a late-night scene out of *The Three Musketeers,* grabbing long-stalked gladiolus from a vase in the front hall and fencing "just like D'Artagnan." At the same restaurant in 1985, Kennedy and drinking buddy Senator Christopher Dodd of Connecticut did "a Mexican hat dance" on their own framed photographs. According to *Washingtonian* magazine, which broke the story, "Kennedy spotted Dodd's framed photo [on the wall] and shouted 'Who's this guy?' Laughing, he grabbed the photo from the wall and threw it on the ground, breaking the glass in the frame. Dodd, not to be outdone, located Kennedy's photo and returned the favor." A new Kennedy photo adorns the wall today, inscribed with "*Laissez les bons temps rouler*—Let the good times roll."

Lobbyist John Aycoth recalls a recent afternoon meeting he arranged between Kennedy and several of Aycoth's potential clients, representatives of an African government. Aycoth says Kennedy "was incredibly rude" and "was drunk . . . stumbling and slurring his words and red in the face and smelling of alcohol." One of the visiting dignitaries—a Kennedy devotee who had called on JFK at the White House—presented the senator with a necklace to give to his mother for her forthcoming ninety-ninth birthday. Kennedy's appreciation? "When we were walking out, he just pitched it on the desk, right in front of them," says Aycoth. "Didn't open it. Didn't say thanks. Nothing." (After my talk with Aycoth, his associate, former Delaware Congressman Tom Evans, who was also at the meeting, called to say nervously that he had heard what Aycoth had said and that while the account of rude behavior is true, in his opinion Kennedy had been "perfectly sober.")

Kennedy regularly finds himself in unseemly scenes. One East Coast playboy recalls an incident a few years ago in a popular Palm Beach bar when "a definitely drunk" Kennedy shoved him against the bar and spilled his beer as the senator rushed out the door with a blonde so young, the man at first mistook Kennedy for an angry father come to take home an underage daughter. Dropping in for a two A.M. drink in the Manhattan bar American Trash in January 1989, Kennedy reportedly got into a shouting match with an obnoxious (and possibly intoxicated) off-duty bouncer, which climaxed with the senator's throwing his drink in the other fellow's face. Unkind *Boston Herald* columnist Howie Carr writes of Kennedy as "Fat Boy" and says it isn't really considered summer in Cape Cod until the senator drives on the sidewalk for the first time. Reporters wonder at his behavior. "He really will do anything at all," says veteran Washington gossip columnist Diana McLellan, "I think he's mad." Says Bill Thomas, writer of the "Heard on the Hill" column for *Roll Call,* the well-regarded newspaper of Capitol Hill, "He's off the reservation . . . out of control. . . . He has no compunctions whatsoever." Thomas likens Kennedy and Dodd to "two guys in a fraternity who have been loosed upon the world."

Perhaps this seems unfair. From all available evidence, God created our elected officials to drink and screw around. Arrogance, too, is common. So is sexual recklessness (witness Gary Hart, Robert Bauman, and Barney Frank); power dements as well as corrupts. But Kennedy's behavior stands out. The two most infamous Terrible Teddy stories make the point. Both take place at Washington's La Brasserie, where Kennedy is a favorite customer.

Brasserie I: In December 1985, just before he announced that he would not run for president in 1988, Kennedy allegedly manhandled a pretty young woman employed as a Brasserie waitress. The woman, Carla Gaviglio, declined to be quoted in this article, but says the following account, a similar version of which first appeared in *Penthouse* last year, is full and accurate:

It is after midnight and Kennedy and Dodd are just finishing up a long dinner in a private room on the first floor of the restaurant's annex. They are drunk. Their dates, two very young blondes, leave the table to go to the bathroom. (The dates are drunk, too. "They'd always get their girls very, very drunk," says a former Brasserie waitress.) Betty Loh, who served the foursome, also leaves the room. Raymond Campet, the co-owner of La Brasserie, tells Gaviglio the senators want to see her. As Gaviglio enters the room, the six-foot-two, 225-plus-pound Kennedy grabs the five-foot-three, 103-pound waitress and throws her on the table. She lands on her back, scattering crystal, plates, cutlery, and the lit candles. Several glasses and a crystal candlestick are broken. Kennedy then picks her up from the table and throws her on Dodd, who is sprawled in a chair. With Gaviglio on Dodd's lap, Kennedy jumps on top and begins rubbing his genital area against hers, supporting his weight on the arms of the chair. As he is doing this, Loh enters the room. She and Gaviglio both scream, drawing one or two dishwashers. Startled, Kennedy leaps up. He laughs. Bruised, shaken, and angry over what she considered a sexual assault, Gaviglio runs from the room. Kennedy, Dodd, and their dates leave shortly thereafter, following a friendly argument between the senators over the check.

Eyewitness Betty Loh told me that Kennedy had "three or four" cocktails in his first half hour at the restaurant and wine with dinner. When she walked into the room after Gaviglio had gone in, she says, "what I saw was Senator Kennedy on top of Carla, who was on top of Senator Dodd's lap, and the tablecloth was sort of slid off the table 'cause the table was knocked over—not completely, but just on Senator Dodd's lap a little bit, and of course the glasses and the candlesticks were totally spilled and everything. And right when I walked in, Senator Kennedy jumped off . . . and he leaped up, composed himself and got up. And Carla jumped up and ran out of the room."

According to Loh, Kennedy "was sort of leaning" on Gaviglio, "not really straddling but sort of off-balance so it was like he might have accidentally fallen. . . . He was partially on and off . . . pushing himself off her to get up." Kennedy and Dodd "looked like they got caught." Dodd, she adds, "said 'It's not my fault.'" Kennedy said something similar and added, jokingly, "Makes you wonder about the leaders of this country."

Giving Kennedy the benefit of the doubt, it's quite possible he did not intend an assault but meant to be funny, in a repulsive, boozehead way. Drunks are notoriously poor judges of distance, including the distance between fun and assault.

Brasserie II: On September 25, 1987, Kennedy and a young blond woman—identified by several sources as a congressional lobbyist—allegedly got carried away at a wine-fueled lunch in a private room upstairs and succumbed to the temptations of the carpet, where they were surprised in a state of semi-undress and wholehearted passion by waitress Frauke Morgan. The room, located next to the restrooms, is secured only by a flimsy accordion door, which could not be fully closed. Morgan declined to be interviewed for this story or to comment on or refute the accounts of other sources.

However, waitress Virginia Hurt, who says Morgan described the scene to her shortly after witnessing it, recalls, "He was on the floor with his pants down on top of the woman, and he saw her and she just kind of backed away and closed the door. The girl didn't see Frauke. So Frauke went downstairs and told the manager and [another waitress] overheard."

A waitress to whom Morgan spoke just after the incident says, "She told me . . . she went up to offer them coffee and when she opened the door . . . there they were on the floor." Morgan said explicitly, the other waitress goes on, that Kennedy had his pants down and his date "had her dress up," and the two "were screwing on the floor."

Says another waitress to whom Morgan immediately related the episode, "She said she had walked in to ask them if they needed anything else before she gave them the check, and she just sort of found Senator Kennedy on top of this [woman] on the floor and they were sort of half under the table and half out."

A copy of La Brasserie's reservation list for that day shows that a luncheon table for two in the back room was reserved for Kennedy. A copy of the check, signed "Edward M. Kennedy," shows he was billed for two bottles of Chardonnay.

◆ ◆ ◆

Kennedy's friends, family, and aides are a little skittish about questions on any of this. I asked the senator's nephew Massachusetts Congressman Joseph Kennedy II if the man portrayed so scandalously in gossip columns and tabloids was the Ted Kennedy that he knew. "Hey! Hey," said Joe in alarm. "I got—I can't—I, uh, have really no comment on that. . . . There's no answer I can give you that isn't going to be explosive, that's all." Recovering slightly, he added, "You know, Teddy's a grown man and he can do whatever he wants."

When I asked Utah Senator Orrin Hatch—a conservative Republican who nevertheless works closely with and likes Kennedy—if he thought his colleague had a drinking problem, I got a similarly telling response. "I wouldn't comment on that. I wouldn't comment on that. All I can say is that I consider him a friend," said Hatch. "I have found [him to be] a vulnerable human being who has a very good side to him. I think he has some bad sides, too, but there is a good side to him that I choose to look at."

Kennedy's staffers do what they can to suppress unflattering reports. In researching this article (three months, more than seventy interviews, fifteen books, a couple thousand pages of news reports and speeches), I asked for an interview with the senator. After a long, elaborate quizzing by his press secretary, Paul Donovan, and deputy press secretary, Melody Miller, about the nature of the article and the questions I might ask, Kennedy decided to stick to a blanket policy of not doing interviews with "life-style magazines." Donovan explained: "Frankly, he doesn't do interviews with life-style magazines because they tend to ask life-style questions."

I later asked Donovan if he or the senator would like to comment on or deny reports of heavy drinking or unusual behavior by Kennedy, and to comment specifically on the accounts of Kennedy's behavior with the congressional page, the Brasserie waitress, and the luncheon date on the floor. Donovan said Kennedy would stick to his standard reply: "It has been and remains his policy never to comment on this sort of endless gossip and speculation." Donovan did say that the "slight tremor" in Kennedy's hands is attributable not to drinking but to an inherited medical condition that worsens with age. (Brasserie co-owner Raymond Campet also declined to comment on either story involving his restaurant. Asked if he would care to deny the incidents, Campet said, "Did you hear me, sir? I have absolutely no comment." Dodd's press secretary did not return numerous phone calls.)

There is not, really, much else that Donovan can say. Kennedy's personal life has always been a press secretary's nightmare. During his twenty-two-year marriage, his extramarital affairs were numerous and barely hidden. "He was philandering from the moment he was married," recalls old Kennedy-family associate Dick Tuck. "Not one-night stands, but not much more than that. Kind of affairs of convenience. . . . I think most normal people might have more than one affair [during a marriage] but not every week, like Teddy. He was always chasing, looking for the conquest."

Of odd and reckless behavior, there are many examples, including Kennedy's photographed 1982 nude promenade on the public sands of Palm Beach, reportedly in the presence of several old ladies. The columnist Taki, chronicler of Europe's idle rich, still calls Kennedy "a boorish and uncivilized philistine" because of an incident in the midseventies. At the time, Taki was a UPI reporter in Athens and a well-known playboy. One day, he got a call from Kennedy's staffers, who asked him to "round up two dates, American girls preferably," for the senator and his nephew Joe during their brief visit to the Greek capital. Taki says he showed up at the Hotel Grande Bretagne, where the Kennedys were staying, with his girlfriend and dates for the Kennedys. "Teddy was . . . pretty much drunk," says Taki. "In fact, he was really out of it." Taki says he and the others left the senator and his date, a proper young Connecticut woman who was "very, very impressed with the Kennedys," at the hotel while they went nightclubbing. Back home later that night, Taki was awakened by Kennedy's hysterical date. Taki says the drink-befuddled young woman became frightened when she "saw Ted Kennedy coming naked at her," and adds, "that would scare me, too, and I would like to say I am a pretty brave man."

Biographers first note obvious public drunkenness in the terrible aftermath of Bobby's murder. In April 1969, flying back from a congressional trip to inspect the living conditions of poor Indians in Alaska, a hard-drinking Kennedy pelted aides and reporters with pillows, ranged up and down the aisles chanting "Es-ki-mo power" and rambled incoherently about Bobby's assassination, saying, "They're going to shoot my ass off the way they shot Bobby."

Three months later, on July 18, came the defining moment of Kennedy's life, when he drove his Oldsmobile off a bridge on the island of Chappaquiddick, sending young Kennedy staffer Mary Jo Kopechne to her death and drowning his chances of ever getting to the White House. This much-explored accident is worth mentioning because the factors surrounding it are the same ones so apparent before and so apparent still in Kennedy's personal life: a childish belief that the rules of human behavior do not apply to himself, a casual willingness to place himself in a compromising position with an attractive young woman and, most probably, a reckless use of alcohol.

Kennedy has never told anything close to the whole story of Chappaquid-dick, the details of which were covered up by Kennedy associates with the help of compliant local authorities, but he has denied that he was driving drunk, or on his way to an assignation when he turned down the deserted dirt road that led to Dike Bridge. No writer who has seriously studied the events of the night—and there have been many—has believed him. Leo Damore, whose 1988 book, *Senatorial Privilege: The Chappaquiddick Cover-Up,* is the most thorough examination of the accident, offers strong evidence that Kennedy was probably drunk behind the wheel and probably on his way to a tryst (not, as he claimed, to the ferry to Martha's Vineyard). Indeed, it is otherwise difficult to explain the actions Kennedy himself called "irrational and indefensible and inexcusable and inexplicable": leaving the party alone with Kopechne and without his driver; failing to notice that he had taken a ninety-degree turn that led down a very bumpy dirt road away from the smooth asphalt road that led to the ferry; never calling the police for help in rescuing the trapped and dying Kopechne but relying solely and clandestinely on his two closest aides; and failing to report the accident until after it was discovered ten hours later.

There have been many theories advanced to explain Kennedy's behavior, all of which make much of the extraordinarily competitive and amoral atmosphere (especially as far as the treatment of women was concerned) in which the Kennedy boys were raised. As Garry Wills makes clear in his elegant *The Kennedy Imprisonment,* Ted Kennedy was born and bred to act like the last of the Regency rakes: to be a boor when it pleases him, to take what he wants, to treat women as score markers in the game of sport fucking, and to revel in high-stakes risks. Joseph Kennedy Sr. flaunted his affairs in front of his wife and children, made crude passes at his sons' dates, and well past his middle years was still chasing doxies. John Kennedy's mad womanizing—frolicking with nudettes in the White House swimming pool, banging a call girl in Lincoln's bed, carrying on barely secret affairs with admitted mobster girlfriend Judith Campbell Exner, with Marilyn Monroe and Jayne Mansfield—was beyond anything Teddy has ever done or, for that matter, anything anybody has ever done. Neither Joe nor Jack was punished by church, state, or wife for such behavior and the late-born Teddy, coming into the family when its adult behavior patterns were already mythologized, presumably figured that neither the rules of decency nor of retribution applied to a Kennedy. The boy grew to manhood without learning how to be an adult. His drinking suggests nothing so much as a frat boy on a toot. His actions with women seem to be more evidence, as writer Suzannah Lessard put it in 1979, of "a severe case of arrested development, a kind of narcissistic intemperance, a huge, babyish ego that must constantly be fed."

Kennedy's only real grown-up job has been serving as a U.S. senator, and the greatest men's club in the world became his second family, giving him the same kind of special privileges and protections as his first. Michael Barone, coauthor of *The Almanac of American Politics,* sees Kennedy as a victim of environmentally induced inertia. "In the old days, you could get away with this stuff," says Barone. "The senator would be at his desk and there would be a pair of high heels sticking out from underneath and you weren't supposed to notice it. Maybe Ted Kennedy didn't realize times have changed."

But arrested development doesn't explain why Kennedy seems to be getting worse as he gets older. According to a theory currently popular in Washington, such incidents as Brasserie I and II are evidence that Kennedy, freed at last by the knowledge that he will never be president, is simply giving his natural inclinations full vent. In the opinion of *Roll Call's* Thomas, "He's beyond caring about anything since he knows he's not going to be president. . . . He's what Kennedys always were, and [as] the only thing that kept them under control was the ambition for higher office . . . he's no longer under control." Says another Washington reporter, "He seems to be going through a second adolescence. . . . I think he realizes his day in the sun is over. Whereas he might have made a pretense of being a good family man years ago, he doesn't have to pretend anymore. . . . He figures he is never going to run for president again. He has no great ambition beyond being the once almost prince." In short, with nothing left to lose politically (he'd have to hit the pope and pee on the Irish flag to lose his Senate seat) and long inured to ridicule, he has become the Kennedy Untrammeled, Unbound.

All the theories, however, still leave you wondering. Neither family history nor generational attitudes nor a lifetime as one of the privileged elite nor the liberation of renouncing the presidency fully explain Kennedy's behavior, although all play a part.

A longtime associate of Kennedy's thinks the full explanation must take into account one other factor. He says, "The problem with Kennedy theories is that people are looking for psychological Rosetta stones when the answer is a far more common malady. If you forget he's a Kennedy, it's textbook, it's just textbook."

This man, who asked that he not be identified, is a recovering alcoholic who spoke because he believes Kennedy needs help. He thinks Kennedy's episodes of disgraceful behavior are due to the simple fact that he periodically drowns his few, faint natural inhibitions in a sea of booze. "He's what we call in the trade a binge drinker," says this man, who says he has seen Kennedy drunk enough to lapse into baby talk with his young dates. "We are talking serious binge drinking, really pouring it down." He adds, "There is an extensive conspiracy effort" among Kennedy's close friends "to make him face up to the fact that he's got a problem. . . . There are occasional plots of confrontation and one thing or another to shake some sense into him. The conversation is far more than idle and it involves just about anyone you can think of who has been exceptionally close to him, especially in the last five or six years." There have been, he says, "hints dropped here and there. You put a hook in the water and see if he bites."

This man, who has known the senator for many years, says Kennedy goes for relatively long periods without drinking "and then, every once in a while, *kaboom*"—a binge triggered by the breakup of a brief affair or a break in work. Is drinking the sole explanation for his behavior? Obviously, no. Lots of men, including some of his fellow senators, get tanked pretty regularly and don't end up on the floor of a restaurant. A cosseted upbringing, a juvenile nature, a powerful sexual greed, the liberation of putting aside the White House, the arrogance and vanity inherent to a Kennedy, the tragedies of his life—they all play a big part, too. But periodic excessive drinking does seem to be the catalyst that brings those forces together and releases them.

Certainly, the anecdotal evidence relating to Kennedy's drinking suggests relatively long periods of sobriety interrupted by bouts of excessive drinking. Younger son Patrick says his father has "the most disciplined life of anybody I know as far as the seriousness with which he takes his work." There are "other times," says Patrick, when he is less disciplined, but "those represent such an infinitesimal part of who my dad is that I get disturbed when people get a misunderstanding from it." Many who speak of his drinking talk of his ability to hold great amounts of liquor and his discipline about exactly when he drinks. "He can control when he drinks," says longtime associate Milton Gwirtzman. "He never drinks when he's working." Former legislative aide Thomas Susman says he has never seen Kennedy drink except socially at night, and he adds, "I have been at his house as early as six in the morning and he's up. He may have been slosh-faced until four [but] he's never staggered in, he's never had trouble getting started, he's never had to have a little hair of the dog before he could work."

On the other hand, eyewitness reports of heavy drinking are also plentiful. *Washington Times* editor John Podhoretz recalls seeing Kennedy, at La Brasserie in 1986, drink a bottle and a half of wine by himself in twenty-five minutes. A recent dinner guest at Kennedy's home recalls with similar amazement Kennedy's guzzling three screwdrivers in one twenty-minute period. "I was chugging to keep up with him," the guest says. "I've drunk with the best of them, and he's the best I've ever seen."

A former La Brasserie waitress calls Kennedy and Dodd "drinkers' drinkers" whose demands led management to put a makeshift bar near their habitual table. "They drank so much you couldn't get to the [regular] bar fast enough," she relates. In a "standard evening," she says, each man would knock off half to three quarters of a bottle of hard liquor, then switch to wine or champagne, and sometimes then to after-dinner drinks: "They would [sometimes] stay at the restaurant till three o'clock in the morning, just drinking and drinking. By the time they got up, they could hardly stand."

A woman in her midtwenties who dated Kennedy steadily a few years ago also describes the senator as largely controlled, occasionally drunk. It was true, she says, that "when you go out with Chris Dodd, go out with the boys, you do get drunk and so on." But Kennedy drank little when he was with her, and the couple would often spend the evening by the fire at the senator's home, reading books or talking. The Ted Kennedy she knew was not the Bad Boy of La Brasserie but "a golden retriever," a "romanticist" who let her have the last bite of his dessert at night and kissed her good-bye on the forehead in the morning. Yet it is hard to believe that this picture is wholly accurate. At the time this woman was dating Kennedy, she was a fixture on the nightclub scene and a heavy partyer.

But even giving the woman the benefit of the doubt and assuming that she and Kennedy did pass many quiet, contented evenings together, I question whether it could have been that fascinating for the fifty-seven-year-old senator to sit cozily around the fire, engaged in conversation with a woman who says that she developed a crush on him largely because they both had "blue eyes and fair hair" and who was surprised to learn that her ex-boyfriend had been the subject of several biographies. I wonder whether Kennedy is even really enjoying any of this anymore.

As the former girlfriend and I were finishing up our talk, she told me of a big party to which she was going that night. "It's going to be reeelly, reeelly great!" she said. "They're going to have these drinks called sharks, which are reeelly, reeelly fun. You have this plastic shark in your glass and you also have a plastic mermaid and you push the shark and the mermaid together and then pour some red stuff over the mermaid that looks like blood."

"Grenadine?" I said.

"I think so," she said.

At what age does it stop being fun and start being hell on earth to spend your evenings with someone who gets reeelly, reeelly excited about novelty cocktails?

The recovering alcoholic quoted earlier thinks Kennedy has passed that point: "He is a very unhappy man personally. He's very unhappy and lonely [because of] his inability to find someone after his marriage fell apart. . . . Getting laid has long since ceased being fun."

Fun? A Boston reporter recalls seeing Kennedy on a morning after: "I had to cover him taking part in the Hands Across America thing on Boston Common and, Christ, it was like someone had poured Jack Daniel's in his hair. It was like he was *shvitzing* Jack Daniel's. And he's holding hands with these two fifty-year-old ladies, and it was just really pathetic. You look at the guy and you think, My God, he must be dying for a drink. You think, He's really killing himself."

Fun? "He has the kind of personal wealth where he can do just about anything he wants to do," says Orrin Hatch. "But I wouldn't trade life with him for ten seconds. I'd rather be poor and in the condition that I'm in than trade with Ted."

The better part of Ted Kennedy's life is found, as it is with so many men, in his work and in his children. When Teddy came to the Senate in 1962, inheriting the seat his big brother John had vacated when he was elected president, he was conspicuous only in his youth and inexperience. Twenty-eight years later, he is the fifth-ranking member and the liberal leader of what remains, despite all its current confusion, the most important legislative body in the world.

The American Enterprise Institute's Congress watcher, Norman Ornstein, only goes a little beyond others when he declares that "Kennedy is going to go down as one of the most significant senators in history, in terms of concrete things accomplished and things put on the agenda that will get accomplished in years to come." Illinois Democrat Paul Simon calls his colleague one of the "three or four shapers of what happens in the Senate," and adds, "in terms of moving the agenda of the Senate, I can't think of anybody who has had a greater impact." Republican Hatch calls Kennedy "the most powerful, effective liberal in the Senate" and says history will view him as "one of the all-time-great senators."

Even a partial listing of the major bills in whose passage Kennedy has played a part is impressive. Whether you admire them or not, these are the measures that transformed—mostly liberalized—America in our time: the first Immigration Reform Act; the Voting Rights Act and its extensions; the Freedom of Information Act; the Gun Control Act; the Campaign Financing Reform law; the Comprehensive Selective Service Reform Act; the Eighteen-Year-Old Vote law; the Occupational Safety and Health Act; the War on Cancer bills; the recodification of federal criminal laws; the Bilingual Education Act; the Fair Housing Acts; the Age Discrimination Act; the Airline and Trucking Deregulation bills; the Job Training Partnership Act; the South African sanctions; and the Grove City Civil Rights Restoration Act.

Far more than either of his brothers, who were lackluster senators, Kennedy, over the past three decades, has been responsible for changes in the complexion of this country and in the lives of its citizens. He has been an ally of blacks, American Indians, the poor, the sick, the aged, the mentally ill, starving refugees worldwide, and immigrants. He has been an outspoken liberal, unafraid to take the controversial positions—on issues such as busing, abortion, gun control, the Vietnam War (late but forcefully), the nuclear freeze, and capital punishment—that other senators clearly avoided.

Since Kennedy assumed the chairmanship of the Labor and Human Resources Committee in 1986, upon the Democrats' regaining control of the Senate, his power has grown markedly and he is now, by all accounts, in the prime of his career. He has become not only the most consistent counterforce to the long-running Republican administrations in pushing for government activism in health, education, labor, and science, but has also become adept at building Republican-Democrat, Right-Left coalitions that can ensure passage of compromise domestic-policy legislation. Hatch, for instance, says he "came to the Senate to fight Ted Kennedy." Yet, because Hatch likes him and trusts him—and because with Kennedy behind it, a bill automatically receives serious attention—he now often joins Kennedy in sponsoring relatively uncontroversial measures.

Kennedy has abandoned the costly utopian reforms he pushed in the seventies—such as government-financed universal health insurance and welfare payments that guaranteed an income above the poverty level for all—and now focuses on less-budget-busting programs. He is increasingly successful and increasingly prolific. The one-hundredth Congress (1987–88) was the best period he or almost any senator has ever had: Kennedy moved more than twenty major pieces of his own legislation through the Senate, including a comprehensive plan to ensure medical care, support services, and discrimination protection for people with AIDS.

A great part of his legislative strength comes from the fact that he likes his colleagues and they like him. A clubman at heart and endowed with a youngest son's natural deference, he is as uncommonly decent toward his peers as he is uncommonly indecent toward his lessers. Senator Joseph Biden, the Delaware Democrat who chairs the Judiciary Committee, says he will never forget the way Kennedy treated him during the seven months in 1988 that Biden was recovering from a brain aneurysm. "He would call my home and speak to my wife and offer to make contacts with doctors he thought were good," Biden recalls. "Once, he got on the train and came to the house in Wilmington, sat up here all day with me, talking. He brought a gift, too—a lovely engraving of an Irish stag." Much more importantly, says Biden, Kennedy did not take advantage of his associate's illness and reassert his authority over the Judiciary Committee, which Kennedy had previously chaired.

Another great strength is his staff—the best and probably the hardest-working on Capitol Hill—which numbers about a hundred people, including committee staffers. Kennedy depends heavily on four or five top advisers, while dozens of midlevel staffers work under great pressure to keep churning out the bills. His public appearances are carefully scripted and stage-managed. For committee hearings, Kennedy's staff provides him with big black briefing books that can run to more than a hundred pages, with an opening statement, detailed questions, background on the issues involved and bios of the speakers he will hear. More-over, Kennedy has continued his brother John's habit of gathering experts from Harvard and elsewhere for informal briefings, holding frequent "issues dinners" at his home. No senator has ever had greater access to a wider range of paid and free counsel.

But no matter how excellent it may be, staff work can take you only so far. Much of what Kennedy does every day he must do himself, no matter how he feels in the morning. And you can't look at his labors without being impressed by his willingness to stick to the tedious daily tilling of the legislative field. Take congressional hearings. Please. As chairman of the Labor and Human Resources Committee and of the Judiciary Committee's Subcommittee on Immigration and Refugee Affairs, and as a member of the Armed Services Committee and of the Joint Economic Committee, Kennedy must chair or attend a couple hundred hearings a year. And while some of them are fascinating, a great many more are dull morality plays. Still, unlike many senators, who are content to make only brief appearances at these hearings, Kennedy often plays an active role even in the hearings that he does not chair.

"He *does* work at being a senator," says Michael Barone of *The Almanac of American Politics*. "And that's impressive. He could easily sink into a life of alco-holism and do-nothingism. He doesn't have to do anything to get elected."

There are times, however, when patience and collegiality do not meet the occasion. When it comes to a clear-cut Left-versus-Right fight, says Hatch, Kennedy "will murder you, he'll roll right over you. . . . He'll trample you in the ground and then he'll grind his heel in you."

Robert Bork still has Kennedy's heel marks on his forehead. Forty-five min-utes after president Reagan nominated Bork for a Supreme Court seat in 1987, Kennedy was on the floor of the Senate and on the attack: "Robert Bork's America is a land in which women would be forced into back-alley abortions, blacks would sit at segregated lunch counters, rogue police could break down cit-izens' doors in midnight raids . . ."

It was, in the words of Kennedy's former aide Thomas Susman, "outra-geous . . . pretty tough and pretty early on and pretty judgmental and very ag-gressive." Bork recently told me with still-hot bitterness, "There was not a line in that speech that was accurate. . . . It was a series of untruths. I didn't want po-lice breaking down your door. I didn't want evolution banned from public schools. I didn't want to force women to have back-alley abortions. The whole thing was false."

Even Judiciary Committee Chairman Biden, Kennedy's close ally, and co-leader of the stop-Bork forces, says Kennedy's speech was "technically accurate but unfair" and that it "drew lines in ways that were starker than reality." Biden says he wouldn't have made such a speech. But, he admits, he is glad Kennedy did. Both he and ranking Republican committee-member Hatch say that without that speech, and without Kennedy's aggressive personal lobbying against Bork with hundreds of civil-rights leaders and liberal activists around the country, the candidate probably would have been confirmed.

Kennedy's role in the Bork fight stems from and illustrates his overarching position in American politics. In a rare moment of irritation with the American Civil Liberties Union, the senator once said, "The ACLU thinks that it defines liberalism in this country. I define liberalism in this country." He was exaggerating only a little. In the religion of liberalism, Kennedy is the guardian of orthodoxy. He is the voice of the interest groups that define the Democratic Party: the black activists, the trade unions, the feminists, the environmentalists, the teachers' unions, and the perennial progressives.

Kennedy is strong and unswerving in his beliefs because they are personal, rooted not in theory but in an emotional commitment to government activism—a continuation and expansion of the leftward direction in which his brother Robert had been heading before his murder. Milton Gwirtzman, who wrote speeches for both Bobby and Ted, says the latter does not have "an articulated set of principles" that rises to the level of an ideology. "There's no such thing as 'Kennedy's thoughts,'" says Gwirtzman. "It's reactions, gut instincts. And they've been bent occasionally, but they have always remained the same."

The world, however, has changed. For all of Kennedy's achievements as a senator, there is a strong sense of anachronism about him as a politician. Alvin From, executive director of the centrist Democratic Leadership Council, among other critics, says Kennedy's "soft, cuddly liberalism, his politics of entitlement," have achieved a viselike grip on the mind of the Democratic Party. And perhaps that is true; as one Democratic National Committee insider says, "It's not as if we're all sitting around thinking we've got to do more for [Kennedy's] cause. It's just that everyone [on the committee] thinks the same way he does."

But while Kennedy's politics may be influential in the party hierarchy, the party hierarchy isn't influential with the voters—or even with other elected Democratic officials. Says former party chairman John White, "It's the dilemma of Teddy Kennedy and it's the dilemma of the party.

"Kennedy is always invited to speak at the convention, always makes a speech in prime time, but when it comes to the general-election campaign, if you bring

Kennedy to Texas, you send him down to Rio Grande Valley to speak to the Hispanics," says political reporter Jack Germond. "If you bring him to Florida, you send him to Miami to talk to the blacks. He is always used exclusively to talk to special interests. And not all of that is related to Chappaquiddick; it is related to issues."

Patrick Kennedy says his father gets depressed about feeling left out in the cold as the political climate shifts. "He genuinely gets sick when the country doesn't go in the right direction in his view," says Patrick. "He gets upset because you know, he's trying to change it and he just feels as if he's run up against the wall sometimes."

There is a solution available, of course. Kennedy could escape dinosaur status by doing what the oldest male Kennedy is supposed to do—run for president. A lot of people, including many of the aides and advisers close to Kennedy, say he is content in the Senate. But Patrick and his cousin Michael Kennedy, Bobby's fourth son, say Ted would, in fact, very much like to run for president again. "I think he still says, you know, I could be a better president than these other jokers," Michael says. "I mean, who else is on the horizon, particularly on the Democratic side?" He says his uncle knows that Chappaquiddick remains "the first question out of the box, so that would make it very difficult for him to run on a national level" but that Ted holds out hope that there will come a "backlash" against the reporting of "this personal stuff" that is so damaging to him and thinks "therefore, I'll be able to run in 1998, or whatever."

My own guess is that Kennedy does still harbor presidential dreams of varying degrees of seriousness, depending on his mood (he has apparently never accepted Chappaquiddick as the career killer it was; he seriously considered running in 1984 and 1988, despite the fact that the voters had made their feelings brutally clear in 1980), but ultimately he won't run. It's time to sink gracefully into the tar pits; the next chance goes to the next generation.

In the end, dynasty is everything. Joseph Kennedy Sr. is the only man in history who ever consciously set out to make one of his sons the president of the United States of America—and succeeded. The father taught his children that that goal could be won. They have never let it be forgotten. To the Kennedys, the White House is the once and future home. It is Ted's duty to help make sure one of them gets it back. There are twenty-eight members of the up-and-coming generation of Kennedys, and they are coming up fast. Joe II, elected twice to the House, makes no secret of his hopes to step higher. Michael, who succeeded Joe as the head of a Boston-based nonprofit company that sells fuel at a discount to the poor, did not make an expected run for state office last year but says he "would not be averse to serving in politics" in the relatively near future. Kathleen Kennedy Townsend, Michael and Joe's sister, lost in her 1986 bid for a Maryland congressional seat but plans to run again. In New York, crown prince and teen heartthrob John F. Kennedy Jr. is being groomed for a big job—if he can ever pass the bar exam.

And, of course, there are Ted's own sons. Ted junior, twenty-eight, harbors ambitions in Massachusetts. And Patrick, a sweet-natured twenty-two-year-old senior at Providence College, was elected to the Rhode Island Legislature in 1988, despite opposition to his candidacy even within the Democratic camp. After all, Jack Skeffington, the man who had held the seat for nine years, had lived in the blue-collar Ninth District all his life, was backed by the state Democratic Party and was a Kennedy supporter as well. Some raised eyebrows over the fact that young Patrick's expenditures were the greatest in the history of the state to win one of the $300-per-year jobs: $87,694, or $66 for each of the 1,324 votes he won. And, some people said, the emphasis on the fact that Patrick was a Kennedy was a little naked, what with the kid's dad and mom and brother and sister and cousins John, Joe, and Michael posing for snapshots with everybody at the polling booths on Election Day.

But let them say what they want. They said the same kind of stuff about Teddy twenty-eight years ago, when the family gave him his first job. The family is the thing. The family is everything. No man is a failure if he does right by his children. And even if the senator was a lousy husband, he is, by all accounts, a caring father.

Sitting in his district office in Providence, Patrick—a fair, fragile-looking young man, gentle like his mother and with a shy, skinny kid's way about him—talks about his father. His voice is as soft and as loving as a puppy's. "I don't think I can ever be as giving a person as he has been to me," he says. "He's the most important person in my life." On the wall of Ted Kennedy's Senate office, prominent among all the pictures of his famous brothers, hangs one of himself and Patrick taken the day Patrick won his seat in the state legislature. Patrick has inscribed on it "To my dad, my friend and my hero."

◆   ◆   ◆

"Ted Kennedy never was born to be president or wanted it terribly," says Milton Gwirtzman. "I think the reason he ran has to do with something his father once said to him: 'If there's a piece of cake on the plate, take it. Eat it.'"

The last Kennedy had so few choices, really. He was born to be the baby of the family, not the patriarch; the fourth brother, not the only one; the also-Kennedy, not the president Kennedy. When he was a chubby-cheeked little boy, the family was packed with grown-ups. They all went away. Joseph junior died when Teddy was twelve. Kathleen died when he was sixteen. Jack died when he was thirty-one. Bobby died when he was thirty-six. The king himself, Joe senior, died when he was thirty-seven.

"To be truly human," Ted Kennedy once said, "is to shape your own world." And he has, far more than most men dream of, done just that. He has made laws. He has been at the front of sweeping change, improving the lives of many people. He has helped perpetuate a dynasty. The truth is, however, the world shapes us far more than we shape it. The truth is, the forces of the world—the rules of primogeniture, the warp of genetics and the woof of environment, the killing power of bullets and the grip of alcohol—shaped Ted Kennedy and shape him still. It is the sad irony of his life that while he has wrought his will on the world at large he remains unable still to control his own life. He started out in this world dangling from strings held by his father and his brothers. They're gone now, but Teddy dangles still, dancing to the echoes of an old and tired tune.

Truth Be Told

◆ ◆ ◆

Pundits who wish to be regarded as scrupulously fair and honest folks like to occasionally toss into their verbal wake a parenthetical clause known in the trade as the Full Disclosure.

A typical Full Disclosure usage reads something like this: "Jones may be the most incompetent—and is certainly the least impressive—judicial appointment put before a Senate since Caligula trotted out his horse. (Full Disclosure: Jones offered a somewhat negative review of my most recent collection of essays, characterizing my work as 'the driveling drool of a diseased and degenerate mind.')" Or, conversely, "Jones is an extraordinarily able nominee—a man of great probity, learning, and humanity. (Full Disclosure: Jones, my college roommate, is married to my beloved younger sister, and he and I have played tennis together almost every Saturday morning for seventeen years.)"

As full disclosures go, these are no monties. And this is pretty much as far as it goes. Pundits do not operate under truth-in-packaging rules. What if they did? Herewith, for the remainder of this column, an experiment in true Full Disclosure:

WASHINGTON—In a climate where the "dismal science" seems ever more aptly named, Wall Street's relapse into the land of the diminishing Dow has sparked fears of a so-called double-dip recession—fears that are quite justified and have their roots in a systemic and decade-long abuse of the public trust by corporate malefactors and their political enablers.

(Full Disclosure: The author knows diddly about the stock market. He went through college on a journalism program, for God's sake. He last understood the mathematics curriculum in the fourth grade. Like most journalists, he only vaguely and dimly grasps the economics of his own business. He did not know the difference between a bull and a bear market until he was in his midthirties. His father-in-law has several times explained to him the concept of a "put," yet it remains to him a mystery. His wife handles all aspects of the family's financial life. He does not even have his own checkbook. He has an ATM card, which he frequently loses.)

And this gnawing fear over the nation's prosperity joins an equally grave, and likewise growing, worry over its prospects for peace. George W. Bush's "war on terror" started out "mit a bang und a boom" over Kabul, but it is now some months later, and Osama bin Laden is still out there and no doubt planning some more bangs and booms of his own. Meanwhile, Pentagon planners squabble-by-leaking over the plans for a war with Iraq the president seems determined to pick, even though he doesn't have a plan for waging it.

(Full disclosure: The author has never served in any branch of the armed services. He was never even a Boy Scout. He has fired a gun precisely four times in his life. As a boy, he was taken rabbit hunting and the slaughter of the bunnies greatly upset him—indeed, still bothers him. As a reporter, he has observed some combat, but he is aware that being in combat is to observing combat as being in an orgy is to being the guy who stands by the CD player and changes the discs. The author has no secret sources in the Pentagon and everything he knows or thinks he knows about war plans for Iraq, he gets from reading the same newspaper accounts that you read.)

The double whammy of a double-dip recession and a seemingly dippy war has had a predictable—but not, except in this space, predicted—effect on the political game. What had seemed only months ago an impossibility now seems to many—even Republican stalwarts—a real probability: Come this November, the Democrats may well take back the House.

(Full Disclosure: The author has never worked in a political campaign. The closest he ever came was a brief stint selling "Nixon Eats Grapes" bumper stickers in support of the 1968 campaign of Hubert Humphrey for president. He contributed half of the proceeds of the sales, $17, to the Humphrey campaign, and in return received a nice genuine cloth handkerchief signed by a machine with the initials HHH. In his first political assignment as a reporter, the author covered a campaign speech by Jimmy Carter in 1976, at the University of New Hampshire, for the school paper. Afterward, he was heard to say, authoritatively: "That man will never be president." On the other hand, the author believed Michael Dukakis stood an excellent chance of being president. He also liked the odds for Bob Dole in 1996.)

Well, I don't think we'll be trying this again.

III

· · ·

The Age
of Clinton

A Man Who Wants
to Be Liked, and Is

◆ ◆ ◆

I t is 2:30 in the morning of Election Day, and Bill Clinton, a middling amateur saxophonist, is playing his true instrument, the crowd.

Thousands of people have come to see him in Fort Worth, and they are wild with emotion, straining so heavily against the heavy steel barricades set up to keep them apart from the candidate that it takes half a dozen large police officers to keep the fences from toppling forward.

The candidate, his boyish face beaming in the moonlight, plunges along the line, grabbing every hand he can, reaching up over the heads to touch in the second and third ranks. The crowd swells and surges as he goes by. In the press, a young woman faints, slumping blank-eyed to the tarmac, but Clinton is already ten feet away, still moving and touching, and he doesn't notice.

Garry Mauro, Clinton's Texas campaign manager and a friend since he and Clinton entered politics working in the 1972 presidential campaign of George McGovern in this state, watches in mild wonder. "He's decided he doesn't want to be president," Mauro says. "He wants to be a rock star."

The communion between William Jefferson Blythe Clinton and the people is the central fact of his life, and of his race for the goal he pursued for three decades, the presidency.

Thirteen months ago, when Clinton stood in front of the Old State Capitol

in Little Rock and announced his candidacy, he was considered by many an unlikely prospect. He had been elected to five terms as governor of Arkansas, but
running a state with an annual budget smaller than that of the District of Co-
lumbia did not seem much of a qualification. Republicans dismissed him, and the
Democrats, hoping to regain the White House that had been denied to them for
twelve years, pined for someone more glamorous.

After an old friend named Gennifer Flowers and an old letter by the young
Bill Clinton raised questions about his integrity, the consensus grew that the candidate was dead, and would be buried in time.

Clinton, who was always the chief strategist of his campaign, banked on the
central faith of his political life: If he could meet enough people, talk to enough
people, make the essential connection enough times, he would win. The people
would like him. After all, so many had before.

"We met in the playground at Ramble School, when we were both eight
years old," recalled David Leopoulos, a childhood friend from Little Rock. "He
came walking up with his hand extended and said, 'Hi, I'm Bill Clinton.' I remember saying to myself, 'Who is this guy?' Not many people are that extro-
verted at that age in that way. But we became good friends right away. The truth
is, you can't not become good friends with Bill Clinton. I don't mean that just
about me. I mean anybody. It's just the kind of person he is."

Born into a family shattered by death and reared in one crippled by alco-
holism, the president-elect is, his friends say, a man who has always wanted to be
liked, and who has always succeeded in that desire.

His way with people, combined with a formidable, organized intelligence,
has won Clinton a lifetime of prizes: delegate to Boys State and Boys Nation,
winner of the Hot Springs Elks Youth Leadership Award, Rhodes Scholar, Attorney General of Arkansas, youngest governor in the nation, chairman of
the Democratic Governors' Association, chairman of the Democratic Leadership
Council.

Now that quality has won him the office Clinton has sought since the age of
sixteen, when he met his political idol, President John F. Kennedy.

To Clinton's many friends, his success is proof that there is something about
the man—empathy is a word often used—that moves people in an extraordinary
fashion. To his many critics, it is proof that slickness is its own reward.

The face of Bill Clinton does not seem the sort to excite adulation. He is reasonably handsome, with bright blue eyes, a strong chin and a slightly pouting
lower lip that lends him sensuality. But allergies make him as puffy and red as a
colicky baby, and his nose tends more toward W. C. Fields than Errol Flynn.

And Clinton tends to run to poundage—his slow and lumbering morning run seems an act of contrition rather than of grace.

His allure becomes clear when he opens his mouth. When Clinton speaks—which he does in torrents; the act of speaking is at the heart of his vocation, his faith—when he speaks, the parts of himself come together in seamless synchronicity.

His voice, a lightly graveled baritone, glides over the words with easy modulation. His big hands work in varied counterpoise, the right forefinger stabbing his points home, the palms cupping, the fists clenching. His smile runs a dizzying gamut, from open-jawed wonder to lip-biting coyness and to beaming boyish delight. His eyes work with the smile, opening wide when he drops his lower jaw, crinkling when he grimaces.

In his favorite political setting, the Donahue-esque television forum he calls a town meeting, Clinton positions himself with the skill of Phil himself, using a series of small movements and gestures welcoming unto himself the immediate questioner and the viewer on the other side of the camera lens.

Clinton's most conspicuous strength, however, lies in a talent for language that is rare in politicians. He involves himself heavily in the writing of his formal speeches, but most often speaks without a script. On the stump this election year he demonstrated a touch with words that is remarkable, and in a way peculiarly fitting to these times.

In a nation so factionalized that each voting block has its own political language, he is multilingual. He does not speak the language of the masses but of each diverse subset.

In farm country he talks of "ol' Bush squealing like a pig stuck under a gate," and of Republicans "who don't know 'come here' from 'sic 'em.'" In the West he pokes fun at federal bureaucrats as lazy bumblers, and hails himself as "the only one running for president who's never been part of the Washington establishment."

Speaking to members of the United Automobile Workers, he talks of "walking the line" at a strike and of the German and Japanese "eating our lunch." At a black college in North Carolina, he preaches of "one nation under God" that is going to "have to decide we need each other, that we care for each other, and that we are going up or going down together," his voice sliding naturally into the cadence of a Southern minister.

People who have known Clinton for a long time agree that his gift for touching those he meets is unusual, and is at the core of his character. Beyond that, opinion is divided.

"There is a presence about him," Leopoulos said. "He has this effect. When he says something, when he looks in your eyes, you just don't question his sincerity. You cannot, because it is so pure. He is the most genuinely empathetic man I have ever known. People respond because they sense that he really, truly cares."

Paul Greenberg, an Arkansas newspaper columnist who has been highly critical of Clinton during his five terms as governor, said, "He knows where all the buttons are in his audience's mind, and how to use the answer to just one question to push several buttons at once."

Greenberg, who gave Clinton the nickname he hates, "Slick Willie," added: "He has a way with language that is extraordinary. He can take any comment, any question, and reshape it to his own desires and advantage, and he is unscrupulous in the arguments he uses. There is a breathtaking quality to the artfulness with which he uses words, and it inspires in me a sense of envy and fear."

Clinton was born William Jefferson Blythe 4th on August 19, 1946, into a shattered family. Three months before the boy's birth, his father, a young traveling salesman named William Jefferson Blythe 3rd, died when the car he was driving left a wet Highway 61 in southern Missouri and crashed, throwing Blythe to his death in a rain-filled ditch.

Blythe's widow, Virginia, was obliged to leave Billy with her parents in the small town of Hope, Arkansas, while she finished her nursing studies in New Orleans. In interviews, Clinton has said that his earliest memory, from the age of three, is of his mother kneeling and weeping as she parted from him at a train station.

He has also said that his father's early death filled him with a sense, as he grew older, of pressing mortality, filling him with a passion to make his mark while young.

"For a long time I thought I would have to live for both of us in some ways," he said in an interview with the *Washington Post* early this year. "I think that's one reason I was in such a hurry when I was younger. I used to be criticized by people who said, 'Well, he's too ambitious,' but to me, because I sort of subconsciously grew up on his timetable, I never knew how much time I would have."

In 1950, when her son was four years old, Virginia Blythe married the second of eventually four husbands, a car dealer named Roger Clinton. A few years later, the new family moved an hour up the road from Hope to Hot Springs. It is the quiet, bucolic town of Hope that Clinton celebrates as the place of his roots, but it was in Hot Springs, a city of gamblers and gangsters (Lucky Luciano, Meyer Lansky, and Al Capone were among the regular visitors) where he was reared.

There, Bill Clinton, as he had come to call himself, was exposed to the second traumatic force his friends say shaped his character and personality: the secret and sometimes violent alcoholism of his stepfather.

Betsey Wright, a longtime close aide to Clinton, sees his desire to be liked, and to conciliate between warring factions, as partly a result of his childhood and adolescence in a home dominated by alcoholism.

"Part of him can be explained by this syndrome of codependency that happens to the children of alcoholics," she said. "It is the feeling that, 'If I am a very good person this will go away.'"

But she rejects the notion that the abusive behavior of Clinton's stepfather toward his mother—behavior that Bill Clinton says he saw regularly, and put an end to at the age of fourteen, a year before his mother divorced her husband—explains all of him.

"The only perspective I can see is that he doesn't believe that he, as a person, is worthy of being liked, but that he has these accomplishments that will make people want to like him and make him worth liking," Wright said. "In some ways he is a person who cannot be set apart from his credentials."

She said Clinton came to terms with this aspect of himself in family counseling sessions after the arrest of his half-brother, Roger Clinton, on cocaine charges several years ago. "He came to acknowledge the peacemaker role that he plays," she said. "He became fully aware that he was not ever going to stop being like that, and began to use it far more constructively, in such things as negotiating with the Arkansas Legislature."

Clinton's critics regard his willingness to conciliate and compromise in terms far less flattering and far more political, pointing as evidence to his record as governor.

After a political apprenticeship that included clerking for J. W. Fulbright, then a United States Senator from Arkansas, while attending the Georgetown University School of Foreign Service and running unsuccessfully for Congress in 1970 while teaching law at the University of Arkansas, Clinton was elected attorney general of Arkansas in 1976. Two years later, at the age of thirty-two, he was elected governor, the youngest person to hold that office in the state's history.

In his first term Clinton sought rapid change, pushing for restrictions in the clear-cutting of lumber, doubling fees for automobile license plates to pay for improvements in education, and in general adopting an aggressive, openly liberal stance. He hired his main aides from out-of-state, drawing from the friends he had made in Washington, at Oxford as a Rhodes Scholar, and at Yale Law School.

The brash, young, long-haired style of the first Clinton governorship alienated large numbers of voters in a state that was poor, rural and conservative. It was noted, with disapproval, that the governor's wife, a fellow Yale Law School graduate, went by her maiden name, Hillary Rodham. (The Clintons have a daughter, Chelsea, now twelve years old.)

The governor's reputation further suffered from an episode of rioting by Cuban refugees sent to the army base at Fort Chafee, by President Jimmy Carter, whose Arkansas campaign Clinton had managed.

In the 1980 election Clinton's Republican opponent, Frank White, ran on the slogan "Car tags and Cubans" and on the fact that White's wife was "Mrs. Frank White." At thirty-four, Governor Clinton was thrown out of office.

The governor's critics say it was this political trauma, not any childhood scars, that made Clinton what he is today. "He sat down and walked around, and thought and thought about it, and figured it out," Greenberg said. "He decided that you ought to go through life not offending anybody."

Clinton cut his hair, and Hillary Rodham became, for political purposes at least, Hillary Clinton. In 1982 he regained the governor's seat.

In the decade that followed, the governor won a number of measures that he points to as evidence that he remains committed to reform government, even in the face of strong political opposition. The two he most often notes are education legislation that included a toughening of requirements for the state's teachers, and a modest program to encourage those on welfare who were able to work to do so.

But he also won a reputation in some circles as a man who, in his desire to not offend—to be liked, and reelected—was far too willing to tell people what they wanted to hear, at the expense of the truth.

"I think he's the best politician I've ever seen," John Brummett, an Arkansas newspaper columnist who was once an admirer of Clinton, said in an interview earlier this year. "I just don't know if there's much there in terms of abiding principle. Reinventing the Democrats is about one thing—getting elected. That's what he is about."

The Making of a First Family:
A Blueprint

◆ ◆ ◆

In late April, the political professionals working to make Bill Clinton president realized they had a potentially fatal problem: at least 40 percent of the voters did not much like Clinton. They saw him as a "wishy-washy," fast-talking career politician who did not "talk straight."

They liked Hillary Clinton even less, regarding her as "being in the race for herself," as "going for the power," and as a wife intent on "running the show."

Arguing that these images were wrong and unfair, the Clinton organization's polling expert, Stan Greenberg; its chief strategist, James Carville, and its media consultant, Frank Greer, set out in a confidential memorandum to Clinton an ambitious political rehabilitation. They proposed the construction of a new image for Mr. and Mrs. Clinton: an honest, plain-folks idealist and his warm and loving wife.

Retooling the image of a couple who had been already in the public eye for five battering months required a campaign of behavior modification and media manipulation so elaborate that its outline ran to fourteen single-spaced pages.

The "General Election Project—Interim Report" as the confidential plan was called, covered a wide array of topics. It set out basic tenets like "The candidate needs to communicate in a way that sounds less political."

And it offered highly specific suggestions that Clinton appear on a television talk show to play the saxophone, for instance, and that he make fun of himself for having said he had tried marijuana but not inhaled.

On a grand scale, it outlines the themes and strategies on which Clinton would ride to triumph in his autumn campaign. The memorandum set forth the thematic message that Clinton was an aggressive, middle-class-oriented agent of change ready to stand up to the special interest groups. And it presented tactics to drive that point home, like pitching his message in town-hall style forums, through live talk television and in several speeches challenging specific interest groups.

On a more intimate level, it included ideas for making the Clintons seem more warm and cuddly, like "events where Bill and Hillary can go on dates with the American people." Examples included arranging an event where "Bill and Chelsea surprise Hillary on Mother's Day," or "joint appearances with her friends where Hillary can laugh, do her mimicry."

These suggestions, and a great many more, were sent on April 27 by the three consultants to Clinton, his campaign chairman, Mickey Kantor, and his campaign manager, David Wilhelm.

A copy of the memo was obtained by the *New York Times* and its authenticity was verified by a campaign strategist. Although the memo is identified as a draft version, he said no subsequent drafts had significantly altered its contents.

"This memo informed the rest of the campaign, everything that happened in the later primaries, in June, in the convention," the strategist said. "It was taken very seriously by Bill and by Hillary, and it was acted on."

Looking back on the Clinton campaign from May to October, it is clear that this is true. In ways large and small, the memo served as a blueprint for the construction of the image of Bill and Hillary Clinton that began to emerge in May and June, and is now firmly established.

What the memorandum told the Clintons to do, and what they did, does not show chicanery; for the Clintons and their advisers, the goal was not to present a false image of the couple but to replace an existing untrue image with one painstakingly built to showcase the true Clintons.

But a reading of the document provides an unusually vivid glimpse into the secret ways of a campaign that succeeded because of a mastery of image packaging on a par with the wizardry that created the public Ronald Reagan.

The memorandum also, by implication, illuminates the reasoning behind the unsuccessful Republican strategy to defeat Clinton. The Republican surveys and focus groups surely showed the same problems with the Clintons' image that the Democratic study had seen.

Armed with information that showed a plurality of voters did not trust Clinton and did not regard with favor his marriage and family life, the strategists for President Bush had reason to feel confident in attacking Clinton's "family values," his integrity, and his wife's personality at the Republican National Convention in August.

Clinton's strategists expected this, as they made clear in a passage about Mrs. Clinton in the memo, writing that the perception of her as unaffectionate and preoccupied with power and career "allows George Bush (and probably Perot) to build up extraordinary advantages on family values."

But by the time the Republicans made their move, the program of image modification drafted by Clinton's consultants had so changed the Clintons' public persona that the feared attack failed to wound him at all.

At the heart of the document is a simple fact, developed by the authors on the basis of a national survey conducted by Greenberg for the Democratic National Committee and by a round of conversations with focus groups, or people selected and brought together by political consultants to talk about a given candidate.

"Bill Clinton is viewed unfavorably by a sizable minority of Democratic primary voters (about 30 percent) and a plurality of general election voters (about 40 percent)," the authors wrote. "The questions about personal morality matter, but their larger impact is contained in the general impression that he will say what is necessary and that he does not 'talk straight.'"

These perceptions, they noted, were fed by Clinton's opponents, but were also the creation of Clinton himself.

"The impression of being the ultimate politician is reinforced by Clinton's presentation (evasive, no clear yes or no, handy lists, fast talking and all that political analysis)," they wrote. "Clinton's political nature leads voters to a number of critical and debilitating conclusions."

The conclusions were indeed critical: "Clinton is not real," "Clinton is privileged like the Kennedys," "Clinton can't stand up to the special interests," "Clinton cannot be the candidate of change," "Clinton's for himself, not people," "Clinton's message/ideas are discounted."

To replace the impression that Clinton was "not real" and was "packaged, created by image makers," with a view that he was "a human being who struggled, pulled his weight, showed strength of character, and fought for change," the candidate's image makers offered a package of Clinton as a child whose "father died before born, mother worked and struggled," who later "interceded to stop an alcoholic stepfather who abused his brother and mother," and who went on to oppose institutionalized racism, teachers' unions, and the perpetuation of a failed welfare system.

The consultants gave examples of television appearances by Clinton that made their point. "The TV clips shown to focus groups suggest the extraordinary power of Bill Clinton when he talks about his mother and alcoholic stepfather (interview with Gabe Pressman), education (Maryland debate) and when he shows what he cares about (Act Up confrontation)."

To put questions of character behind him, Clinton's consultants advocated "immediately and aggressively scheduling the popular talk shows to introduce the real Bill Clinton," noting that "these shows must introduce these elements of the biography, our principal message and the human side of Bill Clinton (e.g., humor, sax, and inhaling)."

Arguing that Clinton was being hurt by "our current style, which too often suggests compromises to organized political support," the consultants recommended "challenge speeches," addresses that would directly challenge specific interest groups and "draw in the press," with Clinton appearing as a "leader who lacks strings and is strong enough to challenge powerful interests."

Turning to Hillary Clinton, the consultants found a "remarkably distorted" view of the Clinton marriage and family. "Bill and Hillary need to talk much more of their own family, including Chelsea, and their affection for each other," they said.

And, the memo went on, "There is a suggestion that Bill and Chelsea surprise Hillary on Mother's Day."

What is most striking about the memo is the degree to which its ideas were adopted, and were successful. In the months that followed, the Clintons did many of the things that their consultants advised. (But not all. They did not, as suggested, vacation in Disneyland, and no media-minded Mother's Day surprise was arranged for Mrs. Clinton.)

Clinton did appear on the *Arsenio Hall Show* on June 3 to play the saxophone and joke that he had really wanted to inhale marijuana when young but he just had not known how.

Also that month, in criticizing the rap performer Sister Souljah before a meeting of the Rev. Jesse Jackson's Rainbow Coalition, Clinton gave his most dramatic show of "aggressive counter-scheduling."

Even before the Democratic National Convention in July, the new image had begun to replace the old. On July 20, as the convention opened, the smiling faces of the Clintons beamed from the cover of *People* magazine, which featured "At Home with the Clinton Family," and *U.S. News & World Report* wrote about "The Bill Clinton Nobody Knows."

By the time Clinton and Gore took to the highways on bus trips with their wives—double dates with the American people—the old Clinton image was so faded it hardly remained.

Saint Hillary

◆ ◆ ◆

Since she discovered, at the age of fourteen, that for people less fortunate than herself the world could be very cruel, Hillary Rodham Clinton has harbored an ambition so large that it can scarcely be grasped.

She would like to make things right.

She is forty-five now and she knows that the earnest idealisms of a child of the 1960s may strike some people as naive or trite or grandiose. But she holds to them without any apparent sense of irony or inadequacy. She would like people to live in a way that more closely follows the Golden Rule. She would like to do good, on a grand scale, and she would like others to do good as well. She would like to make the world a better place—as she defines better.

While an encompassing compassion is the routine mode of public existence for every first lady, there are two great differences in the case of Mrs. Clinton: She is serious and she has power.

Her sense of purpose stems from a world view rooted in the activist religion of her youth and watered by the conviction of her generation that it was destined (and equipped) to teach the world the errors of its ways. Together, both faiths form the true politics of her heart, the politics of virtue.

She is spurred now by a personal matter—the death of her father—and two considerations of practical politics: She recognizes that issues of public values and personal behavior are coming to dominate the politics of this millennial age—but that so far those issues have been mostly defined and championed by conservative Republicans; she is moved by the impatient conviction that moderates and liberals have wanly surrendered the adjective "religious" to the right. She recognizes, too, the need to provide some sort of overarching theme around which the many and varied proposals the Clinton administration spins out to an increasingly doubtful public may be made to seem neatly fitting parts of a coherent whole.

The first lady's vision is singular, formed by the intellectual passions and experiences of a life. But it is also the most purely voiced expression of the collective spirit of the Clinton administration, a spirit that is notable both for the long reach of its reformist ambitions and the cocky assurance of its faith in the ideas of its own design. It is very much a work in progress, but its emerging shape is, even by the standards of visions, large.

Driven by the increasingly common view that something is terribly awry with modern life, Mrs. Clinton is searching for not merely programmatic answers but for The Answer. Something in the Meaning of It All line, something that would inform everything from her imminent and all-encompassing health care proposal to ways in which the state might encourage parents not to let their children wander all hours of the night in shopping malls.

When it is suggested that she sounds as though she's trying to come up with a sort of unified-field theory of life, she says, excitedly, "That's right, that's exactly right!"

She is, it develops in the course of two long conversations, looking for a way of looking at the world that would marry conservatism and liberalism, and capitalism and statism, that would tie together practically everything: the way we are, the way we were, the faults of man and the word of God, the end of Communism and the beginning of the third millennium, crime in the streets and on Wall Street, teenage mothers and foul-mouthed children and frightening drunks in the parks, the cynicism of the press and the corrupting role of television, the breakdown of civility and the loss of community.

The point of all this is not abstract or small. What Mrs. Clinton seems—in all apparent sincerity—to have in mind is leading the way to something on the order of a Reformation: the remaking of the American way of politics, government, indeed life. A lot of people, contemplating such a task, might fall prey to self doubts. Mrs. Clinton does not blink.

"It's not going to be easy," she says. "But we can't get scared away from it because it is an overwhelming task."

The difficulty is bound to be increased by the awkward fact that a good deal of what Mrs. Clinton sees as wrong right now with the American way of life can be traced, at least in part, to the last great attempt to find The Answer: the liberal experiments in the reshaping of society that were the work of the intellectual elite of . . . Mrs. Clinton's generation.

The crusade of Hillary Rodham Clinton began on April 6 [1993] in Austin, Texas. There, speaking from notes she had scribbled on the plane, she moved swiftly past the usual thanks and jokes to wade into an extraordinary speech: a passionate, at times slightly incoherent, call for national spiritual renewal.

The Western world, she said, needed to be made anew. America suffered from a "sleeping sickness of the soul," a "sense that somehow economic growth and prosperity, political democracy and freedom are not enough—that we lack at some core level meaning in our individual lives and meaning collectively, that sense that our lives are part of some greater effort, that we are connected to one another, that community means that we have a place where we belong no matter who we are."

She spoke of "cities that are filled with hopeless girls with babies and angry boys with guns" as only the most visible signs of a nation crippled by "alienation and despair and hopelessness," a nation that was in the throes of a "crisis of meaning."

"What do our governmental institutions mean? What do our lives in today's world mean?" she asked. "What does it mean in today's world to pursue not only vocations, to be part of institutions, but to be human?"

These questions, she said, led to the larger question: "Who will lead us out of this spiritual vacuum?" The answer to that was "all of us," all required "to play our part in redefining what our lives are and what they should be."

"Let us be willing," she urged in conclusion, "to remold society by redefining what it means to be a human being in the twentieth century, moving into a new millennium."

It is easy to mock this sort of thing, and some people immediately did. What, asked the *New Republic* in a question the first lady finds to be a perfect small example of the cynicism she deplores, was all that supposed to mean?

Mrs. Clinton has been groping toward an answer to that question for much of her life. She has read her way from the Methodist founder John Wesley to Paul Tillich, Reinhold Niebuhr and Dietrich Bonhoeffer, three left-of-center theologians who sought to link their religious beliefs to a critical involvement in politics and government, to, most recently, Michael Lerner, a liberal Jewish thinker who coined the phrase "politics of meaning," which Mrs. Clinton adopted in her Austin speech.

She gropes still. "I don't know; I don't know," she begins, when asked to define her philosophy. "I don't have any coherent explanation. I hope one day to be able to stop long enough actually to try to write down what I do mean, because it's important to me that I try to do that, because I have floated around the edges of this and talked about it for many, many years with a lot of people, but I've never regularly kept a journal or really tried to get myself organized enough to do it."

But she is well along in her musings. Working her way through a thicket of theologies and ideologies, she offers in language that is a mix of Bible and Bill Moyers, of New Testament and New Age, a tentative definition of what she believes.

"The very core of what I believe is this concept of individual worth, which I think flows from all of us being creatures of God and being imbued with a spirit," she says. She speaks carefully, sitting upright and leaning slightly forward at a small table in a neat and modest White House garden.

"Some years ago, I gave a series of talks about the underlying principles of Methodism," she goes on. "I talked a lot about how timeless a lot of scriptural lessons were because they tied in with what we now know about human beings. If you break down the Golden Rule or if you take Christ's commandment— Love thy neighbor as thyself—there is an underlying assumption that you will value yourself, that you will be a responsible being who will live by certain behaviors that enable you to have self-respect, because, then, out of that self-respect comes the capacity for you to respect and care for other people.

"And how do we just break this whole enterprise down in small enough pieces? Well, somebody says to themselves: 'You know, I'm not going to tell that racist, sexist joke. I don't want to objectify another human being. Why do I want to do that? What do I get out of that kind of action? Maybe I should try to restrain myself.'

"Or somebody else says: 'You know, I'm going to start thanking the woman who cleans the restroom in the building that I work in. You know, maybe that sounds kind of stupid, but on the other hand I want to start seeing her as a human being.'

"And then maybe the next step is I say to myself: 'How much are we paying this woman who works the three to eleven shift. And who's taking care of her kids while she's here working? And how do we make it possible for her to be able to both be a good parent and perform a necessary function?'

"And these are little pieces, and a lot of those little pieces can be done on a very small scale that then aggregates. So I think what we're basically, what we're really looking at is, you know, millions and millions of changes in individual behavior that are motivated by the same impulses, even if we're not doing a very good job of describing them."

This rambling passage seems to validate the *New Republic*'s impertinence. What does it all mean? This is, as it turns out, a fair question. The meaning of the politics of meaning is hard to discern under the gauzy and gushy wrappings of New Age jargon that blanket it. Michael Lerner, who has been expounding on the subject for several years in the pages of *Tikkun,* a magazine of liberal Jewish thinking, has described the new politics as all about "how to build a society based on love and connection, a society in which the bottom line would not be profit and power but ethical and spiritual sensitivity and a sense of community, mutual caring and responsibility."

Mrs. Clinton says the right language remains to be invented. "As Michael Lerner and I discussed, we have to first create a language that would better communicate what we are trying to say, and the policies would flow from that language."

The problem with the language goes right to the core of the question of what it all means. Is there one unifying idea that is at the heart of the politics of meaning? "I don't think there is one core thing," Mrs. Clinton says. "I think this has to be thought through on a variety of planes. I don't think there is one unifying theory."

Meanwhile, words somewhat fail her. "It is like when you tell someone for the first time that you love them," she says. "You're not fully aware of what that means, but it's the best effort you can make to kind of convey the full range of emotions and feelings and intentions and expectations that you can articulate at the time."

◆   ◆   ◆

But there actually is, as the mists of New Age mysticism slip away, a clear line to Mrs. Clinton's message. It is, fundamentally, an old and very American message, one that goes purposely beyond the normal boundaries of politics into the territory of religion. It is concerned not just with how government should behave but with how people should. It is the message of values, not programs. It is the message of the preacher, a role Hillary Rodham Clinton has filled many times delivering guest sermons from the pulpits of United Methodist churches.

It seems odd at first to contemplate Mrs. Clinton in such terms. The public debate over her that swirled throughout the 1992 presidential race centered on two lesser questions—how left-wing was she and how hungry for power—but failed to consider the larger point of her life.

She appeared before the public in a series of roles, some of the news media's design, some of the Republicans' and some of her own. She was, by bewildering turns, a calculating and radical feminist lawyer and a cookie-baking mom, Lady Macbeth and the little lady.

In an election that Republicans failed to win on the strength of much the same sort of "values" issues that Mrs. Clinton now talks about, one thing the Democratic candidate's wife was not was a moralist.

"American women don't need lectures from Washington about values," she said then. "We don't need to hear about an idealized world that was never as righteous or carefree as some would like to think."

Now, questions of values and matters of morals are the heart of what Mrs. Clinton sees as the way toward national salvation. In truth, they always have been at the core of what she is about, but the many faces of the Hillary of 1992 obscured the larger point of her life.

The politics of Hillary Rodham Clinton are indeed largely liberal (although, the postelection evidence indicates, no more so than those of her husband), but they are of a liberalism derived from religiosity. They combine a generally "progressive" social agenda with a strong dose of moralism, the admixture of the two driven by an abundant faith in the capacity of the human intellect and the redeeming power of love.

They are, rather than primarily the politics of Left or Right, the politics of do-goodism, flowing directly from a powerful and continual stream that runs through American history from Harriet Beecher Stowe to Jane Addams to Carry Nation to Dorothy Day; from the social gospel of the late nineteenth century to the temperance-minded Methodism of the early twentieth century to the liberation theology of the 1960s and 1970s to the pacifistic and multiculturally correct religious Left of today.

The true nature of her politics makes the ambition of Hillary Rodham Clinton much larger than merely personal. She clearly wants power, and has already amassed more of it than any first lady since Eleanor Roosevelt. But that ambition is merely a subcategory of the infinitely larger scope of her desires.

Hillary Rodham was born in 1947, into the world she wishes to restore, a place of security and community and clear moral values, to Hugh and Dorothy Rodham and raised in the solidly upper-class, solidly conservative Chicago suburb of Park Ridge, Illinois. Her childhood was, by all accounts including her own, grounded in the old-fashioned, uncomplicated absolutes of her parents' ethical code.

"My father was no great talker and not very articulate, and wouldn't have known Niebuhr from Bonhoeffer from Havel from Jefferson, and would have thought a conversation like this was just goofy," Mrs. Clinton said in an interview several weeks after Rodham's death on April 7. "But he gave me the basic tools, and it wasn't fancy philosophical stuff.

"He used to say all the time, 'I will always love you but I won't always like what you do.' And, you know, as a child I would come up with nine hundred hypotheses. It would always end with something like, 'Well, you mean, if I murdered somebody and was in jail and you came to see me, you would still love me?'

"And he would say: 'Absolutely! I will always love you, but I would be deeply disappointed and I would not like what you did because it would have been wrong.'"

The lesson Mrs. Clinton drew from this is one she says is at the core of her philosophy: "It was so simplistic, but it was so helpful to me, because, I mean, it gave me the basis of unconditional love that I think every child deserves to have—and one of our problems is that too many of our children don't have that—but it also gave me from the very beginning a set of values based on what I did."

Mrs. Clinton says the sixteen days she spent in Little Rock as her father lay dying led her to give the Austin speech. Her reflections went back to 1961, when she was fourteen and began attending Sunday-evening youth sessions conducted by the Rev. Donald G. Jones, the youth minister at the First Methodist Church in Park Ridge. It was Jones who taught her the lessons that would most profoundly shape her idea of the way things ought to be.

Jones, who now teaches social ethics at Drew University in Madison, New Jersey, was thirty years old, "just out of the seminary, full of vim and vigor," and a believer in the theology of Paul Tillich, whom he considers a theological mentor. Tillich had propounded a theory that sought to redefine the Christian role in the modern world.

"He said that the two major problems of contemporary society were the crisis of meaning and alienation," Jones said in a recent interview. "He contrasted this with the sixteenth century, where the two major problems were death and guilt.

"The point he was making was that because death and guilt were the two major problems back then, Protestantism had defined grace in terms of answers to those problems: eternal life and the forgiveness of sins. But now, with the two major problems being the crisis of meaning and alienation, he said, our religious language should speak in terms of unity, of connectedness, of overcoming alienation, of giving meaning."

When Jones read the texts of Mrs. Clinton's Austin speech, he was struck by the obvious parallels between the oratory of the first lady and the teachings of Tillich on alienation and meaninglessness: "These were precisely the terms Hillary struck in that speech in Austin. She talked of the discontent lurking beneath the surface and the politics of meaning."

Indeed, this theme runs deep in Mrs. Clinton's sense of things.

"If you go back and read the correspondence that existed in the nineteenth century between people of all different walks of life," she says, "you know, it may not be some kind of heavy theological inquiry, but there will be all kinds of flashes about what happened in a way, that, that, you know, that the whole cycle of life and its meaning is tied into their daily life.

"And you know, by the nature of how we spend our time today, we have walled ourselves off from that. I mean, we get up in the morning and we go to work and our children don't know what our work is, because they don't see us plowing a field or making a quilt. We go off and push papers and then come home and try to explain it. Our relatives age and die often in places far away from our homes. We've compartmentalized so much of our lives that trying to find even the time to think about how all of it fits together has become harder and harder."

Jones was a dedicated proponent of the idea, then and now the driving force of the United Methodist Church, that Christian duty lay in taking a direct, helpful interest in the lives of the less fortunate. He organized the white, suburban children of Park Ridge to help provide babysitting for the children of migrant workers in the Chicago area. Hillary was among the students he took on an eye-opening visit to talk with young black and Hispanic gang members at a community center on Chicago's South Side and also among those taken to meet the Rev. Dr. Martin Luther King Jr., who was speaking in the city.

Now, asked if she has always been impelled by what she called, in a recent interview with the *Washington Post*, "a burning desire" to "make the world . . . better for everybody," Mrs. Clinton says, with a slight, self-conscious laugh: "Yeah, I always have. I have not always known what it meant, but I have always had it."

Then, on a moment's reflection, she amends her answer in a way that shows clearly the effect Jones's field trips had on the sensibilities of a child of well-off suburbia: "Especially since I was in junior high and high school and got a sense of what people were up against, and how lucky I had been, a sense, you know, that I was a very lucky person in what I had been given."

But there was more to Hillary's education than the inculcation of a guilt-induced sense of obligation. Jones also exposed her to the writings of Niebuhr, who argued that the tragedy of history proved that the hope for a better world could not depend on any sentimental view of human behavior but must encompass the legitimate use of power.

"My sense of Hillary is that she realizes absolutely the truth of the human condition, which is that you cannot depend on the basic nature of man to be good and you cannot depend entirely on moral suasion to make it good," Jones says. "You have to use power. And there is nothing wrong with wielding power in the pursuit of policies that will add to the human good. I think Hillary knows this. She is very much the sort of Christian who understands that the use of power to achieve social good is legitimate."

There is a Niebuhrian hardness under the fuzzy edges of Mrs. Clinton's discourses on the politics of virtue—an acknowledgment that some sorts of behavior are acceptable and other sorts are not, that every right is married to a responsibility, that a civilized society must be willing to condemn those who act in ways destructive of that society.

"We do this in our own lives," she says. "I mean, we pass judgments all the time. I can remember sitting in a law school class years and years ago in which a hypothetical was being discussed about terrorists. . . .

"And I remember sitting there listening to the conversation as so many people tried to explain away or rationalize their behavior. And I remember saying, 'You know, there is another alternative. And the other alternative is that they are evil. I mean, you know? There are evil people in the world. And they may be able to come up with elaborate rationalizations to attempt to explain their evil, and they may even have some reasonable basis for saying their conduct needs to be understood in the light of preexisting conditions, but their behavior is still evil.'"

Mrs. Clinton argues passionately for a "reaffirmation of responsible behavior rooted in what I view as a value system in which people respect one another and in which they care for one another."

She offers an example of what she sees in society as the opposite sort of value system. "We have two friends who just moved out of a big city to a smaller town, because they found that their high-school daughter was basically being shunned because she had a curfew, she was not permitted to run wild with other kids, she was not permitted to go out to dance clubs till two or three o'clock in the morning. She was basically being made fun of for being a good kid.

"Now, it is not government's fault that the parents of those other kids are letting their kids engage in behavior and court dangers that they are not emotionally or psychologically prepared to do," she says. Rather, it is the fault of individuals: "affluent parents in this society who drop their ten- and eleven-year-olds off at the mall, that let their thirteen- and fourteen- and fifteen-year-olds go off to places that they've never met the parents of the kids, they've never met the kids or anything like that—that is a failure on the part of the adult community to care for our children."

A critical aspect of Mrs. Clinton's analysis suggests the rejection of rights-based liberalism as it now exists. She favors, as does the president, welfare reform, and she argues that society has extended too freely rights without responsibilities, which has led to a great decline in the standard of behavior.

She cites a recent article by Daniel Patrick Moynihan on what the New York senator called "defining deviancy down."

"Senator Moynihan argues very convincingly that what we have in effect done is get used to more and more deviant behavior around us, because we haven't wanted to deal with it," she says. "But—by gosh!—it is deviant! It is deviant if you have any standards by which you expect to be judged."

This line of argument, central to Mrs. Clinton's view, is, of course, precisely what social conservatives have been saying for years. Social liberals, who dominate the national Democratic Party, have held that it is not the place of either government or society to lay down a set of behavioral standards based on moral absolutes, and that individual freedom necessitates moral relativism.

"I think that is a theoretical and to a great extent an elitist argument," says Mrs. Clinton, with some heat. "I think a person would have a hard time making that argument to the kind of people who I know who are working hard and living in fear and are really taking the brunt of a lot of the social and political decisions that we've either made or failed to make in the last twenty years. There are standards. We live by them. We reward them. And it is a real fallacy to jump from what we do in our individual and work lives to expect us not to have standards in our social community lives."

Those standards are, it is suggested, the standards of the Ten Commandments.

"That's right," she says. "And in nearly every religion I am aware of, there is a variation of the Golden Rule. And even for the nonreligious, it is a tenet of people who believe in humanistic principles."

We could do a lot worse, she says, than live according to the Golden Rule. "That means: Should we let whole sections of our city be like Beirut? Would we want that to be the place where we live with our children? Of course not. Well then, what would be reasonable policies to pursue in order to avoid that? Would we want young children to be exposed to a lot of the dangers that might lead to drug addiction or abuse or violence or all of the problems we face, if there were ways we could band together as adults to help them avoid that? Of course, we would much prefer that."

◆ ◆ ◆

It is at this point that some awkward questions arise:

If it is necessary to remake society, why should Hillary Rodham Clinton get the job?

Can someone who helped lead the very generation that threw out the old ways of moral absolutes and societal standards now lead the charge back to the future?

At Wellesley College, from 1965 to 1969, Hillary Rodham gradually moved away from the conservatism of her parents and embraced the predominant attitudes of a campus that was steeped in the tradition of liberal, social service–oriented Protestantism and heady with the conviction that the young people of the moment were fated to remake the world.

The times encouraged dreaming of great, sweeping change. Alan Schechter, who taught Rodham political science and remembers her transformation from a Goldwater Girl to "secular liberalism," recalls: "The aura of the martyred Kennedy was strong on the campuses then, and everyone was full of talk about doing something about the race crisis, about the Peace Corps. The mood was one of youthful idealism, commitment, that clichéd line of Kennedy's—ask not what your country can do for you."

By the time she graduated from Wellesley to head on to Yale Law School, Hillary Rodham had become a radical, in the true sense of the word: dedicated to the imperative of profound societal change, and confident in her own ability to direct that change.

She began thinking then about the ideas she is giving voice to now. The student commencement speech delivered by Hillary Rodham for the class of 1969 is the direct ancestor of the Austin speech delivered by the Hillary Rodham Clinton of today. They share all the same traits: vaulting ambition, didactic moralizing, intellectual incoherence, and the adolescent assumption that the past does not exist and the present needs only your guiding hand to create the glorious future.

Then, she spoke of "attempting to come to grasp with some of the inarticulate, maybe even inarticulable, things that we're feeling." Today, she speaks of the struggle to "put into words what is often for most of us inarticulate or inarticulable."

Then, she spoke of the attempt "to forge an identity in this particular age." Today, she speaks of "redefining who we are as human beings in this postmodern age."

Then, she spoke of "our questions, our questions about our institutions, about our colleges, about our churches, about our government." Today, she asks, "What do our governmental institutions mean? What do our lives in today's world mean?"

At the heart of the Wellesley speech, she argued for what she then called the "experiment in human living" and would come to call "excessive individualism" and "rights without responsibility."

The "prevailing, acquisitive, and competitive corporate life," she said, "is not for us. We're searching for a more immediate, ecstatic, and penetrating mode of living."

When asked if the social experiments of the 1960s and 1970s led to the systemic problems she now sees in the 1990s, Mrs. Clinton replies, "I don't know if it's unfair to say that, but it's probably incomplete."

The roots of the problems go back further and spread wider than that, she says. But still, she carefully acknowledges that the questioning and searching of her generation did produce some "excesses" and "wrong decisions."

It is suggested that for Hillary Rodham Clinton, a career liberal activist and former seeker of ecstatic living, to sound the call for a return to traditional ethics will strike some people as a bit much. As easy, moralistic preaching. After all, the last person who tried this sort of thing, Dan Quayle, was mocked for his pains. And he, at least, had been elected.

The first lady jumps hard on the point.

"That's irrelevant to me," she snaps back. "I know that no matter what I did—if I did nothing, if I spent my entire day totally disengaged from what was going on around me—I'd be criticized for that. I mean, it's a no-win deal, no matter what I do, or try to do.

"But from my perspective, there are millions of people who are worried about the same things I'm worried about. I don't care who gets the credit. I don't care who has to be criticized in order to move this conversation forward. I want to live in a place again where I can walk down any street without being afraid. I want to be able to take my daughter to a park at any time of day or night in the summertime and remember what I used to be able to do when I was a little kid."

At that moment, irritation still edging her voice, she doesn't sound at all like the Hillary Rodham of 1969. She doesn't sound like a politician or a preacher. She sounds like just another angry, sincere, middle-aged citizen, wondering how everything went so wrong.

Which brings up the second difficult question.

What exactly can Mrs. Clinton and the new politics do about it all?

It is clear that there will be immense practical problems in making the transition from theory to practical politics.

The reason harks back to the question of language. Several weeks ago, when Michael Lerner accepted Mrs. Clinton's invitation to come to the White House and talk about the politics of meaning, they agreed that, he says, "the question was how to take, in a practical, hard-nosed way, the sum of the ethical ideas of the Bible and apply them to this moment in time."

They fell into disagreement, however, as soon as they began talking about how that might be done. "I proposed that the Clinton administration establish a policy where, for any proposed legislation or new program, there would have to be written first an Ethical and Community Environmental Impact Report, which would require each agency to report how the proposed legislation or new program would impact on shaping the ethics and the caring and sharing of the community covered by that agency."

Mrs. Clinton, Lerner says, "liked the idea, but was worried about using words like 'caring' and 'sharing' and 'love' in talking about government policies. And this concern became the central question of our discussion: Would the press kill us on this?"

Unintentionally hilarious Big Brotherism is, in fact, a hallmark of Lerner's ideas for implementing the politics of meaning. In the May–June issue of his magazine, *Tikkun,* Lerner offers a series of specific proposals by which the Clinton administration could turn the theory of the politics of meaning into reality in the workplace.

These include: that the Department of Labor order "every workplace" in America "to create a mission statement explaining its function and what conception of the common good it is serving and how it is doing so"; "sponsor 'Honor Labor' campaigns designed to highlight the honor due to people for their contributions to the common good," and "train a corps of union personnel, worker representatives and psychotherapists in the relevant skills to assist developing a new spirit of cooperation, mutual caring and dedication to work."

The reason Lerner's proposals for the application of the politics of meaning focus so heavily on bureacratic irrelevancies is the same reason Mrs. Clinton is struggling still with words.

Any clearly expressed, serious proposal to do anything to improve public values runs immediately against the fundamentals of social liberalism that are the guiding ethos of Democratic policies.

Mrs. Clinton argues that the concepts of liberalism and conservatism don't really mean anything anymore and that the politics of the New Age is moving beyond ideology. But that is not at all true in the area of values where she seeks to venture. It is easy for social conservatives, who have been writing and debating for years about the moral values Mrs. Clinton is now addressing, to speak bluntly about what is morally right and what is not. Conservatism is purposely, explicitly judgmental. But liberalism, as defined by Mrs. Clinton's generation and those who came after, has increasingly moved away from the entire concept of judgment and embraced instead the expansion of rights and the tolerance of diversity.

Returning to moral judgment as a basis for governmental policy must inevitably mean curtailing what have come to be regarded as sacrosanct rights and admitting a limit to tolerance. And that will bring the politics of meaning hard against the meaning of politics.

The President's Past

♦ ♦ ♦

A good place to begin thinking about how Bill Clinton became who he is today is the Arkansas town of Springdale, where a short, red-faced man known as Mr. Chicken sits in a room modeled after the Oval Office of the president of the United States (although not precisely; the White House's Oval Office does not have doorknobs shaped like hen's eggs) and tells a story about the political education of a bright young fellow.

It may seem an act of considerable vanity for a chicken farmer to build himself a copy of the president's office. But Don Tyson is a realist to his thick fingertips, as befits a man who presides over the largest abattoir the world has ever seen—every week, Tyson Foods reduces 25 million chickens to plucked and gutted shadows of their former selves—and he sees politics as a series of unsentimental transactions between those who need votes and those who have money. His office decor is an accurate, not immodest statement about where, in a world where every quid has its quo, power lives.

Moneymen like Tyson are strong in politics everywhere, but the realities of Arkansas favor them particularly. Power in Arkansas rests upon two enduring conditions complicated by an enduring contradiction. The first condition is that most people in Arkansas have very little money while a few people have a great deal. The second condition is that Arkansas is not really a democracy. It has been ruled for almost all of its existence, and is largely ruled still, by a thin upper crust of Democratic Party officials and Democratic legislative leaders and important landholders and businessmen. This elite, bound together not by party or even ideology but by mutually advantageous relationships, holds sway over a small and politically disorganized middle class and a large but well-beaten population of the poor. The contradiction is that Arkansas voters, in a class-based reaction against this condition, perpetually favor politicians who are "common" in touch, populist in theology, and reformist in policies.

What results is a system in which voters consistently reward candidates who promise change, but in which men like Tyson consistently reward those who preserve the pro-business status quo. Because each candidate must, in the absence of real party politics, build his own organization, and because the money men are the only dependable sources of the heavy financing that this requires, Arkansas's wealthy corporatists possess far greater clout than they would in a state with a strong party system, large professional class, or powerful unions. They are the equivalent of Broadway's angels, determining who appears on the big stage and who does not. There are a few Republicans among the angels, and perhaps one or two mild ideologues, but most of the heavenly host fit the description Don Tyson applies to himself: "businessman's Democrat," which means they support Democrats who support them.

"The Arkansas system had always been able to find some good young people and encourage them to work on the local level," Tyson ruminates by speaker-phone from his oval office. "The system kind of weeds them out, and out of that comes a United States senator or a governor. . . . It's like a horse race. You back three or four, so you always got a winner."

The Tyson family has been backing winners in Arkansas politics since 1954, when John Tyson, Don's father and the founder of the family business, bet on a promising young man named Orval Faubus. "Orval was my dad's first political deal," Tyson recalls, speaking of the six-term governor with the nostalgic affection of an old horseplayer remembering a 5-to-1 shot that paid off. "Orval was a little newspaper editor twenty-five miles east of here in Huntsville. He got over here one day and had a lunch with a bunch of Springdale people here in a restaurant. He said, 'I want to run for governor and I need $1,500 and don't have it.' Dad was one of the three people who gave him $500 apiece so he could pay his filing fee."

The generation that entered Arkansas politics in the 1970s was exceptionally rich in talent, but even so, Bill Clinton caught Tyson's eye. "He was young and he was impressive," Tyson recalls. "I don't believe we ever talked about his politics; hell, he was a Democrat." Tyson put a modest sum of money on Clinton in his yearling race, a congressional run in 1974. Although Clinton lost that election, he showed excellent form, and Tyson backed him again in his successful 1976 run for state attorney general; and again in 1978, when the thirty-two-year-old ran as the overwhelming favorite for governor.

But before Tyson made his gubernatorial choice for 1978, he posed a ques-tion. In the relentless drive of expansion and acquisition that would make Tyson Foods the largest poultry processing company in the world, Tyson faced a serious obstacle. In recent years, most other states had raised their legal truck weight lim-its from about 73,000 to 80,000 pounds. Arkansas, though, still stuck to the old limit, which put the state's poultry and trucking companies at a disadvantage with their out-of-state competitors and cost them millions of dollars. Would a Governor Clinton take care of that problem? Candidate Clinton, recalls Tyson, said he would be happy to.

"Bill promised a bunch of us that he'd raise the weight limit on trucks," Tyson remembers. "Damn right he did. He promised me, personally, in my car driving to the airport three or four months before the election. He said that if he was elected, he'd do it. He said he'd take care of it. Now, there's a bunch of chicken folks in this state, and we all had a big interest in this weight thing, so we sup-ported Clinton."

It was, by Tyson's account, several months after this private talk that a great windfall came into the lives of a young and relatively poor couple named Bill Clinton and Hillary Rodham. The windfall fell from the hand of the Clintons' close friend James Blair, an important Arkansas Democrat of the back-room genre and a Springdale lawyer whose most important client was Don Tyson and Tyson Foods.

Blair was a man who greatly desired to be rich. In 1977, he began plunging deep into a string of commodities speculations that he expected would make him so. Trading in cattle futures through the Springdale branch of the Ray E. Fried-man and Company (Refco) chain run by Robert (Red) Bone, a commodities broker (and former Tyson executive) of dubious reputation, Blair had already made several hundred thousand dollars by October 1978, and expected to make millions more. With Clinton up 30 points in the polls less than a month before Election Day, Blair approached Hillary Rodham to urge her to invest in his sure-thing scheme, telling her that "it was one of those rare chances to put aside some money," and that "she wouldn't have to be the expert. I'd give her advice."

Mrs. Clinton put up $1,000, and on her first day made a postcommission profit of $5,300, trading on ten cattle futures contracts. She continued to invest with Blair and Bone for nine months, during which time her husband was elected and sworn in as governor. Although Mrs. Clinton was a small, inexperi-enced and cash-poor customer, Bone's Refco office accorded her privileged treatment generally reserved only for investors with deep pockets or proven records. The Blair-Clinton investments ended in July 1979, having netted $99,537, a nearly 10,000 percent return.

On April 22, 1994, Hillary Rodham Clinton, soft-edged in a warm pink sweater and smiling sweetly at the badgering White House reporters, acknowledged that she had opened her account at Blair's "very strong recommendation," that Blair had always guided her about which trades to make and that "often" he had simply placed the trades for her. Her role, as she described it, was largely limited to approving Blair's suggestions. But, Mrs. Clinton insisted, Blair had done this large favor only because he and his wife were "among our very best friends." Scorn crisping the edges of her voice, Mrs. Clinton dismissed the idea that Blair might have meant to guarantee good will toward Tyson Foods with his $100,000 boon to the governor and his wife. "I found it a little bit surprising that anyone would suggest that," Mrs. Clinton said, "because, in 1980, right during the time that this was all going on, when my husband ran for reelection, Tyson supported his opponent."

Mrs. Clinton's artful explanation notwithstanding, the records show that she had concluded her commodities trading with Blair by July 1979—more than a year before the next gubernatorial campaign. For his part, Tyson says today that he never knew about the financial arrangements between his attorney and the Clintons until he read about them in the *New York Times* earlier this year. But Tyson also says the reason he didn't support Bill Clinton in 1980 is not because he couldn't buy Clinton's favors in 1978. It was because Tyson thought he had indeed obtained a favor—the promised truck weight increase. But Clinton had failed to deliver his part of the bargain. "He didn't raise the limit," Tyson says.

The fact is, even if he had wanted to, Governor Clinton could probably not have pushed the higher truck weight through the legislature. The opposition of the powerful Arkansas Highway Commission—on the grounds that heavier trucks would damage the state's highways—was just too strong. But Tyson blamed the young governor for not even making the fight. "He never even tried to get it through," Tyson says.

And so, when Clinton ran again for governor in 1980, against a little-known Republican businessman named Frank White, Tyson took revenge: "I said, 'Hell, I'll support Frank White.'"

Clinton lost the 1980 election, a defeat that threatened to end his political career. But in 1982, after a brutal campaign against White, he won back the governor's seat. Tyson, who had backed White a second time, watched with interest to see what the resurrected governor would do about the truck weight limit, which remained unchanged despite White's support of an increase. Almost immediately after taking office again in 1983, Clinton maneuvered the 80,000-pound limit through the legislature by linking it to a special tax on the heavier trucks, to pay for potential road damage. And when Clinton ran for reelection in 1984, Tyson supported him, as he has in every election since. He is refreshingly candid about why. "He started running the state better and learned a few lessons," Tyson says, "And, hell, my trucks were running full, 80,000 pounds."

◆ ◆ ◆

The forty-second president is an impressive thinker, a talented political performer and something of a visionary. Indeed, although Bill Clinton has been largely successful (for better and worse) in presenting himself as a moderate, he is, in a true and unpejorative sense of the word, a radical, committed to a level of change far more ambitious than that of most presidents. Through his ability to speak with both uncommon intelligence and a common touch, he has advanced issues that had been frozen for years in a Left–Right stalemate, most notably health care, welfare, and crime. The expanded earned-income tax credit program he won from Congress last year was a historic measure, the government's first real attempt to guarantee that no one who works full time and has a family to support would fall below the poverty line. The health care reform he is trying to get through Congress this year would be the most significant expansion of entitlements since the creation of Social Security and among the most ambitious efforts at social engineering in the nation's history. The Clinton administration is the first to openly (if at times gingerly) embrace the idea of according protected minority status to homosexuals. The Clinton welfare-reform bill may not entirely meet the grand campaign promise of "ending welfare as we know it," but it nevertheless represents a genuine attempt to impose the toughest work requirements ever attached to welfare, the first serious effort by any president, Democrat or Republican, to stop the disastrous generational cycle of America's dole society. Because Clinton is president, it has become harder now for criminals and lunatics to arm themselves, and easier for parents to take time off work without losing their jobs.

So why doesn't all of this seem to matter more? Why doesn't Bill Clinton get more credit for his successes, and less vilification for his failures, which seem to loom so large? Why does the president get so little respect? The problem is not just criticism from the right, where many passionately loathe Clinton. That is to be expected; conservatives understand, if liberals do not, how serious the president is about dramatic change. What threatens this president seems to be much larger than mere partisanship. There is a level of mistrust and even dislike of him that is almost visceral in its intensity. In Washington, where power is generally treated with genuflecting reverence, it is no longer surprising to hear the president spoken of with open and dismissive contempt. In mainstream journalism and even more so in popular entertainment, President Clinton is routinely depicted in the most unflattering terms: a liar, a fraud, a chronically indecisive man who cannot be trusted to stand for anything—or with anyone.

Bob Woodward, in his book *The Agenda: Inside the Clinton White House,* describes the president as a lost leader, berating himself and his aides for selling out the populist promise of his campaign to satisfy Wall Street, being berated in turn by his own vice president to "get with the goddamn program." At a television town-hall gathering in North Carolina, a woman confronted the president: "Many of us Americans are having a hard time with your credibility. How can you earn back our trust?" At another public event, a newspaper editor informed the president that his explanations on Whitewater reminded him of his young daughter's excuses for undone homework. The political columnist Joe Klein, once one of Clinton's great fans, writes that the president's idea of character is "adolescent, unformed, half-baked," and that "with the Clintons, the story is always subject to further revision," as "trust is squandered in dribs and drabs."

Much of this is unfair, some of it is irrational and some of it has more to do with the savagery of an angry and fearful time than it does with Clinton personally. It is true as well that Clinton suffers from a fundamental handicap; in the unusual three-way race of 1992, he was elected with only 43 percent of the vote, putting him in office with one of the weakest bases of support any president has ever had. But there is a fundamental reason for Clinton's plight. Bill Clinton is the first president since Richard Nixon to be threatened with the awful intimacy of rejection not simply as a leader or as a politician but as a person. As was also true with Nixon, this threat flows from a deep source, an abiding public doubt about the ethical content of the president's character. Such doubt is quite different from the criticisms of job performance that plague every president. It is an assessment of the man as a whole, of what is bred in the bone, one of those national gut decisions that happen in politics, something that solidifies after the accumulation of evidence passes some unseen tipping point: Lincoln is honest, Carter is weak, Reagan is decent but doddering, Bush is a wimp. Only Richard Nixon and now Bill Clinton have been tagged with nicknames that reflected a popular suspicion that the president of the United States could not be fully trusted: Tricky Dick and Slick Willie.

What plagued Nixon, and now Clinton, is that this sort of judgment is extremely difficult to overcome; it is almost entirely impervious to the machinations of speechwriters and political consultants, and even to substantive achievements of office. Bill Clinton ran for president promising to revive the economy and bring about universal health care. Less than halfway through his term, the economy is in strong shape and health care reform in some form is almost assured. Most Americans acknowledge these achievements. According to a *New York Times*-CBS poll in mid-July, 53 percent of Americans view the economy as healthy, compared with only 23 percent when Clinton took office. Seventy-nine percent think universal health care is "very important." Yet the public is strongly disinclined to give Clinton credit. The *Times*-CBS poll found that 63 percent of Americans think Clinton has made no progress in improving the economy. Even more startling, 60 percent say Clinton has made no progress in advancing health care insurance. The president's overall approval, which has never risen more than about 10 points beyond the 43 percent mark, has dropped precipitously in the past six months; 47 percent of the public disapprove of the way Clinton is doing his job and only 42 percent approve.

Nixon's problems were rooted in the record of his life, and Clinton's are, too, in the things he has said and done to get where he is today. Clinton's life trails him like a peculiarly single-minded mugger, popping out from the shadows every time it seems the president is for a moment safe—to whack the staggering victim anew. The past has slugged Clinton so often, so publicly and so brutally, that its attacks have become known, in the pop-culture shorthand that signifies universal acquaintanceship, by their tabloid handles: Gennifer, the Draft, I Didn't Inhale, Whitewater, Troopergate, Hillary's Commodities, Paula Jones. Each episode has moved the national assessment closer to the tipping point.

What makes this sad, even tragic, rather than merely sordid, is that Bill Clinton's predicament owes itself directly to Bill Clinton's promise. The president's problems did not come about because he was a cheap political hack. They came about because he was not. For what has happened to Clinton has happened because he wanted, more than anything in life, to get to where he is today, and because he wanted this, at least in part, in order to do good—and because the great goal of doing good gave him license to indulge in the everyday acts of minor corruption and compromise and falsity that the business of politics demands. Bill Clinton was perceptive enough to master politics—but not perceptive enough to see what politics was doing to him.

◆ ◆ ◆

Circumstances of both nature and nurture set Bill Clinton up for a life in politics. The Hollywood version of Clinton's life, produced for his 1992 presidential campaign, centered on his early childhood "in a place called Hope," a parable of small-town innocence and working-class roots. But Clinton really grew up in the old gangster city of Hot Springs, where his mother, Virginia, had moved when he was seven. As she describes it in her recent, posthumously published memoirs, *Leading with My Heart,* Hot Springs was "a town in which the con job was considered an art form," and the home of some of the most thoroughly crooked politics in America. The city of Clinton's youth was a place where whorehouses and illegal gambling halls thrived under police protection, where the retired New York mobster Owney Madden was a celebrated citizen and the town's leading madam was another, where illegal gambling and liquor sales were routine—a place, Virginia writes, "where gangsters were cool, and rules were made to be bent, and money and power—however you got them—were the total measure of a man."

Virginia and her second husband, Roger (Dude) Clinton, were not peripheral citizens but successful members of the Hot Springs business and political establishment. Virginia built what was for three decades a successful practice as a nurse-anesthetist, and Roger was employed at his brother Raymond's thriving Buick dealership. In her memoirs, Virginia Kelley (as she was known at the time of her death in January) describes a family that always had a big, comfortable home, at least one late-model Buick convertible in the garage and enough spending money to indulge in frequent nightclubbing and gambling with a group of "running buddies" that included many of the men who ran Hot Springs. Indeed, the Clintons themselves were important political players: Roger's brother Roy was a member of the state legislature from 1951 to 1954, and his brother Raymond, the family leader whom Clinton has described as a father figure, was a behind-the-scenes power in town. He made his Buick dealership "a gathering place for powerful, politically savvy men in Hot Springs," Kelley writes. "The big wheels."

One critical point that the young Clinton could not have failed to notice was that people who had power and connections could do things that other people could not. Kelley's unblushing account makes it clear that Roger Clinton and his friends had a long history of getting away with crimes and acts of drunken violence. She writes, offhandedly, that before she met Roger, Raymond had used his influence to get Roger out of trouble with the Hot Springs police after he had "bashed a Puerto Rican boy in the head with a cue stick." In later years, Kelley recounts, there was a litany of violent occasions: "the night I danced with a man at the Tower Club and Roger Clinton beat him to a pulp"; Roger punching and kicking her at a public dance; Roger and his drinking buddies driving roaring drunk down the highways; nights the cops were called to the Clinton home to protect her and her sons.

And the lesson was not merely that the right people could get away with doing wrong. As Kelley describes her philosophy, the right people—herself, her family, and friends—couldn't really do wrong.

In the two years and eight months of her marriage to her first husband, Bill Blythe, Kelley writes, he never told her of his previous three marriages or that he had fathered at least one child besides Bill. Of her third husband, Jeff Dwire, Kelley writes that her friends suspected him of being "a con man," and of running a house of prostitution out of his beauty salon. Kelley says she "never believed" those "awful rumors." In 1961 Dwire was indicted on twenty-five counts of stock fraud (for which he was ultimately convicted and sentenced to nine months in prison) for his part in a scheme in which he and a partner bilked small-time investors of more than $32,000 by pretending they were producing a movie on the life of the gangster Pretty Boy Floyd. As far as Kelley was concerned, "that one mistake wasn't a reflection of the inner man."

Kelley calls her approach to life "brainwashing," and describes it in clear terms: "Inside my head, I construct an airtight box. I keep inside what I want to think about, and everything else stays beyond the walls. Inside is white, outside is black. . . . Inside is love and friends and optimism. Outside is negativity, can't-doism and any criticism of me and mine."

Also outside the parameters of Kelley's construct were the past and the future; she insisted on living in the present. "I've always felt the past is irrelevant," she writes. "I've always maintained that whatever's in someone's past is past, and I don't need to know about it." As for the future: "I've trained myself not to worry about what-ifs, either. . . . And when bad things do happen, I brainwash myself to put them out of my mind." Kelley's relentless accentuation of the positive must have been a great help in dealing with years of adversity, and Bill Clinton clearly owes much of his own optimism, tenacity, and resilience to his mother's inspiration. Clinton also may owe to Kelley the character trait that was perhaps the essential determinant of his political success—an unusually large need for adulation, a hunger for affirmation from others so intense that approval is seen almost as an entitlement. "I think Bill and Roger and I are all alike in that way," Kelley writes. "When we walk into a room, we want to win that room over. Some would even say we need to win that room over, and maybe that's true. Roger says the three of us, if there are one hundred in a room and ninety-nine of them love us and one doesn't, we'll spend all night trying to figure out why that one hasn't been enlightened."

This powerful need doubtless had a great deal to do with turning Clinton into the remarkable political performer he is, a campaigner driven to treat each encounter with a prospective voter as an occasion for seduction, an opportunity to win another's love. But this need also made him peculiarly vulnerable to the universal temptation of political life—to tell people what they want to hear. Kelley's philosophy could only have encouraged this behavior. Her world view taught, ultimately, that people are not to be judged by their actions, but are endlessly free to reinvent themselves, to be whatever the moment demands. Since "what ifs" do not exist, one needn't worry that the promise of the moment cannot be met in the future, or that the action of the moment might have a harmful consequence. Since the "irrelevant" past does not really exist either, the actions of the moment cease to exist once the moment becomes the past, and cannot be held against one later.

Kelley describes herself as a natural performer who craved to be the center of admiring attention, and it is noteworthy that the early ambition of both of her sons was to be a popular music star like Kelley's idol, Elvis Presley. Roger Clinton never advanced beyond that adolescent dream; Bill Clinton, recognizing his true talents, put aside his saxophone and turned to politics.

Clinton's career began while he was still a student at Hot Springs High School, where he was president of his junior class, the Beta Club (for academic achievers) and the Kiwanis Key Club. By his late teens, Clinton was already a semiprofessional politician, so greatly in demand as a civics club speaker and leader of charitable fund drives that his high-school principal had to limit his engagements in order to protect his schooling.

It was clear early on that Clinton possessed great political gifts. He was intelligent, charming, and driven, and he had an extraordinary gift for intimacy, a chameleonlike quality of immense value in politics. All sorts of people, meeting Clinton, saw someone much like themselves. Like his hero, John F. Kennedy, he was at home on stage or in front of a camera.

Moreover, Clinton was precisely the kind of budding politician to appeal to the Arkansas powers. In an age of radicalism, he was an instinctive establishmentarian. He was a joiner: the calculus club, the advanced math club Mu Alpha Theta, DeMolay (an organization of "future leaders"), the Junior Classical League, the Bio-Chem-Phy Club, the marching band, concert band, stage band, and pep band. He was the right kind of achiever: a National Merit Scholarship semifinalist, winner of the Hot Springs High School Civitan Junior Businessman Award and the Elks Youth Leadership Award for Arkansas, accepted at Georgetown, Oxford, and Yale. He was not a bomb thrower or even a boat rocker. He ran for his first college office, the 1964 freshman class presidency of Georgetown University, on a platform of solid, modest reform. After his victory, he informed the college newspaper that "the freshman year is not the time for crusading, but for building a strong unit for the future. You must know the rules before you can change them."

A young man of such obvious promise would have been encouraged in any state, but in a poor, chronically put-upon state like Arkansas, he was particularly prized. As A. J. Liebling once noted, the states of the old Confederacy are always searching for those exceptional "national" political talents, the bright young men who will go to Washington and make those damn Yankees stop their endless sneering. But neither Clinton's inarguable appeal nor his inarguable talent for wooing support explains why so many people were willing, and would always be willing, to do so much to further his ambitions. The real explanation lies in the conviction, held by Clinton's elders and friends, as well as by Clinton himself, that he was ambitious for the right reasons—because he wanted power in order to do good.

"We all believed, at that time, that the most noble direction we could take was to serve in elective or appointive office," recalled David Mixner, a longtime Clinton friend and liberal political activist, in an interview with the Clinton biographer Robert E. Levin. "He really deeply believed that government could feed people, that we could end war, that poverty did not have to be a permanent condition, that we could make our country great and prosperous and that our generation would be the one to do it."

The danger in this admirable thought was that it led, almost inevitably, to a logical successor: that the advance of a generational idealist like Bill Clinton was a moral imperative—one that justified any means necessary. The acceptance of this rationalization was the signal event in the development of Clinton's character—the ur-compromise from which all later compromises would flow. It occurred when Clinton was only twenty-three, in response to the first great crisis in his life, the Vietnam War.

For Clinton, as for so many men of his generation, Vietnam would be the crucible, the testing ground that would shape their characters forever. Clinton's successful multiyear effort to avoid the Vietnam draft reached its apex in April 1969, when he was a Rhodes scholar at Oxford and received an induction notice from the Hot Springs draft board. At his request, the induction was postponed for two months so that he could finish his term. That summer, he returned to Arkansas and won a deferment on the strength of his pledge to enroll in the Reserved Officers Training Corps program at the University of Arkansas, whose law school he said he planned to attend once he'd finished at Oxford. It was a move of desperation. The ROTC deferment could protect him for four more years, but would at the same time commit him to two undesirable courses of action: attending the University of Arkansas Law School instead of the far more prestigious one at Yale and serving a lengthy stint in the army reserves after graduation. The deferment was granted on August 7, 1969, and was put into effect immediately, protecting Clinton from the draft for two crucial months in which the Hot Springs draft board inducted two younger men.

On October 30, Clinton was reclassified 1-A. He has said that this was his idea, and that he took this step because he had come to feel, after several years of maneuvering to avoid the draft, a moral obligation to take his chances along with the other young men of his community. But Clinton's timing suggests otherwise; he changed his draft status only after President Nixon had announced that inductions would be sharply decreased and that graduate students, like Clinton, would be allowed to finish the school year even if drafted, thus guaranteeing protection through the late spring of 1970. Moreover, Nixon had begun winding the war down; 25,000 troops had already been withdrawn, and the administration was reportedly considering withdrawing all troops by the end of 1970. On November 26, Congress enacted the new draft lottery system, and on December 1, Clinton's birth date was assigned the number 311, high enough that he knew he would never be called. On December 2, in violation of his promise to enroll in the ROTC program at the University of Arkansas, Clinton applied to Yale Law School. On December 3, he sent a letter explaining his actions (and seeking the approval he craved even from someone he had deceived) to Col. Eugene Holmes, the army ROTC commander at the University of Arkansas.

The now-famous Holmes letter, made public during the 1992 campaign, captures the young Clinton at a crossroads. On one hand, the writer of this letter is obviously and passionately concerned with doing, and being, good. But the letter also captures, with shattering clarity, a young man learning to rationalize acts of deception and compromise as necessary in the pursuit of that good—which Clinton now regarded as inseparable from his own political advancement.

In his carefully crafted explanation of his thinking, Clinton made clear that he regarded the draft as "illegitimate," and the Vietnam War as immoral. He described two close friends who had openly resisted the draft as heroes, and portrayed the path of the conscientious objector as the honorable one for anyone opposed to the war. But in the end, Clinton wrote, he decided to put the moral imperative of his political success above his principles:

"I decided to accept the draft in spite of my beliefs for one reason: to maintain my political viability within the system. For years, I have worked to prepare myself for a political life characterized by both practical political ability and concern for rapid social progress. It is a life I still feel compelled to try to lead."

Here, astonishing in its hubris, is the idea at last expressed in its all-excusing force. Other young men of Clinton's generation might justify their actions regarding Vietnam on the grounds of simple self-interest: They did not want to lose their lives to a stupid war. Clinton decided that his self-interest was the same as his country's. He was acting for the sake of the nation's future.

The Arkansas that Bill Clinton came home to in the summer of 1973 after getting his law degree at Yale was in the middle of the most significant generational reform movement since the late 1940s. Clinton plunged immediately into it, with a 1974 challenge to the popular Republican representative John Paul Hammerschmidt of the Third Congressional District, which covered most of northwestern Arkansas. That included Fayetteville, where Clinton had accepted a teaching position at the University of Arkansas Law School. Although Clinton was unlikely to win against Hammerschmidt, he nevertheless attracted strong backing, beginning with his family connections and expanding quickly throughout the Democratic establishment.

In the Democratic primary and in the general election, both the AFL-CIO and the Arkansas Education Association supported Clinton, as did consumer groups, the United Mine Workers and some of the angels of Arkansas politics, most notably Don Tyson. According to Meredith Oakley, the author of *On the Make: The Rise of Bill Clinton,* Clinton was able to outspend Hammerschmidt by $20,000. In his campaign, Clinton was much aided by his de facto campaign manager and wife-to-be, a young woman whose reformist zeal surpassed even his. By running hard on an anti-big-business platform and by unfairly tarring Hammerschmidt with Watergate, the young candidate nearly pulled off what would have been a tremendous upset, winning almost 49 percent of the vote.

Falling back on his teaching job, Clinton immediately began planning his next race, a run for attorney general that he won as expected in 1976. The new attorney general was a populist reformer in the classic Arkansas style: anti-utilities, anti-big-business, pro-environment, pro-working class. Every week, he and his young staff attacked the utility companies over rate hikes and other issues, pushed environmental issues and energy conservation and sued local dairy farms and General Motors. He worked all the time, and kept his name before increasingly impressed voters through frequent photo ops and media shows that demonstrated his deepening understanding of the new performance art of television politics. After only one two-year term as attorney general, Clinton won the governor's seat, becoming, at thirty-two, the youngest chief executive in the nation.

Much of what the new governor did in his first term, in 1979 and 1980, was relatively uncontroversial. For instance, he increased spending on public education by 40 percent and expanded legal, health, and social services for the elderly. But a good deal of it directly challenged the moneyed interests. Clinton did not merely alienate Don Tyson and his fellow poultry barons; he took on the entire host of Arkansas angels: the utilities, the timber interests and the trucking companies.

The administration's most famous and popular battles were fought against the Arkansas Power and Light Company, a perennial target of reform governors. The so-called whiz kids who ran Clinton's new Energy Department—Scott Trotter, Walter Nixon 3rd, Basil Copeland, and Jerry Lawson—made headlines with a suit that forced the utility to refund to its customers $8.5 million in overcharges, and challenged the company over its secret plans to pass on to Arkansans up to one-third of the cost for the Grand Gulf nuclear plant, which was being built near Port Gibson, Mississippi, by AP and two other southern utilities.

Thus, in 1980, when the first-term governor ran for what was expected to be an easy reelection, it wasn't just Don Tyson who was looking for revenge. Much of the entire corporate establishment of Arkansas lined up behind Frank White, a Little Rock investment banker and political neophyte. The timber companies and the Stephens family, financiers who wielded immense political power, either supported White or sat on their wallets. Both AP and Southwestern Bell openly endorsed White, contributing heavily. When financial disclosure reports were filed a few weeks before election day, Clinton, who had expected to far outraise his relatively unknown opponent, was shocked to learn that White had collected an impressive $400,000.

The fat cats' backing allowed White to run an aggressive, late-campaign series of television commercials attacking the arrogance and incompetence of the Clinton administration. White won the election, and Clinton became the youngest ex-governor in the nation. White's first official act as governor was a gift to AP: He abolished the Energy Department and fired the whiz kids.

Clinton brooded about his first real political setback, potentially fatal to his long-term ambitions. Publicly, he blamed himself for losing touch with the people. In private conversations with friends, he attributed his failure at least equally to losing touch with the moneyed interests.

"During his lame-duck period, I went to his office to visit him," recalls Trotter. "He was in this real funk, and he told me that after the news got out about Grand Gulf, AP went out and raised a lot of money for Frank White, and that this money had enabled White to run the negative TV ads late in the campaign that Clinton figured cost him the race. The message was: If we hadn't done this thing, he'd still be governor."

Clinton's traumatic defeat took its place alongside the Vietnam draft as a watershed in his development. His first term as governor had been a grand experiment in reform, motivated both by ideals and by political instincts that told him change was what the voters wanted. Where had all this got him? The voters had paid little attention to his successes, and had held his failures greatly against him. The angels, on the other hand, had paid close attention to what Clinton had done, and had punished him for it.

The lesson was clear: to be successful, a politician had to appear hugely concerned with bettering the lives of ordinary citizens but had to be careful to avoid acting on those concerns so aggressively that they threatened the interests of the business elite. Exiled to an office in the Little Rock law firm of Wright, Lindsey & Jennings, Clinton pondered how he could win votes as a populist reformer and still raise money as a businessman's Democrat. Arkansas political observers credit two people, Jim Blair and a tough political operative from Texas named Betsey Wright, with teaching the defeated governor how to walk the line between the two competing demands. "It was Betsey who taught him—hammered it into his head, really—the idea that perception was reality," recalls Brownie Ledbetter, president of the reformist Arkansas Fairness Council. "That became the battle cry of the new Clinton approach."

Bill Clinton had never been much good at the old style of populism, the bellowing, wisecracking, denunciatory style practiced by Arkansas candidates since the days of Jeff Davis. But his own natural style—his intuitive desire to please, his chameleonesque habit of becoming whoever he was with, his talent for losing himself in the moment—was ideally suited to the new style of perception-based populism, primarily defined by television. The small screen did something perverse. It diminished and distorted the traditional thunderers of politics, translating their grand oratorical sweeps and outsize physical gestures into cartoons. Clinton realized that the new medium permitted a much more sophisticated level of communication with voters, by playing intimate scenes before the camera as if the camera weren't there. He understood that the camera rewarded the evocation of a different kind of sincerity in politics. It transmitted more than words; it transmitted performances, and the performances it transmitted most effectively were all about seduction.

The right words and the right nonverbal signals—the way in which a politician stood, sat, listened, laughed, smiled, frowned—combined to create a message that overrode the content of the words alone. If a politician was good at this, he could create not only a political reality out of perception, but also several conflicting realities at the same time, subtly manipulating the nuances of language, voice, expression, and body posture so that each member of his audience saw and heard what he wanted to see and hear. It was possible to speak even on a subject that aroused sharp division—abortion or affirmative action or welfare—and have people on opposing sides perceive the speaker to be one of them.

Bill Clinton was beyond good at this new political performance art. When he spoke, perception was not only reality. It was a reality that changed, quicksilver quick, from eye to eye and ear to ear. "You and Clinton might disagree totally on a subject and you'll never know it unless you listen closely to every word," marveled Robert S. McCord, executive editor of the *Arkansas Democrat,* in 1978. "Most people don't. They rely on tone of voice and facial expressions, which from Clinton, will never be harsh or unpleasant. . . . Liberals and conservatives alike go away from him thinking he's one bright fellow."

In the 1982 campaign to regain the statehouse, Clinton appeared to run hard as a populist. He accused White of being the tool of the moneyed interests, telling a Democratic women's club audience: "He's got half a million dollars because the people who wanted decisions from the governor's office paid for them." Diane Blair, an Arkansas political scientist (and the wife of Jim Blair) later wrote that Clinton's ads "portrayed White as an untrustworthy, interest-dominated plutocrat who might run with the good-old-boy hounds by day but slept with the utility foxes at night, while Clinton was just a caring and concerned, down-home Baptist family man who wanted nothing more than another chance to fight the fat cats on behalf of the little guys."

Publicly and frequently, Clinton embraced his former energy whiz kids Trotter and Nixon, who were themselves campaigning for a 1982 ballot referendum to reform the state's regulation of the utilities. "Clinton made a big media deal out of signing our petition to put the reform on the ballot, and during the primary season, he exploited the hell out of the issue," Trotter says now. "We had a flat commitment from him that he would enact our reforms if he got back in."

But offstage, Clinton took pains to establish a cordial and lucrative relationship with the big-money interests against whom he was railing. To that end, he appointed as his finance chairman a small-town banker named W. Maurice Smith, a second-generation political heavyweight and formidable fund-raiser. "Smith's wealthy friends were numerous," the Arkansas columnist Oakley has written. "His selection as finance chair in the 1982 campaign—and all subsequent Clinton re-election campaigns—was one of the smartest decisions Clinton made." With Smith's help, Clinton raised more than $1 million, then a record.

When Clinton regained office, Smith came along as the resurrected governor's executive assistant.

From 1983 until he resigned halfway through his fifth term to seek the presidency, Governor Clinton achieved a number of moderate reforms. He opened up high-level government jobs to blacks and women. He helped win passage of the first ethics law for elected officials in Arkansas's history. He greatly increased spending on social services. He developed tax-credit and bond-issuing programs to create thousands of new jobs, although most of them were low paying. He and his wife, who had established herself as a powerful figure in Arkansas political and legal circles, worked to fashion a settlement that ended a long-running lawsuit over Little Rock schools, which had resegregated along residential lines. He established some regulatory controls on Arkansas's largest pollution problem, animal wastes. His showpiece act, the 1983 education reform, primarily designed and sold by Mrs. Clinton, won large increases in tax-generated financing for state schools and established a mandatory competency test for public-school teachers and standarized testing of students. He sponsored improvements in the prison system, the child-welfare system and the administration of juvenile justice.

But he would never again take on the angels with anything like the vigor of his first term. "A big intersection of interests—timber, farms, AP, the Stephenses—was aligned against Clinton when he took office again in the early eighties, and I think there was basically a conscious decision not to antagonize any of these guys anymore," says Ernest Dumas, a veteran Little Rock political writer and editor. "Clinton, in essence, said, 'Fellas, I'm going to concentrate all my energies on education reform.' Well, that was fine with the interests. They were for education reform. It would be nice to be able to hire people who could read and write, and it didn't hurt them any."

And Clinton's other reforms—many of which came about as a result of federal court decisions forced by class-action and interest-group litigation—often turned out to be much grander in the selling than in their real effects. Clinton's 1983 education reform was a classic case in point. With the promise that teacher testing would rid the schools of incompetent educators, Governor Clinton had won broad public support for a tax increase to finance his education program. What was actually delivered struck many in Arkansas as a cynical exercise: a test that could be passed by teachers possessing only eighth-grade-level skills in language and math. Teachers were coached in special workshops, and those who failed were allowed to retake the test.

Perhaps the most striking example of the discrepancy between what Clinton the populist governor promised and what Clinton the businessman's Democrat governor delivered came in his handling of issues involving Arkansas Power and Light.

Two of the original energy whiz kids, Scott Trotter and Walter Nixon, maintain that Clinton won reelection in 1982, at least partly, on the strength of his opposition to the utilities. "But when he was reelected, we did not go back to work," Nixon recalls. "He did not recreate the Energy Department, did not reengage on the energy issues which he believed had helped get him defeated in 1980, never followed through again with any fervor on energy reform."

Publicly, Clinton remained committed to the fight. In his first month back in office, the governor introduced eight utility reform bills that encompassed many of his campaign promises. But only three of the weakest bills passed, and the four that were the centerpieces of his reforms were killed. Trotter charges that Clinton, while officially urging passage of the bills, never really fought for them. "We pushed and pulled and poked, but he was completely dilatory," Trotter said. "He and I argued about it in his office before I quit, and he just said that he didn't need the utility issue anymore. He was going into education."

Clinton's handling of Don Tyson evolved similarly. During the 1980s, Tyson Foods grew at an explosive rate, climbing to $4.2 billion in sales in 1993. It became the largest chicken processor in the world, controlling more than 20 percent of the American market and churning out more than 80 million pounds of chicken products every week. Critics among Arkansas's environmental and labor groups found much to object to in the way Tyson did business. One growing complaint was that the huge volume of animal waste—especially the euphemistically named "litter" from chicken houses, much of it generated by Tyson's ever-expanding empire—was seriously polluting Arkansas's crystalline rivers and streams. In one famous incident that took place shortly after Clinton was restored to office in 1983, the sewage system in the town of Green Forest, which had been for years overloaded by Tyson-produced animal waste, dumped so much raw sewage into Dry Creek that a giant sinkhole formed, sending largely untreated sewage into the aquifer that supplied much of the local drinking water at a rate of one million gallons a day.

Clinton's response to the pollution issue was typical of his new style. Seventeen months after the Green Forest crisis, he declared a state of "disaster emergency." That same year, the state environmental agency, which had been given enforcement powers for the first time by Clinton, began enforcing long-ignored directives to Tyson to pretreat waste from its Green Forest processing plant. But the state failed to levy any fines against the company or to sue it for damages. That was left to a group of outraged citizens, who eventually prevailed in a 1989

judgment that found Tyson Foods guilty of forty-three violations of the Clean
Water Act.

On the question of how poultry wastes should be handled in general, Clinton waited until 1990. He appointed a commission, the Animal Waste Task
Force, which deliberated until November 1992 and then issued guidelines that
called for state-enforced regulation of the liquid animal wastes produced by cattle and hog farmers, while allowing the poultry industry to comply with the
guidelines voluntarily. "Thousands of Arkansas poultry producers should be
pleased," declared *Poultry Times,* the industry newspaper.

Certainly, the people at Tyson Foods noticed a difference in the governor. "I
think the defeat of 1980 was a watershed in his political career," says Archie
Schaffer, a Tyson public relations official. "He came back in eighty-two with a
different attitude, much less confrontational with the business community and
others in the so-called establishment, much more conciliatory. . . . After he was
reelected, he pushed some mildly controversial, progressive things, but I don't remember him ever again pushing any big controversial thing that he was willing
to die for."

Clinton and his supporters have long argued that these sorts of compromises
were necessary in a chronically poor state like Arkansas, where the urgencies of
economic growth necessitate concessions to business. The point is, to a degree,
valid. But it is also true that early in his career Clinton began to garner a reputation in Arkansas that now besets him nationally, a reputation for slipperiness and
waffling in excess of even the norms of politics. The nickname Slick Willie,
originally made popular by the Arkansas columnist Paul Greenberg in 1982,
passed into common usage among the governor's critics on the Right and the
Left and soon stuck with the public. Jokes about Clinton's honesty, about his
predilection for saying whatever his listener of the moment wanted to hear,
about his willingness to reverse himself, were common midway through his second term and grew steadily through his five terms as governor.

One Clinton characteristic that attracted increasing critical attention was his
readiness to do favors for current or potential financial supporters. There were
two paradigmatic cases, both involving revenue bonds issued by the Arkansas
Housing Development Agency and its 1985 successor, the Arkansas Development Finance Authority.

In 1989, the nation's largest nursing home company, Beverly Enterprises, was
in deep financial trouble. The company, with more than one thousand nursing
homes in forty states, had suffered crippling losses in 1988 and 1989, and had
agreed to a restructuring requiring it to sell off some facilities to pay off its debt

by 1991. The fate of Beverly was of intense interest to the Stephens family, whose brokerage house, Stephens Inc., held all of the company's preferred stock, worth approximately $100 million. Three Stephens appointees sat on Beverly's eight-member board, and the Stephenses also served as Beverly's well-paid financial advisers.

Beverly, guided by the Stephenses and the Rose Law Firm in Little Rock, where Hillary Rodham Clinton had become a partner, put together a $149 million plan to sell off all of Beverly's nursing homes in four states. A Rose lawyer, William H. Kennedy 3rd, served as counsel to Beverly in the matter. (Kennedy, who had joined Mrs. Clinton, Vincent Foster, and Webster Hubbell to form a powerful clique at the firm, is currently serving as an associate White House counsel.) The deal worked out by Beverly, with advice from Stephens and the Rose firm, was precisely the sort of arrangement the future first lady would have called a health care rip-off. It was designed to take advantage of a loophole in the 1986 Tax Reform Act by using government-issued bonds to finance the sale of Beverly's nursing homes to nonprofit shell companies that were, in fact, fronting for for-profit companies.

The first sale was completed in August 1989, when Beverly sold forty-five nursing homes to a Texas investor named Bruce Whitehead. The deal, essentially a tax-exempt, leveraged buyout, was structured around a series of transactions that ended with Whitehead holding most of the homes in a nonprofit shell company called Care Initiatives. Whitehead put up no money in the deal; the creation of Care Initiatives was capitalized almost entirely through the issuance and sale of $86 million in tax-exempt bonds from the Iowa Finance Authority. Iowa courts later ruled that the entire transaction had been designed to generate "millions of dollars of excessive profits" for the principals in the transaction—at the expense of Iowa taxpayers. All told, the courts found, the businessmen, lawyers, and underwriters involved made in excess of $20 million, a profit that District Court Judge Gene L. Needles called "unconscionable."

The second deal put together by Beverly, the Stephenses, and the Rose firm was a replication of the first, involving the same parties and structure. The only difference was that it was set up in Arkansas. Pride House Care Corporation of Dallas, another Whitehead concoction, would buy Beverly's thirty-two nursing homes or leases. The sale was to be financed by $81 million in revenue bonds issued by the Arkansas Development Finance Authority.

The Finance Authority's preliminary limited-offering memorandum describing the proposed bond issue made it embarrassingly clear that the state agency knew Whitehead's companies were nothing but shells. As the offering put it,

Whitehead's Pride House Care "has no assets and has not acquired any facilities, nor does it operate any" and has "no current operations and therefore has no employees." The state justified the sale on the grounds that Arkansas could not afford to see Beverly collapse and that the large institutional investors who would finance the deal through their bond purchases would, in any case, bear all the risks. As was the case in Iowa, the proposed deal would greatly enrich those who fashioned it. Whitehead was to make an immediate $1.9 million profit, and lawyers and underwriters would make off with $6.4 million. The Finance Authority, presided over by its Clinton-appointed president, Robert Nash, had already tentatively approved the transaction when news reports began to raise serious questions.

Clinton, who, as governor, had the power to stop the Finance Authority bond issue, remained silent through weeks of mounting public outrage. It was not until the Arkansas attorney general, Steve Clark, announced that "a Beverly-Stephens Inc. representative" had offered him $100,000 in campaign contributions if he would end his opposition to the deal that Clinton urged the agency under his control to kill the bond issue. (The lobbyist maintained that his offer did not constitute a bribe, and Stephens denied any connection with the incident.)

Afterward, Clinton claimed he had opposed the deal from the beginning. Writing in his *Arkansas Gazette* column, John Brummett declared: "The Governor's assertion that he was against this proposal all along is false. The fact is that Clinton sat by as Nash and the board approved this deal September 21—back when it contained those personal profits for Bruce Whitehead that the Governor now says are so obscene."

The second controversial Finance Authority–related affair centered on a well-known Little Rock figure named Dan Lasater. A flashy young millionaire—at the age of twenty-two, he had founded the Ponderosa Steakhouse chain—Lasater, in 1980, opened a bond house that, within a year, was selling $1 billion worth of bonds a month. In the tradition of Witt Stephens, Lasater quickly made himself a prominent figure in local politics and society, contributing heavily to the campaigns of Governor Clinton and other politicians. In three consecutive Clinton gubernatorial campaigns, Lasater contributed thousands of dollars personally, and hosted fund-raising events that netted many thousands more. But the services did not stop there. Lasater provided Clinton use of his private jet and hired the governor's famously unemployable brother, Roger, as his driver and stable hand. Once he even lent the governor's brother $8,000 to pay off Roger's debt to his cocaine wholesalers.

In 1982, after strongly supporting the campaign that reseated Clinton in the governor's office, Lasater and his partners asked to be included in Arkansas state bond issues. Clinton agreed. "They wanted to do some business, and I said I thought they ought to be able to compete for it," Clinton told *U.S. News & World Report* in 1982. The name of Lasater and Company first appeared as an underwriter of an Arkansas Housing Development Agency bond issue in 1983, after Clinton was sworn in for his second term.

Over the next three years, until Lasater was convicted of distributing cocaine in the fall of 1986 and served six months in prison, the company won assignments to co-manage thirteen bond issues from the Arkansas Development Finance Authority, handling a total of $664 million worth of bonds, and received brokerage fees of $1.6 million.

As in the case of Beverly nursing homes, what is telling about the Lasater affair is Clinton's evident willingness to risk the reputation of his state and his administration in order to benefit a powerful financial supporter. Dan Lasater was, to put it mildly, a known quantity in Little Rock. In the 80s, he was the king of the city's "bond daddies," hustlers who used high-pressure, dishonest sales tactics to peddle wildly overpriced and risky bond deals on the telephone, and who became so famous that they gave Little Rock a new nickname in financial circles: "Slam City," a term derived from the daddies' word for a successful hustle—"slamming."

Lasater and Company was one of the most prominent of the bond daddy firms, with a downtown office where seventy-two salesmen worked the telephones from desks arranged in tiers around a central pit. There, Lasater hosted after-hours, high-rolling parties where cocaine was passed around on silver trays. "They were crooks pure and simple," said Vernon Giss, a longtime adviser to Witt Stephens at Stephens Inc. "They would sell bonds that had been defaulted, absolutely crooked stuff."

Warren Stephens, the president of Stephens Inc., is among the many in Little Rock who say Bill Clinton had full knowledge of Lasater's character but allowed him to win state business anyway. "You didn't even open the door to these places, 'cause of all the snakes down there," Stephens says. "These guys, these firms, smelled to high heaven."

Asked if he believes Lasater's campaign support and his helping Roger Clinton had anything to do with the governor's failure to oppose Lasater, Stephens says dryly, "I would think they played a role in it, I would."

The criticism Governor Clinton faced over the Beverly and Lasater affairs were part of a larger pattern. One of the great paradoxes of Clinton's career is that during the years he was winning a national reputation as a courageous truth teller—particularly about the problems of Democratic politics and policies—he was winning a reputation at home as someone who, as John Brummett writes in his forthcoming biography of Clinton, *Highwire,* "seems to have an almost pathological inability to tell the whole truth."

Politics, in its own strange fashion, is an honest business. The rules of the game allow small lies of omission, waffling, fudging, and any amount of hedging. But flat-out lying and acts of direct betrayal are much rarer than cynics believe, and greatly frowned upon. The survival of the system demands this. Every relationship in politics—whether between voter and candidate or between lobbyist and elected official—is based on the assumption that a bold statement of fact or an unhedged promise can be taken as true. And almost every statement or promise, from the back-room deal to the campaign pledge, is unwritten and therefore vulnerable. A politician who blatantly goes back on his word threatens the entire fragile structure, and is likely to be punished harshly. Consider the example of George Bush and his "read my lips" promise. Long-term successful politicians typically measure the consequences of their words, carefully couching the language of every pledge they make and deal they cut in the knowledge that no one ever forgets, and almost no one forgives, anything.

What became increasingly clear in Arkansas was that Clinton was different, blithely and flatly promising what he couldn't deliver, reversing himself on a position to which he had been, only moments before, firmly committed. It sometimes seemed he would say anything to win support, or even to get through a conversation without conflict, ignoring the consequences.

One famous evening in 1985, for example, the governor vetoed a bill providing a tax credit for private contributions to Arkansas colleges and universities. After the bill, stamped "Disapproved," had been slipped under the door of the legislative clerk's office, Clinton called the state's university presidents to explain his decision. When they protested vehemently, the governor sent a state trooper to retrieve the bill. With a coat hanger, the trooper fished the bill out from under the door and returned it to Clinton, who crossed out the prefix "Dis" and had the trooper return the bill to the clerk's office, now "approved." Later, after the bill caused the state unacceptable financial losses, as the governor's advisers had warned, Clinton was forced to call a special session of the legislature to amend it.

Of all the bonds of politics, the handshake deal made to ensure the passage of legislation matters the most. As governor, Bill Clinton quickly earned a reputation as someone who didn't understand that these agreements between professionals were inviolate. During the legislative battles to pass the 1983 education reform, J. Bill Becker, president of the Arkansas AFL-CIO, and Brownie Ledbetter of the Arkansas Fairness Council, led a successful effort in the Arkansas House to block the one-cent sales tax increase Clinton needed to finance his program, complaining it would hurt the poor and working class. The governor then proposed a deal in which he asked that Becker and Ledbetter agree to drop their opposition in exchange for his support of an amendment offering a rebate to poor people for the sales tax they paid on groceries. "Bill called Becker and me in," recalls Ledbetter. "And he said, 'If you let me get this through the House with the low-income rebate on it, I'll help you in the Senate so the tax bill will come out in the end with the rebate attached.' So we did, and he shafted us. When it came to the Senate, the governor's man on the bill made no effort at all." Clinton, speaking to reporters, explained that his promise to Becker and Ledbetter had been nothing more than "a twenty-four-hour commitment." (In retrospect, Ledbetter says, it is clear that Clinton never had the power to effect senate passage of the amendment but should not have made a commitment he couldn't meet.)

In 1983, Clinton said that the tax increase he was seeking for education reform would be earmarked entirely for primary and secondary schools. But after personal lobbying by Jim Blair, then chairman of the University of Arkansas board of trustees, Clinton peeled off a third of the allocation for higher education.

In 1987, Clinton promised several journalistic organizations that he would kill a bill that had been proposed to deny public access to previously available tax records, including those of the state's corporations. He then turned around and supported passage of the measure. Carol Griffee, an Arkansas reporter who was then regional director of the Society of Professional Journalists' Freedom of Information Committee, spoke openly of the "betrayal by the governor."

By 1990, when Clinton ran for his fifth and final term as governor, his honesty had become an open issue. It was in this race that the AFL-CIO president Becker memorably described Bill Clinton as a man "who will pat you on the back" and micturate down your leg.

The candidate found himself dogged by a well-founded suspicion that he would not serve out his four-year term if reelected governor, but would instead use the job as a platform from which to run for president in 1992—a move he had publicly considered in 1988 and for which he had been busy positioning himself with his work on the Democratic Leadership Council. In a televised debate, Craig Cannon, a reporter, asked Clinton a simple but encompassing question: "Will you guarantee to us that, if reelected, there is absolutely, positively no way that you'll run for any other political office and that you'll serve out your term in full?"

This was exactly the sort of question that most politicians would have answered with an un-Shermanesque hedge: "I have no intentions of running for president. . . . I certainly am not planning to run for president."

But Clinton responded with a stunning lack of equivocation. "You bet," he said. "I told you when I announced for governor I intended to run, and that's what I'm gonna do. I'm gonna serve four years. I made that decision when I decided to run. I'm being considered as a candidate for governor. That's the job I want. That's the job I'll do for the next four years."

When a year later Bill Clinton announced his candidacy for president, not many in his home state were surprised. "He has always wanted to be president—that was his whole idea in life, and Hillary's whole idea was to be Mrs. First Lady," says the veteran Little Rock liberal activist Edwin Dunaway. "He talked a good game and he had big ideas, but he never followed through. I fell out with Bill because he never followed through on anything. His word is no good."

The *Newsweek* writer Joe Klein recently quoted the president on the subject of character: "Character is a journey, not a destination." No, Klein responded, life is a journey; character is a destination reached by the actions of a life. What you are, by the time you are the president's age, is the cumulative result of all that you have done, all the thousands of decisions that build an adult. Bill Clinton's problem isn't merely that his past haunts him. It is that his past has made him what he is today.

But Clinton's definition of character reveals an essential truth about him. The president does still seem to be on a journey to maturity; he is a brilliant young man who has not quite arrived at a clear understanding of himself. It is as if, in the hard, ambivalent business of getting to where he is, he has somehow put off the business of who he is, of what he stands for and of what he will not stand for.

A line of consequence runs from the Draft to "I Didn't Inhale" to Whitewater to Hillary's Commodities to Dan Lasater to Lani Guinier to Somalia to Bosnia to Haiti: The episodes of rationalization and compromise from Clinton's Arkansas past are the progenitors of the indecision and betrayal that have done so much damage to the White House present. Bill Clinton is today, as he was twenty years ago, clearly concerned with doing the right thing, and his presidency still holds some of the promise that stirred so many Americans to such hope in 1992. But there is a hollowness to the Clinton presidency, a sense that it lacks a center because the man at its center lacks one of his own.

No one is surprised any more when the president reverses himself on a matter of policy, or breaks a promise, or axes an old friend. In both houses of Congress, controlled by Clinton's own party, there is a nearly collective assumption that the president's stated intention on a policy or a piece of legislation is not to be taken as his final word; the legislators all remember how the White House whipped Democratic House members into line to vote for the unpopular BTU energy tax in 1993, and then dropped it when it encountered strong resistance in the Senate Finance Committee. After the administration's flip-flops on Haiti, Bosnia, Somalia, and China, the conventional diplomatic wisdom is that the pledges of the president of the United States are to be regarded more as well-meaning sentiments than actual commitments.

The president is a ubiquitous electronic presence, always on the go and on the tube, in some vivid new tableau that is a masterwork of the campaigner's art. But the scenes that Clinton so brilliantly conjures seem more and more disconnected from the realities of his actions. The president evokes the memories of World War II to warn against the dangers of appeasement, isolationism, and cowardice while his administration declines to call the slaughter in Rwanda "genocide," for fear such honesty would force America to do something to stop it. The president denounces the influence of big-money special interests in politics while the Democratic National Committee, under his de facto control, raises $40 million in "soft money" contributions from the rich, corporations, and unions.

Two contrasting events from the Clinton presidency perfectly capture the disunity of the man's character:

On November 13, the president delivered a passionate and, in part, extemporaneous address to a group of black ministers in Memphis. He asked them to imagine Martin Luther King Jr. suddenly appearing by his side on stage, to issue a report card on the progress of black America over the last twenty-five years.

King would tell the ministers, Clinton said, that they had done a good job in creating a large black middle class: "But he would say: 'I did not live and die to see the American family destroyed. I did not live and die to see thirteen-year-old boys get automatic weapons and gun down nine-year-olds just for the kick of it. I did not live and die to see young people destroy their own lives with drugs and then build fortunes destroying the lives of others. That is not what I came here to do. . . . I fought for people to have the right to work, but not to have whole communities and people abandoned. This is not what I lived and died for.'"

Seven months later, Bill Clinton walked on Omaha Beach, in Normandy, with three veterans of the bloody D-Day battle that had been fought there. The walk had been planned by the president's media advisers as part of an overall attempt to reshape the president's image as commander in chief, a mantle that had never rested comfortably on his shoulders. The event, staged as carefully as a small movie, was duly noted in the White House press schedule of the day: "6:15 C.E.T. President Clinton visits Omaha Beach with the American veterans of that beach. Note: no remarks are planned during this walk."

The president and three men who had fought on the beach walked slowly along, talking in hushed tones among themselves, as a dozen or so photographers and television cameramen walked backward in front of them, recording the scene. After a few minutes, White House aides pulled the veterans off to one side, so that the president could continue his beach walk in Kennedyesque solitude. At a certain point, where some beach stones had been gathered into a small pile to form a marker, the president stopped, and the photographers took up their positions so that he was nicely framed by the hulks of the old warships in the sea behind him.

The president stood for a moment, staring silently out to sea. Then he knelt down, his knees not quite touching the ground, in a pose that suggested worship. He reached for the pile of stones in front of him and slowly began rearranging them into the shape of a cross. A journalist who was there watching the scene recalls "getting that sick feeling you get sometimes with him, thinking 'Oh God, please don't do this.'"

As the cameras clicked and rolled, the president bowed his head as if to pray. Later, White House aides said the moment of silence had been planned, but that the cross of stones had been entirely the president's own idea.

The problem with Bill Clinton is that the same man is capable of playing both of these scenes. He is capable of delivering, as he did to the ministers, a message of breathtaking clarity, candor, and courage. And when he does, it is impossible to doubt that he believes utterly in what he is doing. He is equally capable of kneeling on a beach where two thousand American men were slaughtered and acting out an intimate communion with God in front of a platoon of cameras. And when he does this, it is also impossible to doubt that he believes utterly in what he is doing.

A former friend says, bitterly, that Clinton has become "a performer of empathy." The president's face is a screen upon which plays a loop of expressions that have become insistently familiar: the open-mouthed grin of joyous wonder; the scowl of righteous but controlled anger; the lip-biting, eyes–lowered glance of pondering humility; the near tears of a man who is not afraid to show that he feels. In an important sense, these expressions are entirely honest; Clinton's empathy is wholly real. But it exists only in the moment. The president's essential character flaw isn't dishonesty so much as a-honesty. It isn't that Clinton means to say things that are not true, or that he cannot make true, but that everything is true for him when he says it, because he says it. Clinton means what he says when he says it, but tomorrow he will mean what he says when he says the opposite. He is the existential president, living with absolute sincerity in the passing moment.

Clinton's Escape Clause

◆ ◆ ◆

On a bright, fat-pumpkin morning in late September, an odd little parade made its orderly way from the House office buildings onto the grounds of the Capitol and along the side of the building and the western steps to gather in neat ranks before twenty-three television cameras and a small crowd of reporters, Republican staffers, and incidental tourists. The assembled stood framed by bunting, but they would have made a patriotic tableau in any case, being almost entirely white, and dressed almost entirely in suits of blue (the men) and red (the few women). Over the years, the Capitol has seen many armies of protest: Coxey's, in 1894; the Kluxers of 1925; the Bonus Expeditionary Force of 1932; and the vast anti–Vietnam War demonstrations of the late sixties and early seventies. It had never seen anything like this. Traditionally, marching on Congress has been a privilege reserved for people who were not themselves members of Congress. After all, that has always been the point of the exercise: A march on Congress was an expression of anger by the citizenry outside the Beltway toward the crowd within—a public act of denunciation and exposure. This day represented the first time the insiders had marched to denounce and expose themselves.

If American life had not vaulted beyond parody some time back, the scene would have seemed a joke, of sorts: a hundred and fifty members of Congress and some two hundred people who would very much like to be members of Congress standing in front of the institution they served, or wished to serve, in order to rail against it, as if they were Free Silverites or Dust Bowl farmers come to smite the corruption of Washington. The day was lovely and the mood of the speakers was correspondingly lighthearted, but the scripted rhetoric was meant to sound angry and radical; each politician rose to declare the nation on the edge of disaster, Congress a disgrace, the president a fool, the people betrayed. The ge-nial House minority leader, Robert Michel, who has dwelt comfortably in the belly of the beast for thirty-seven years, damned the "decades of neglect and mismanagement" in the House he helped run. The white-haired Henry Hyde of Illinois led the convocation in a prayer that the Capitol where he has worked for nineteen years "will once again be a place of honor and a temple of freedom." Dick Armey of Texas, who, with Newt Gingrich of Georgia, was a leader of the pack, declared the Congress in which he has served for nine years to be "cor-rupted by absolute power, a House of Representatives that now routinely stifles free and open debate, cobbles together thousands of pages of bills behind closed doors, and refuses to live by the laws it imposes on everyone else."

Citizen Gingrich took the final turn at the mike, and he was the angriest of all. Technically, Gingrich represents the Sixth District of Georgia, but really he is the representative of the permanent state of Madderthanhell—a state that in this election autumn has become the most powerful in the Union. Gingrich has been a congressman for fifteen years, but age has not withered, nor custom staled, his infinite capacity for outrage toward the Democratic majority. While Gingrich may occasionally allow himself the grace notes of "my honorable colleague" and "my learned friend," he makes no real pretense at collegiality. He is, in all appar-ent sincerity, at war. He wants the Democrats out, he wants their way of doing things finished. With the help of a growing number of fellow believers—the most important being his Senate counterpart Phil Gramm of Texas—Gingrich has reshaped the congressional Republican Party, an entity that was once strongly inclined to follow former House Speaker Sam Rayburn's advice about going along to get along, into a force for the advancement of a grand agenda: the destruction of Democratic policies and politicians, and the fulfillment of Ron-ald Reagan's promise to reverse the liberalization of America that began six de-cades ago.

Gingrich's speech was not clever or well written. In a shotgun marriage of Mario Cuomo's metaphor of the nation as family and Ross Perot's of the nation as automobile, he asked the audience to "think of America as a giant family of two hundred sixty million people of extraordinarily diverse backgrounds riding in a huge car down the highway trying to pursue happiness and seek the Amer-ican dream"—an exercise that would make the Joads look like specialists in trav-eling light. Its unblinkered anger lent it a measure of force nevertheless. Gingrich is one of those men for whom anger appears to be the natural condition; he seems true to himself when his face reddens and his voice takes on a razored edge and he snipes, as he did on this day, at "the usual carping, the usual complaining, the usual negativism from an all too cynical Washington press corps," and chortles over the "collapse" of the Clinton administration. The speech was also forceful because it painted the sort of apocalyptic picture that has an immense resonance these days. Gingrich proclaimed that "America is in trouble," and that, with "twelve-year-olds having babies, fifteen-year-olds killing each other, seventeen-year-olds dying of AIDS, and eighteen-year-olds getting diplomas they can't even read," we are facing "a crisis of our entire civilization." He warned that "if America fails, our children will live on a dark and bloody planet."

What was needed to rescue the republic, Gingrich declared, was revolutionary change: the end of the forty-year Democratic control of Congress; the weakening of Congress itself (through constitutionally mandated term limits and spending controls); the utter rejection of Democratic policies as embodied by the Clinton administration; and the passage of ten legislative proposals, most of them controversial and some apparently unconstitutional. The highlights: A Gingrichite 104th Congress would, on its first day, strike a series of blows against itself, including the cutting of House committee staff members by a third and the imposition of a three-fifths-majority requirement for the passage of any tax increase. In the course of the next ninety-nine days, the 104th would bring to the floor, among other measures, a radical welfare-reform act, a crime bill far more hard-nosed than the one passed this summer, constitutional amendments to mandate a balanced budget and to give the president a line-item veto, a bill limiting the terms of congressmen, and one cutting the capital-gains tax by 50 percent.

Not one of these notions was new; some, such as the balanced-budget amendment, the term-limits requirement, and the capital-gains tax cut were hoary to the point of permafrost. What was new, and was meant to be attractive, was the bright idea of collecting all the promises into a "Contract with America," an idea dreamed up by Armey, Gingrich, and the former Perotista pollster Frank Luntz, which all the assembled Republicans signed. In the GOP flackery that accompanied the event, much was made of the supposedly binding nature of what the Republicans capitalize as the Contract. "A campaign promise is one thing, a signed Contract is quite another," one press release noted, and another said, "If we don't do what we say, throw us out. We mean it."

◆ ◆ ◆

Two weeks later: It was seven o'clock in the evening, at the end of another trying day in the life of Gene Sperling, quintessential Clintonian. Sperling is thirty-five years old, and, although he is a lawyer, not an economist, he is a deputy economic adviser to the president. Like most of the young men and women of the Clinton White House, Sperling is partisan to the bone: He has been working for liberal policy groups (the NAACP, the Legal Defense Fund, and the National Abortion Rights Action League) and Democratic politicians (Michael Dukakis, Mario Cuomo, and Bill Clinton) since his Yale Law School days. He occupies an interesting niche at the intersection of policy and politics: a job that epitomizes the endless symbiosis—and confusion—between governing and selling that is the hallmark of the modern White House. Gene Sperling is a political numbers cruncher. One of the first policy aides to be hired by the Clinton campaign, he created the mathematical blueprint for "Putting People First," the economic agenda cum political pamphlet that provided the foundation of Clinton's pitch to the voters.

When, in 1993, the White House mobilized behind an economic plan that, as Bob Woodward has written in his book *The Agenda,* neither the president nor his senior advisers fully supported, the political consultant Paul Begala wrote the script for selling the proposal to the public—a memo, headlined "Hallelujah! Change Is Coming," that said Clinton's plan would boost the economy "by finally paying down the deficit." Actually, the plan was designed to shrink the deficit for only a few years, after which it was projected to balloon once again. Details such as this were to be glossed over, Begala warned administration officials in his memo. "Anytime you're asked about a specific in the economic plan, look for ways to bring it back to the general points that this is good for the country, and this is real change," Begala wrote, as his memo is quoted by Woodward. Gene Sperling provided the statistical muscle behind Begala's prose—what Woodward describes as "a spokesman's bible, a half-inch thick document of graphs, tables, pie charts, quotes, and lengthy arguments totalling 86 pages. [A] manual for all-out political war."

Sperling and the White House won that congressional budget battle, though by just one, reluctant vote. In the year since, however, the tide has gone heavily against the administration, and the Clintonites have lost much of the cheerful blood lust that once energized them. Now, thanks to the Contract with America, Sperling was a happy warrior again. With his pinstriped suit coat draped over the back of his chair, he sat at the long wooden table in his West Wing basement office, his glasses off, and rubbed the bridge of his nose as he scratched hasty mathematical notations on the backs of documents he had prepared to refute the promises of Newtian law.

"Take a look at this," he said, jabbing his pen at an item in the Republicans' proposal. "Note the language here, where they talk about what spending cuts they would employ to achieve a balanced budget. It contains, for God's sake, a *double* caveat: 'Examples of possible cuts.' They're not saying these are cuts they are going to make, or even possible cuts; they are *examples* of possible cuts! Or take a look at their line where they talk about the cost of the balanced-budget amendment. This is maybe the best political line I have ever seen for sheer dishonesty: 'Balanced Budget Amendment/Line Item Veto—No Cost.' Or take a look at their line item for defense: 'Strengthening Defense—No Cost.'"

Scratch, scratch went the Sperling pen, burrowing deeper and deeper into the mysteries of political budgetry. "Why, just consider their proposal for back-loading super IRAs. Here, let me show you some numbers. You can see here, the back-loaded super IRA would cost the treasury six billion dollars per year; it's designed to fool the budget window, designed to get a good federal-deficit number in the early years, while passing on the cost to the out years."

It is the media wisdom of the moment not to take the Contract with America seriously. But, as Sperling's urgency suggests, within the Clinton camp the Contract is taken with utmost seriousness, if not necessarily in the way its creators intended. The White House has seized upon the Republicans' gambit with loud cries of outrage and quiet sighs of relief. What Newt Gingrich proposed on September 27 on the steps of the Capitol is now being used by Bill Clinton and his political strategists in a last, desperate attempt to redefine the 1994 elections and to rehabilitate the reputation of his presidency. As a wholly unexpected result, these midterm contests have become, in their last month, what an election is supposed to be—a battle of ideas, a choice between two competing visions of the role of government in America.

◆ ◆ ◆

To understand how this has happened, it helps to look back to where matters stood with Clinton and the Democrats on the morning Gingrich rolled out the Contract. That day, the president and his party were staring glumly at disaster. After years of trying, the Republican Party appeared to have finally reversed Tip's Law—to have made all politics national. In congressional and gubernatorial races across the country, Republican challengers were hammering Democratic incumbents. Men who had been in office so long that their desk chairs were form-fitted to their bottoms were falling, or threatening to fall, to challengers nobody in Washington had heard of before, it seemed, last Tuesday. The very foundation of the O'Neill universe—the understanding that the ability of an incumbent to bring the bacon of Washington home to his district ensures reelection—seemed suddenly shaken. The voters in Tom Foley's district, infuriated by his lawsuit against a term-limits referendum, were, the polls indicated, seriously considering giving up the privilege of being represented by the Speaker of the House. In Massachusetts, Ted Kennedy had become the personification of Bloated Washington, heaving his besuited bulk from stump to stump, his face as fat and red as a Big Boy tomato, in the company of aides toting giant stage-prop checks that represented examples of his tax-dollar largesse to the folks back home; the senator of thirty-two years' standing was running barely ahead of the millionaire novice politician Mitt Romney. In New York, the three-term governor, Mario Cuomo, was threatened by the former mayor of Peekskill, George Pataki, and, in California, Senator Dianne Feinstein by the stealth candidate Michael Huffington. In the Tennessee race for former Senator Al Gore's seat, the Democratic representative Jim Cooper was getting clobbered by Fred Thompson, a lawyer-lobbyist cum movie actor running as a populist in a pickup truck, while the incumbent senator Jim Sasser was facing a surprisingly tough challenge from William Frist, a rich Nashville surgeon who had been so little involved in politics that he hadn't registered to vote until 1988. In Oklahoma, Representative Mike Synar, after eight terms in the House, lost the Democratic primary to Virgil Cooper, a seventy-one-year-old retired schoolteacher who had spent less than seventeen thousand dollars on his campaign.

In these races, and in many others, almost every challenger was running on a platform directly in line with the Gingrich pitch. Frank Luntz, whose voter surveys and focus groups were instrumental in framing the Contract, calls it the "to hell with you" message: to hell with Congress, to hell with Washington, to hell with Big Brother government, to hell with taxes, to hell with the liberal elites, to hell with welfare mothers and street gangsters and bad schools and the mess of the cities.

"The editorial writers in Washington, they don't understand the mood out there," Luntz said. "They write the word 'anger' as if it were a five-letter word. It's not. It's a four-letter word and a three-letter word—'Fuck you.' In all my focus groups, people are saying 'Fuck Washington.' They don't even bother to correct their language. There are different types of anger all around the country, all coming together against Washington. There is a conservative religious anger in the South, and that is quite different from the antifederalist Washington you find west of the Mississippi. The South is a moral anger, a moral indignation; the western anger is: 'Get off my back.' The urban anger is gritty and blunt. All these things are evident, in one way or another, in various races. The Oliver North vote in Virginia is: 'To hell with the system. The system is evil. It has to be changed.' The Marion Barry vote in D.C. is: 'Screw the white establishment.' It's all the same phenomenon."

The anger against Washington, Luntz argues, is all-encompassing. "It's anger not just against the federal government but against congressmen, senators, journalists, even pollsters," he says. Still, the Democrats bear the brunt of it because "people see in growing numbers that Democrats are the party of big government, so the way to vote against big government—against Washington—is to vote against Democrats."

As the White House and Democratic Party strategists were unhappily aware, Bill Clinton had come to personify for many voters what it was that had made them so angry about Washington in the first place. Two years earlier, Clinton had been elected by a bare plurality—43 percent of the vote—in the first wave of the same anti-incumbent, antigovernment fervor that now threatens him and his party. Catching that wave perfectly, Clinton had promised voters the sort of radical change they were demanding: to reform the financing of national politics, to run an administration of spotless ethical character, to effectively address America's huge problems of crime and underclass pathology, to reject the special-interest politics with which his party had become identified, to end congressional gridlock, to "grow" the economy, to work toward balancing the federal budget, and to effect a national health care plan offering universal coverage.

To a larger extent than it is usually given credit for by voters, the administration had met its goals, boosting the economy with the passage of a deficit-reducing budget and the North American Free Trade Agreement and enacting an array of social reforms. It had also, however, committed large and frequent blunders, not only in its general failure to manage Congress but also in its particular failure to pass health care, welfare-reform, or ethics legislation. Abandoning a promised middle-class tax cut, the Clintonites had imposed new taxes. In such matters as gays in the military, health care, and affirmative action, they had exhibited a remarkable insensitivity to the public dislike of federal efforts at social engineering. Clinton himself had come to be regarded with widespread animus, for both his personal and his governing style.

Finally, dismally, the promise of sweeping change petered out in the debacle of the 103rd Congress's closing months, in which weak Democratic support, strong Republican opposition, and chronic White House ineptitude had combined to kill health care and political-financing reforms. When Congress went home two weeks ago, it left behind an exhausted, battered administration. "I had a dream the other night," Secretary of Health and Human Services Donna Shalala told me. "Congressmen were running out the door, and Harold Ickes and I were holding onto their legs, trying to pull them back, saying 'Please, you can't leave until you pass some kind of first step on health care.'"

For all this Clinton reaped the blame; he became, fairly or not, the great white albatross of his party. "He is a victim of this feeling out there," Don Sweitzer, the political director for the Democratic National Committee, explained. "He has become the person you can point to for your anger over the state of things, because he is the president." A liberal Democratic representative, who predicts "more Democratic losses than people think in the House," was more direct. "Clinton has come to symbolize the people's mistrust of government," he said. "Many of them feel duped by him, and these are people who tend to be swing voters." To the dismay of Democratic candidates, the 1994 elections were shaping up as a referendum on what was wrong with government, as symbolized by the leader of the Democratic Party. "People are disgusted at government," said Tony Coelho, the former California congressman whom Clinton has made the de facto Democratic national chairman, "because government misled them, and they feel very strongly about it, and what they sense is that Clinton has not delivered on change."

There did not seem much that the president and the national Democratic Party could do about all this. Clinton was so profoundly unpopular, particularly in western and southern states, that many Democratic candidates refused to be seen in public with him, and were running television commercials assuring voters that they, too, opposed the president's policies. For weeks, Clinton had been arguing privately that he should go on the offensive—that the White House should mount an aggressive campaign in defense of his record, pointing to legitimate achievements like the deficit-reducing 1994 budget, the Family Leave Act, the National Service Corps, and the 1994 crime bill as evidence that the administration was living up to its grand campaign promise of change. But among the president's own advisers there was deep concern that a Clinton offensive would only serve to intensify the albatross effect.

"We had trouble," Coelho told me. "What was happening was that our people were trying to fight on a local basis, which is the way most off-year races are fought, and the Republicans were trying to elevate the election to a national anti-Clinton election and make all our candidates run as Clintonites, and they were trying to take it from the normal losses for the party in power in an off year to major losses. And they had convinced the press that this was indeed more than a normal off-year election, and the press was writing it, and the more the press wrote it, the more our Dems believed it. Our base was demoralized. Our members were frustrated and running scared, as opposed to aggressively defending. There was a psychology in place that we were having a hard time containing."

A senior White House strategist summed up the situation in similar terms:

"The Republicans were blessed with a situation in which they had complete control of the field, they had the issues on their side, they owned the game. They were running candidates who did not have to stand for anything except not to be Bill Clinton. Every race was dominated by a negative discussion about us. We did not have anything going for us. We had nothing."

In this bleak environment, the Contract with America struck many in the White House as something close to a gift from Heaven, delivered unto Clinton and the Democratic Party by one of God's more unlikely handmaidens, the scowling Old Testament figure of Newt Gingrich.

"We are absolutely grateful for it," senior presidential adviser George Stephanopoulos told me. "It clearly shows what they are for and why they have been blocking things in Congress for the past couple of years. They are blocking things not just for the sake of blocking things but because they have different ideas, and if people look at their ideas they will realize they are bad. There is now a clear contrast in the 1994 race, and the president will be out there several days a week between now and Election Day drawing a clear contrast between the start he has made in getting Congress to work for ordinary people and the Republican alternative, which is taking us back to trickle-down economics and Reaganomics."

What the Contract with America did, White House strategists figured, was give Democratic candidates a chance to shift the conversation, at least slightly, away from the subject of Bill Clinton. "All of a sudden, Dems out there who had nothing to run on except defending Clinton—all of a sudden, they had something else to run on, and, in so doing, could get an audience to accentuate the positive side of the administration's record," Coelho said. "If the Republicans hadn't done this, the whole conversation would still be the Republicans going anti-Clinton and us defending Clinton, which is not a winning conversation for us."

According to Coelho, the Democrats first learned of the Contract's broad outline in August. "We realized right away they were giving us a softball," Coelho said. "So we immediately went into gear and started coming up with the data on what this would mean." By September 20, a week before the Contract was actually unveiled, Sperling's National Economic Council office had churned out a not-for-distribution "Preliminary Budget Analysis of House Republicans' Contract with America," a twenty-four-page argument setting forth the essential points of what would become the Democratic offensive: that the Contract represented a return to Reaganomics, with tax cuts for the wealthy at the expense of the middle class; that the Republicans' plan to balance the budget while simultaneously cutting taxes would necessitate a trillion dollars' worth of budget cuts over a five-year period; and that the only way the Republicans could achieve those savings would be to dramatically reduce Medicare or Social Security, or both, since these two huge entitlement programs make up fully half the projected budget for the fiscal year 2002.

◆ ◆ ◆

The first unsubtle clue that Gingrich's gift was not going to be the salvation that the Democrats were hoping for came the first time the president took the offensive outside Washington. On October 11, Clinton went to Dearborn, Michigan, to speak to a group of workers at a Ford Mustang plant. Standing in front of a giant Ford emblem, he derided the Republicans' proposal as "the Contract *on* America": "I hope the American people will have a simple answer to this contract. We've been there. We've seen that. We've tried it. And we will not be fooled again. No one would want to go back to the days when we exported jobs, not products. No one would want us to go back to the days when the deficit was exploding and our economy was going downhill. That is exactly the decision that all of you are going to have to make on November eighth: whether we keep going in the right direction or go back to the nineteen-eighties' trickle-down economics."

The event should have been a hit. The American auto industry is once again enjoying fat times, and the Dearborn plant is running at full tilt. The United Auto Workers had secured a paid morning off so that members could attend the president's speech. Before the speech, White House officials had told reporters to expect a crowd of four thousand. According to press reports, however, fewer than a thousand workers bothered to show up, and the *New York Times*'s Michael Wines called their response to Clinton's words "lackluster." To make matters worse, the local Democratic candidates Clinton had come to Michigan ostensibly to help treated him like a leper. Representative Bob Carr, who was trailing the Republican candidate, Spencer Abraham, in the race for Michigan's open Senate seat, declined two opportunities to stand next to Clinton, and made a point of telling reporters, "I did not invite the president here." Lynn Rivers, the Democratic candidate for the congressional seat of Representative William D. Ford, a Democrat who is retiring, skipped a White House invitation to join the president at a gathering with union officials.

What made Dearborn a sign of catastrophe, rather than merely a humiliation, was the fact that Michigan auto workers are exactly the sort of voters the Democrats are trying to reach with their last-ditch effort. Although White House officials like to talk about the Gingrich opening as an opportunity to galvanize great numbers of voters, it is doubtful whether many of them really believe that. The truth is that the entire Democratic campaign over the next few weeks— featuring more presidential speeches, a blizzard of demagogic television commercials accusing the Republicans of secretly plotting to cut Medicare, and the reprise of Vice President Gore's 1992 role as attack dog—is designed solely to scale back the scope of disaster, to arouse enough traditional Democratic voters, such as unionized factory workers, so that losses will be kept to a minimum on November 8. "This whole thing is about motivating our base to cut our losses," Coelho told me. "For us to activate our base, this is exactly what we need. Our base understands Reaganomics totally. We'll remind them what it was like in the eighties."

In attempting to recast the 1994 elections as Reaganism versus Clintonism, as the eighties versus the nineties, the Democrats may have seized their only chance to turn the conversation at least partly away from the subject of Clinton. But in so doing they have grasped a weapon that cuts against them as much as for them. "I hate to see us encourage people to start comparing how they feel about the Reagan era and the Clinton era," Al From, the director of the centrist Democratic Leadership Council, one of whose founding fathers was Bill Clinton, told me. "That will give Democratic loyalists energy, but that's all." From sounded as if he were mystified by the White House political thinking. "They think people hate Ronald Reagan, but I don't think people do," he said. "People like him. And the people who buy the notion that you can't balance the budget and cut taxes at the same time are the forty-three percent who voted for Bill Clinton in the first place."

One of the Democrats' top political strategists regards the president and his senior White House advisers as hopelessly self-deluded. "They don't see the true scope of it," he told me. "The president and his political people do not understand what has happened here. Not one of them ever comes out of that compound. They get in there at seven A.M. and leave at ten P.M., and never get out. They live in a cocoon, in their own private Disney World. They walk around the place, all pale and haggard, clutching their papers, running from meeting to meeting, and they don't have a clue what's going on out here. I mean, not a clue."

Both Stephanopoulos and Coelho told me they were sure that the Republican ideas, as outlined in the Contract with America, were unpopular with voters. Democratic pollsters had conducted extensive surveys and several focus groups on the subject, they said, and the answers always came back the same. "People don't want to go back to those economic policies," Stephanopoulos said. The result of the polls, he said, indicated strong disapproval of the Republicans' ideas. "It was not close," he said.

What Stephanopoulos did not mention was that the Democratic pollsters had framed key questions in ways bound to produce answers the president presumably wanted to hear. When the pollsters asked in simple, unadorned, neutral language about the essential ideas in the Republican agenda—lower taxes, a balanced budget, term limits, stronger defense, etc.—respondents approved in large numbers. "If we asked a question that said 'Do you support balancing the budget and giving a tax credit to people who have children?' people supported them overwhelmingly," explained Celinda Lake, a Democratic pollster, who conducted surveys on the Contract with America in five congressional districts around the country.

But Lake knew from previous experience that voters readily believe the stereotype of Republicans' favoring tax breaks for the wealthy and cuts in Social Security and Medicare. And so, she acknowledged, she used this stereotype in her polling to, as she put it, "frame the question very powerfully." She gave me the specific language of one such question: "Candidate X"—the Republican— "signed on to the Republican Contract with their national leadership in Washington saying that he would support more tax cuts for the wealthy and increase defense spending, paid for by cuts in Social Security and Medicare. That's the type of failed policies we saw for twelve years, helping the wealthy and special interests at the expense of the middle class. Do you approve?"

When I suggested to Coelho that asking questions in such a loaded manner hopelessly distorts the picture of what voters want, he replied, "That's what polling is all about, isn't it? You poll to get a response. The Republicans polled to get a response, and we polled to get a different response, and we did." When I pressed the issue, he said huffily, "Ideas are not the issue. The ideas are wonderful. Of course the ideas are popular. Tell me, who would not support cutting taxes? Tell me, who would not support balancing the budget? Tell me, who would not support a strong defense? It's taking the ideas and putting them together and enacting them that is the problem. Ideas are not the issue. It is putting all these ideas together that is the issue. That is what the Contract is. The Contract isn't ideas. It's putting all the ideas together and saying 'We can do this' that's the issue."

But the ideas in the Contract do matter. The Contract itself is a silly, obvious gimmick. It binds the Republicans who signed it to nothing; they are promising only to consider such steps as passing a balanced-budget amendment, not to actually vote one way or the other. It purports to limit congressional terms of office but neglects to mention that Gingrich intends to put forward legislation that would protect current members of Congress through a grandfather clause; Gingrich and his fellow signatories are bravely promising to throw out the next generation of bums—not themselves. The ideas in the contract, however, are popular. That's why they are in there. The Contract was based on polls from its inception; every idea in it was there because Republican surveys told Republican politicians that people liked it.

"As we put the Contract together, we had input from all of our candidates in and out of the House," Representative Armey told me. "On each issue, we asked if it had good standing with the American people. There is not a single one that pulls less than sixty percent. We wouldn't write a contract that didn't have great standing with America. These issues have been around a long time, and have a long history of pulling."

The Republicans are counting on stereotypes, too. I asked Chuck Greener, director of communications for the Republican National Committee, if he was worried about the fact that some of the anti-immigrant, antiwelfare, antipoor legislation that the Contract calls for a Republican 104th Congress to vote on during its first hundred days might strike some voters as too harsh, too cold-heartedly Republican. Greener replied, "No, you're missing the point of it. We *know* that maybe the Dole soul of the party is showing here. We think it's time for that to show. We think the Dole personality—'I'm a mean son of a bitch'— is maybe something the American public *wants* at this time. We think the American public is feeling, We need guys like that up there. We need some mean sons of bitches in Washington. We've got too many of the other kind as it is. So people look at Dole and Gingrich and they think, We need more like you up there. They think, You say you want to take on welfare? Cool. Let's get a mean son of a bitch up there and do the job right."

As for the Democrats' hope that the Contract will anger voters who remember the Republicans' cynical bait-and-switch tactics on taxes in the past, Greener said, "Maybe the voters' attitude is, All right, you guys go ahead and promise me a tax cut and that's fine, because I know you're going to take away from me in the end what you give me today. But the other side isn't even promising to give me anything at all; it's just promising to keep on taxing me. Maybe with you I'll get something at least in the short run, and I'll take what I can get."

◆ ◆ ◆

Three weeks after the Clinton forces joined battle with Gingrich's marchers to remind voters, in the contrast between Bill and Newt, just what Democrats and Republicans stand for, every sign suggests that the voters perceive the distinction—and a majority prefer the hard-edged anger of Gingrich to the president who feels their pain. On October 12, a Times Mirror survey of registered voters found that 52 percent said they were more likely to vote for a GOP candidate next month; only the 40 percent who can be presumed to compose the diehard Democratic constituency said they would back a Democrat. The last time numbers like that came up was in 1954, when a Gallup poll shortly before Election Day found the GOP leading the Democrats 53 percent to 47.

These results indicate the real scope of Bill Clinton's problem, and his party's. Deflecting the national political conversation from Clinton personally does not help much, because the anger toward the Democrats is inspired not simply by a dislike of Clinton but by a dislike of liberal Democratic federalism wearing Clinton's face. The president could easily improve his own reputation with the voters before Election Day—given his performance skills, and also given his recent foreign-policy successes (so far) in standing down Saddam Hussein and restoring Jean Bertrand Aristide to power in Haiti. Through these triumphs, Bill Clinton has finally appeared strong and decisive in crisis. But even a Clinton rise in the polls is unlikely to benefit any other Democrats much next month. The 1994 races really are about ideas—some of them half-baked ideas, self-contradictory ideas, cynically arrived-at ideas, perhaps, but ideas all the same.

In 1954, at the last moment the Democrats came back. They went on to regain control of the House, which they had lost in 1947, thus beginning the forty-year reign that the Gingrichites hope to end this year. It is possible that 1994 will see a similar outcome. The combined efforts of Gingrich and Clinton to transform the elections into a national referendum may ginger up enough Democrats and scare enough swing voters to keep Gingrich out of the House Speaker's office, and perhaps even deny Bob Dole the Senate majority leader's seat. If that happens, some of the more sunny-sided citizens of 1600 Pennsylvania Avenue will ballyhoo the victory. They will be missing the point. Even modest GOP gains in November will serve to reinforce what the congressional Republicans already possess—the power to block most, if not all, of the legislation Bill Clinton needs to appear an effective president, while retaining the all-purpose alibi they have wielded so devastatingly this fall: It's a Democratic Congress, after all, so don't blame us. Whether their victory is big or small, they'll have the tools they need, and there's no doubt they'll have the will to use them. Gingrich's awkward speech on September 27 was not the culmination of a war but its declaration. If you thought the 103rd Congress was the last word in bloody-minded divisiveness, wait until you see the fratricidal 104th.

Bob Dole's Last Hurrah

◆ ◆ ◆

It was around sunset on the day before Halloween, a cloudy, windy evening in New Orleans, and Bob Dole was giving his second, and final, speech of the day. In his position—there were five days to go until the election, and he was still trailing Bill Clinton almost everywhere in the country—he should have given four or five speeches that day. But he didn't want to do that, and so he hadn't. He was doing only what he wanted to do now. The day before, he had quit campaigning, again after only two speeches, in midafternoon, in order to beat the curfew at National Airport, in Washington, to which he insisted on returning so that he could spend the night in his own bed. His advisers had protested, but he had ignored them. "National, here we come!" Dole had shouted gleefully as he left his second speech in Denver to rush to the airport.

Dole was ignoring his advisers in other ways as well. His senior staff members were united in the belief that it was crucial for him to go out of the 1996 race on an upbeat note, offering voters an affirmative reason to choose him over Clinton. Every day, the campaign provided Dole with a positive, issues-oriented speech. The advance texts of these speeches were dutifully put up on the teleprompter and handed out to reporters. Sometimes Dole delivered the speeches, but more often he didn't. He used whatever he wanted from them and discarded the rest. He said, it seemed, whatever he pleased, whatever popped into his mind. What pleased him most was to rail against Clinton, so that was what Dole was going to do, no matter what his advisers said.

Standing on the stage at the Pontchartrain Center, in the suburbs of New Orleans, he faced a relatively small crowd that, as usual, had been wedged into an even smaller space to look large. He rambled and harangued and exhorted. He grinned grimly as he spoke, and he had a look about him that was faintly odd. Dole has always been a lean man, and the rigors of campaigning seemed to have slimmed him further, to a point approaching gaunt. His cheeks were hollow, almost sunken, advertising the fact of his seventy-three years. But they were also tanned, almost umber. The disjunction in Dole's appearance echoed in his words.

"I'll tell them the truth, and they'll think it's hell," he said. "How about that?

That's what Truman did, and he won, too. Remember, he was behind in the polls, and he won. Keep your eye on me. I'm going to be the second Harry Truman. You watch and see. . . . Now, remember, this is one of my home states, because a long time ago I was at Camp Polk, Louisiana, marching around there in the summertime. Boy, it was hot. It was hot. Even when you're twenty years old, it was hot. But I learned a lot. I finally found the base. I got lost for a few hours. But Clinton's been lost all his life. I was only lost a few hours. And if he were here today you could join his retirement party right here. . . . This is D Day. This is decision day. November 5, not far away. . . . I've always kept my word. And my colleagues in the Congress or wherever else I've been, regardless of their political affiliation or party affiliation, will tell you that Bob Dole keeps his word. Bob Dole keeps his word. Keeps his word. And I know that there are some who say that character doesn't make any difference, that the public trust doesn't make any difference, that when you're president of the United States you can do everything you can get away with, when you're in the White House nobody cares. I don't believe it for a moment. I don't believe it for a moment. We're going to find out on November fifth."

As Dole was speaking, his campaign manager, Scott Reed, stood behind a blue curtain that made the backdrop for the stage, listening with half an ear to the candidate and ruminating on the final days of a nearly lost cause. Dole had accepted, Reed said, that he was most likely not going to win. "I give him the polling number every morning, and I give him the electoral strategy every morning," he said. "And I have told him—I tell him every morning—I say, 'It looks like we may not win.' And he says, 'You're right.'"

Reed shook his head and went on, "The truth is, nothing has changed for a long time. Four or five months. We were never able to jolt the race. We thought we jolted it when he left the Senate. Then we thought we jolted it with our convention. But we didn't, and we had a string of bad luck. The Clinton train trip was very successful, moved a lot of votes. Then came Saddam Hussein. *Boom!* Knocked us out of the news for seven days. Then Congress gives Clinton everything he wants. *Boom!* Knocks us down again. Then the Middle East blows up. *Boom!* Knocks us out of the news for four days. Every time we turned around— *boom!*—we're knocked on our ass." He paused, then added, "And it's hard to jolt a race against those guys. They're very, very good. Their negative ads were very successful, drove us into the ground. They shaped this race—they really did. They made it Dole-Gingrich and Medicare."

But if Dole knew that it was nearly impossible for him to win he still believed there was a chance, Reed said. Every losing presidential campaign has its forlorn hope. Usually, it is a tactical hope—that their voters will turn out in vast numbers and the other side's will stay home, that the precise, magical combination of states will all fall together to pick the electoral lock. Dole shared that hope, of course (politicians are gamblers, and while they believe devoutly in the odds, they also believe in the million-to-one shot coming home), but his larger dream was much more personal. He believed that at the last minute millions of voters would look at the choice facing them and would suddenly decide that they could not vote for a dishonest man over an honest one. This was always the bottom-line strategy of the Dole campaign, and the fact that it had never been realized was a mystery to Dole. (It was also a mystery to George Bush, who tried and failed with the same approach against Clinton in 1992.) By this point, most of the people around Dole no longer believed in the hope—no longer believed that Dole had any real chance of winning—but Dole would not let it go. It wasn't really even about winning. He refused to accept that a man he regarded as a routine liar—a man he believed most voters regarded as a routine liar—was entitled to beat him. He would rant and rail, against all advice, because it simply galled him too much not to. "This is his campaign, and he's going to finish it the way he wants to," Reed said. "And nobody is going to stop him."

◆   ◆   ◆

Bob Dole's campaign for president was, in a sense, always a protest campaign: Dole's protest against everything—the culture of politics, the culture of his country, the values of a nation that appreciated a man like Clinton more than a man like Dole. And it was a protest against the business of campaigning itself. Dole always ran in a state of agitation against what he was doing every day, as if he were determined to have an opponent worthy of himself: himself. A successful campaigner is like a donkey on a treadmill. He does what he is supposed to do when he is supposed to do it, he masters the essential arguments of his side, he stays on message, he works sixteen hours a day, he obeys the advice of his aides. When political consultants talk about their favorite clients, their ideal campaigners, what they talk about are people who, as they say, take direction well. Nobody has ever taken political direction better than Clinton: He governs by it. Dole never took direction at all. He never learned to accept the standard relationship between the candidate and his manager, which is akin to the relationship between a defendant and his lawyer. And Dole never mastered the sloganeering of his side, let alone the core intellectual arguments. His formula for convincing voters of the validity of his plan for a 15-percent tax cut was emblematic of his entire approach. "If you have the will, you can do it," he would say. "I have the will and I can do it." It wasn't a defense of the tax-cut plan but an eccentric, quixotic refusal to defend the plan: Take me on trust, or don't take me at all.

Normally, in a presidential campaign the candidate travels with at least three or four senior advisers. Most of the time, Dole traveled with one senior adviser—his press secretary, Nelson Warfield. The other people on the plane were mere functionaries, and they were, in terms of Dole, children: political novices who were forty or fifty years younger than the senator. "He insisted on controlling the manifest, so he could control the road operation, so you had all along a plane operation that was kept separate from the rest of the campaign—it was just Dole and his press secretary and the kids," one senior staff member said. "And, obviously, having a presidential operation run in such a fashion that the most senior person on the plane is the press secretary is not how successful campaigns have been waged previously."

What Dole did in the last days of his run was the logical, final extension of his protest. Deeply frustrated, he turned completely away from his staff, and inward, toward himself—the only adviser he has ever really listened to—and waged what one senior campaign official called "a renegade campaign," running as much against his own operation as against Clinton. His staff gave him the usual advice given to losing candidates in the final stretch. "We all had the same desire, to have Dole speaking positively, not succumbing to the irresistible temptation to continually comment on Clinton's ethical woes—to go out classy," the campaign official said. "But it was as if he just said to himself, 'It's the final goddam weeks and I'm going to do this the way I think I can win, and to hell with what anyone else says.'"

Dole's speeches as he entered the last week of his campaign were Dole untrammeled. He abandoned any pretense of formal structure. He spoke in phrases and fragments that interrupted one another at his whim, like a call-waiting system gone awry, non sequitur giving way to non sequitur. Sometimes he seemed lost in his utterances, wandering through the boneyard of his mind, picking up an idea here, waving it for a moment, dropping it for another a few feet away.

"We learned in our little hometown—I see other hometowns represented here today—to keep our word," he said in Denver. "We also learned not to say four-letter words. My mother always had a bar of soap handy for that. But in any event, we learned a lot. We learned about honesty, integrity, and generosity and love and your family, and honor and duty and country—all these basic things we want to teach our children, we learned. That's what this election is all about."

When he lit upon a word or a phrase that struck him as especially important, he would yell it out two or three, or even four, times in a row. "You are the polls!

You are the polls! You are the polls right here!" he hollered at a crowd in western Tennessee. "The federal government is too big and spends too much of your money. Your money! Your money! Your money!"

But then in the same speech, and sometimes in the same paragraph, he would slide suddenly into the groove—into a funny, evocative riff, slashing Clinton's White House for its scandals. He would imitate the former White House security chief Craig Livingstone "down in the White House basement, drinking a beer," and calling for another round—"Set 'em up, boys. Have another beer!"—as he amused himself with FBI files. Or he would conjure up a picture of Al Gore pocketing "a hundred and twenty-two thousand dollars" at a Democratic fund-raiser in a Buddhist temple—"the Buddhist temple in Los Angeles, where you take a vow of poverty," he marveled in a California speech. "Creative. Innovative. There must be a laundromat next door. I wouldn't be surprised to see them holding fund-raisers in homeless shelters, the way this money is coming in."

◆ ◆ ◆

As the campaign entered its last few days, it achieved, finally, a sort of Dolean purity—a state of perfect antic formlessness. On Thursday morning, with four days to go, Dole, after deliberating with Reed on Wednesday night, made his last big decision as he was preparing to leave Tampa: to throw himself and his campaign into a final ninety-six-hour marathon of campaigning, winging across the country, making it up as he went along. "At that point, Scott Reed called us here, and said, 'It's on, put it together,'" a somewhat harried Dole campaign adviser in Washington said. "The official start is noon Friday. Between then and one A.M. on Saturday, there will be nine stops. Between Saturday morning and midnight Saturday, there will be another eight stops, ending in Las Vegas. Dole leaves Las Vegas for San Diego at five A.M. Sunday, and we don't have it mapped out from there, but my guess is there will be four or five stops in California, and then sometime Monday morning they will fly from California and hopscotch their way east, probably hitting Phoenix, Albuquerque—get into Russell, Kansas, late Monday night."

There was a kind of beauty in it all, a rare pleasure in seeing, in the age of triangulated politics, a candidate who had come so thoroughly apart from his packaging. But such a creature couldn't expect to fare very well against the most perfectly packaged candidate anyone had ever seen. The funny and sad thing is that it was, in the end, the breathtaking depth of Clinton's cynicism that fired Dole's last hope. The Dole adviser said, "It is not so much a feeling of 'I can't believe I am losing to this guy' as it is 'I can't believe a guy who is this much a phony and who has this sheer magnitude of ethical scandals all around him is going to be able to pull this election off.'" And it was this emotion that drove Dole forward with a freedom, and even a kind of joy, in his final days.

His own people were saying that it probably wouldn't be enough against Clinton. Still, it would be closer than most people expected, the adviser said. The campaign's polls showed the race had finally begun to significantly tighten. "We're heading toward beating Bush in percentage, in electoral vote, and in the number of state victories," he said. "We're heading for a very respectable loss."

The adviser laughed. "It's renegade perversity against effective cynicism. And effective cynicism will mow down renegade perversity every time."

Class

◆ ◆ ◆

Taking time off from the *Washington Post*'s latest story about how the Riady family purchased FOB status, and tearing myself away from the *Washington Times*'s item on Roger Clinton's apparent reluctance to properly support his apparent love child, to read the unanimous decision by the Supreme Court to the effect that "petitioner, the current President of the United States," was not protected by his office from a lawsuit alleging that he one day had espied respondent, Paula Jones, at the Excelsior Hotel in Little Rock and had ordered a state trooper to procure Jones and bring her up to "a business suite where he made abhorrent sexual advances," I pondered what exactly was the elusive quality that set this White House crowd apart from their predecessors. Class, I decided. That's what it is. They're just so classy.

Actually, the case of *William Jefferson Clinton v. Paula Corbin Jones* is all about class, his class and hers. His is the class that did not go to Vietnam, and for the most part did not forthrightly refuse to go to Vietnam either, because one must preserve one's "political viability." Hers is the class that did go, and that, in 57,000 instances, lost not merely political but mortal viability. His is the class that came of age possessed by a conviction that it was equipped to remake the world, a destiny so manifest and so manifestly good that those who shared it comprised a new elite, the elite of the deserving, privileged for the sake of us all.

When a member of this class does something a little eyebrow raising—makes $100,000 on a sweetheart commodities deal, say, or exercises his droit du seigneur with a working girl—the better sort of people avert their eyes. It would be not merely unseemly to notice, it would be wrong. Unpatriotic, really. Thus, when Paula Jones, a citizen of the other class, accused Bill Clinton of exposing himself to her in a hotel room and asking her to bestow upon his person a particularly intimate kiss, she was greeted with a vast silence punctuated by occasional expressions of open class contempt. She was, said *Newsweek*'s Evan Thomas, "some sleazy woman with big hair coming out of the trailer parks." (To Thomas's credit, he later took a swipe at himself in print for this "elitist attitude.") James Carville sneered "drag $100 through a trailer park and there's no telling what you'll find." The establishment press mostly ignored Jones, and the feminists who had championed Anita Hill mostly dismissed her. Jones was a gold-digging tart, ran the storyline. (And so in some circles it still runs; the *New York Times,* in its coverage of the Supreme Court decision, saw fit to print a profile shot of Jones looking slightly come-hitherish in a tight sweater.) She had her nerve.

She certainly had. She had the nerve to fight the president of the United States all the way to the Supreme Court. And her nerve is all the more admirable for the modesty of her desires. All she wanted was a little recognition that even people like her have rights. Tight sweater and distinguishing characteristics aside, *Clinton v. Jones* is about egalitarianism.

"Petitioner, William Jefferson Clinton, was elected to the presidency in 1992, and reelected in 1996," wrote Justice John Paul Stevens in the Court's opinion. "In 1991 he was the governor of the State of Arkansas. Respondent, Paula Corbin Jones, is a resident of California. In 1991 she lived in Arkansas, and was an employee of the Arkansas Industrial Development Commission. . . . These allegations principally describe events that are said to have occurred on the afternoon of May 8, 1991, during an official conference held at the Excelsior Hotel in Little Rock, Arkansas. The governor delivered a speech at the conference; respondent—working as a state employee—staffed the registration desk. She alleges that State Trooper Danny Ferguson persuaded her to leave her desk and to visit the Governor in a business suite at the hotel, where he made abhorrent sexual advances that she vehemently rejected."

Stuart Taylor Jr., in his climate-changing *American Lawyer* article defending Jones's case, concluded that "the evidence supporting Paula Jones's allegations of predatory, if not depraved, behavior by Bill Clinton is far stronger than the evidence supporting Anita Hill's allegations . . . against Clarence Thomas," and included "clear proof . . . that then-governor Clinton's state trooper-bodyguard . . . took Jones to meet Clinton—the boss of Jones's boss—alone in an upstairs suite at Little Rock's Excelsior Hotel, for the apparent purpose of sexual dalliance."

But Jones apparently never would have forgotten her place to the extent of complaining about this had not Trooper Ferguson, and later Clinton's shills, besmirched (in Jones's opinion) Jones's reputation. Initially she asked not for monetary damages, but only for an admission by Clinton that he had met her in that hotel room that day, and that she had done nothing improper. And, initially, Clinton was prepared to agree; Jones's lawyers and Clinton's lawyer Bob Bennett settled on a statement in which the president would say that he did not recall meeting Jones "in a room," but would add that "I do not challenge her claim that we met there," and that Jones "did not engage in any improper or sexual conduct."

But the president's very brilliant advisers could not resist, as they can never resist, spinning the story their way, and they leaked to the press the untrue charge that Jones was settling because she knew her accusations would not stand up to examination. That tore it, and Jones sued.

Clinton's argument that Jones's case should be postponed until after he leaves office was nothing but an expression of the theory of the deserving class. In Justice Stevens's words, the president's claim was that "in all but the most exceptional cases, the Constitution affords the president temporary immunity from civil damages litigation arising out of events that occurred before he took office." In other words, Clinton couldn't be sued like any other citizen, even for actions taking place out of and utterly unrelated to office, because he was too valuable to the country. He couldn't be sued because he had to preserve his political viability.

No, said the entire Court, in tones of polite astonishment. "We have never suggested that the President, or any other official, has an immunity that extends beyond the scope of any action taken in an official capacity." It seems odd that the Supreme Court had to inform the president that, as it noted in the syllabus of its opinion, "the President . . . is subject to the same laws that apply to all citizens," and that the imperative to do public good does not exempt one from those laws. Clinton thought that he was hitting on a woman, but he was hitting on an American.

The Reich Stuff

◆ ◆ ◆

I claim no higher truth than my own perceptions. This is how I lived it.
—FORMER CLINTON LABOR SECRETARY ROBERT B. REICH, IN A NOTE TO
THE READER IN HIS MEMOIR, *Locked in the Cabinet*

"For God's sake, man, get a grip on yourself!" The secretary of labor's voice cut like the crack of a whip through the cabinet room. Robert B. Reich stood towering over the treasury secretary, who lay curled in the fetal position on the fine Aubusson carpet, whimpering and mewling like a kitten. "And take your thumb out of your mouth, Bentsen! You're in the presence of the president of the United States!" Robert B. Reich raked one coolly calculating ice blue eye around the room. The president was ashen. The vice president was oaken. The other cabinet secretaries were on the edge of panic, the fear shining in the little pig-eyes that were the only sharp features in their pasty, plump faces.

Robert B. Reich wheeled on his heel. "You, and you!" he barked at two hulking Secret Service agents. "Get the secretary of treasury out of here. Take him by the underground tunnel to his office. Take the president's doctor with you. I don't care what you have to pump into this man—coffee, B complex, oxygen, extract of pineal gland—but I want him clean, sane, and sober by 0100, ready to face Congress." The agents glanced at each other and traded a quick, satisfied grin. "Blue Steel to the rescue again," said one, referring to Robert B. Reich by his Secret Service code name. As they were bearing the broken, drunken treasury secretary from the room, the craven figure turned back to face Robert B. Reich. "Bob, I know I've never played straight with you, but I'm begging you now. Only you stand between us and the greatest global depression in history. Please, Bob. I'm not asking for the country. I'm asking for myself. It would kill me to be poor."

"Get him out of here now," Robert B. Reich snapped to the agents, his Lincolnesque features contorted in a grimace of disgust. He turned to the others and motioned for them to sit. Robert B. Reich folded his own lean six-foot-four frame into his chair, and for a moment the silence in the room was nearly absolute, punctuated only by the nervous drumming of the president's fingers on the cabinet tabletop: *pocketa-pocketa-pocketa*. Robert B. Reich faced the frankly frightened leader of the free world. "Sir, the situation is this," he said. "In one hour, the foreign gold markets will open, and we will see the greatest run on the American dollar in history—unless we do exactly what I say. Now, first . . ."

◆　◆　◆

"Bob? Bob? Did you hear me? Hellooo. Earth to Bobby, anybody home?"

"Wha? Huh?" said Robert B. Reich. He looked at the president with blank wonder. The other cabinet secretaries were snickering. "Christ, he's got the attention span of a four-year-old," Bentsen whispered loudly to Christopher. Robert B. Reich blushed scarlet. "Bob, what I was asking was, do you know what the unemployment figures for next month are going to show?" the president asked.

"Uh, no, uh, I mean yes, I mean I'm sure I have it here somewhere." Robert B. Reich leaned hastily forward to fumble through the pile of papers in front of him and watched with paralyzed horror as a hand that seemed to be attached to somebody else's flailing arm knocked over his coffee cup, sending a brown stream onto Health and Human Services Secretary Donna Shalala's lap. "Oh, God! Bob, you idiot," wailed Shalala, leaping up, "that's the third time this month!" Robert B. Reich found himself, for the third time in a month, rushing from the cabinet room as fast as his legs could propel him, the sound of laughter ringing in his burning ears.

◆　◆　◆

"Oh, God! Bob, you animal! That's the third time this hour!" Robert B. Reich looked fondly at Clarissa Woods-Bourke, the beautiful and brilliant Oxford-educated sociobiologist who had replaced Shalala in order to rebuild a department shattered by scandal. Clarissa stretched sinuously, so that her long, lithe body rippled against Robert B. Reich's own lanky yet muscular form. "You're ruining me," she murmured. Robert B. Reich allowed himself the rare luxury of a satisfied smile. Famous in Washington as his own harshest critic, he almost never let himself think any but the most self-critical thoughts. But Clarissa made him feel good about himself. He hadn't felt this way in years—not since those fourteen terrible months in the Hanoi Hilton.

Robert B. Reich's wrist chronometer, the gift of a grateful queen, gave voice to its subtle alarm: *"pocketa-pocketa, ching! pocketa-pocketa, ching!"* "Well, rest in the ruins, honey," he said. "I've got to go face the dogs." Ten minutes later, showered, shaved, and impeccably but simply dressed in his invariable uniform of gray flannel suit and crisp white shirt, Robert B. Reich stood before the White House press corps. He stood tall.

Robert B. Reich stared down at the slavering pack before him. It was after eleven A.M., so he knew that two-thirds of them were already drunk. Some of them were still clutching their snifters of expense-account brandy in their pudgy ink-stained hands. The air was a thick, ugly funk made up from the stench of the reporters' unwashed bodies and the illegal Cuban cigars they favored. The over-powered air-conditioning system labored noisily but in vain: *pocketa-pocketa-urp-pocketa-pocketa-urp.* The reporters leered at him, and several of the older and drunker ones were literally smacking their lips in anticipation. The questions came in a great, shrieking wave: "Mr. Secretary, why are you so stupid?" "Mr. Secretary, if this administration can't handle a simple task like ending poverty in one week, why shouldn't the president be impeached?" "Mr. Secretary, you sorry bastard, how can you even stand to look at yourself in the mirror?"

Robert B. Reich waited for the poltroons to pause for breath, and when they did, he was ready. "You miserable curs," he said. "There isn't one of you fit to lick the boots of this administration. Remember this: You may hate your country, but the rest of us love it. And we'll keep on doing our level best to move it forward, and you may be damned." Robert B. Reich turned to leave, and a snarling, slob-bering weasel-faced fellow, a *Times*man by the look of him, leaped up to land a sucker punch from behind. Without even glancing in the coward's direction, Robert B. Reich lashed his powerful right arm backward, catching his misguided assailant on the point of his chin and sending him in a crumpled heap to the floor. Robert B. Reich walked on.

For the second time that day, as he strode in long, manly strides through the mess of scribblers slinking away, Robert B. Reich allowed a slight smile of satis-faction to play across his craggy face. He had less than a minute to get to the sit-uation room. Pyongyang had finally done it. The missiles were already in the air.

The Artful Dodger and the Good Son

◆ ◆ ◆

It turns out that Albert Gore Jr. was not the model for Oliver Barrett IV, the sensitive yet two-fisted, foul-mouthed yet well-bred athlete cum poet who starred in Erich Segal's romantic tale *Love Story.* To be precise, Gore was partially the model for Barrett, but only the uptight-young-preppie-struggling-with-an-overbearing-old-poot-of-a-father part, not the cool stuff.

The vice president's suggestion, as reported in *Time* magazine, and his belated, clumsy retraction of the claim that he and his then-girlfriend Tipper had been the models for Segal's tedious young lovers should not have been a consequential event. Yet Segal's correction of Gore was given substantial play in Sunday's *New York Times,* and the subsequent admission and apology from Gore's office made the *Times,* the *Los Angeles Times,* and the *Washington Post.*

What this suggests is that Gore may, in one critical sense, have a good deal harder time of it in his run for the presidency than did his boss. The critical sense is in the area of, pardon me, honesty. In this regard, Clinton has been from early on in the national eye a settled figure. A hard core of supporters thinks the world of him, and an equally hard core of detractors can't stand him, but most voters are comfortable with a more ambivalent view. They don't believe that Clinton is very honest and they don't entirely trust him with the running of the country, but they think he is in other ways decent—well-meaning, big-hearted, open-minded—and they figure he is smart enough to do more or less what they want him to do, if they keep an eye on him.

This dynamic has twice elected Clinton and twice denied him a majority, putting him in the White House but also, by means of a Republican Congress, keeping him in his place. And this dynamic has been unchanging. If Clinton's successes in office have not erased doubts about his integrity, neither have his scandals much heightened those doubts. Nothing has seriously affected the basic equation—not the story of the young Clinton and the Vietnam draft, nor Gennifer Flowers, nor Whitewater, nor Hillary Clinton's commodities deal, nor the travel office affair, nor Paula Jones, nor Ron Brown's fly-me Commerce Department, nor Johnny Chung, nor Charlie Trie, nor Mike Espy's indictment, nor Henry Cisneros's.

Figuring they had Clinton's number from the beginning, the voters have always accorded him a certain slack. Everyone knows, or thinks he knows, someone like Clinton: fast on his feet, full of big ideas and full of himself, in some ways immature, something of a rogue. Maybe a sincere guy, but also a guy who practices his sincere look in the mirror. When Clinton gets caught in even a very large fib, it isn't a revelation but a confirmation, and it is accordingly discounted. If Clinton had told reporters that he was the model for Oliver Barrett, everybody would have said: That's our Bill; next week he'll probably say he was the model for Ben Hur.

It's quite different with Gore. Gore is the good son, not the prodigal. He is not about the art of seduction; he is about the importance of being earnest. He is, in his public persona at least, a tremendous moralist—pious, even sanctimonious. Thus, when he gets caught in even a minor moral transgression, it is treated as news. It's a tricky business being a preacher, and politics has no bigger preacher than the man whose stated mission in life is to save the planet.

And Gore not only has the wrong persona to get away with every little thing, he has the wrong personality, too. Clinton is a true natural at manipulating language to his ends. Pinning down a misstatement in a Clinton statement is an exercise in deconstruction; and in the end, it often turns out that there is, tucked away in a clause, a neat little conditional that gives the president a neat little out.

Gore is a nonnatural; he has no ear for the music of evasion, obfuscation, and embellishment. He embarrassingly overplays his hand (as he did in his lachrymose Democratic Convention speech about his sister's dying of cancer teaching him the evils of Big Tobacco). He forgets to build his out (Clinton, telling the *Love Story* story, would have said himself that he was sure it wasn't true, and laughed at his own vanity before anyone else could have). He recites verbatim what is supposed to be his subliminal message. ("No controlling legal authority" was the exact equivalent of George Bush's "Message: I care.")

Al Gore has always been a very good student, but some things can't be learned, and artful dodging is one of them.

I Believe

✦ ✦ ✦

I believe the president.

I have always believed him. I believed him when he said he had never been drafted in the Vietnam War and I believed him when he said he had forgotten to mention that he had been drafted in the Vietnam War. I believed him when he said he hadn't had sex with Gennifer Flowers and I believe him now, when he reportedly says he did.

I believe the president did not rent out the Lincoln Bedroom, did not sell access to himself and the vice president to hundreds of well-heeled special pleaders and did not supervise the largest, most systematic money-laundering operation in campaign finance history, collecting more than $3 million in illegal and improper donations. I believe that Charlie Trie and James Riady were motivated by nothing but patriotism for their adopted country.

I believed Vice President Gore when he said that he had made dunning calls to political contributors "on a few occasions" from his White House office, and I believed him when he said that, actually, "a few" meant forty-six. I believe in no controlling legal authority.

I believe Bruce Babbitt when he says that the $286,000 contributed to the DNC by Indian tribes opposed to granting a casino license to rival tribes had nothing to do with his denial of the license. I believed the secretary when he said that he had not been instructed in this matter by then White House deputy chief of staff Harold Ickes. I believed him when he said later that he had told lobbyist and friend Paul Eckstein that Ickes had told him to move on the casino decision, but that he had been lying to Eckstein. I agree with the secretary that it is an outrage that anyone would question his integrity.

I believe in the Clinton standard of adherence to the nation's campaign finance and bribery laws, enunciated by the president on March 7, 1997: "I don't believe you can find any evidence of the fact that I had changed government policy solely because of a contribution." I note with approval the use of the word "evidence" and also the use of the word "solely." I believe that it is proper to change government policy to address the concerns of people who have given the president money, as long as nobody can find evidence of this being the sole reason. I believe the president has lived up to his promise to preside over the most ethical administration in American history. I believe that indicted former agriculture secretary Mike Espy did not accept $35,000 in illegal favors from Tyson Foods and other regulated businesses. I believe that indicted former housing secretary Henry Cisneros did not lie to the FBI and tell others to lie to cover up $250,000 in blackmail payments to his former mistress. I believe that convicted former associate attorney general Webster Hubbell was not involved in the obstruction of justice when the president's minions arranged for Hubbell to receive $400,000 in sweetheart consulting deals at a time when he was reneging on his promise to cooperate with Kenneth Starr's Whitewater investigation. I believe Paula Jones is a cheap tramp who was asking for it. I believe Kathleen Willey is a cheap tramp who was asking for it. I believe Monica Lewinsky is a cheap tramp who was asking for it.

I believe Lewinsky was fantasizing in her twenty hours of taped conversation in which she reportedly detailed her sexual relationship with the president and begged Linda Tripp to join her in lying about the relationship. I believe that any gifts, correspondence, or telephone calls and the thirty-seven postemployment

White House visits that may have passed between Lewinsky and the president are evidence only of a platonic relationship; such innocent intimate friendships are quite common between middle-aged married men and young single women, and also between presidents of the United States and White House interns.

I see nothing suspicious in the report that the president's intimate, Vernon Jordan, arranged a $40,000-per-year job for Lewinsky shortly after she signed but before she filed an affidavit saying she had not had sex with the president. Nor do I read anything into the fact that the ambassador to the United Nations, Bill Richardson, visited Lewinsky at the Watergate to offer her a job. I believe the instructions Lewinsky gave Tripp informing her on how to properly perjure herself in the Willey matter simply wrote themselves.

I believe that the *Washington Post,* the *Los Angeles Times,* the *New York Times, Newsweek, Time, U.S. News & World Report,* ABC, CBS, NBC, CNN, PBS, and NPR are all part of a vast right-wing conspiracy. Especially NPR.

I Still Believe

◆ ◆ ◆

I've just finished reading the six hundred pages of material released last Friday by Paula Jones's lawyers, and I've just finished watching Kathleen Willey on *60 Minutes,* and I've just finished reading Bill Clinton's statement that he didn't bother to watch Ms. Willey on TV but that he knows what she says isn't true anyway. And I still believe the president. Truly, madly, deeply, I believe. Also verily.

I believe that the president is "mystified" by Ms. Willey's claim that he sexually assaulted her when she visited him in the Oval Office on November 29, 1993, to ask him for a desperately needed job. I believe the president did not grab Ms. Willey, kiss her, touch her breasts, and place her hand on his genitals, against her will. I believe that Ms. Willey is perjuring herself to hurt the president, even though the record shows that she supported and liked Clinton very much, and continued to support and like him even after the alleged assault, and that she only talked in the end because she was compelled to by Jones's lawyers.

I believe Ms. Willey is, like Paula Jones and Gennifer Flowers and Dolly Kyle Browning and Sally Purdue before her, and like the women who will come after her, a bald-faced liar. If Monica Lewinsky sticks to her affidavit that she never had sex with the president, I believe her. If she instead confirms the long hours of recorded conversation in which she detailed a sexual affair with the president and affirmed her intention to lie in the affidavit—well, then, I don't believe.

I believe all this because I am assured of it by Robert Bennett, the president's sexual misconduct mouthpiece, which is a distinguished position. It is distinguished from David Kendall, his personal-finance corruption mouthpiece; from Lanny Davis, his campaign-finance corruption mouthpiece; from James Kennedy, his White House general scandal mouthpiece; from James Carville, his "independent" general scandal mouthpiece; and from Michael McCurry, his don't ask, don't tell mouthpiece. I believe that all presidents require, for the handling of daily press inquiries, enough mouthpieces to outfit the wind section of the National Symphony Orchestra.

I believe, as the White House whispering campaign already has it, that Ms. Willey is a bit nutty, and a bit slutty. I believe that, the way things are going, David Brock will write an article to this effect for *Esquire*.

I believe White House communications director Ann Lewis is right to suggest that Ms. Willey's desire to work in Clinton's 1996 campaign casts doubt on her claim that Clinton abused her in 1993. I also believed Ann Lewis in 1991, when she explained why Anita Hill continued to work for Clarence Thomas after he allegedly harassed her: "You don't know what it's like to be a young working woman, to have this really prestigious and powerful boss and think you have to stay on the right side of him, or for the rest of your working life he could nix another job." I believe Ann Lewis is not a rank hypocrite. I believe that it is not despicable for the president's henchmen and henchwomen to smear the reputations of others in order to protect their boss from allegations of misconduct.

I believe that Clinton-Gore fund-raiser Nathan Landow did not try to pressure Ms. Willey to lie in her deposition in the Jones case, and that there must be some perfectly innocent reason why, after Ms. Willey was subpoenaed in the Jones case, Landow's real estate company chartered a plane to fly Ms. Willey to Landow's Eastern Shore estate.

I believe Ms. Willey is lying even though her account of Clinton's amatory approach is remarkably similar to the account Ms. Jones offers of the Clinton modus operandi on May 8, 1991, in a room in the Excelsior Hotel in Little Rock, Arkansas. I believe Ms. Jones is lying even though her sworn account of what happened to her that day is supported, in graphic, pathetic detail, by sworn contemporaneous accounts from her sister, Lydia Cathey, and by her friends Pamela Blackard and Debra Lynn Ballentine. I believe Ms. Willey and Ms. Jones are lying even though their stories are buttressed by the sworn deposition of Judy

Stokes, alleging a similarly sudden and unwanted sexual approach by Clinton against a former Miss Arkansas, Elizabeth Ward.

I believe that L. D. Brown, Larry Patterson, and Roger Perry, three former Clinton bodyguards, were all lying in their sworn depositions in which they described, to varying but conforming degrees, Clinton as a sexual adventurer of great recklessness and a man who used the resources and perks of office to further his sexual pursuits.

I believe everybody is lying except my Bill.

A Pathetic Speech—and Untrue

◆ ◆ ◆

Well, now we know exactly what it takes to get our president to approach the act of telling the truth: a federal prosecutor and a posse of deputy prosecutors, a grand jury, the Supreme Court, the confession of his chief co-conspirator, the testimony of a couple of dozen other witnesses, the urging of his lawyers and his advisers, the ministering of the Rev. Jesse Jackson and, one assumes, the possession by the FBI of conclusive physical evidence.

Bill Clinton went on television Monday night and admitted that he had "misled people," and had given "a false impression" in his seven months of public denial of a sexual relationship with Monica Lewinsky. Because, you see, he did, actually, "have a relationship with Miss Lewinsky that was not appropriate." And, actually, this was not a good thing to have done: "In fact, it was wrong." And Clinton was "solely and completely responsible" for it.

Certainly true. You see, the president really sort of did give a false impression when, on January 26, he wagged a scolding finger and said: "I want to say one thing to the American people. I want you to listen to me. I'm going to say this again: I did not have sexual relations with that woman, Miss Lewinsky." He really kind of did mislead people when he lied under oath, lied on camera, lied in private, lied in public, lied to the nation, lied to his wife, lied to his friends, lied to his cabinet, lied to his staff, lied to his party, lied to the world, and sent out his staff and surrogates to lie on his lying behalf.

And, now that he mentions it, I guess our Bill really did do something a little bit wrong in exploiting a silly and star-struck young female employee as a sexual service station. And he maybe shouldn't have encouraged his girlfriend to join him in perjury. And he maybe also shouldn't have obliged Vernon Jordan and Bill Richardson and Betty Currie and Bruce Lindsey and the rest of the gang to help him hide his bit of Oval Office fun.

And it probably wasn't the perfectly moral thing, knowing that he was lying through his teeth, for the president to countenance a long and vicious campaign by his henchmen to savage those who were telling the truth. And it wasn't 100 percent appropriate to force all those innocent people to suffer through grand jury inquisition, and to trash the presidency, and to make fools out of Al Gore and Madeleine Albright and Paul Begala and James Carville and Mike McCurry and Ann Lewis and everyone else who insisted for seven months that the perjurer in chief was telling the truth. And, oh yes, groping Kathleen Willey when she came to the Oval Office to ask for a job was probably not a good thing to do. Maybe it wasn't right to lie about that also, and to sic the smear team on Kathy. Ditto Paula, ditto Gennifer. Sorry about all that.

No, not really. Our Bill has never really apologized for anything in his life, and he didn't now. He never used the words "I'm sorry," and he acknowledged "regret" only glancingly and euphemistically. Indeed, as he made quite clear, he wasn't sorry, except, as all adolescents are, for getting caught. His passing imitation of an apology lasted for all of one sentence. By contrast, he devoted nearly nine full paragraphs to offering excuses for his actions, to once again attacking Ken Starr and to urging that the mess he had created be put aside—without, of course, any punishment for himself. The poor boy, he let us know, has suffered enough. This speech wasn't a mea culpa. It was an everybody-else culpa. It was an insult. It was pathetic.

And it was a lie. Even in confessing his lying, Clinton lied. He said that in the Paula Jones deposition that started it all, he had given answers that were "legally accurate," but that he did not "volunteer information." What he was referring to was his answer to one question about sex with Lewinsky—sex as defined in narrow and confusing terms by a legalistic definition. In denying sex as defined, he may have managed to stay just barely inside the borders of what was "legally accurate." But Clinton was also asked a question in which sex was described in commonly understood language, not in legalese: "Did you have an extramarital sexual affair with Monica Lewinsky?" To this, the president simply and perjuriously replied: "No."

This man will never stop lying. To borrow a hyperbolic description of another of the century's historic prevaricators, every word he utters is a lie, including "and" and "the." He will lie till the last dog dies.

"Hairsplitting"

◆ ◆ ◆

On September 11, as he awaited the release of a report that would, quite credibly, accuse him of perjury, abuse of office, and obstructing justice, President Clinton, under cover of an apology, served notice that he was instructing his lawyers to "mount a vigorous defense, using all available appropriate arguments."

It is now clear what the president considers "appropriate": more lying. The euphemism is that the president's lawyers are engaging in "hairsplitting." No, they are engaging in lying, in perpetuating and elaborating Clinton's past lies, the lies he insists he regrets. In its depravity, in its cynicism, in its sneering disdain for the law and for truth, it is an astonishing thing to witness.

The central question in the Clinton–Lewinsky case is whether Clinton committed perjury in his January 17 deposition in the Paula Jones sexual harassment case, and later in his August 17 testimony to Starr's grand jury.

In the January deposition, Clinton flatly and repeatedly denied that he had any sort of sexual relations with Lewinsky. In his grand jury appearance, he admitted, vaguely, to an improper sexual relationship with Lewinsky, but continued to insist that he had not perjured himself in the January deposition. The president's lawyers pretend that Clinton's statements were not perjury because the sex acts that took place between the president and the intern (the latter performing oral sex upon the former) did not fit a tortured legal definition of sex that had been agreed upon by the court.

But here, so to speak, is the rub: Even under the definition of sex that provides Clinton with his tissue of cover, Clinton clearly did have sex with Lewinsky. The definition says that "a person engages in sexual relations when the person knowingly engages in or causes contact with the genitalia, anus, groin, breast, inner thigh, or buttocks of another person with an intent to arouse or gratify the sexual desire of any person." Lewinsky told the grand jury that in her ten sexual encounters with Clinton, the president did indeed knowingly engage in contact with her genitalia and breasts with intent to arouse or gratify.

Thus, Clinton's testimony in the Jones deposition was perjury even under the terms of the agreed-upon definition. And so was his testimony to the grand jury:

Q: The question is, if Monica Lewinsky says that while you were in the Oval Office, you touched her breasts, would she be lying?

A: That is not my recollection. My recollection is that I did not have sexual relations with Ms. Lewinsky . . . as I understood this term to be defined.

Q: Including touching her breast, kissing her breast, touching her genitalia?

A: That's correct.

On Sunday, Clinton's lawyers defended this perjury by uttering false statements across three networks. On ABC's *This Week,* Sam Donaldson reminded David Kendall of Clinton's grand jury statement denying that he had sexual relations with Lewinsky, as defined, "including touching her breasts . . . touching her genitalia."

"And you say that's not a lie," said Donaldson.

"That is not a lie," said Kendall. Oh yes, it is, and Kendall must know it is.

On *Meet the Press,* Tim Russert put a question to Charles F. C. Ruff, White House counsel: "Did the president lie before the grand jury when he said he did not have sex with Monica Lewinsky?"

Ruff: "Absolutely not. The president testified before the grand jury truthfully." Oh no, he did not, and Ruff must know he did not.

That Clinton, through his mouthpieces, continues to lie proves, finally, that he must be impeached. He must be impeached not merely because he is a pig and a cad and a selfish brute. He must be impeached not merely because he sexually exploited and then discarded an employee under his supervision, nor because he used government resources and personnel to facilitate and cover up his sorry little affair. He must be impeached not merely because he abused the office entrusted to him by the people.

He must be impeached because he shows an utter and absolute contempt for the truth and for the law he has twice sworn to uphold. He must be impeached because, in a judicial proceeding, he knowingly lied under oath with intent to deceive, because he was given a chance to correct that lie in a second judicial proceeding and he lied again, because he persists in lying even still. He must be impeached because, in his pathology, he does great and heartless violence to other people and to the nation, and because he has made it clear that he is perfectly prepared to do more violence. He must be impeached because to not impeach him is to declare that this is what we accept in a president. He must be impeached because we are a nation of laws, not liars.

Farmer Al

◆ ◆ ◆

He taught me how to clean out hog waste with a shovel and a hose. He taught
me how to clear land with a double-bladed ax. He taught me how to plow a
steep hillside with a team of mules. He taught me how to take up hay all day
long in the hot sun.

—VICE PRESIDENT AL GORE JR. IN THE *Des Moines Register,* MARCH 16, 1999, ON
HIS LIFE EXPERIENCES GROWING UP AS THE SON OF SENATOR AL GORE SR.

It wasn't yet dawn, a good two hours to go till first light, but young Al was already up, out of his warm little bed high up in the eaves of the Fairfax Hotel
on Embassy Row. He could see from the frost on the windowpane and the ice in
his wash basin that it was going to be another cold one. Al shrugged. He didn't
care. He had work to do, no matter the weather. That was the Gore way.

Moving fast, before the chill could seduce him back into bed, Al shrugged on
his shirt, a simple homespun linsey-woolsey smock. He jumped into his old
leather breeches and tied tight the piece of rope that held them up around his
waist. Some folks lately had taken to putting buttons and belts and even those
newfangled zippers on their trousers, but the Gores didn't hold with that sort of
thing. They didn't even entirely hold with left legs on their trousers. Up until a
few years ago, the Gores had always insisted that a right leg was enough for anybody. If God had meant for trousers to have two legs, He wouldn't have given us
the gift of hopping, the Gores had always said. But change comes to all places
sooner or later, even to the top floor of the Fairfax Hotel.

Al thought of the day that lay ahead. Farming was hard work, backbreaking
hard, and it never stopped. But it was good, honorable work, and there was
money in it, too. "And there's money in not doing it, too," Al's father, Senator
Al, liked to say. The Gore spread ran from the rich bottom land down by the
State Department, up through the loamy meadows of Massachusetts Avenue
clean to Spring Valley. And every acre of it was not farmed; it was subsidized
instead.

"Yep," Senator Al would say. "I could be raising corn on Dupont Circle and clover in Foggy Bottom, but the guvvamint would rather pay me not to do it. Seems a mighty funny way to spend the taxpayers' money. Gonna have to have the Agriculture Committee look into that one day." But he never did. It wouldn't have been the Gore way.

But enough mental woolgathering, thought Future Senator Al. It was time to herd the sheep over to Dupont Circle. Time to be doing some real woolgathering, Al riposted to himself with the easy wit that had won him the joshing nickname Oak Head among the other farmers' sons at St. Albans School for the Better Class of Boys. Al ran through the vast apartment. (The Gore farmhouse occupied six big rooms on the top floor of the Fairfax, and Al was proud of that; there weren't many farm families in Washington whose penthouses boasted views of sunrise and sunset.) Al grabbed biscuit and ham from the plate on the table and dunked it in the red-eye gravy in the skillet on the wood stove. He ate as he ran, just pausing to grab his trusty two-bladed ax from the umbrella stand.

As he called for the elevator boy to hold the door, Al heard the cock crow. He smiled. It was a Gore point of pride to make the morning elevator by the cock's first crow. Senator Al kept a cock handy, right there in the hallway, for just that purpose, and damned annoying it was to the other patrons of the Fairfax. Al shrugged. The Gore clan owned the hotel, so to heck with them.

In the lobby, Al saw that the hotel manager had sneaked some of that Louis XV furniture back in. Al couldn't abide the prissy Frenchified stuff. He figured that it was getting about time to take the two-bladed ax and clear the lobby again. His hands itched to do the job then and there, but there really wasn't time, not with slopping the congressional pigs, stacking the Supreme Court hay, and cutting the winter wheat down at the Spinster Reno's place.

The sun shone bright on Embassy Row. Al hoisted himself up into the seat of the wagon, pulled by his father's matched mules, Checks and Balances. He turned to his faithful servitor. "Drive, James," he said, and Carville gee-upped the mules out across the green, green grass of Massachusetts Avenue.

Starr Wars:
The Twenty-first Century

♦ ♦ ♦

Independent counsel Kenneth W. Starr has decided against giving Congress an interim report on his investigation of President Clinton. . . . Starr will submit a report only when—and if—he determines there is substantial and credible information that crimes have been committed.

—*Washington Post*, JULY 6, 1998

LETTERS TO THE EDITOR

September 17, 2011

The September 16 article by reporter Susan Schmidt concerning our client Mr. Bruce Lindsey's testimony on September 15 in his 732nd coerced appearance before Kenneth Starr's grand jury to the effect that the former president had—on or about May 2, 1998, August 8, 1998, March 17, 1999, May 12, 2000, February 27, 2001, December 11, 2002, and on all other occasions up to and including any conversations that may or may not have taken place on or about April 2, 2011—urged Mr. Lindsey to "stonewall till the last dog dies," was not based on information provided by Mr. Lindsey or his counsel. Therefore, it could only have been provided via the continued, illegal, and unethical leaking campaign that is being conducted by Mr. Starr. That this leaking campaign is in clear violation of Rule 6(e) of the Federal Rules of Criminal Procedure has been established by numerous independent legal experts (see "I Was a Slut for a Renegade Lawman: How the Media Lusts for More, More, More from Starr," by Steven Brill, *Brill's Judgment,* Summer beach issue, pp. 12–28).

Sincerely,

ROBERT BENNETT AND DAVID KENDALL,

Bennett, Kendall, Davis, Marsh, Clinton & Clinton Partners at Law

October 2, 2011

Just a quick note to say that I still have nothing to say, really. I am just sitting here and waiting for my turn and being very quiet. Also very good, not like some people.

With a deep and patient sincerity, your friend,

AL GORE

November 23, 2011

I tell you what Ken Starr is. Ken Starr's a sex pervert, that's what Ken Starr is. Sex! Sex! Sex! It's all he ever thinks about! I never think about sex my own self. I just think about Ken Starr. All the time! Day and night! Got a doll made up, looks just like him, do some stuff to that doll, make your teeth curl! Not sex stuff, though. Just good clean hatin' stuff. Let me show what I'd do to Ken Starr if he were here right now. Yow! I just bit my thumb off, how about that!? Yow! I bit my other thumb off! I'm gonna mail my thumbs to Ken Starr! What you think about that, Ken Starr? What you say now?

Forever yours,

JAMES CARVILLE

December 18, 2011

I would only like to say that my most esteemed and treasured dear friend Mr. Bill Clinton has a good imagination. He has vision. He can visualize. He can imagine a future that is different from the present. This is a quality that is profoundly important at this moment in our history when there is so much change going on, and I am of utmost confidence that this quality will enable my friend Mr. Bill Clinton to triumph over the deviationist and hegemonic forces of Mr. Kenneth Starr, who is an enemy of the people and whom we would know what to do with over here, you bet.

Yours in strategic partnership,

JIANG ZEMIN,

President, the New Democratic People's Republic of China and Taiwan

January 2, 2012

I was not dumped. Not, not, not. I am still the most important person in the world.

Until next week,

WILLIAM H. GINSBURG

February 20, 2012

Although I was pleased that the *Post* chose to so prominently review the book of memoirs *Girlfriends* (Random, Simon, Schuster, Bantam, Little, Brown & Bertelsmann), by my clients Monica Lewinsky (Mrs. Larry King) and Linda Tripp, I must say that I do not think that the choice of Maureen Dowd as reviewer was a fair one, nor do I think that the tone of Ms. Dowd's review ("Faster Pussycat! Kill! Kill!," December 29) at all reflected the nature of a book that other respected critics have hailed as "a work of healing and spiritual growth" (Linda Bloodworth-Thomason, *People*), and "an important artifact of a debased media culture" (Larry Sabato, *Harper's*).

Respectfully,

LUCIANNE GOLDBERG

Literary Agent

November 1, 2012

The characterization of our client Mr. Sidney Blumenthal by columnist Michael Kelly—a writer who makes no secret of his dislike for our client—as "a man who gave duplicity a bad name," and "Sid the Human Ferret," to repeat only two of Mr. Kelly's more recent in a long series of outrageous, false, and defamatory statements, was yet another clear violation of Rule 6(e) of the Federal Rules of Criminal Procedure.

Sincerely,

ROBERT BENNETT AND DAVID KENDALL

Bennett, Kendall, etcetera

That's Entertainment

◆ ◆ ◆

The news that Patrick J. Buchanan is seriously considering tossing his comb-over into the Reform Party ring is of course splendid. As we regard a race dominated by Al Gore, Bill Bradley, and George W. Bush (Tweedledull, Tweedleduller, and Tweedlejunior), we feel a sore need for electoral amusement. It is a long, long way to November, and we are not going to be able to sustain ourselves, entertainment-valuewise, with these three.

For real spectacle in our presidential melodramas, we depend on the Reform Party, which has never failed to delight since the very first day that Ross Perot made his way onto the national stage, barking like a dog and occasionally biting off small pieces of himself. What pleasures that man and his movement have given us—the tales of assassins and of plots to wreck weddings; the vice-presidential candidacy of Admiral James "Who Am I?" Stockdale; our first governor with a boa.

The bolting of Buchanan from the Republican to the Reform Party feels so right. Buchanan would be going home, going to where he has, in his heart, been all along. Here, in the funhouse that Ross built, everybody knows about the One World Order and a lot of people have actually seen the black helicopters. In the liberating air of Perotland, Buchanan will be all that he can be. Pat, unfettered. This is what we have been waiting for.

But is it enough? It is not. Candidate Buchanan is always entertaining—he is, after all, an entertainer—but his material is old. Pat, you've already told us that the Jews have all the money. (Actually, Pat, it's us, the Irish; we've got it all; we've just been very clever about hiding it.) No, we need something fresh.

And, there he is. Warren Beatty, enter stage left. Mr. Beatty penned a wonderful little penseé for the *New York Times* a few weeks ago. "Why Not Now?" the essay was entitled, and it was, for the heights of its vanity, the depths of its incoherence, and the reach of its banality, a thing of rare beauty.

Every word was to savor, beginning with the opening phrases: "Aware of my 35 years of liberal activism as a Democrat, some have urged me to spend 40 years of fame on a presidential campaign." This is a man who gets a telephone call from Barbra Streisand and thinks he hears America singing. This is a man who has been so long under the lights that he thinks fame is accomplishment. This is a man who believes his press clips, his agent, his manager, and his personal trainer when they tell him that the people pine for him. This is a man of whom it can be boldly asserted: He is no less intelligent than Alec Baldwin.

This is also a man, it turns out, who is almost (but not quite) too good for the job of saving the Democrats from their sorry selves. "I have no wish to diminish the capable, cautious centrists Mr. Gore and Mr. Bradley, who have unselfishly devoted much of their lives to public service when they could so easily have enriched themselves in the private sector, as I have," Beatty writes with plodding condescension. "But when a Roosevelt-Truman-Stevenson-Kennedy Democrat, comfortably continuing a career of writing and directing movies, accepts the megaphone tossed to him, it will be to challenge the present party to admit its timidity in protecting those who need help most."

And so, blah-blah on for almost another one hundred words to end the sentence, in the manner of a teenage girl's note about a reeely, reeely cute boy, with one long phrase written entirely in capitals. Mr. Beatty ends on a teasing note: "Stay tuned. We'll be back after this message." Back for what, it is not entirely clear. Beatty is reportedly favoring entry as a Democrat. But he could challenge Buchanan for the Reform Party slot. Beatty's presidential Web site suggests "a winning scenario: Beatty runs as a Democrat, later converts to the Reform Party." Whatever.

But, oh, Warren, accept that tossed megaphone. Let us have more, much, much more of this. Stand before us and grin that sixty-two-year-old boyish grin and let us join you in basking in you. Speak to us, Warren. Give to us your deepest thoughts, and as your lovely lips flap, we will listen to the wind whistle from ear to Beatty ear. Give us the real thing, Warren. We are tired of making do with a president who merely acts like an aging movie star. Give us a leader with some real numbers to boast about. Give us that scene from *Shampoo* on the evening news. Give us the logical conclusion of our politics. Give us the movies.

Conan the VP

◆ ◆ ◆

George Bush won Tuesday's debate by a nose—not his, the one Al Gore spent ninety minutes looking down. Both men came into this with a clear imperative: Bush had to show he was at least minimally competent to think through the decisions of leadership. He met his mark, handing in a performance that was by no means brilliant but adequate to convince open-minded voters that he is serious enough for the job. Gore had to show that he was something resembling a real, likable, more or less regular human being. He failed.

Gore was so programmed, so artificial, that it seemed as if he had been put together with an Identikit, hurriedly and in the dark. His face, with its leaps from oaken repose to plastic animation, looked like the mirror of a soul that has been through one cosmetic surgery too many. And what has happened to the poor man's body? How did Arnold Schwarzenegger get into Al Gore's suit? Someone needs to check the videotape on this, but I am pretty sure that Gore did not used to have a twenty-three-inch neck. It is, I think, fair at this point to ask whether the vice president is a step-in or perhaps a pod person.

Then there was Gore's unfortunate decision to, as Ann Landers used to advise girls, just be himself. That was the real Al up there—the class showoff smirkily displaying his superiority, lecturing, hectoring, interrupting, bullying. And, oh, the pained grimaces, the rolling of the eyes, the sighs! Every time Bush spoke, it seemed, Gore would haul up another great gust of oh-really-now from his lungs and blow it all over the stage, shaking his new Conan head and pursing his lips to show his frustration in being forced to witness such foolishness.

It was much like the most infuriating of all husbandly marital-argument tactics. You know the one—where you play the part of the patient but pained party in the obvious right, too much a gentleman to say that your wife is spewing pure rubbish, but communicating utter contempt through creative breathing. In marital circles, this usually culminates in a scene like this:

SHE: With a full head of steam, perorating.
HE: Rolls eyes. Grimaces. Makes noise like steam escaping radiator bleed valve.
SHE: "What did you say?"
HE: "I didn't say anything."
SHE: "You sighed."
HE: "Excuse me. I wasn't aware that sighing was a federal offense."
SHE: "!!XX!, Jack."

All in all, an unattractive performance, and damaging to Gore. But was it enough? Not nearly. If Bush is to win, he must in the coming days and debates:

• Keep playing the seven-years card, hard. Bush showed Tuesday night that he finally has a handle on the core of the race for the undecideds. That core consists of an argument revolving around two issues, Social Security and health care. Gore talks a good game on these subjects, but he has a real weakness: He is the number two in an administration that for seven years has failed to address these problems. Bush hammered Gore on this failure, and he should hammer more. To Gore's every promise, Bush needs to say, as he did Tuesday, "Yeah? Why haven't they done it for seven years?"

• Keep studying. Bush was better than ever on substance but still barely good enough. In the next debate, he must get to the next level; he must display a knowledge of the issues (his own issues at least) that goes beyond bare-bones set pieces.

• Make 'em laugh. Having established a measure of gravitas, Bush can now afford to display his easy wit and genuine good humor. Nothing will more effectively highlight Gore's priggishness.

• Turn the argument on taxes. Gore is giving Bush a great opportunity by harping on the charge that Bush's tax plan would give "breaks to the wealthiest one percent." Bush should embrace the fight, to remind voters that his tax plan gives breaks to all people and that Gore's plan only gives breaks to selected people—often people who are doing what the government wants them to do with their lives. If mom and dad in a $78,000, two-kid household both work and put the kids in day care, the Gore plan gives them a break—but if mom stays home with the kids, forget it. Bush's plan covers everyone; Gore's covers only "the right people." That's an effective counter to "the wealthiest one percent."

Clinton Versus Bush

• • •

There are several less than fully flattering reasons one can point to for the steady and large gains in public opinion made by President Bush: (1) He benefits from surpassing exceedingly low expectations; (2) he benefits from surpassing an exceedingly low predecessor; (3) he benefits from an easy and shallow charm, which is useful in winning over an easy and shallow press corps; and (4) he possesses the narrow mind's narrow focus, which naturally concentrates his administration's energies and the public's attention on the priorities of his agenda.

All of this is true, but there is more to Bush's good times. There is, of all things, intelligence. Bush is, on one level, no toy rocket scientist. "Is our children learning?" he asked during the campaign. Oh, they is, but not, we hope, grammar from you, sir. As it happens, the level on which Bush is not intellectually impressive is the only one that most journalists respect: verbal intelligence, the ability to understand and manipulate logic and language. This is precisely the sort of intelligence Bush does not possess, and so, many journalists stupidly thought of Bush as, well, stupid. I include myself in this and hereby renounce and regret my repeated past use, in connection with Bush, of the word "pin-head."

What Bush does possess is political intelligence—the ability to understand and manipulate people and situations. Verbal intelligence and political intelligence are not necessarily connected: Think of the Mayor Daleys, father and son. It appears that this is so with Bush. The best evidence of this is that he has shown a grasp of the same essential dynamic of politics that brought success to his immediate predecessor—the dynamic of triangulation.

What Bill Clinton knew and what it seems Bush knows is that there are three groups of voters: a core who will vote for you if, and only if, you satisfy their nonnegotiable ideological demands; a contrapuntal anticore, whom you can never win over but whom you may discourage; and swing voters. To win, you must satisfy the core; blunt the drive and reach of the anticore; and make yourself minimally acceptable to a majority of the swing.

Obvious, of course, but in practice, not so. Clinton brilliantly grasped the subtleties of the thing. He understood that (a) the core's nonnegotiable needs were actually very few; meet those needs absolutely and always and the core would grant you vast leeway on every other issue; (b) the post-'60s Democratic Party, forgetting this, had assumed all sorts of demands to be nonnegotiable and had thereby saddled itself with all sorts of unpopular positions (in areas such as welfare, crime, and use of military force); thus (c) making it impossible for it to win a majority of the swing. So Clinton made himself the unwavering champion of his core's nonnegotiables (affirmative action, unfettered abortion, identity group representation in the distribution of power and perks). Everything else he threw up for grabs, and in the process threw away all the bad old issues that kept Democrats marginalized, and won back the swing.

Bush is now doing the same thing in reverse. Like Clinton, Bush knows that he must satisfy his core's nonnegotiables; he has moved unwaveringly to do this, most importantly on abortion and on taxes. Like Clinton, he knows that most of the swings want a nondivisive, "nice" president, and that giving ground on contentious issues will please the swing, weaken the standing of the anticore, and be tolerated by the core.

Consider Bush's support for an end to racial profiling in law enforcement. The core might regard that as giving in to race demagoguery, but it doesn't regard this as a nonnegotiable. To Bush's anticore, though, racial profiling is a vital concern—in fact, a nonnegotiable. The swings, meanwhile, just don't want to waste time and energy fighting about the thing. Thus, with one move, Bush's administration weakened its anticore, which is depending heavily on selling the canard of Bush as a racist president, and pleased the swing, while not losing the slightest support with its core.

That is politics played on a high and nuanced plane of intelligence, the sort of level that signifies a natural ability—natural political smarts. George W. Bush: smart guy. Who knew?

IV

⋅ ⋅ ⋅

Wars
and Peace

Before the Storm

◆ ◆ ◆

BAGHDAD—Every once in a while during debate in the Iraqi National Assembly, a delegate or two will actually rise to disagree slightly with the motion put forward. It is a way to show this is a real parliament and not 250 rubber stamps for Saddam Hussein. But the special session called for the morning of January 14 [1991], the day before the deadline, was too important to allow for niceties. Not a speaker varied from script in the call for a holy war against the forces of American imperialism.

"The United States is heading for an evil action to destroy not only Iraq but the entire Arab nation!" declared Speaker of Parliament Saadi Mehdi Saleh. "If the United States wants to fight, we are fully determined to challenge it to a long showdown to destroy the invader!" thundered delegate Anwar Kasira. "America has made a crime against humanity!" read Farouq Abdullah. "With blood, with soul, we sacrifice with Saddam," chanted the entire assembly.

Just after the unanimous vote giving Saddam "all jurisdictional and constitutional powers" necessary to combat "the American threat," the delegate seated behind me tapped me on the shoulder. "Where are you from?" he said.

"Washington, D.C.," I told him.

"Washington!" he exclaimed. "I love Washington! I went to school at Catholic University, and I have a brother at George Washington University." He offered his hand across the seat.

For all I know, surreality is the norm in all third world dictatorships facing the likelihood of suicidal war with the world's greatest superpower. In such a case, schizophrenia may be merely the sane reaction to an insane situation. But it is certainly true for Baghdad on the brink.

On one level, the entire city is a study in denial. On a sunny afternoon four days before the deadline, Femi Azzat Saloom and his best friend, Abdul Emir Abut, sat in their box at the racetrack. "We are not afraid of war," said Saloom. "We have been fighting eight years already with the Iranians. Ha ha! Many rockets came, but we stayed always right here at the races. Ha ha!"

"Yes, we stay," said Abut. "Of course. The rockets of the Americans are no different from the rockets of Iranians." He pointed beyond the horses positioning at the gate. "We saw an Iranian rocket land one day over there, and they didn't even stop the race. Ha ha!"

Even educated people seem unable to grasp the difference between facing human waves of poorly armed Iranians and a force of B-1 bombers and cruise missiles. "We have seen everything in a war that can happen," said Taha Hassan, a war veteran and professor at the Academy of Fine Arts. "Certainly, it will be a difficult war, but we think victory will be with us because our military is very strong. We saw armies like this in the Iranian war."

Every man chose his myth. "I have read many reports from all over Saudi Arabia," confided a newspaper editor. "They say some American privates and sergeants and even some colonels are depressed and do not know what they are doing there." A retired Iraqi army brigadier said, "When you see Saddam on television, he is so sure, so confident of victory. Why? Our army is not so good. We know that. It must be he has a secret weapon, a big surprise."

The newspapers keep up a daily blather. "We will make the confrontation arena a marsh of blood where the American invaders will swim with their corpses floating over, or scattered in, the Arab Sahara," editorialized *Al Qadissiya*. *Al Thrawa,* the official organ of Saddam's Ba'ath party, assured that "the fate of Bush's forces in the Gulf will be nothing but crushed bones in the desert swimming in their blood."

◆ ◆ ◆

As if the natural level of false hopes and fat chances in Baghdad were insufficient, every day brought a new, imported crop of charlatans, scoundrels, fools, and men who had mistaken impotence for importance. The flight I took from New York to Amman, the first step to Baghdad, was packed with such; in economy sat a dozen fresh-faced college students, members of the Fellowship of Reconciliation, a venerable pacifist organization. In first class was a rather more hard-eyed bunch of pacifists: Zhedi Terzi, the PLO's UN ambassador; Louis Farrakhan, leader of the Nation of Islam; and ex-Nicaraguan president Daniel Ortega. The innocents in economy told me they were aware that they could be used for propaganda purposes. Sure enough, before they even got out of the airport in Amman, Farrakhan swooped down on them at the baggage carousel and grabbed them to his breast as the cameras clicked.

It was all as cheap and tinny as an old kazoo. "The people here are very resolute about this holy war business, but we're not sure that's the right way to go," said Farrakhan's aide Leonard Muhammed on January 12, standing in the lobby of the Al Rasheed Hotel and rolling the words off his tongue with grave pontification. "There is no deadline. No deadline!" shrilled Yasir Arafat on January 14. "In my opinion it is only a date. For me it is a very important date because it is the birthday of Nasser."

The wretched reality was bubbling away just under the rhetoric, as, for the first time in many years, state controls loosened under the strain. Criticizing Saddam is a capital offense here, and reporters who went to Baghdad as recently as a month ago found a society so fearful it was virtually impossible to get anyone but government officials to talk. This time they were besieged by people desperate to offer their opinions, most of them making it clear that they did not want this fight at all.

I talked one day to a retired high-ranking military officer, a man who had fought from the first day of the Iraq-Iran war to the last and who had one son in the army in Kuwait, another on the front near Saudi Arabia, and a brother still missing in action in Iran. "We are very tired of war," he said. "I must fight because this is my home, but this is a bad war." He continued, lowering his voice. "From the time I am born here, what have I seen? Many troubles, many wars, many revolutions, many blood. Many men killed. And not only killed—one man I saw they put a rope on the neck and dragged him through the streets." He whispered, "I want to go to America. In America a human is human. In Iraq, a human is not human."

Many Iraqis seemed astonished that America had taken the seizure of Kuwait so seriously and depressed to find themselves heading to war with a people they more or less like. The official hate rhetoric of crushing Americans and making them swim in their own blood had, as far as I could see, no connection with the way the people of Baghdad thought about Americans. It certainly had nothing to do with the way they acted toward the American journalists around town. On the evening of January 13 I dropped by the offices of *Al Jumhuriyah,* the government newspaper whose editorials had been promising the imminent, bloody death of American aggressors. Muhammed Hamza, the front-page editor, spent half an hour recalling his days at the University of Tennessee, dwelling with special delight on the occasions on which he met Tennessee Williams, Edward Albee, and Alex Haley. An editorial writer, Issa Al Abadi, had an agonized question. "Do the American people understand the history and culture of my country? Do they ask themselves what these people who are facing a death that is not right are like?"

As January 15 approached, however, the mood of unreality and bewilderment faded. It was replaced by a despondent acceptance that an unwanted, terrible destruction was very close. The rich began slipping out of town on January 12 and 13, heading to summer homes north of the city or rented villas in the countryside. The middle class headed to cities like Hilla, sixty miles away, to stay with relatives. Many fled to the towns of Najaf and Karbala, which are sacred sites to Shiite Muslims, in the belief the Americans would spare holy land. By January 14 the army had called up every male except necessary government workers, the aged, and the crippled (of which, thanks to the war with Iran, there are a great, great many). The men left behind sent their wives and children to the country and prepared to protect their homes.

One man took me home to show me his setup: two freezers filled with food, a dozen jerry cans of gasoline, propane, and kerosene, a cooler of water, and a spade for digging a hole in the backyard to hide in when the bombs fell. Hidden away, he had, as do many men in Baghdad, a Kalashnikov automatic rifle, to fight the Americans if they ever got to his house. He was not looking forward to the fighting, he said, but what could he do?

The National Assembly declared January 15 "The Day of Challenge," in which the people would take to the streets to demonstrate their defiance of America. Schoolchildren and government workers got the day off and were bused to selected sites. Perhaps as many as half a million people were turned out in Baghdad, and many thousands more in Iraq's other principal cities. The marchers were just about the only folks around. Saddam had tried to keep people in town by passing the word that all government workers who failed to show up at the rally on January 15 would be fired, and all students who skipped it, expelled. It hadn't worked. Baghdad, which is a crowded city of 4 million people, was suddenly full of wide open spaces. Few cars drove on the broad boulevards Saddam built, and the shops were all shuttered and closed.

The day had dawned exceptionally foggy but cleared up somewhat by eleven A.M., when the ministry minders rounded up the reporters to escort them to the protests. The one I went to was in a residential neighborhood near a deserted downtown. Thirty thousand were all lined up when we got there, children and bureaucrats with soldiers to guide them. The marchers had banners—THE CITIZENS OF AL KARKH WILL BE MARTYRS TO DEFEND OUR GREAT COUNTRY AND PROTECT ITS COMPLETE SOVEREIGNTY—and there was a small school marching band comprising three or four drums and a couple of bugles. Everybody walked along slowly and in order for five city blocks, then turned around and walked back. When the cameras pointed at them, they offered the traditional chants: "Yes! Yes! Saddam! Long Life Saddam! Down! Down! Bush!" The children who had gotten the day off from school were terrifically pleased with the whole thing, but most others seemed as glum as guests at a wake.

A small, neat woman of thirty or so came up to me after a chorus of "Down! Down! Bush!" She wanted something understood. "That just means down, down Bush's policies," she said. "Not down, down Bush personally." I asked her how she was enjoying the demo, and she said she was really not. "Truly, we did not want war," she said. "Because we are still getting over our war with Iran. We want to live in peace, have a happy life . . . I want to get married and have children. My God says I must get married and have children. But if the war comes, there will be no marriages, I think."

Blitzed

◆ ◆ ◆

AMMAN, JORDAN—The days of delusion are dead in Baghdad. The city has finally discovered the obvious: a contest between a third world semipower fighting World War II and a first world superpower fighting World War III is no contest at all. The war could well go on for several bloody months or even longer, and kill many soldiers, but its inevitable conclusion is strongly suggested in one fact easily grasped by the people on the receiving end of the American-led attack. This is a war in which, in the very first hour of conflict, the attacking forces were able to destroy specific targets at will, with no losses, in the heart of the defending forces' capital city. And yet there was Saddam, still spouting the big lie. "The infidel tyrant's missiles and aircraft are being destroyed," he said in his first post D-day radio address, on January 20. "His defeat will be certain."

But big lies weren't playing too well in Baghdad after January 16. With allied bombs and missiles redrawing the skyline every hour, the entire city was a reality check. The first morning of the war, I was standing across the Tigris River from the Ministry of Defense, looking at the black smoke pouring out of it from a cruise-missile hit five minutes earlier, when the second missile smacked home, shuddering the ground with the explosion and sending up great new billows of smoke. Five minutes after that, the third missile boomed. In ten minutes the heart and symbol of Iraq's armed forces was a burning rubble. The hospital next to it, though, was untouched, and so were the homes crowded around it. The attack had been so swift that the antiaircraft guns had not even fired.

By the morning of January 20, four days after a U.S. Air Force Stealth bomber opened the war with a 2,000-pound laser-guided bomb targeted precisely on the microwave dishes atop Baghdad's international telecommunications building, the city was crippled. There was no mainline electricity, no running water, no working telephones. The streets were mostly deserted, the shops mostly closed. The few grocery stores open for business were charging extortionate prices for such basics as candles and beer, and were mobbed with panic buyers. The mood of the people could be gauged by the growing number of accidents, the cars of frightened drivers piling up against lampposts and guard rails with every round of antiaircraft fire.

The allied bombs and missiles had destroyed or crippled the Defense Ministry, the telecommunications building, the power station, seven telecommunications microwave relay towers, the headquarters of Saddam Hussein's Ba'ath Arab Socialist Party, the huge (and, for Iraq's economy, vital) Dora oil refinery, a key nuclear research facility, the air force headquarters, and the airport. That's just in greater Baghdad. In the first two days of war the allied forces dropped 5 million pounds of bombs on Iraq and Kuwait, fired 196 Tomahawk cruise missiles, ran two thousand B-52 and Stealth bomber attack missions, and so on and on, to devastating effect.

You couldn't turn around without seeing something get taken out. My drive out of Iraq took about twenty hours longer than it should have, in part because we had to keep pulling over to wait out bombardments. In that one five-hundred-mile drive, we saw allied planes pound the big Al Walid air base in the western Iraqi desert, a major phosphorous plant, and an oil pipeline pumping station. The antiaircraft fire was, as always, spirited and heavy and just about wholly ineffective.

The one-sidedness could be seen in the air. In the nighttime raids, the antiaircraft fire would begin a few minutes before the bombers came, in scenes of incandescent hysteria and beauty, the tracer shells tracking lovely curves, and S's and parabolas of orange-red light against the backdrop of a blacked-out city skyline. Only every fifth or sixth shell was a tracer, which created a spacing that gave the *ack-ack* trails a pleasingly deliberate, almost lazy look. You could see the tracers hit their apogee and then explode in delicate bright white starbursts, like the better sort of fireworks. You could hear the defense, too, in a big sweeping wash of noise, the sharp staccato bursts of the lighter guns punctuated by the thuds of the big ones.

What you could not see, or hear, were the planes at which all this was directed. Those B-52s and Stealths were far, far above the fire and clamor. You might catch just a hint of engine sound, but generally you knew that they had come only when the bombs fell and the big yellow-red bursts ballooned up over the stricken target. Then they were gone, leaving the Iraqi guns firing crazily and hopelessly in the air for another forty-five minutes or more. By Saturday the defensive fire was more controlled, in shorter bursts and focused on a more concentrated area. Whether this reflected more discipline or less ammunition was not clear, but the lack of results was the same anyway.

◆ ◆ ◆

There was one element of attack that was visible, but it was more or less unstoppable, and a glimpse of it was frightening. The sight of Tomahawk cruise missiles moving purposefully two or three stories above the city streets became a recurring nightmare vision in Baghdad. Cruise missiles move at subsonic speeds and can easily be followed with the eye as their lethally single-minded little gyroscopes and computer circuits guide them along to their target. A stunned Reuters correspondent actually saw a missile arrive at a street corner, appear to pause for a moment, and then turn left.

On Saturday a group of reporters standing outside the Al Rasheed Hotel looked up to see a Tomahawk sailing along toward the Foreign Ministry, or perhaps the National Assembly. Suddenly, and directly over their heads, it exploded, sending them diving under parked cars as flaming chunks of engine and cowling rained down. The missile, accidentally detonated or hit by an Iraqi antiaircraft shot, split into two flaming balls; one roared into the disused servants' quarters of the hotel, the other demolished its conference center.

It is pathetically indicative of the shape of things that from this minor stroke of relative luck the Iraqis claimed a great victory. Shortly after the explosion Iraqi soldiers brought into the hotel bomb shelter pieces of the blown-apart missile. Hoisting the debris high, they declared it to be the earthly remains of a fighter bomber, shot down by the great Iraqi gunners. The women in the shelter stopped their weeping and let loose with a high-pitched keening of false triumph.

Such moments of Great Satan defiance were, however, rare. As early as the morning of January 17, after the first night of bombing, the doubts and fears of a truth come home were right out in the open. The most astonishing examples were provided by the people whose job it is to keep up the lies, the serious men of the Ministry of Information and Culture. One reporter approached Saddoun al-Genabi, the affable chief of the "minders" who tell foreign journalists what they may and may not do. "I will see you when I return," said the reporter. "If I am here," said Saddoun. "If I am dead, visit my grave."

◆ ◆ ◆

ABC cameraman Fabrice Moussus had a conversation with a ministry minder that was, in terms of Iraqi politics, apocalyptic. The worried minder of official information asked Moussus first for . . . information. How long would the bombing continue? How could he best protect his family? Then he leaned forward and whispered something that you would never have heard in Baghdad before the bombs. "I will be very happy when this is over," he said. "We do not like this government. I am afraid many Iraqis will get killed, but we hope the [allied forces] will hit the government areas and help us get rid of this government."

It's the beginning of the end for any tyrant when jokes are made at his expense. The morning after Iraq's first missile attack on Israel, one Iraqi said, with a sly smile, "Seven rockets and seven casualties? We could do better with pistols."

This kind of heretical—and, in a state where criticism of Saddam is a capital offense, extremely dangerous—talk was cropping up all over, blooming in the first tentative breakdown of state control. The signs of the breakdown were small but real: a man in a crowd passing an American journalist a note reading, "You are not the enemy. Saddam is the enemy"; a bomb shelter full of people sitting through a night of attack, playing cards, sleeping, and talking among themselves in complete disdain for the address from Saddam playing on the radio.

Saddam's men did their best to make Baghdad put on a happy face. Veteran reporters there could not recall a time of greater freedom and bonhomie. But all species revert to form, and by the end of the first week of war, gangsterism was back. A group of state security agents grabbed three European photographers and took them off for eight hours during which they were blindfolded, handcuffed, and threatened with death. Saddam paraded the seven prisoners of war on the radio and television broadcast, and announced they would be placed as human shields at key industrial locations. The last of the Western press was chucked out, and the people of Baghdad settled down for their punishment, which is, after all, what they know best.

Desert Rat

◆ ◆ ◆

AMMAN, JORDAN—Have you ever danced with the devil in the pale moonlight? Probably not. It's a tough step to master, tougher than the lambada even, and heaven help you if you step on your partner's hoof. If you want to see it done, though—and done right, done by someone who can really trip the black light fantastic, a real Astaire of the sulfuric zones—here and now is where the box seats are going cheap for the performance of a lifetime.

His Majesty King Hussein has ruled the Hashemite Kingdom of Jordan for thirty-eight years, and there may be no one in the world who knows the old fandango better. He has dipped and twirled with Nasser and Arafat and Assad and Qaddafi, with Nixon and Brezhnev and Kissinger—with many, many dark and cunning lords. Quite a few of his partners thought little of him (perhaps because he is a little man, perhaps because he is polite and pleasant and sometimes seems indecisive), and many expressed their disdain by double-crossing him at one time or another. A surprising number went so far as to try to bump the small king off. But most of the old partners are gone, and Hussein of Jordan is still perched, handsomely if somewhat gingerly, on the throne. What's going on now is a study in why, and why it may not last.

Before the Gulf War began, a lot of Amman's deep thinkers said that the conflict would probably widen the gap between the perpetually angry, increasingly fundamentalist Palestinians who make up almost half the population (70 percent in Amman) and the Westernized Jordanian elite who still control the military and most of the political hierarchy. Mayhem was predicted, and anti-American riots, and possibly a serious challenge to Hussein's regime. Two weeks into the war, however, nothing of the sort had occurred. The streets were quiet, and Hussein, by all signs and accounts, had never been more popular.

The reasons why have a lot to do with the king's skilled footwork, and they could be seen on a Friday nine days after the bombing began, in Amman's Baqa'a refugee camp, where some eighty thousand Palestinians live in a teeming, wretched mass. Two weeks earlier, Friday prayers in Baqa'a had ended with a demonstration that was nearly a riot; Western journalists were roughed up, stones were thrown, etc. This Friday the protest attracted at most two thousand people in a brief, orderly, and rather desultory march. Although there was plenty of the usual death-to-America rhetoric, nobody seemed inclined to do violence to anyone. And certainly not to Hussein. Shop windows and walls were papered with posters of the smiling king next to the beaming Saddam, in glossy color against a backdrop of Jerusalem.

Young Ibrahim Khrais took a moment off from a bit of hopeful chanting— "Today, Scuds in Tel Aviv. Tomorrow, Scuds in the White House"—to explain the way things were. "We are all with Saddam. . . . The king, I think, is actually with Saddam, too. But he cannot do anything more about it than he does, because Israel is right next door. The people understand this, so they are not angry with the king." Mohammed Ananiti, a second-generation refugee, was more skeptical, but no less forgiving. "We are totally with Saddam; the king is near Saddam but not with him," he said.

Six months since Iraq attacked Kuwait, two weeks since America attacked Iraq, and His Majesty is still such a dervish even his own people can't quite make out his outline. He was against the taking of Kuwait, but not for the American-led war to take it back. He remains, sort of, a friend of the America that has sustained and armed him all these years. But he turns a benign eye on the bloody anti-American rhetoric that fills the streets of Amman and the parliament of the Hashemite Kingdom. Officially, he is aligned neither with Saddam Hussein nor against him. Really, as the people in Baqa'a correctly sense, he is on Saddam's side, but not so blatantly as to force a showdown with Israel or the United States. (A good example is his wink-and-a-nod approach to the economic sanctions on Iraq. A few days after the bombing began, the officially embargoed oil trucks from Iraq were still crossing the border into Jordan in an unbroken convoy, and the Baghdad stores were still filled with processed foods from Amman.)

Hussein limits his own statements to carefully modulated pitches for peace, leaving the masses' thirst for more bloodthirsty rhetoric to be slaked by the Islamic fundamentalists who have won control of the lower house of parliament, by the protesters, and by the popular press. All do the job with adolescent gusto. "The Arab peoples, who are already pregnant with hatred of the United States, will deliver painful strokes to American interests all over the world," writes Dr. A. R. Malhas in the *Jordan Times*. "Protective chest vests may become standard American underwear!"

◆ ◆ ◆

In all cases, the freedom to speak out was given by Hussein, in a democratization process he and his brother Crown Prince Hassan began in 1989. That process is largely aimed at defusing the extremists by giving them platforms from which to shout and an increasing degree of real power. After a fundamentalist Muslim Brotherhood candidate won the speakership of the lower house in the last elections, Hussein reshuffled his cabinet, giving five seats to Muslim Brotherhood men and two more to independent fundamentalists.

The king's behavior is part of a career pattern directed by the unpleasant realities of Jordan: a poor, weak country of mostly worthless rocky desert, bordered by large, hungry Arab states; in a state of perpetual tension with Israel; stuck with more than a million Palestinians for whom refugee status has become permanent; and dependent on U.S. aid and Arab trade for economic survival. The essential point in governing this mess has always been placating the dangerous and numerous Palestinians, a point Hussein probably grasped at the age of fifteen, when he watched a Palestinian assassin gun down his grandfather, King Abdullah.

Hussein has always met the Palestinians more than halfway, even at the risk of losing all. In 1967, when the mob howled for war with Israel, Hussein joined Egypt, Syria, and Iraq for the disastrous six-day folly that cost him Jerusalem and the West Bank. When, after 1967, the various groups of the Palestine Liberation Organization decided to make Jordan their base for attacks on Israel, Hussein allowed the Fedayeen to stay until they had grown to a well-armed force of more than fifty thousand, had reduced the country to near anarchy, had made clear their intentions of taking over completely, and had tried to kill him. Worked then, works now.

◆ ◆ ◆

But appeasement may not keep the streets quiet indefinitely. For the moment the mob that has accepted Hussein's "near Saddam but not with Saddam" position is happy, because (a) an Arab nation has stood up to the Great Satan for a whole two weeks and is still on its feet, and (b) Israelis are suffering. Both offer immense psychic gratification. (A fair indication of the way Jordanians feel about Jews can be found in the lobby of the Intercontinental Hotel, which boasts the only hotel shop I have ever seen that stocks, along with the Harold Robbinses and Jeffrey Archers, such works as *The International Jew: The World's Foremost Problem*.)

Before too long, however, the war will be over. Saddam Hussein will be defeated and Jordanians will no longer wake to the pleasure of front-page pictures of dead and wounded in Tel Aviv. When that happens, Hussein will be left with a great deal of debris. In 1989 the per capita income of Jordanians was cut in half;

since the Gulf crisis began in August, the complete destruction of the country's tourist trade, the crippling of trade between Iraq and Jordan, and the cutoff of trade between Saudi Arabia and Jordan have left Hussein's kingdom close to economic collapse.

Meanwhile, the fundamentalists will have solidified their power, and they will not be pleased with the notion of going back to a *status quo ante* relationship with Israel. "The threat is from the fundamentalists," said George S. Hawatmeh, the *Jordan Times*'s editor in chief. "These guys came with an agenda. They want to wipe Israel out. . . . What will suffer in the coming months will be the position of the moderates."

Moreover, even moderate Jordanians such as Hawatmeh who believe Israel has a right to exist will demand what they like to call "the new Arab order," a vague notion that covers a transfer of wealth from the richer Arab states to the poorer ones, and the establishment of some sort of Palestinian entity in the West Bank. "We cannot go back. Hussein knows this," said Hawatmeh. "War or peace, things cannot go back to what they were; the people will not tolerate that."

But Saudi Arabia isn't about to allow U.S. troops to die for the privilege of giving up any part of its petrobucks to Jordan. And Israel hasn't restrained itself in the face of Scud attacks for the privilege of giving up territory it has held for twenty-three years. Attitudes had been stiffening on all sides before the war began. There is no reason to think that thousands, or tens of thousands, of deaths will mollify them. The war is likely to end with a hardening of the old order, not the birth of a new one. And then we will see how nimble Hussein can really be.

Souk Kook

◆ ◆ ◆

AMMAN, JORDAN—On a recent Friday afternoon, the big, old, elegant Al-Hussein mosque in Amman was momentarily quiet, its loudspeakers silent between the 11:30 and 3:30 calls to prayer. The sidewalks and streets around the market area were filled with young men in Italian-cut slacks, soldiers in olive drab, women in brilliantly embroidered ankle-length robes, giggling girls, and shy-faced boys. (Think of Manhattan's garment district with ten times its normal quotient of people, but with everybody moving in an unexpected fluid neatness, no one's body ever touching anyone else's body, all gliding and eliding by.) The crowd was there to bargain and buy, one of the great occupations and preoccupations of the Arab world. There was much to purchase: pistachio nuts, peanuts, walnuts, almonds, and raisins; saccharine-sweet white custard by the bowl, with honey dripped on top; sandwiches of shaved lamb, tomatoes, and onions wrapped in greased, hot pita bread; fresh fruit milk shakes and sweet Turkish coffee by the cup; suits made to order on the spot; unheard of perfumes and novelty-brand radios; knock-off cigarettes called Marlbril. And so on, and on. Not much ever changes, except money between hands.

◆ ◆ ◆

But this afternoon there was one little plot of entrepreneurial turf where the bustle (and the hustle) was clearly something special. In front of the little storefront of the Al-Afghani Company, a camera crew was busily recording for history . . . the door. A dozen passersby had stopped to watch this oddity. Inside the shop, three more reporters—a Brit, a German, and a Dutchman—hip-nudged and elbow-poked each other in the tiny, narrow aisle. They watched the scene before them with the hungry attention of the professional voyeur. Being myself one such, I watched, too. At one end of the cluttered glass counter, a man stood working with a hacksaw and a vise, separating a half dozen freshly stamped metal figures from their metal brackets. At the other end, another craftsman was soldering alligator clips onto the back of each pin.

◆ ◆ ◆

Since January 19, two days after Saddam Hussein first dropped Scud missiles on Israel, Fouad Afghani, proprietor, has been doing land-rush business in the mementos of death wish. The metal pins were die-stamped, engraved replicas of the Scuds Saddam fired on Israel. Painted and polished, they would become cheap brooches and key rings. The rafters of Mr. Afghani's little shop, and the walls, are hung with the usual items of Mideast tourist trade—brass and tin coffee pots; costume-bejeweled brass scimitars; sweet, suffering Christs of machine-carved olive wood—but the hot tickets on the exchange now are all about the death and suffering of the folks in Tel Aviv. He sells buttons, too. The samples hung on the door were what the TV crew was filming. Mr. Afghani designs them himself. They are sturdy and well painted, and as big around as beer cans. All of them bear a photo of the smiling Saddam, and a cartoon figure of a speeding Al Hussein missile, as Saddam has renamed his Russian-made Scuds. One says (in English, like them all): "East or West, Scud is best." Another declares, next to the picture of a speeding Scud: "Saddam, One Like You Makes Dream Come True." A third shows the beach at Tel Aviv, with a pair of bare feet next to army boots, and underneath a neon sign that flashes "Israel" with two Scuds bearing down on it. The writing next to them: "Wherever you hide, Al-Hussein ('Scud') is going to FIND!" The most virulent depicts the falling Scuds next to the words, "Israel is Cancer and Al Hussein (Scud) is answer."

◆ ◆ ◆

The key rings, pins, and buttons have been selling very well. Mr. Afghani began making the key rings on Monday, and by Saturday had sold, as far as he could figure, at least three thousand. Of the Scud cartoon buttons, at least two thousand had been sold. Related sales have likewise been booming. Cheap but gaudy watches with Saddam's beaming visage are a steady mover: five hundred sold in the past five months. At the low end of the market, general-purpose Saddam buttons (without the pointed Scud message) have been making the cash register ring nonstop since August 2: about 300,000 sold to date.

◆ ◆ ◆

None of this is a surprise. Jordan is, after all, half Palestinian. The country is filled with people like Mr. Afghani, for whom anger and hatred is bred in the bone. In 1948, when the first Arab-Israeli war was raging and Afghani was six months old, his father moved the family from the city of Jaffa, next door to Tel Aviv. Afghani has never returned, and he will not, as long as going to Jaffa means being questioned and searched first by Israeli soldiers. But there's a twist to the story, one that is both mildly encouraging and, for those interested in the corruptive interaction between the media and that which it covers, mildly interesting. In the whole of Amman's big, bustling downtown, in this city where 70 percent of the population is Palestinian, Mr. Afghani's store was the only one selling Scud key rings and pins celebrating the fall of Scuds on Israel. At the Intercontinental Hotel, where most of the hundreds of Western journalists in town are camping, the location of Mr. Afghani's store is as well known as the location of the hotel bar. That's why the camera crew was there, and the three other reporters, and me. We were there to catch a bit of ugly vox populi on the quick and easy.

◆ ◆ ◆

But listen to what Mr. Afghani has to say about why business is booming. "About eighty percent of our sales, maybe more, are to journalists," he said, pointing behind him to the wall where he hangs the orders he takes over the phone for the hot new mementos. The scraps of paper all bore orders from the press corps: "TV-Spain—10 Scuds . . . Ingrid Tonquist, Marriott Room 827—20 Scuds . . . CNN, Kris—5 Iraqi maps." "Oh, yes," said Mr. Afghani, "it is almost all journalists. Some Jordanians want to buy Scud key rings, because they do not cost so much as the Saddam watches, but I do not sell to them. They only want to buy one or two, and we have too much trouble keeping up with the rush for that. We only take the bigger orders, ten pieces or more, and they are mostly from journalists." After all, he said, with the inarguable logic of a third-generation merchant, "It is much better for me to sell ten pieces to one person than one piece to ten person. Maybe later, we will sell to Jordanians. Right now—to journalists. That is where the business is."

Speech Defect

◆ ◆ ◆

AMMAN, JORDAN—A few days after King Hussein unlumbered himself of the anti-United States, pro-Iraq peroration his grateful subjects call The Speech, a flock of foreign reporters sent a petition to the palace, asking for a royal press conference to discern exactly what the king meant by the thing. Hussein promptly said yes, and at the appointed time, several hundred journalists jumped into a fleet of taxicabs and sped off to the palace. "Oh, but I am sorry, sirs," said the functionary at the castle gates. "His Majesty has developed pressing business. The news conference is postponed." The king, the grumbling hacks concluded, had come to his senses and realized that clarifying his position would be the act of a fool, which he is not.

The ruler of the Hashemite Kingdom of Jordan is gambling his postwar status on a bet that Saddam will lose the war and with it his standing in the Arab world; that the postwar Middle East will be a place of bitter anger, chaos, and rebellion against the United States and the Arab leaders who sided with it; and that a pan-Arab leader named King Hussein ibn Talal will emerge from the flux. The first part of the bet is almost a sure thing, the second is better than odds-on, but hitting the third would constitute a trifecta, and not many players make that score.

This interpretation of The Speech is not, of course, the official one. The king himself insisted afterward that Jordan's position has not budged from the center course of neutrality and desire for peace. He was shocked, shocked, he told David Brinkley and America, that George Bush, Congress, and the Western press had so misread him. "I do not see why my statement, my appeal for peace, has been so misunderstood and misinterpreted," he said.

But the king's own minister of information made his master's thinking clear the morning after the speech, beginning with the royal personage's large view of himself. "In order to understand the speech of His Majesty the king, one must talk about the person himself," said Minister Ibrahim Izzeddin. "He believes he has a historic responsibility. His family has, through ancient and modern history, played a very, very important role in shaping public opinion—going beyond the boundaries of states in which they have rules."

He clarified the king's thinking about the postwar Arab world: "When the war ends, things will change dramatically. . . . The Arab League as an institution is totally shattered now, and the United Nations as a peacemaker is totally paralyzed." And, finally, he suggested the role Hussein hopes to play in the new Arab order: "We would like to build a new Arab consensus, a new Arab cooperation that could face a world that is being shaped without any real Arab input."

This is too big a wager to hedge properly, but that hasn't stopped Hussein, one of the world's great hedgers, from trying. Thirty-eight years as an Arab leader, four assassination attempts, and a quasi war with the PLO leaves a man either dead or possessed of a keen sense of when to do what must be done. Therefore a speech was born unlike anything the mild-mannered monarch had delivered before. On the first—and widely missed—level, it was a concession speech: Hussein of Jordan conceded Hussein of Iraq's war. Not in such blunt terms, but the message was there, and formed the basis for all that followed. The king described Iraq in language that admitted the only possible military outcome to the war was Iraq's defeat. He spoke of Iraq as having already been destroyed in a "third world war" (a fine, if unintended, pun) that "aims to destroy all the achievements of Iraq and return it to primitive life." The only hope he offered to avoid this was not that Iraq might somehow prevail, but that the American-sponsored coalition could somehow be induced to stop fighting.

"Let us join our efforts to stop this catastrophe and save the people of Iraq from the fate that is being planned for them," he said. "The starting point in all this is immediate and serious work to make the alliance accept a cease-fire. . . . The alternative to a cease-fire is the destruction of all Arabs and Muslims, their humiliation, the trampling on their honor, pride, and legitimate hopes. . . ."

Cease-fire is a chimera, and the king must have known that; neither Iraq nor the United States had expressed the slightest interest in backing down.

As implicit as the dismissal of Iraq's chances on the battlefield was the dismissal of its leader. In the speech the king offered an emotional salute to "Iraq, its heroic army, its steadfast people, its glorious women, its brave children, and its aged." Conspicuously missing in the litany was Saddam, whose name never appeared in the twenty-minute speech. In speaking of a country in which the cult of personality is so pervasive that almost every street boasts at least one giant piece of Saddam-analia, this is not the kind of thing one does by accident.

◆ ◆ ◆

But if Iraq goes under, and Saddam with it, why should rebellious Arab masses turn to someone whose modus operandi has always been to play at least two sides against the middle? Well, Hussein used the speech for a bit of image adjustment. Having postulated the need for a new Saladin/Nasser/Saddam, Hussein spent the rest of The Speech fitting himself out as such, carefully hitting every Arab hot button in the process: "If this situation continues, it will only benefit those who covet our lands and our resources, with Israel at their forefront," he said. "There are already signs that the spoils are being divided. We hear and read every day of plans to control our resources, limit our aspirations, and usurp our rights."

He trotted forth every line of every dark conspiracy theory and every hysterical claim. He described the allied bombing of Iraq in precisely the same terms as those employed by Iraq: "Fire rains down upon Iraq from airplanes, from battleships, from submarines and rockets, destroying mosques, churches, schools, museums, powdered milk factories, residential areas, Bedouin tents, . . . [in] a war that aims to destroy all the achievements of Iraq and return it to primitive life." He spoke of plots to keep standing foreign armies on Arab soil and of "a war against all Arabs and Muslims, not just Iraq."

With this talk, he gladdened the hearts of people who need no convincing that what he said was exactly so. Half of Jordan's people are Palestinians, many of them impoverished, who define themselves in terms of permanent victimhood. What is new is the radicalization of the usually complacent upper and middle classes. It was this that made the king's unexpected move toward extremism a political imperative. As his minister of information explained, "In the Arab world it will be very difficult for anyone who has been party to this [U.S.] war camp to have any say in the future."

A few days after the speech I went to a Palestinian refugee camp in Amman, where, at a fund-raiser cum auction, three thousand momentarily happy residents forked over more than $30,000 of very hard-earned money to buy a few hours of revenge in the form of viewing a hunk of a downed American warplane. There were no surprises in the anti-America, anti-Israel rhetoric of the poor and hungry crowd. The surprise was in the words of my young interpreter. Mona is a daughter of privilege, born to an upper-middle-class family, educated in a convent school, comfortable in cashmere jackets and American cowboy boots, and in London, Paris, New York. She is apolitical to the degree that she had skipped watching the king's speech in favor of dressing for a date. This was her first visit to a Palestinian refugee camp.

The day after the speech she and several of her friends went down to a Popular Army registration center and signed up for training. "This is the fight of our lives," she says. "The talk is over. This is the great battle between our people and the Israelis. We must fight. There is no other way." Such talk is in vogue here, in a country that is determinedly staying out of real harm's way in the Gulf War, but whose heart belongs to Saddam.

What Hussein is figuring is that the sort of shift in passion represented in Mona is not limited to his own intensely political country, but is the coming way of the postwar Arab world, and that such a world will need a man who can talk the way he did for the first time in his life on the evening of February 6. It's at least a fair shot that he is wrong. There have been no signs yet that the people of Egypt, Saudi Arabia, and Syria wish to depose their leaders, and there is every reason to think the governments in those countries can squelch all but the most dramatic upheavals. But it's at least a fair shot that he is right, and it is that possibility that has led a natural-born player of the house minimum to take the flier of his life.

Kiss of Victory

◆ ◆ ◆

KUWAIT—I had thought from the moment the first bomb dropped on Baghdad that the matchup between Saddam Hussein and a good portion of the civilized world was wildly one-sided, but the staggering, lunatic scope of the disaster he visited on his people did not actually bring tears to my eyes until the moment here, on the third day of the ground war, when I took my first, and I hope my last, prisoners of war.

I was driving down the abandoned highway to Kuwait City with my friend Dan Fesperman, a correspondent for the *Baltimore Sun*. We were "doing a unilateral," the press corps' term for getting around the Pentagon's press pool restrictions by ignoring them. I'd been told there was no way I was going to get on a good pool anyway—maybe deck space on a ship in the Red Sea, if I was lucky. So we drove to the war—over the desert, past a couple of checkpoints, and into Kuwait, being careful to avoid American patrols. We had heard that the day before a carload of British hacks had been stopped by American troops. Their officer radioed his commander, who told him that reporters not in a pool should be detained and treated as prisoners of war. The officer decided instead to look the other way while the Brits got the hell out of there, but the story made us wary.

◆ ◆ ◆

About fifty miles from the city limits, we seemed to be ahead of allied lines in this sector, but that was of little moment. Iraqi troops all across Kuwait were in a frenzy of retreat and surrender. In two days of driving across the Kuwaiti desert and in and out of various battlefields, we had seen tens of thousands of allied troops and vehicles, watched many hundreds of Iraqis surrender, heard allied guns and missiles fire for hours at a time—and had not seen one shot fired by one Iraqi soldier. We never even saw an Iraqi soldier with a rifle in his hand. They had buried them all, filling the desert with a strange crop that will bloom slowly over the centuries, as the shifting sands uncover the weapons that Saddam promised would make the land a lake of American blood.

Still, we were driving with care. The Iraqis had blown up the highway every quarter mile or so, which forced us periodically to swerve off the road and onto the desert, where we had to watch out for stray minefields. Dan spotted the men first, at a distance of about half a mile, a ragged line of green blocking the road. "They are Iraqis, I think," he said. "You can tell from the uniform. . . . Do you think they're armed?"

We drove on gingerly and stopped the four-wheel drive a few feet from them. They were ten soldiers, most of them in their thirties and forties, unarmed, clearly underfed, unshaven, wearing only light uniforms against the cold, late afternoon desert wind. One waved a white rag tied to a bamboo pole; another fluttered a dirty white handkerchief. They held their hands high over their heads and nervously advanced a few feet as we got out of the car.

"No, no," we said. "We are not soldiers. We are journalists. We are *Sahafi*." It didn't matter. The men begged to be taken in. They were cold, they said in broken English, and had already walked six kilometers from their trenches. "We afraid of Saddam," said one. "Not afraid of Americans. United States is good. United States of America is good." Every other soldier in their unit had fled north, they said. "The Iraqi army is not here. Gone. Gone to Iraq."

We gave the men water and bread and chocolate bars, and cheese and salami, and little square cartons of orange drink, and left them. We said we would send someone to pick them up, and headed on toward the capital city. But it was getting dark, which is a bad time to get lost in a war, and then we came across a giant minefield, blocking the road and the desert for hundreds of yards on both sides. (Minefields, I was interested to learn, are marked—in this case by wire strung on metal posts—so that one's own soldiers won't wander across them and get blown up. This deprives the minefield of the advantage of surprise, but the point of a minefield is not so much to be a kind of static ambush as to slow down an enemy advance.) So we turned back. We found the Iraqis still walking with their white flags before them and decided we could not leave them there. All ten managed to cram into the car: one in the front seat, four in back, and three fitted around the ten jerry cans of gasoline in the rear, with two standing on the bumper.

◆ ◆ ◆

After a couple of miles we came across a supply column of the Fourth Tank Brigade of the Saudi army, heading to frontline headquarters. We flagged down a truck and told the driver the news.

Within moments thirty-five excited Saudi soldiers crowded around the Iraqis, slamming clips of ammunition into their automatic rifles and carrying on in tremendous excitement as they searched the prisoners. They threw the Iraqis' few possessions and the food we had just given them into the sand. One zealous Saudi soldier even grabbed a Koran one Iraqi had been clutching and tossed it aside. They made the terrified prisoners sit in a line, and they shouted and waved their rifles about. Half a dozen prisoners began weeping in fear and begging for their lives. The prisoner whose Koran had been taken away crawled over to retrieve it, and clutched it to his chest for protection as he moaned and rocked back and forth. Another plucked frantically at his hair and his crotch in little agonies of terror, and shouted for his God. But the Saudi troops eventually calmed down, and gave the Iraqis new packages of food, drink, and cigarettes. One young Saudi soldier soothed a distraught Iraqi by placing both hands on his shoulders and kissing him on the forehead. We left the prisoners in the care of a young Saudi lieu-

tenant named Saud Otabi, whose beardless face shone with the pleasure of another glorious, bloodless victory.

It wasn't, after all, the Gulf War. It was the Gulf Rout. The Iraqi troops,
hopelessly outgunned and outmaneuvered, never had the slightest chance. Nor,
it seemed, did many of them want one. They just wanted to quit and go home.
On the second day of the ground battle we drove with the Egyptian army
through the Iraqi front lines, through Saddam's vaunted defense work. The
Egyptian assault began at dawn and by dusk had easily breached the three-foot-
high dirt berm, cleared roads through two minefields, filled in a section of oil-
filled trench, cut the rolls of concertina wire, and taken prisoner almost all of the
defending Iraqi soldiers in the first line of trenches twelve miles inside Kuwait.
There had been some hard resistance, but only in spots, and never for long. Most
of the Iraqis had surrendered as soon as they possibly could.

By midafternoon 530 Iraqi soldiers and twenty-two officers sat barefoot in
the sand by the section of trench they had given up, their belongings dumped in
a pathetic litter nearby: some cheap plastic combs, a few letters, a coin or two.
Two men lay dead on the ground, one with blood soaking through his shirt front
and back, his mouth gaping at the sky. When several Iraqi prisoners had to urinate, a guard led them a few feet away and stood over them with rifle and bayo-
net as they pissed in the trench they had given up only an hour earlier.

"Personally, I did not fight at all," said one Iraqi lieutenant in quite good English. "Not one bit, and I urged my men not to fight either. We had no wish to
be attacked. When we saw we were safe, that was enough. We did not wish to
fight. Why to fight? For what?" He smiled a small, bitter smile, and gestured at
the barren land around him. "For Kuwait?"

The lieutenant and his men had only stayed in the trenches, he said, because
"otherwise Saddam would hang our families—babies, girls, brothers. They did it
many times." Even if the Iraqi soldiers had wished to fight, the impossibility of
their plight was staggeringly obvious on the ground. It could be seen in the
Egyptian attack, which—on just this one relatively small and lightly defended
stretch—encompassed two battalions totaling ten thousand troops, hundreds of
tanks, armored personnel carriers, self-propelled 155-millimeter howitzers, jeeps,
half-tracks, supply trucks, and so on and on in an ever moving supply line that
stretched by day's end sixteen miles to the Saudi lines.

◆ ◆ ◆

The attacking forces filled the eye to the horizon in every direction, and filled the
ear, too, with the thuds and booms and the shelling punctuated by the soft, sibi-

lant whistle of ground-to-ground missiles, which left a puffy white trail against the gray sky. Arrayed against all this was a thin line of demoralized troops, in the kind of fixed defenses that went out with the Maginot Line. Iraqi prisoners said almost uniformly that they had been living in fear and hunger and great fatigue since the war began, and some of them complained that Saddam had pulled back the big guns that were to defend their positions before the attack even began. A garrison in the western desert town of Al Abraq, liberated on the third day by most of an entire Egyptian division, had only one, possibly broken, armored personnel carrier to defend it.

The four hundred Iraqi soldiers left to defend the town were so eager to surrender that some of them ran out from their bunkers and gave themselves up to the division's commanding officer while he was making a tour of the perimeter accompanied by only two aides and a soldier. It is a measure of how weak the resistance was that the Egyptian attack was waged without any air support at all. By the end of the third day of battle, the day Saddam announced that he was, really and truly this time, pulling out of Kuwait right now, the fight was over. The allied generals were saying their troops would liberate Kuwait City within two days at most, but that was a very conservative estimate.

The invasion had become something akin to the world's largest cross-country drive. That afternoon we drove to the head of the lead Egyptian column, and for a while amused ourselves and the troops by taking a position in our Nissan Safari at the very front of the front. Behind us stretched an unbroken line of men and matériel that now went back forty-some miles without a worry in the world, or at least in the nineteenth province of Iraq.

The Rape and Rescue
of Kuwait City

◆ ◆ ◆

KUWAIT CITY—One sunny afternoon in the week of liberation, I went to the theater. The hall at Kuwait University's school of music and drama is a place of conspicuous civilization, a big cantilevered room with modestly elegant blue cloth seats trimmed in gold, rich wood-paneled walls, and a deep, broad stage set above a large orchestra pit. I expected to be alone there but instead found a British television crew videotaping the statement of twenty-nine-year-old Abdullah Jasman, Kuwaiti citizen, University of Pittsburgh graduate, and victim of a torture session in this unlikely place. He was standing in the balcony, talking and crying. Here and there, the tile floor was spotted with drops of dried blood, little trails that went no place in particular.

"On the stage," Jasman said, pointing to a large section of steel set scaffolding, "you can see the metal frame. They put you on that, naked, with both legs spread and they spread you open all the way. . . . They raped one of my friends here. They raped him. They were laughing. They said, 'This is what your emir did to you.' There were a bunch of us brought here. You sat in these chairs, waiting to be tortured, blindfolded, and couldn't see anything. You'd hear the voices, loud, and the screaming and begging."

He pulled up his pant legs and showed the camera his calves, mottled with deep black burn wounds. "They put the wires on your legs and put your feet in the water, so your whole body is electricity," he said. "They would put you with the electricity in the water for twenty seconds, thirty seconds, and you would go unconscious and they would throw water on you and revive you, and then do it again." He began crying, in short, harsh, shuddering sobs, and he could not stop for many long, videotaped seconds.

After it was over, the British reporter thanked him. "It must have been terrible for you to go through this," he said. "But it is important. Your story is really something else." Actually, the terrible thing is, it really wasn't. It was as common as sand in Kuwait. It was, in one variation or another, simply the story of living in Iraq's nineteenth province for seven months under the rule of Saddam Hussein.

One of the new, postliberation pieces of graffiti here is a two-foot-high, three-foot-long message in red spray paint on a concrete wall, along the formerly lovely Gulf Street, amid the debris of the Iraqi army's elaborate and worthless beachfront defenses. It reads: "Diarty Iraqis." Apart from the slight misspelling, it is a commendable statement: accurate, succinct, and restrained. What the Iraqi forces did to this place was profoundly dirty; was filthy, vile, obscene; was one long, vast crime.

The city the Iraqis left behind appeared to have been worked over by a huge army of drunken teenage vandals. They stole everything they could, from air conditioners to cigarettes, in a citywide smash and grab. The huge and superb medical library at the city's teaching hospital, Mubarak Al-Katib, was stolen in its entirety. So was the library at Kuwait University, along with the school's big mainframe computers and everything else worth a cent. Standing near the library, where a few thousand bedraggled books (*Henry the Fifth, The Italian Renaissance and Its Historical Background,* etcetera), along with hundreds of thousands of index cards, remained scattered on the floor, Omar Samman, an eighteen-year-old student, described the looting: "They came in with lorries and took everything—the computers, the books, the carpets, the chairs, the keyboards, the carrels, the microphones, the podiums. It took them nearly a whole month, with men in lorries every day, before they got it all."

What the Iraqis could not steal, they destroyed, in an astonishingly savage and thorough rampage. They torched every major hotel, the banks, car dealerships, almost every store in the downtown shopping district, a score of major office buildings, the fishing marina and all its boats, the National Museum, and a great deal more. They ruined the beachfront with lines of concertina wire, bunkers, pillboxes, and mines, and turned Gulf Street's luxury apartment buildings into high-rise bunkers, cinder blocking the windows into gun ports. They shot up and burned down the emir's office and residential palaces, as well as the parliament building, smashing the windows and doors and breaking the furniture for kicks.

Kuwaitis were stunned by the Iraqi soldiers' habit of turning every place they went into a sty. At Kuwait University every office, it seemed, was ankle- to calf-deep in debris; the contents of desks and files dumped on floors, paintings ripped from walls, chairs and tables overturned. In one room was a great pile of gold- and azure-trimmed academic robes, sodden and stinking of urine. At the Al-Ahadat police station, which the Iraqis converted into one of many makeshift prisons, as many as two hundred men were locked in one 30-by-30-foot room, with no beds or blankets. The prisoners slept on a filthy tile floor and used scraps of styrofoam for pillows. As elsewhere, the Iraqis' own living quarters in the prison contained layer on layer of grime; half-eaten, rotten plates of food flung into corners, trash and garbage covering the floors, graffiti (HOSNI MUBARAK IS A SON OF A BITCH) covering the walls, the stench of feces and urine heavy in the air.

It was the human factor that hurt most, though. The Iraqi forces treated the people here as they did the property. They trashed them. "They killed the people and threw their bodies in the dirt," said District Attorney Nassar Seleh. "They killed the people like they were chickens."

When I first got here, a day and a half after most of the Iraqi troops had fled in the middle of the night, and a day after Kuwaiti troops had entered, I met on the road into town a polite, middle-aged newspaper writer named Abdullah Al-Khateeb. He led me to a grubby little piece of ground, a few blocks from his home, and across the street from a building where the Iraqi state security agents had one of their headquarters. We walked about twenty yards in from the sidewalk. Behind us, the street was filled, as it would be for days, with uproarious celebration; gunshots, horns, shouts, and whistles, and dark-robed women ululating—the high-pitched series of rapid tongue and glottal stops that is an Arab noise of public emotion. We stopped by a bloody red and white kefiyeh, the Arab man's common-wear headdress. Next to it were two sets of scuff marks in the dirt, and two big patches of rusty, dried blood.

"Here," said Khateeb, pointing, "is where the two boys kneeled. And here, to the side, is where the Iraqis stood. They shot the boys here, one with a pistol in the forehead, and one with a pistol in the back of the head. The boys died here."

Abdul Rahman Al-Awadi, Kuwait's minister of state for cabinet affairs, claims that 33,000 people have disappeared since August 2. The Iraqis are reliably estimated to have taken as many as 20,000 prisoners to Iraq to serve as slave laborers, and another 3,000 to 5,000 as hostages and shields in the days just before the allied ground offensive. By the minister's reckoning, that would put the number of murdered between 8,000 and 10,000. This figure is improbable, but not wildly so. The precise number was still being worked out at the end of the first week of liberation, but it was clear by the evidence that it would amount to at least a couple of thousand. The dead were everywhere.

In a cemetery in the southern suburban district of Rigga, mass graves, each reportedly containing seven or eight men or boys, stretched for long rows. Cemetery workers said the slots contained about one thousand bodies. There are ten major hospitals in Kuwait City, and all report having handled atrocity victims. At Mubarak Hospital, one of the city's largest, the chief of surgery, Dr. Abdullah Behbehani, said that from late August through October his emergency room received groups of five to ten corpses almost every day. At the Al-Amira Hospital, Dr. Sabah Al-Hadeedi said he can document, with photographs and fingerprints, thirty-eight executions.

Subhi Younis, an ambulance driver and the chief morgue attendant at Sabah Hospital, said he had handled at least four hundred and perhaps as many as seven hundred executed bodies over the seven-month occupation. One day, he said, forty-five bodies came in; another day, seventy. On days like that, the twenty-two refrigerated steel drawers in the morgue would fill quickly, and bodies would be laid out in a bloody, twisted carpet on the tile floor and the courtyard outside. When I visited, the morgue was still home to seven or eight unclaimed victims.

The corpse in drawer 12 had been burned to death with some flammable liquid. The body was curled like a fetus, and what remained of the head was still barely recognizable as a skull, but a skull that seemed to have been slathered in a brown viscous material and then baked in a kiln. It was received by the hospital on October 9, and its identity was unknown.

The corpse in drawer 16 was that of a handsome man with a full, proud black beard. His white shirt was stiff with clotted blood, as were his hair, beard, ears, lips, and nostrils. He had been shot twice, execution-style, in the head and chest. He was brought in on February 19, and he was also labeled unknown. Two men looking for a lost relative peered down at him. "That's not who I want," said one of the men. "But I know him. I can't remember the name, but I know the face. He lived in the neighborhood." He sighed and shrugged. "What can you do?"

The corpse in drawer 3 had its yellowed hands tied behind its back with a strip of white rag. The body had been beaten from the soles of the feet to the crown of the head, which had been staved in by a club, the apparent cause of death. The legs were covered with deep purple and black bruises, some six inches or more long, and the chest was scored with a crosshatch of purple welts.

The corpse in drawer 17 had been so badly burned it did not look like a body at all. It looked like something you might find on the beach on an early morning walk, in the smoldering remains of a driftwood fire. It came in on November 3, unknown.

Corpses 18 and 19 were two brothers, Amir Abbas and Hanza Abbas, brought in on January 20. Excited by the thought of the land war, the young Abbas men reportedly had led a small, bloody insurrection against an Iraqi police station in their suburban neighborhood. Their bodies came in with those of five of their neighbors, who were rounded up and killed for good measure, hospital officials said. Those men had been shot in the head, and Amir's eye sockets were bloody holes. "We believe the eyeballs were plucked out with fingers while he was alive," said Saba Hospital surgeon Ali Nassar Al-Serafi, with a sorry little shake of his head.

◆ ◆ ◆

Drs. Behbehani and Hadeedi charted, in the precise way of professional accountants of casualties, the patterns of death. The first pattern is chronological, with the execution of civilians beginning several weeks after the August 2 invasion, in response to resistance efforts, and drastically increasing from mid-September on, after Saddam Hussein's brother-in-law, Ali Hassan Majid, arrived as the new governor. Majid reportedly brought in squads of trained killers from the Iraqi state security agency, the Mukhabarat. "The executions began in earnest after they sent in the special execution squads from Baghdad," said Dr. Behbehani. "We started seeing a lot of young men between the ages of seventeen and thirty-two. They arrived, not as patients to care for, but as bodies to bury."

The second pattern is one of style, identical in almost every case. After arrest, a victim would be imprisoned and interrogated for several days or weeks. Upon release, sometimes secured with bribes solicited from the family, the prisoner would be returned home and shot in the head, neck, or heart, in front of family members. Alternatively, his body, with ankles and hands bound, would be deposited near his home. The families were generally barred from retrieving the bodies from the street or doorstep until the next day, so that many might see them, and fear.

The third pattern was one of even worse brutality. "There started in late September something more severe. We started getting mutilated and tortured bodies. Not simply shot, but eyeballs taken out, heads smashed, bones broken," said Dr. Behbehani. "You would see heads that were completely unvaulted, with no brains in the skull, or multiple fractures in each arm, or severe burns in the face and body, or fingernails removed."

"The signs of torture I saw from the thirty-eight executions this hospital handled were electrical burns, where wires had been put on the chest wall and near the genitals, and cigarette burns anywhere on the body, massive bruising, and nonlethal bullets in the shoulders, kneecaps, hip, and legs," he said. At about the same time, the doctors also began seeing more cases involving women, often raped and mutilated before death. "In November a woman I know personally was brought in," Dr. Behbehani recalled. "The top of her head was gone and bullets were in her chest." Sitting at his desk, a neat, polished man reflected in a neat, polished surface, the doctor wept. "She was—my God—she was completely mutilated. There was no brain inside her skull. Why should they take her brain? Why do such a thing?"

◆ ◆ ◆

Rape and torture not resulting in death were also common. Almost everyone I talked to in four days had a story of some friend or relative being so abused. One day a man handed me his business card, which said he was Bassam Eid Abhool, assistant electrical engineer at Kuwait International Airport. His fingernails were perhaps one-eighth of an inch long: tiny, soft, fragile little strips of ragged cuticle. "Ah, you see my fingers," said Abhool. "Iraqis, of course." His story was typical: picked up at random walking in his neighborhood; taken to a police station; hung upside down naked; beaten, tortured, interrogated; released with a warning. Much of the questioning was political. "They would say, 'You know what your emir do for your people? Marry two hundred women and take all your money—is this not true?' I would say, 'I don't know.' They would say, 'The Iraqi people have come to give freedom to people of Kuwait; is this not true?' I would say, 'I don't know.' "

On Abhool's second day in prison, his interrogators got down to serious work. "Two guys take my hands and they close my eyes, and they take pliers and they take out, one by one, my fingernails. Then they put my fingers in water with salt," Abhool recalled in a soft, dispassionate voice. On the third day, his captors crushed his fingertips with the pliers, but on the fourth day they let him go. "Later, I see them in supermarket, and they say, 'How are your fingers, are they good?' I say, 'No, they are not good.' They say, 'Come back to the police station, we will make them good.' They laugh and laugh."

There was real resistance here, and it was never completely overcome. Dr. Hadeedi and his colleagues entered wounded resistance fighters into the hospital as car accident victims to fool Iraqi watchers and hid an entire fifty-bed ward and operating theater in three basement storerooms. Five-person resistance cells worked in a loose food and money distribution network that provided those in need with staples and cash every week. Some people fought with arms up to the end, despite an Iraqi policy of collective reprisals that meant half a dozen Kuwaiti deaths for every Iraqi death. A favored tactic was to invite a lonely Iraqi soldier home to dinner and at evening's end stab him and bury him.

But for most people here the seven months were mostly a time for hiding. The postliberation boasts of opposition were often about how the rich hired cranes to put their Ferraris on their rooftops, how every neighborhood was stripped of street signs and house numbers, how valuables were secreted in backyards and young men in cubbyholes.

The liberation was, above all, a release from the grinding daily horror of hiding. I went to the street where the Iraqi governor, Ali Hassan Majid, had lived in a commandeered mansion. The women who lived across the street hadn't been outside in months, because of fear of the Iraqi guards who leered at them. Two women, one older, the other just eighteen, showed photographs of themselves from before the invasion, portrait shots in full hairdo and makeup. "Look at us now," said the older one. "We are ugly now. Look at our clothes. We could not wash." "Look at my hair," said the younger one, holding out a tousled rope of henna-rich auburn. "It is terrible, is it not?"

◆ ◆ ◆

The release from captivity took the form of that most pleasant of releases, a party. The bash began unexpectedly, early in the morning of February 26. "We woke up and saw the Kuwaiti flag flying from the police station," said Nassar Seleh. "You cannot imagine our feelings when we realized the Iraqi troops had gone from the city. In the night we had heard the tanks moving in the street, and we had dared hope they were going. But to wake up and find all of them gone—the city is ours again!"

Suddenly everyone was a rebel. The streets were filled with young men firing rifles and pistols, making the celebration almost as dangerous as the battle for liberation itself. Early reports cited six such deaths in the first two days; I know of three, whose fresh graves I visited in Sulaibikhat Cemetery. ABDULLAH JASSIM, WHO DIED FOR KUWAIT read the stone on the mound of a man hit on top of the head by a falling round.

Suddenly everyone could be brave. People tore the Iraqi license plates from their cars; two days before, that had been a jailing offense. They displayed photographs of the emir, wrote anti–Saddam graffiti (SADDAM, PUSHED BY BUSH), waved Kuwaiti flags, shouted "Kill Saddam!"; those had all formerly been hanging offenses. One car sported twenty-three photos of Kuwait's leader, his smiling face plastered on the trunk, hood, and windows, all of it festooned with bright gold and silver Christmas tree garlands. Pickup trucks dragged effigies of Saddam by the neck through the streets, and a group of laughing teenage boys led a skinny white donkey labeled "Saddam" down the boulevard.

At Al-Amiri Hospital a long line of cars queued up to take souvenir shells from an Iraqi antiaircraft gun, and families posed for pictures next to it. In a heavy rainstorm four young women sat in a row on the trunk of an Impala, having made a seat by knocking out the rear window. They waved to the crowd like princesses, and yelled over and over, "I am Kuwaiti! I am Kuwaiti!"

For Americans the party offered the novel sensation of being adored in a foreign land. An American couldn't pay for anything that week in Kuwait, couldn't walk ten feet without being stopped to accept thanks, couldn't talk to anyone without getting an invitation to dinner or lunch. "Welcome, soldiers, you are welcome" three little girls in party frocks serenaded the U.S. Marines at the newly reopened American Embassy. "George Bush, very, very, very, very, very, very, very, very, very good," an old man offered. Two women jumped from a car to proffer a daisy and a tray of cookies. "Thank you! Thank you! And thank Mr. Bush," said one. "Welcome to your country," said the other.

At one raucous do, centered on three Kuwaiti armored personnel carriers

whose crews stood unusually erect in the manner of young men posing for pos-
terity, four teenage girls wearing sweaters covered with photos of Bush, John
Major, and Margaret Thatcher (each framed with little red and gold and silver
spangles) worked the crowd of American soldiers and reporters with their auto-
graph books. I wrote, self-consciously, "To Maha, on a wonderful day, 3-1-91,"
under an inscription from a "Captain Henry Douglas: 'To a lovely Kuwaiti girl.'"

◆ ◆ ◆

There were few Iraqis left in Kuwait City against whom retribution could be ex-
acted. But on the outskirts of town I did see one scene of vengeance—pretty
much the last thing I saw there. Five days after liberation I drove up the road
toward southern Iraq, the route Saddam's soldiers had taken in flight. Every fifty
or one hundred yards there was a fresh kill from the slaughter the allied forces visited on the fleeing Iraqis. From each charred and trashed vehicle the belongings
of the dead Iraqi driver and the dead Iraqi soldier-passengers were spread in a
dirty plume on the asphalt.

Most of the bodies had been carted away, but a fair number remained. At
every spot where there was still an Iraqi corpse, a crowd had gathered. Every few
minutes a new group would approach, and someone would pull the blanket
down to see the enemy's face. The corpses were already decomposing, their faces
yellow and black and green, their features melting together under the buzzing of
flies. One by one the Kuwaitis moved cautiously forward and paid their last respects. One middle-aged man bent down, over half of a machine-gunned body
wedged upside down in the driver's seat of a stolen Toyota. He spat, carefully, on
the face. His friend got it all on videotape. They pulled the blanket back up and
got in their car, heading up the road to spit on the next of the waiting dead.

Highway to Hell

◆ ◆ ◆

ALONG THE KUWAIT-IRAQ BORDER—Captain Douglas Morrison,
thirty-one, of Westmoreland, New York, headquarters troop commander of
First Squadron, Fourth Cavalry, First Division, is the ideal face of the new Amer-

ican army. He is handsome, tall, and fit, and trim of line from his Kevlar helmet to his LPCs (leather personnel carriers, or combat boots). He is the voice of the new American army, too, a crisp, assured mix of casual toughness, techno-idolatrous jargon, and nonsensical euphemisms—the voice of delivery systems and collateral damage and kicking ass. It is Tom Clancy's voice, and the voice of the military briefers in Riyadh and Washington. Because the Pentagon has been very, very good in controlling the flow of information disseminated in Operation Desert Shield/Storm, it is also the dominant voice of a war that will serve, in the military equivalent of *stare decisis,* as the precedent for the next war.

In the one-hundred-hour rout, Captain Morrison's advance reconnaissance squadron of troops, tanks, and armored personnel carriers destroyed seventy Iraqi tanks and more than a hundred armored vehicles. His soldiers killed many Iraqi soldiers and took many more prisoner. In its last combat action, the company joined three other American and British units to cut in four places the road from Kuwait City to the Iraqi border town of Safwan. This action, following heavy bombing by U.S. warplanes on the road, finished the job of trapping thousands of Saddam Hussein's retreating troops, along with large quantities of tanks, trucks, howitzers, and armored personnel carriers. Standing in the mud next to his Humvee, Morrison talked about the battle.

"Our initial mission was to conduct a flank screen," he said, as he pointed to his company's February 26 position on a map overlaid with a plastic sheet marked with the felt-tip patterns of moving forces. "We moved with two ground troops [companies] in front, with tanks and Bradleys. We also had two air troops, with six O-H50 scouts and four Cobra attack helicopters. It is the air troops' mission to pick up and ID enemy locations, and target handoff to the ground troops, who then try to gain and maintain contact with the enemy and develop a situation."

The situation that developed was notably one-sided. "We moved into the cut at 1630 hours on Wednesday [February 27, the day before the cease-fire]," Morrison said. "From 1630 to 0630, we took prisoners. . . . They didn't expect to see us. They didn't have much chance to react. There was some return fire, not much. . . . We destroyed at least ten T-55s and T-62s. . . . On our side, we took zero casualties."

There hadn't been much serious ground fighting on the two roads to Iraq because, as Morrison put it, "the air force had previously attrited the enemy and softened target area resistance considerably," or, as he also put it, "the air force just blew the shit out of both roads." In particular, the coastal road, running north from the Kuwaiti city of Jahra to the Iraqi border city of Umm Qasr, was "nothing but shit strewn everywhere, five to seven miles of just solid bombed-out vehicles." The U.S. Air Force, he said, "had been given the word to work over that entire area, to find anything that was moving and take it out."

◆ ◆ ◆

The next day I drove up the road that Morrison had described. It was just as he had said it would be, but also different: the language of war made concrete. In a desperate retreat that amounted to armed flight, most of the Iraqi troops took the main four-lane highway to Basra, and were stopped and destroyed. Most were done in on the approach to Al-Mutlaa ridge, a road that crosses the highway twenty miles or so northwest of Kuwait City. There, marines of the Second Armored Division, Tiger Brigade, attacked from the high ground and cut to shreds vehicles and soldiers trapped in a two-mile nightmare traffic jam. That scene of horror was cleaned up a bit in the first week after the war, most of the thousands of bombed and burned vehicles pushed to one side, all of the corpses buried. But this skinny two-lane blacktop, which runs through desert sand and scrub from one secondary city to another, was somehow forgotten.

Ten days after what George Bush termed a cessation of hostilities, this road presented a perfectly clear picture of the nature of those hostilities. It was untouched except by scavengers. Bedouins had siphoned the gas tanks, and American soldiers were still touring through the carnage in search of souvenirs. A pack of lean and sharp-fanged wild dogs, white and yellow curs, swarmed and snarled around the corpse of one soldier. They had eaten most of his flesh. The ribs gleamed bare and white. Because, I suppose, the skin had gotten so tough and leathery from ten days in the sun, the dogs had eaten the legs from the inside out, and the epidermis lay in collapsed and hairy folds, like leg-shaped blankets, with feet attached. The beasts skirted the stomach, which lay to one side of the ribs, a black and yellow balloon. A few miles up the road, a small flock of great raptors wheeled over another body. The dogs had been there first, and little remained except the head. The birds were working on the more vulnerable parts of that. The dead man's face was darkly yellow-green, except where his eyeballs had been; there, the sockets glistened red and wet.

◆ ◆ ◆

For a fifty- or sixty-mile stretch from just north of Jahra to the Iraqi border, the road was littered with exploded and roasted vehicles, charred and blown-up bodies. It is important to say that the thirty-seven dead men I saw were all soldiers and that they had been trying to make their escape heavily laden with weapons and ammunition. The road was thick with the wreckage of tanks, armored personnel carriers, 155-millimeter howitzers, and supply trucks filled with shells, missiles, rocket-propelled grenades, and machine-gun rounds in crates and belts. I saw no bodies that had not belonged to men in uniform. It was not always easy to ascertain this because the force of the explosions and the heat of the fires had blown most of the clothing off the soldiers, and often, too, had cooked their remains into wizened, mummified charcoal men. But even in the worst cases, there was enough evidence—a scrap of green uniform on a leg here, an intact combat boot on a remaining foot there, an AK-47 propped next to a black claw over yonder—to see that this had been indeed what Captain Morrison might call a legitimate target of opportunity.

The American warplanes had come in low, fast, and hard on the night of February 26 and the morning of the twenty-seventh, in the last hours before the cease-fire, and had surprised the Iraqis. They had saturated the road with cluster bombs, big white pods that open in the air and spray those below with hundreds of bomblets that spew at great velocity thousands of razor-edged little fragments of metal. The explosions had torn tanks and trucks apart—the jagged and already rusting pieces of one self-propelled howitzer were scattered over a fifty-yard area—and ripped the men inside into pieces as well.

The heat of the blasts had inspired secondary explosions in the ammunition. The fires had been fierce enough in some cases to melt windshield glass into globs of silicone that dripped and hardened on the black metal skeletons of the dashboards. What the bomb bursts and the fires had started, machine-gun fire finished. The planes had strafed with skill. One truck had just two neat holes in its front windshield, right in front of the driver.

Most of the destruction had been visited on clusters of ten to fifteen vehicles. But those who had driven alone, or even off the road and into the desert, had been hunted down, too. Of the several hundred wrecks I saw, not one had crashed in panic; all bore the marks of having been bombed or shot. The bodies bore the marks, too.

◆　◆　◆

Even in a mass attack, there is individuality. Quite a few of the dead had never made it out of their machines. Those were the worst, because they were both exploded and incinerated. One man had tried to escape to Iraq in a Kawasaki front-end loader. His remaining half body lay hanging upside down and out of his exposed seat, the left side and bottom blown away to tatters, with the charred leg fully fifteen feet away. Nine men in a slat-sided supply truck were killed and flash-burned so swiftly that they remained, naked, skinned, and black wrecks, in the vulnerable positions of the moment of first impact. One body lay face down with his rear high in the air, as if he had been trying to burrow through the truckbed. His legs ended in fluttery charcoaled remnants at midthigh. He had a young, pretty face, slightly cherubic, with a pointed little chin; you could still see that even though it was mummified. Another man had been butterflied by the bomb; the cavity of his body was cut wide open and his intestines and such were still coiled in their proper places, but cooked to ebony.

As I stood looking at him, a couple of U.S. Army intelligence specialists came up beside me. It was their duty to pick and wade through the awfulness in search of documents of value. Major Bob Nugent and Chief Warrant Officer Jim Smith were trying to approach the job with dispassionate professionalism. "Say, this is interesting right here," said one. "Look how this guy ended up against the cab." Sure enough, a soldier had been flung by the explosion into the footwide crevice between the back of the truck and the driver's compartment. He wasn't very big. The heat had shrunk all the bodies into twisted, skin-stretched things. It was pretty clear some of the bodies hadn't been very big in life either. "Some of these guys weren't but thirteen, fourteen years old," said Smith, in a voice fittingly small.

We walked around to look in the shattered cab. There were two carbonized husks of men in there. The one in the passenger seat had had the bottom of his face ripped off, which gave him the effect of grinning with only his upper teeth. We walked back to look at the scene on the truckbed. The more you looked at it, the more you could imagine you were seeing the soldiers at the moment they were fire-frozen in their twisted shapes, mangled and shapeless. Smith pulled out a pocket camera and got ready to take a picture. He looked through the viewfinder. "Oh, I'm not gonna do this," he said, and put the camera away.

Small mementos of life were all around, part of the garbage stew of the road. Among the ammunition, grenades, ripped metal, and unexploded cluster bomblets lay the paltry possessions of the departed, at least some of which were stolen: a Donald Duck doll, a case of White Flake laundry soap, a can of Soft and Gentle hair spray, squashed tubes of toothpaste, dozens of well-used shaving brushes, a Russian-made slide rule to calculate artillery-fire distances, crayons, a tricycle, two crates of pecans, a souvenir calendar from London, with the House of Lords on one side and the Tower on the other; the dog tags of Abas Mshal Dman, a non-commissioned officer, who was Islamic and who had, in the days when he had blood, type O positive.

◆ ◆ ◆

Some of the American and British soldiers wandering the graveyard joked a bit. "Crispy critters," said one, looking at a group of the incinerated. "Just wasn't them boys' day, was it?" said another. But for the most part, the scene commanded among the visitors a certain sobriety. I walked along for a while with Nugent, who is forty-three and a major in the army's special operations branch, and who served in Vietnam and has seen more of this sort of thing than he cares for. I liked him instantly, in part because he was searching hard to find an acceptance of what he was seeing. He said he felt very sad for the horrors around him, and had to remind himself that they were once men who had done terrible things. Perhaps, he said, considering the great casualties on the Iraqi side and the extremely few allied deaths, divine intervention had been at work, "some sort of good against evil thing." He pointed out that there had not been much alternative; given the allied forces' ability to strike in safety from the air, no commander could have risked the lives of his own men by pitching a more even-sided battle on the ground. In the end, I liked him best because he settled on not a rationalization or a defense, but on the awful heart of the thing, which is that this is just the way it is. "No one ever said war was pretty," he said. "Chivalry died a long time ago."

Rolls-Royce Revolutionaries

◆ ◆ ◆

KUWAIT CITY—Six days after the Iraqis stole away in the night, the U.S. Army Corps of Engineers brought in the first supplies requested by the Kuwaiti government to rebuild its stripped and junked country. Food for the hungry? Water for the thirsty? Generators for the darkened city? Well, no. The first convoy carried furniture for the emir.

The truckloads of new sofas, beds, tables, and chairs were not for His Majesty Sheikh Jaber Al-Ahmad Al-Sabah's primary home. The occupiers had, in the hallmark style, looted, burned, and shat up that pleasant old palace. The Bayan Palace, where the emir is hanging out these days, is not even his second home. It is either number three or number four, and he rarely stays there. Still, the emir's new house is really a very, very, very fine house.

From the outside it looks rather like a community college campus, a collection of squat concrete boxes grouped around trim lawns and simple gardens. But inside it's all Trump Tower and Rodeo Drive. The architect's principal idea seems to have been: Say it with marble. The hallways and staircases are marble. The bathtubs and sinks are marble. Even the trash cans are marble. All of this marble comes from the quarries of Carrara, cut there in what the Italian stonecutters call matchbox, so that each polished piece precisely matches its neighbors, in creamy slabs of white, beige, pink, blue, and black, with rich Roqueforty veins running from panel to panel in perfectly synchronized streaks. The look is so buttery rich it seems you could scoop out a little spoonful of wall and spread it on a piece of bread, if there were any bread in the emir's city.

The palace's main buildings are situated in clusters of three; each named after a Kuwaiti island in the Persian Gulf. Every building has a ground floor reception area and three floors of suites, two to a floor and each comprising five bedrooms, a like number of bathrooms, a kitchen, a dining room, a cabinet-level conference room, and a couple of sitting rooms. The bedroom and sitting room walls are dressed in watered silk or blond wood; the bathroom fixtures are gold-plated; the private kitchens are state-of-the-art in techno-cuisine; the beds are appropriately king-sized, the bathtubs are oval; the carpets are toe-wriggling plush. The flatware is sterling, each piece engraved with a crest that denotes which building it belongs to. The tablecloths and napkins are Irish linen, and they, too, are embroidered with crests. The doorknobs are brass, the bolsters and valences are satin, and the big chandeliers are crystal.

All of this had to be fixed up properly—stolen marble balustrades and gold showerheads replaced, denuded walls resilked, the 2-million-gallon reservoir linked up—before the emir, who sat out the war in the Saudi Arabian resort town of Taif, would come home. Some people suggested that Kuwait's leader had not returned to lead his struggling nation until fifteen days after its liberation because he was concerned about his security in a city where the streets were filled with youths with guns and the air with falling bullets. Not at all, assured Sulaiman Al-Mutawa, Kuwait's minister of planning. The delay was entirely caused by the need "to find a suitable place for him to live in."

The job of rendering the Bayan Palace suitable fell to Wayne Urbine, a Corps of Engineers supervisor from Savannah, Georgia. On the afternoon of March 14, a few hours before the emir's plane was to touch down, Urbine showed me around the second building in the Bubiyan cluster. The place was due for completion the following afternoon, and it was hopping, the only scene of intense reconstruction work I saw in two weeks in Kuwait City. On the door to every room a little yellow Post-it note was stuck, enumerating the details within left to be attended ("Remove valence, replace molding on bathroom door"). One hundred and twenty workmen were moving about, from room to room, floor to floor, and as they finished each chore, one of Urbine's undersupervisors would check it off.

The crews, Urbine said, generally worked twelve-hour days but had pulled some all-nighters in order to finish the million-dollar job in its allotted ten days. Members of the royal family, he said, visited regularly—"a constant circus"—to check on progress. "Everything has to be visually outstanding," he said. "The cousin of the crown prince is here all the time. . . . The crown prince also came by last weekend to check it out and was very delighted with the way it was coming. The minister of labor was here yesterday. He sat down in the chairs to test them and made a few comments about the wallpaper. He said the chandeliers looked okay."

The whole scene bothered Urbine a bit. "It's sort of a value question," he said. "You go out there and see thousands of people in line to make a phone call and you come here and see all this opulence and someone is complaining because there aren't enough damn gold fixtures."

◆ ◆ ◆

There did seem to be, on the day of the royal return, plenty of concerns of a more pressing moment than bathroom accessories. Garbage lined the streets in smelly, rotting hills. Running water existed only in some city mains and a few of the big hotels. There was no electricity other than that provided by generators, and there were very few generators. Food distribution finally had begun several days before but was limited mostly to a bare list of basics: rice, milk, sugar, cooking oil, and tomato paste. Trucks carrying electric generators, water, and food had been stalled for days at the border of Saudi Arabia and Kuwait, thanks to the Kuwaiti government's insistence on changing its customs requirements, it seemed, about every two hours.

Then there was the misplaced enthusiasm that the government, or at least young gun-toting men in army uniforms purporting to represent the government, seemed to have for the most unsavory aspects of life under martial law. Although the State Department professed ignorance of any mistreatment of Palestinians and other non-Kuwaiti residents, U.S. officials here said otherwise. Andrew Natsios, the director of disaster relief for the Agency for International

Development and a major in the army's Kuwaiti emergency task force, put the number of disappeared Palestinians at "on the low side, between two hundred and three hundred, on the high side, between five hundred and six hundred." At the Iraq-Kuwait border town of Safwan, U.S. military police officers said men dressed as Kuwaiti soldiers had taken to dumping busloads of Palestinian, Iraqi, and North African prisoners in the no-man's-land. "They dumped twenty-five yesterday," said MP Steve Eaton. "They came up here, stopped, and told them to get out and start walking. The prisoners didn't have any food, any blankets. Some of them didn't even have shoes."

Apart from roughing up and chucking out undesirables, the Kuwaiti soldiers passed the time demanding identification papers at countless checkpoints and firing clips of machine-gun bullets into the air, the slugs of which bounced down on the sidewalks and bored through the occasional skull. They took a more laid-back approach to the real work of reestablishing control. On the day of the emir's arrival, the beaches, the countryside, and various crannies of the city were still littered with unexploded Iraqi land mines, American bomblets, and other objects suitable for maiming and killing curious children. Huge numbers of weapons, everything from pistols to armored personnel carriers, had disappeared into private homes, garages, and warehouses in the chaotic days after the war's end. Tales of both random and organized violence were common. A major political opponent of the Sabah family had been shot in the chest in his doorway. Unpleasant rumors swirled about: A secret group called the Men of Jaber was threatening and killing liberal political figures; a secret Syrian army hit team had moved in to do the same. The gloomy conventional wisdom predicted a serious round of bloodletting once the Americans went home.

◆ ◆ ◆

Returning to a devastated land filled with subjects who had strayed when he had left, and who had suffered greatly for seven months under Iraqi rule, the emir said . . . nothing at all. He knelt and touched his forehead to the tarmac, greeted the several hundred family members, senior government officials, and diplomats he had allowed to attend the homecoming, and was whisked away. The masses were not permitted entry to the heavily guarded scene.

This is, of course, just the sort of thing, right down to the clichés (has there ever been a fabulously wealthy, unfeeling potentate who did not favor gold-plated toilet gewgaws?), that has gotten other rulers their heads handed to them. So it was not surprising that, as the emir sped off to his palace, mutterings of dark discontent could be heard all over town.

At one neighborhood supermarket four hundred or so people, mostly women, waited in long lines for a chance to get the few meager supplies the government's new food distribution plan was offering. Unfortunately, the supermarket had closed for the day at noon, and most of those who had waited since five A.M. were going home empty-handed. Inside, a store manager lied with broad and smiling abandon. "At home, the people already have everything they need," he said. "Fresh fruits, vegetables, all stored in their homes."

Not far away several hundred Kuwaitis buzzed angrily about a police station. They were trying, they said, to get permission to leave the country temporarily, to buy food, generators, and other necessities. The martial law imposed by the government upon Kuwait City's liberation made that impossible without special permission. "They told us to come here for the piece of paper," said one man. "We have been here since eight-thirty this morning, and there is only one little window for us to go to, and now they say the window is closed, so come back tomorrow. It is an outrage!"

The talk of the town hinted at some species of revolution. The Sabah family, which numbers about two thousand, has run Kuwait since the turn of the century, and run it absolutely since Jaber, who acceded to the throne in 1977, dissolved the 1986 National Assembly, and suspended the 1962 constitution. There has been some opposition, most seriously in 1989, but political upheaval is not naturally popular in a country where vast oil wealth is spread around in one of the world's most generous welfare systems. A fair idea of the general attitude toward serious political change can be gathered from the 1981 elections, called to form the first National Assembly since 1976. Of the 6 percent of the population allowed to vote (only male Kuwaiti-born citizens, and not all of them), half didn't bother.

Now the family's political opponents were suddenly uttering the unutterable. "This government should resign," said Abdul Aziz Sultan, a banker and a leading opposition figure. "A government of defeat cannot be a government of reconstruction. . . . The emir has done nothing, and the prime minister is spending all his time going to *diwaniyat* and bullshitting." A few days later the cabinet of the prime minister, who is also the crown prince, submitted its resignation. The new cabinet is to be formed by the crown prince, who is also still the prime minister.

Political discussion—indeed, all discussion—in Kuwait is centered on *diwaniyat,* late-afternoon gatherings of men drinking endless cups of tea and sitting in comfortable couches around the walls of large, and generally quite elegant, rooms. A few days before the emir's return, I went to one where I was promised I would find hotheaded, revolution-minded souls. I found a young man named Ahmed

Al-Issa. He took me for a ride in his lovely, late-model Mercedes Benz. We went to his house, where he introduced me to two pretty young women who were playing pool in a big room that had white carpets and a superbly stocked bar. He talked moderately rough while the girls poured and posed with cue sticks. "The Sabah family has a problem," he said. "We all see that the failure of the government has been quite clear, and the government sees that we see this, so they come in with the whip now. But they are incompetent people. All is chaos."

Indeed, there was a striking contrast between the efficiency of the unofficial government established by the Kuwaiti resistance under occupation and the bumbling, lackadaisical approach of the reconstruction. By all accounts the resistance delivered the goods, at least to fellow Kuwaitis. An underground banking system kept hundreds of millions of Kuwaiti and Iraqi dinars in circulation and provided money on a regular basis for those Kuwaitis who had not fled the country. A food distribution network provided ample supplies of canned goods and other basics. Volunteers picked up garbage and policed neighborhoods.

The Marafies, owners of hotels, stores, and other businesses, are one of Kuwait's top families, a leader in the group of twenty-five that the emir formally visits twice a year. They live exceedingly well. Thanks to their money and foresight, they even made do, on T-bone steaks, shrimp, and pâté, during the occupation. They do not normally complain about their good friends the Sabahs. But at a *diwaniyah* just before the emir's return, the mood was a touch bitter. "The Sabah family said they would be ready to go as soon as Iraq left Kuwait," said Nader Marafie, moistening his lips with a little sip of tea. "We expected them to take two or three days to get things ready, not three or four weeks. We were told trucks of food were waiting to roll in. They were not. We were told the police force would be ready to come back right away. It was not. This is not good."

The real problem, of course, is the Palestinians. The 450,000 Palestinians of Kuwait, many of whom have been here for decades, made the country work. "The people who know how to run things, the people who always did all the work here, were almost all Palestinians," said one U.S. official involved in the reconstruction. "They were the judges, the doctors, the dentists, practically all the engineers, all the middle managers. The Kuwaitis in charge of things now are politically well connected, but not well versed in technology." A Red Cross official marveled at his difficulties in establishing a coherent relief system. "The people we are dealing with have no concept of the mechanics of actually getting jobs done," he said. "They are very good at talking and sitting and drinking tea all day, but they don't have a clue about things like how to get a lorry from point A to point B."

The obvious solution would be to encourage the 150,000 Palestinians remaining in Kuwait to get back to work, and encourage the thousands who fled to Jordan and elsewhere to return. This is not the solution the emir has in mind. Instead he and his government intend to reduce greatly the number of Palestinians and other foreign-born workers (the Filipino maids and gardeners, the Pakistani hoteliers and sales managers, the Sudanese trash collectors) and replace them with hard-working Kuwaitis. "We proved during the occupation that Kuwaitis are not ashamed of sweeping streets, collecting garbage, working in gas stations," said Nader Marafie, as he lit another cigarette and settled back in the cushions. "So what the government should do is supplement wages in the private sector for people like garbage collectors, and then you will see lots of Kuwaitis doing this."

◆ ◆ ◆

I changed the subject. Why, if the government was botching the job of getting food and water to Kuwait City, did not the Marafie family, with its vast resources and empty stores waiting to be filled, organize its own shipments? "It is not easy," demurred Nader. "There is no official exchange rate yet, so how could we know what to charge people? Besides, it is not easy to get food. How can we get to Saudi Arabia? Where would we get trucks?"

No, it isn't easy. Although probably not any harder than it was for the Palestinian proprietors of the Al-Sultan Saleem Restaurant, a humble joint in the poor Hawalli neighborhood. By the time the emir came home the Al-Sultan Saleem had been open for a week, serving rough bread, tea, and the Arabic fava-bean dish called *fool* to standing-room-only crowds, taking payment in Kuwaiti dinars, Iraqi dinars, U.S. dollars, and Saudi royals.

Nader continued: "The government must organize things to make it less difficult." As he was speaking, two members of the royal family dropped in for a surprise visit. They were seated in places of honor, and served tea and ice water, with much bustling and courtesy. The conversation picked up its pleasant hum again, as the *diwaniyah* settled into its fourth hour. No one said anything to the royals about the balky pace of the reconstruction, or what the government must do. It would have been impolite, and Kuwaitis are very polite, at least to fellow members of the ruling class.

The Other Hell

◆ ◆ ◆

SARDASHT, IRAN—In war there are winners and losers, and then there are the truly screwed. Meet Majid Abdullah. He is thirty years old, and up until a month or so ago he was a soldier in the Iraqi army. When the ground war started in Kuwait, he ran away from a fight he wanted no part of anyway, and made his way back to his home in Kirkuk, a city in the Kurdish north. Soon after he arrived, his neighbors, Kurds like himself, decided to seize the moment against their old enemy, Saddam. Abdullah says they had an idea, based on listening to George Bush, that the United States might lend a hand. This proved fatally false, and in no time Saddam's helicopters, Abdullah recalls, "were killing, killing, killing—killing people in the streets."

Abdullah ran again, this time with about a million and a half of his fellow Kurds, to the sanctuary of Iran. And this is where he is now, on a late April afternoon, standing shivering and sockless in the mud on a hilltop in a refugee camp that looks like a place for prisoners of war, where a meal of a few potatoes and water and a little bread is daily fare, where the weak and the sick are dying at a slow but steady clip, and where, it turns out, he and his kind are not welcome at all.

◆ ◆ ◆

The Kurds who fled Iraq's butchery for Iran's mercy have escaped hell to land in purgatory. Their brethren who fled to Turkey are, relatively speaking, the lucky ones. America has promised them protection; decent camps are being built; the marines are watching over them.

Sorrow does have its gradations. The saddest place I came across in the hundreds of miles of western Iran over which the refugees have been scattered was the camp of lost children. This place, located just outside of the farm market city of Saqqez, in the province of Kurdistan, was set up by the Iranian government to care for the thousands of Iraqi Kurdish girls and boys who have lost their mothers or their fathers or both. Some of them saw their parents gunned down by helicopters. Others misplaced them in the terrible exodus through the snowy mountain passes to Iran. Now they live here—infants, toddlers, and teens, together with aunts and occasional uncles; five thousand thoroughly wretched souls. In happier times the camp was a farm, and it must have been a fine and pleasant place, situated as it is in a lovely green and broad plateau ringed by gently rounded hills and old, soft mountains. Now it is guarded by armed soldiers and surrounded by metal fences and shining, slice-to-the-bone new rolls of concertina wire. The first thing I saw there was a pretty little girl, maybe four years old, sitting alone at the front gate against a big roll of the razor-edged steel, smiling in the afternoon sun.

In the old bucolic days the concrete and corrugated tin barns held beasts. Now they hold humans treated like beasts. Each building has been divided into pens, with sheets of tin tied together with twine. The pens fill the barns and the people fill the pens. I counted twenty-three in one ten-by-twenty-foot square. The refugees sleep in the pens, on worn and dirty blankets on the concrete floor; the children play in them; the women cook in them, on crude kerosene stoves that are tipsy on the uneven floor. The sick lie still, staring or sleeping, and the others fit themselves around them, in a squalid, squirming zigzag. Rain leaks through the roof and through the windows and doors that are covered only with plastic sheets. The air is fetid and close, rich with the stink of sweat and kerosene and the shit that is everywhere, and that peculiar smell of apple-sweet rottenness that emanates from the lungs and pores of the gravely ill.

I walked, with another reporter, through the beast homes. A refugee and mechanical engineer named Barham Abbus pointed out one hollow-cheeked woman lying curled on the floor in a fetal position, with two young children lying next to her. He said, "You see her? You see these children? They have had diarrhea for twelve days. They are going to die." The people swarmed, shouting for attention, each one trying to tell what horrified him or her the most. "Mister, mister! There are no showers. . . . Mister, mister! We have no freedom to leave. Mister, mister! This is a place for cows and chickens. . . . Mister, mister! There is no food. . . . We are sick. . . . The water is bad." Very soon after we arrived in the camp, the Iranian official accompanying us decided this was not a fit sight for the foreign press. "Come," he said, pushing and prodding. "Enough. Must leave now." The soldiers escorted us out and shut the gate.

◆ ◆ ◆

Lesser horrors greeted the eye everywhere. The dirt roads and green pastures leading from the mountain passes were thronged with dirty, tired, hungry people. On a path thirty miles north of this western Iranian city, thousands camped in rough tents made from tree branches and plastic sheeting. On a warm afternoon the women washed clothes against the rocks in a brook swollen by spring melt. The dirt road was a bizarre bazaar, the result of private enterprise rushing in to supply food and goods that the government and relief agencies had not. Small boys walked down the road tempting the hungry with boxes of pastries and cookies and hard-boiled eggs (a pinch of salt included). A stand of aluminum tent poles stood next to a shish kebab brazier that was bordered by a display of ladies' plastic pumps. To pay for such goods, the refugees had opened a medieval trading route, carrying on foot from Iraq into Iran anything of value they could take from their home. Every ten or fifteen minutes, another importer would come trudging down the road from the mountains. One old man, perhaps five-foot-three-inches tall and weighing maybe 130 pounds, was bent double from the refrigerator strapped to his back. Another labored under a load of four large television sets, still in their cardboard factory boxes. The men said they had walked six or seven miles with their loads.

In the towns and small cities near the border, the wandering homeless over-whelmed the streets, searching for food, resting by small fires along the sides of the road, joining roosters and hens and just sitting and scratching in the dirt. Here the only care seemed often to come from the local Iranian Kurds. "We get noth-ing from government," said Muhammed Kidur, standing on a street corner in Sardhast. "No medicine, no food. We haven't seen meat, we haven't seen bread, we haven't seen anything. We are not even allowed to go to the market to buy food." Others rushed around, a cacophony of complaints, but the Iranian media minder hurried a few policemen over to shoo the witnesses away.

◆ ◆ ◆

It is not that no one was trying to care for the refugees. By the second week of the crisis, the large foreign relief agencies—principally the International Com-mittee of the Red Cross and the French group Médecins Sans Frontières—had done much good. But they were nowhere close to coping with the scope of the problem. No one knew the basics: how many refugees were still arriving, where they were going, how many camps had sprung up and where they were located, how many people were dying, and from what. I talked one afternoon with the Red Cross's chief delegate in the refugee-swamped province of Azerbaijan. I mentioned the fact that in at least some of the Iranian government-run camps, refugees were guarded by soldiers who seemed to treat them as prisoners. He de-murred. "In the camps I have been in, I have seen them come and go as they please." It turned out he had not been to any camps except the one operated by his own agency, and one or two others. "I don't really have the time."

What the international relief workers did know was enough to make them gloomily sure that things were going to get worse. In the only camps where medical teams had made a complete survey, the mortality rate among children was found to be four times the level considered "acceptable": two deaths per ten thousand people per day. "The rate should stay the same for the next week or so, but because of food supplies being insufficient, it should rise after that," said Dr. Bitar Dounia, the Médecins Sans Frontières epidemiologist who analyzed the survey results. "To what extent it will rise, I have no idea."

The insufficiency of food is the heart of the problem. Foreign relief supplies, arriving in the regional capitals of western Iran, mostly by cargo planes, are not enough. By the third week of this crisis, an estimated 150 planes had landed, bringing 500 tons of food, blankets, medicine, and other supplies. But, said Pierre Sarant, chief field administrator in Azerbaijan for Médecins Sans Frontières, "This is not going to work. There are 500,000 refugees here. Under these circumstances, 500 tons is nothing. It is rain in the desert."

Which brings the issue back to the Iranian government, whose resources in manpower and at least such basics as bread dwarfed that which the foreign relief agencies can bring to bear. From the beginning of the flood, the government, first in the form of the wholly controlled Iranian Red Crescent and then through the interior ministry, has insisted on handling all food distribution. Privately, Red Cross and other foreign relief workers complained that the government's role seems to have focused on maintaining bureaucratic protocols and stockpiling food, rather than speeding it to the remote refugee camps and border areas.

The Iranian government has contended that a modest third world nation cannot be expected to do any better caring for such multitudes of guests. But a number of the international relief experts working with the Iranians said they did not believe a paucity of resources was the real reason why, for instance, the children in the Saqqez camp were being fed nothing but potatoes and bread, why they were being given drugs that had expired as long ago as 1964, why they had only eleven toilets for five thousand people.

"The real truth," said an angry Red Cross official, "is they don't want these people here. They only want to give them just enough to survive and make them get the hell out of town and the hell out of the country."

Which is why Majid Abdullah, sockless in the mud of Sardasht, is truly screwed. Because if you are an Iraqi Kurd in Iran, it may be some time before you can go home again.

Back to the Hills

◆ ◆ ◆

MOUNT AZMER, IRAQ—The Kurdish rebel stronghold here consists of a few dozen men on a little scrabble patch of dirt on the edge of a small plateau just below the top of the hill. The men have Kalashnikov automatic rifles and a 106-millimeter antitank gun, and two mortars that look like lengths of old, green pipe some careless plumber left in the rain too long. Near the mortars, on the ground, are a couple of hundred loose rounds of antiaircraft ammunition that likewise have been scabbed over with rust.

But high ground covers a multitude of sins. The mountain overlooks the big Kurdish city of Sulaymaniyah, fifty miles from the Iran-Iraq border, about 180 miles north of Baghdad. About six miles distant, the city is home to thirty thousand Iraqi army troops. When, in a series of attacks between April 7 and April 12, Saddam Hussein's soldiers left the safety of Sulaymaniyah and tried to take this sorry little outpost, they couldn't do it. The *pesh merga* (as the rebel fighters call themselves) claim that their 150 defenders held off 500 to 600 army troops, three tanks, and a helicopter attack, killing 110 of the enemy and taking only 15 dead on their side.

Press reports on the post–Gulf War Kurdish uprising in Iraq have tended toward the view that the Iraqi army crushed the rebellion in a massively one-sided victory. The view from Mount Azmer suggests a more complicated truth. The real nature of things is a delicate balance of power between Saddam's men in the cities and the Kurds in the hills. "The weapons we have are defensive mainly," said Derwish Ibdula Arhma, a military strategist for the Kurdish Democratic Party, one of the top two of Kurdistan's five political parties. "A few anti-tank weapons and light weapons, five or six partially damaged tanks. It really is not much, while the army still has major offensive power in its helicopter gunships and advanced tanks." It would be extremely difficult, Ibdula figures, for the *pesh merga* to retake a major city by force. "On the other hand, the army cannot retake all Kurdistan," he said. "The more spread out it gets, the less control it has."

Saddam's forces, immeasurably aided by U.S. complicity, did indeed crush the rebellion in the large cities of the region, most notably Kirkuk and Sulaymaniyah. They bombed the cities with helicopter gunships, inflicting much death and driving as many as 3 million people into the countryside and toward the dubious sanctuary of Turkey and Iran. (At least in the case of Kirkuk, *pesh merga* leaders say, U.S. fighter jets watched from overhead.) The Iraqi army then occupied the big cities and held them by sheer force of numbers.

◆ ◆ ◆

But the story outside the few Iraqi army strongholds is precisely the opposite. Here, in a broad swath of land running the length of Kurdistan along the Iraq-Iran border and along much of the Iraq-Turkey border, the *pesh merga* completely hold the field. These rebel-controlled territories, which the Kurds call "freedom places," are rarely less than thirty miles wide and generally stretch up to sixty miles or more inland from the borders. Within these, the Iraqi army is limited to a very few cites, such as Dahuk, fifty miles from the Turkish border, from which American forces were attempting to oust them in the first two weeks of May.

In eight days of traveling through the Kurdish countryside, I never saw an Iraqi soldier, except as a distant, binocular-viewed bug on the horizon. I saw many hundreds of rebel fighters, well-armed with AK-47s, RPGs, heavy machine guns, antiaircraft guns, and mortars taken from captured government caches. They thronged the roads and villages, and had established a large network of camps and checkpoints that kept in touch through sophisticated shortwave radios, also courtesy of the Iraqi army.

Neither the Iraqi army nor the Iraqi civil authorities can operate at all in the countryside of Kurdistan. The well-armed men of the *pesh merga* own the turf, and act like it, lolling about in their hidden hilltop camps, tearing about in their liberated Toyota Land Cruisers, shooting their guns about in the evening air, and all in all strutting high, wide, and handsome.

One afternoon a local *pesh merga* chief (who looked unexpectedly like George Bernard Shaw) suggested we take a break from drinking cocoa by the waterfall and visit the front lines. We went in the usual caravan—forty or so men, with one hundred or so assorted rifles and pistols, in seven or eight four-wheel drive machines, including a pickup with a .50-caliber machine gun in the back. It took two hours to cover the twenty miles, because all the *pesh merga* military leaders are politicians, or all the Iraqi Kurdish politicians are *pesh merga* military leaders, and they brake for handshakes. We drove through the usual sort of scenery: past meadows of Ireland-green grass and purple thistles and glorious yellow wildflowers, past ten thousand desperately sick, dying people, past countless blown-up houses, past the shot-up and abandoned outposts of the Iraqi army.

After a while we stopped at a widening in the road where a group of ten or twelve men with guns stood around to form a checkpoint. We walked with them a few hundred yards to a second checkpoint in the road, where a smaller group of men stood next to two .50-caliber guns and a rocket-propelled grenade launcher, both set on tripods. Manning the machine guns was a young man who had wrapped so many overlapping bandoliers of ammunition around his torso that he seemed to be wearing an extremely well-armored cummerbund up to his armpits.

This, it turned out, was a major position of the Kurdish southern front line. The Iraqi army was five kilometers distant, standing guard over its own more elaborate front. Through binoculars you could see a line of seven dug-in tanks stretched along a ridge, and a few dots that were presumably enemy soldiers. Traffic moved freely through the two checkpoints. The *pesh merga* guards, at least, hardly slowed the cars and trucks for the most cursory of checks. A small flock of black mountain sheep, with curly horns and witchy white and black eyes, moved slowly and stupidly by. "As you can see, this is a pretty relaxed situation," said the commander, in a slightly apologetic tone. "The fact is, the Iraqi army is more afraid of us than we are afraid of them."

This may have been an exaggeration, but it is extraordinary it could be said with a straight face at all. The checkpoints manned by the careless young Kurds were Iraqi army posts; two months ago they were the property of Saddam's gunsels. The land we were driving through—like all of the land that makes up the *pesh merga*–held territory—had been under the total control of the Iraqi army for years, in some cases for a decade or more. This country is the heart of Kurdistan. To realize what it means that the Kurds have taken it back, it is important to understand exactly what Saddam did in taking it away.

◆   ◆   ◆

The Iraqi regime has always taken care to keep foreigners out of Kurdistan, and it is easy to see why they would want to hide what they did. Jelal Talibani, leader of the preeminent Patriotic Union of Kurdistan, and others who claim to have kept track of the wreckage, say the Iraqi army, enforcing Saddam's plan to depopulate rural Kurdistan and relocate its people in the more easily controllable big cities, dynamited twenty-eight Kurdish cities and at least four thousand villages from 1974 to 1990, with the greatest carnage in the late 1980s. I don't know if the figure is inflated, but it is certain the destruction was vast and thorough.

When I first walked into Iraq, over a mountain pass from Iran, I asked a Kurdish refugee traveling part of the way with me to point me first in the direction of one of those destroyed villages everyone talked about. "Why, you are in one now," he said. I looked around at the steep hillsides and, after a moment, the jumble of stones strewn everywhere organized themselves into lines and squares, like one of those trick drawings that changes from a wine goblet to two faces, and I realized I was looking at the foundations of a village of many houses. This was the town of Terwella, built a long, long time ago, on the banks of a gin-clear brook, blown up in 1986.

Around the bend of the road were the remains of Dara Kaysar and Naranjala. "Look what has happened to my people. Look what Saddam has done," said the old man who took me there, looking at the rubble spread over three hillsides. Every mile brought the sight of another ruin: Hormal, built in 1977 to house Kurds moved from previously destroyed villages, in turn dynamited in 1985. Nawprez, situated in an especially pleasant spot near where a single sliver pour of water falls straight into a turquoise pool, destroyed so thoroughly it would take a team of archaeologists just to reconstruct the outlines. Penjwan, a good-sized city of seventy thousand people, reduced in 1983 to a messy pile of stones and concrete jumble and rusting iron and steel. Saed Sadek, with forty thousand homes, which took fifteen days to blow up completely and where now almost nothing tops three feet.

The dynamiting was preceded by the forced evacuation of the people who lived in the wrecked towns. First they were moved from their old, isolated hillside villages to new cities built on flatland more accessible to the Iraqi army and security forces. Then those were TNTed, too, and the people were moved again, to settlements in and near the major Kurdish cities. The destroyed areas were sealed off and guarded by numerous checkpoints, and no one but soldiers and government men were allowed to go there. By 1991 most of Kurdistan was a military zone.

◆ ◆ ◆

The *pesh merga* reclamation has brought, remarkably quickly, a return of people to the places where no Kurds were ever supposed to live again. In every ruined village and city, hundreds and thousands of families now huddle in pancaked buildings, in tents, in lean-tos made from tree limbs and plastic sheets and scraps of metal. Most of the people are refugees from Kirkuk and Sulaymaniyah, desperate for any shelter, even a broken slab of concrete. Many, however, are people who seized the chance to return to their hometowns and begin building something new. The man who looked like Shaw, for instance, had been a wealthy businessman in Baghdad and a commanding officer of a thousand men in the

Iraqi Popular Army. He left, he says, a $400,000 house in Baghdad, and brought his wife, three young children, and most of his troops to a spot not far from where he was born. He lives in a big tent in the middle of a leafy, sun-dappled clearing in the woods, and he says he is having the best time of his life.

Indeed, the life of the *pesh merga* leaders, returned to the land, had a hard but lovely charm. One evening a local commander took me home for dinner at his family's hilltop camp. As his wife made a small fire, we walked down the hill to bathe in a pool of cold, clear water. As I washed, my host slipped off into the brush, stalking dinner. He rested his Kalashnikov on a tree branch and took a long, steady sight on a blackbird perched on a limb sixty yards away. He fired once, and the bird fell. He showed it to me, so I could marvel at his shooting. Since a direct hit would have exploded the tiny bird, he had shot just to graze its breast, the bullet plowing a neat, bloody furrow a quarter-inch deep. Back at the camp, as he prepared the body of the bird for supper, he cut off the head and gave it to his delighted three-year-old daughter. She played with her toy, opening and shutting its tiny yellow beak, stroking its fine black feathers.

Nowhere was this serenity and recovery more evident, or more poignant, than in Halabja, the scene of Kurdistan's greatest crime. On March 17, 1988, according to witnesses, Iraqi warplanes used bombs and rockets with chemical warheads against the people of this city, killing about five thousand and forcing the rest to flee to Iran. It was three days before it was safe to return, and by then the dead clogging the streets and roads were so far gone that the burial parties had to use bulldozers to shovel them into mass graves. The graves are on the edge of town, a series of big, slightly misshapen mounds, each holding a couple of hundred bodies, covered in lush, tall grass and abundant thistles.

In 1990 the troops returned to dynamite the buildings. On March 18, 1991, the *pesh merga* took back the city. When I visited it in late April, it was for the first time in three years home to more living people than dead. At least six thousand were camping out in the shattered hulls of the city's one-story houses, and in tents and lean-tos among them. The central market area was alive with the buzz of hustle among the ruins.

On one corner a butcher whacked great hunks from a freshly skinned sheep hung from a tripod of poplar branches. On another, a barber had set up a rickety chair and a mirror in a shell of a storefront and was giving a close haircut to a small boy. A restaurant of sorts was selling an excellent chicken soup that the chef-proprietor brewed in a big pot suspended over the burning end of a log on which he sat and stirred. The owner of a battered minibus stood nearby bellowing his destination, and a boy trundled past him with a wheelbarrow of sticky, furry figs.

Down the street Dr. Fayak Muhammed, who lost his mother, brother, and sister in the attack, had returned and opened a clinic, where he was seeing two hundred patients a day. I spent that night at Dr. Muhammed's house, which was one of the few in town still more or less intact. After a dinner of rice, bread, and tomatoes, the men sat around and drank tea and talked. The conversation was an incompatible mixture of yeasty hope and leaden worry. One young man, a writer of the school of magic realism, who had written two (unpublished) anti-Saddam novels, talked of the mimeographed newspaper *Freedom,* which he had put out in the brief period the rebels held Sulaymaniyah. "I wrote about the important things," he said. "The function of censors in a fascist structure and the nature of democracy and the meaning of totalitarianism. We published one issue, maybe three hundred, four hundred copies."

All of which—the young men and their shining bandoliers, the fine talk, and the real strength of the *pesh merga*—raises a question. If things are so full of promise, why did the Kurds agree to sit down and bargain with Saddam? The answer is that apart from the military situation, things are terrifyingly bad.

There are, Kurdish leaders say with perhaps some hyperbole, 3 million refugees scattered in the border areas. At least several hundred thousand are within Iraq's borders. These are not the poor, huddled masses you saw on television. Those are the luckier, or stronger, ones who were able to make the trek all the way to Turkey or Iran. These wretched souls are the ones who couldn't or wouldn't make the exodus. They have almost no food or medicine. They live in filth and hunger and misery. There are too many of them crowded together with too few toilets, which has contaminated the usually good mountain water. Diarrhea diseases are epidemic. "You may say, at this point, that everyone has diarrhea," said Dr. Muhammed. As if to prove him right, the next day I got it myself, and learned why the few doctors of Kurdistan are afraid they could lose half the children if more medical help does not arrive before the full heat of summer.

It was a remarkably fast and violent sickness. In the morning, the first faint flutterings in the stomach; six hours later, ceaseless diarrhea and a 103-degree fever. The next afternoon I found a *pesh merga* doctor who hooked me up to an intravenous drip for four hours to rehydrate me and gave me the course of antibiotics that would soon cripple the amoeba enough to allow me to function. The doctor was Talibani's own, which is why he had such things as saline and antibiotics. Ordinary doctors, such as Fayak Muhammed, had run out weeks before.

Those without such good treatment may easily die of dehydration. The sickness makes it impossible to retain any fluids. One day, walking up a dirt road near Penjwan, I came upon a ten- or eleven-year-old boy lying in the dust, barely conscious. His face was burning hot, and thick ropes of mucus ran from his nostrils. He lay with his head turned to the side and his feet splayed outward, and he could not move. When we lifted his head and tried to pour water in his mouth, he stared uncomprehendingly and let the liquid dribble from the corners of his cracked lips. A medical student, the closest thing to a doctor in that place, flagged down a passing pickup and we laid the boy in the back, for a twenty-mile trip to a *pesh merga* clinic. "But there won't be much they can do for him there," the student said. "They have nothing to give him."

There was plenty of food available, but here, as elsewhere in Kurdish Iraq, it is too expensive for many families. At the stands along the road in Penjwan, a can of Isomil powdered milk costs three dinars; a kilo of rice or flour, two. The average Iraqi salary in the wake of the war is between six and eight dinars per day. These deadly circumstances dictate the position of the Kurdish leaders. They are willing to talk terms with Saddam because they have no other choice if they wish to get their people back into their homes and avoid mass casualties from hunger and disease. "At this point the only thing that is important is the survival of three million refugees," said Talibani. "We are facing the biggest catastrophe in our history."

The Iraqi regime likewise cannot afford not to talk. Saddam can't get away with keeping the dispirited remnants of his army indefinitely stuck on police duty surrounded by well-armed young men eager to shoot them. A German photographer who managed to sneak in and out of Sulaymaniyah a few weeks ago says he found Iraqi troops eager to talk to him, and to tell everyone how miserable they were, how much they wanted to go home, how tired they were of fighting. I interviewed three Iraqi army POWs in a *pesh merga* camp one day. "You tell Mr. Bush he must do something to get rid of this Saddam," said a lieutenant. "He must do something to help us all go back to our homes." He and his colleagues berated the United States for calling off the ground war before destroying all of Saddam's military machine. But more fighting would have meant a great many more deaths of Iraqi soldiers, I said. "Yes," said one of the men. "Kill ten thousand, twenty thousand. Fine. It is worth it as long as Saddam is dead too."

◆ ◆ ◆

And here, of course, is the problem in the precarious equation of power in Kurdistan. It can exist as it is, or be tipped one way or the other, only by the actions of the most powerful force in Iraq these days, the U.S. armed forces. The United States might prefer the United Nations fulfill this role. The Kurds, who would just as soon possess the only army around, would prefer this, too. But Iraq has rejected a UN peacekeeping force in Kurdistan. And the United States is already the de facto cop on the beat, holding territory fifty miles deep inside northern Iraq in a 3,600-square-mile "security zone."

The point of the zone is to make the refugees feel secure, thus enticing them home. But it only covers the area along the Turkish-Iraq border and does not protect the many more refugees on both sides of the Iran-Iraq border. The Kurds want a larger zone, as the United States found out in Dahuk. This undestroyed city is roughly sixty miles from the Turkish border. Secured, it would serve, the U.S. planners decided, as a magnet to attract 200,000 refugees home. But the Iraqis, already pushed out of the cities of Zakho and Amadiy, dug in the heels of 1,000 troops. The United States suggested a compromise that would allow the Iraqis to stay in Dahuk and keep U.S. forces out, while protecting the returning refugees with a force that might include UN troops and *pesh merga* fighters. The Kurds said that wasn't good enough.

Things will probably work out in some stopgap fashion, because everyone wants it to. Saddam and the Kurds want to sign a truce. The Iraqi army doesn't ever want to fight American troops again. Everybody wants the Kurds to go home. But working it out is going to mean, at least in the immediate future, the presence of an armed third party strong enough to handle both groups of men with guns. If I were an American soldier stationed in Zakho, I'd be planning on celebrating my Labor Day the Kurdish way.

· FRONT LINES ·

The Fear of Death

· · ·

In the summer and autumn of 1995, as the war in Bosnia was winding uncertainly down, I spent a couple of months in and around the town of Bihac, a small, handsome mountain city in the northwest corner of the country then entering its third year and last days under Serbian siege. Bihac was defended by the Bosnian army's V Corps, which had built itself up from a few platoons of local volunteers armed with Kalashnikovs and hunting rifles into a great if unconventional fighting force. For more than two years, the V Corps held off a much larger and vastly better armed encircling force, and the war they fought was more like 1917 than 1995.

The soldiers at the front lived for weeks and months at a time in slit trenches and scant bunkers of sandbags and tree branches dug in along the wooded ridges and hills that surround Bihac. They had, for most of the war, so little ammunition that it was common for troops to go into battle with twenty rounds apiece. They fought in short, furious bursts, emerging from their holes in the mud to charge the enemy line in shooting, stabbing, shrieking onslaughts that usually ended in minutes with everyone on one side or the other dead or wounded—the wounded to be carted out of the woods by hand and by horse, a lengthy ordeal that served as a rough triage, finishing off the lingering doomed along the way.

These soldiers were mostly young and mostly untrained, but they had become greatly familiar with war. Many of them had killed people and almost all of them had seen people killed, and familiarity had bred its usual contempt.

While they still feared death, they no longer respected it. This had some unhappy consequences. There was a lot of mental depression in Bihac, and the local sense of humor tended toward the gallows (Bihacians swapped black little ironic stories of death the way Washingtonians swap black little ironic stories of lawyers), and I met a few young soldiers who had become sickly enamored of killing.

But the devaluing of life had also served its great purpose: It had freed the people from their normal inhibitions about killing and being killed, and this in turn had kept them from being killed. If the citizens and defenders of Bihac had not come to more or less comfortable terms with death, they would become overwhelmed, and unable to summon the wherewithal to fight for their lives. Accepting death, it turned out, was indispensable to defeating death.

This is a troubling idea to contemplate as the United States worries, again, about what to do about Baghdad. Saddam Hussein's ability to agitate America rests on his understanding that America has developed a phobia of military death. While we have become weirdly numb to the horror of death in the civilian sphere (on the streets, in the movies), we have evolved what amounts to a zero tolerance policy for death on the battlefield; and not just American death, any death. In Bosnia, we watched the Serbs conduct a genocidal campaign, and did nothing of practical import for three years, because we didn't want to be responsible for anyone being killed—not even the perpetrators of genocide.

The Persian Gulf conflict was, per capita, probably the most death-free war ever waged. In all the war, there was only one scene of really troubling mass slaughter, the savaging by air and by tank of the armed Iraqi forces fleeing on the roads home from their rout in Kuwait. And this scene ended the war.

Looking at the burned, exploded bodies a few days after the attack, it seemed obvious to me that the war must instantly end; there could be no justification for continuing unilateral slaughter. This seemed obvious to a lot of other people, too, some of them professional military men and some of them advisers to the president. So the war ended, abruptly and disastrously, with Saddam Hussein in power and protected by the well-paid, heavily armed Republican Guard, which American forces could have destroyed in a few days then.

It seems obvious to me now that what seemed obvious to me then was the usual result of a little knowledge intruding suddenly on total ignorance. I had never seen the results of war, and the results horrified me out of my wits. In this, I was, of course, typical of my generation of reporters. The result is, in matters military, a press corps that is forever suffering a collective case of the vapors. At the least exposure to the most unremarkable facts of military life—soldiers can be brutes and pigs, generals can be stupid, bullets can be fatal—we are forever shocked, forever reaching for the *sal volatile.*

Fortunately, not many people pay much attention to us anyway anymore. But the media's generational horror at war's truths reflects the larger society's views, and this larger society includes the military itself. Not since Vietnam has America faced a serious war, involving a serious level of death (and Vietnam's 58,000 American coffins were a fraction of the butchers' bills paid in the great wars), and that conflict ended a quarter century ago. We are a nation in which there are fewer and fewer people, and they are older and older people, who accept what every twelve-year-old in Bihac knows: That there are things worth dying for, and killing for.

So, we will let Hussein stall us until he has hidden what weapons of mass death he needs to hide, and then he will let the UN inspectors back in, and we will live with that. Or we will inflict some suffering on Iraq, and kill some people, but not too many, because the people—our people, not theirs—will not be able to stand the pictures. And we can live with that, too. But one of these days, somebody—the North Koreans come to mind—is going to start a real war. And we will find out what we can really live with.

Where Are the Dead?

◆ ◆ ◆

One afternoon in the early autumn of 1995, as the war in Bosnia was entering its last weeks, I was driving in a slanting thick rain on a back road from the city of Bihac to the city of Cazin, and I stopped to pick up a soldier who was hitchhiking to the front, about fifteen miles away. The soldier belonged to the 511th Brigade of the Bosnian army's V Corps, one of the two best brigades in what was by far the best corps in the army. He wore a uniform rigged out of castoffs from other armies, and sneakers on his feet. I guess he was eighteen or nineteen years old. He had no hair on his face, except a straggling of thin black shoots on his upper lip, and he was thin, like most people in the Bihac area at that time. His skin was faintly yellowish from malnutrition, which was also common.

He climbed into the back seat and lit a cigarette. It was late in the day, almost dusk, and chilly. I had the heat on, with my window open only a few inches, and the cigarette smoke and the steam from his rain-wet clothes made a homey smell of burning tobacco and damp wool. When he had finished the cigarette, he stubbed out the butt in the ashtray in the door handle and began talking. He spoke in Serbo-Croatian—or Bosnian, as he would have said—and the translator retooled his words into English, which lent a slightly unreal and theatrical distance to them, as if they were coming from the radio.

He said that a few days before, in the aftermath of the V Corps's successful effort to drive the Serbs out of Bosanska Krupa, he had been walking in the woods of a hill overlooking the town when he had come unexpectedly upon a Serb soldier, whom he captured without incident. As he stood there, pointing his rifle at his prisoner, he realized that he knew the man. They had grown up together, and had gone to school together, in the city of Prijedor, about fifty miles from where they now stood, a place where both Muslims and Serbs had long lived as neighbors. In April 1992, near the beginning of the war, the Serbs of Prijedor took control of the city in a swift, brutal coup, and began killing and expelling the Muslims there, as part of an ethnic-cleansing sweep throughout northern Bosnia. The captured Serb soldier had taken part in this.

The Bosnian soldier who was telling me this story in the car on the way to Cazin had fled Prijedor with all his family, except for his father. His father had refused to leave their home, and he had been missing ever since.

"What happened to my father?" the Bosnian soldier asked the Serb soldier. The Serb was silent for a moment, and then he said, "I am sorry to say he is not alive. He died soon after you left Prijedor." He did not say, but neither did he have to say, that the Bosnian soldier's father had died because the Serbs had killed him.

"You remember that we were friends," the Serb said. The Bosnian didn't say anything. "You remember that we were classmates." The Bosnian still didn't say anything. "Is there a future, do you think, for Bosnians and Serbs together in this country?" the Serb asked.

At this point, my passenger, sitting there in the backseat, in the washing-day warmth, said, "So I said to him, 'Yes, there is, but not for you and me.' And then I shot him."

◆ ◆ ◆

Before the war in Bosnia, the city of Prijedor had 112,000 inhabitants. Today, 1,022 of its residents—all of them Muslim, or, as is said, Bosniac—are listed by the International Committee of the Red Cross as missing.

What happened in Prijedor happened all over Bosnia and Herzegovina. The Red Cross, which uses the most conservative accounting, lists 19,323 people as missing from the war. Most of these are presumed to be dead, and most died in ethnic-cleansing operations. The great bulk of the missing, 16,152 people, are classified as Bosniac. Their disappearances created in some towns a hole of 100 people, in others a loss of 1,000 or more. Occupying its own magnitude of disaster, there is Srebrenica, a city of 40,000 people that fell to the Serbs on July 11 and 12, 1995. The Red Cross lists 7,364 people as missing from Srebrenica.

The idea in ethnic cleansing is not simply to get rid of an undesired population but, more precisely, to get rid of the problem cases among the undesired population—the political, social, business, and religious leaders, and all potential armed resisters. In practical terms, this means getting rid of the men, especially the men between the ages of eighteen and fifty. More than 92 percent of the missing in Bosnia—17,842—are men. Places like Srebrenica have been stripped of three generations: the potential husbands, the husbands, the fathers. It is not very unusual in Bosnia to meet a woman who has lost both her husband and her father, or her husband and her sons.

Many of the survivors assume the worst, but they need to know for sure; they need to know which body in which mass grave belongs to them. Others believe that the missing must still be alive somewhere. They speak of hundreds or thousands of "hidden detainees" in secret underground prisons. They are easy marks for crooked government officials and con artists posing as middlemen between the governments, who pocket the money they pretend to pass on as bribes in deals that never quite come off.

Conventional warfare most often produces relatively small numbers of missing people, scattered over time and place. (There are 2,097 Americans still missing from the Vietnam War, which was fought over a period of ten years and which involved 2 million U.S. military personnel in Vietnam or offshore.) Ethnic cleansing produces relatively large numbers in isolated times and places. And it produces them through a process that is illegal. These two factors lend to the task of finding the missing an array of difficulties. The difficulties begin with the criminal aspect. Most of the missing were murdered, and were buried in hidden mass graves. These graves and any information about who is in them represent evidence of capital war crimes. So right away any investigation runs up against the natural disinclination of government officials to provide evidence that can be used toward the eventual hanging of themselves. In the past four years, only 1,421 of the cases of people missing from the war in the former Yugoslavia have been resolved.

◆ ◆ ◆

Given all these difficulties, the task of hunting for the missing requires a special person. You need someone who is at least a little desperate for something to do with his life, someone with a solid streak of perversity, someone who is attracted to failed causes and dismal realities. You need, in a sense, a loser. Early last fall, it occurred to President Clinton that Bob Dole would be ideal for the job.

The job, specifically, was that of chairman of the International Commission on Missing Persons, a committee that Clinton had formed in the summer of 1996 and which was composed of distinguished elder statesmen with time on their hands. Under its first chairman, former Secretary of State Cyrus Vance, the commission held a few meetings and made a few fact-finding trips, and established an office in Sarajevo. It did not, however, accomplish much in the way of actually solving the cases of the missing. Some critics said that was at least partly the fault of Chairman Vance, who was in his late seventies and did not seem to bring much energy to the job. Vance's term ended on November 8, and Clinton appointed Dole, who is seventy-four, to replace him.

Dole was happy to get the call from the president. He has been one of Bosnia's most serious supporters in American politics, and his commitment is emotional, that of someone who has a visceral knowledge of war. When I asked him why he had gotten involved, he replied, with a sort of stream-of-consciousness disgust, "You know, nobody was paying attention. Things would happen, the president wouldn't do anything, nobody was doing anything. And you would have terrible things happen—Srebrenica, women and children not able to walk the streets in Sarajevo—and you just see more and more of it every day on television, you hear more and more of it, you have to do something, you really do."

Dole had another, more personal reason for wanting the job, and he talked about it recently, sitting up late on the twelve-hour flight aboard one of the Boeing 707s used as Air Force Two, which carried him to the former Yugoslavia on his first official tour as chairman of the commission. "My dad, you know, he was a working man, wore his overalls every day, he worked for forty some years, but he finally quit," Dole said. "And he'd go home and get up and there's no place to go. So he'd take out the garbage and sweep the walks and mow the lawn. You know, you can only do that once or twice a day, mow the lawn a couple of times a day."

It is not really the case that Bob Dole has had nothing to do since November, 1996, except cut the grass. He has a job at the Washington law firm of Verner, Liipfert, Bernhard, McPherson & Hand. It is an easy job—Dole neither litigates nor formally lobbies; his primary function is simply to attract rich clients—and it pays well, reportedly $600,000 annually. Dole still enjoys the perks of public life. He has a suite of ten rooms in Verner, Liipfert's downtown Washington offices, a press secretary, and a chauffeur who drives a Cadillac with Kansas plates. He also enjoys at least some of the attention of public life. Since the election, Dole has appeared on the *David Letterman Show* and has made television commercials in which he gently mocks himself in the service of Visa check cards and Dunkin' Donuts. He is popular enough to command a fee of up to $50,000 per speech, and last month he spent three days shaking hands and accepting thanks on a "farewell tour" of Kansas.

None of this, though, has much meaning beyond the pursuit of money. What has meaning is that, on the evening of January 16, Dole stood in the VIP room at Andrews Air Force Base, waiting for the vice president's plane to take him to Sarajevo, and the telephone rang, and it was the president, for him. It was only a courtesy call, good luck and bon voyage, but it made Dole beam.

◆ ◆ ◆

"It's good to be going here," Dole said as the plane began its descent into Sarajevo. "I could get elected in Bosnia." This reminded his young press secretary, Joyce Campbell, of a remark Dole made on another recent trip: "I'm just flying around looking for a country that needs a president."

The next day, Sunday, January 18, Dole and his fellow commissioners—Max van der Stoel of the Hague; Cornelio Sommaruga, the president of the International Committee of the Red Cross; and Sahabzada Yaqub-Khan, the former foreign minister of Pakistan—hosted the public centerpiece of their visit to Sarajevo, a meeting with members of the associations of the families of the missing of Bosnia and Herzegovina. The meeting took place in a conference room in the Hotel Grand, which is a nice, modern hotel that has opened since the end of the war. There were twelve groups represented around the table: the missing of Srebrenica, the missing of Mostar, the missing of Bugojno, and so on. Erwin Böhi, a dapper and officious Swiss gentleman who is the commission's Sarajevo staff director, opened the meeting by telling the witnesses that they would be limited to three minutes' speaking time per group. Then the testimony began.

It was awful, desperate stuff. "We come before you as the saddest population in Europe," the first speaker, Branko Panic, began. "We are all people looking for our beloveds, some hoping to find them alive, while many will be satisfied just by finding their bodies. Many mothers have said they will be happy just to find three ribs belonging to their sons. They will be happy just to know where to bring candles with which to mourn them."

Vlada Erkapic, of Bugojno: "Between the eighteenth of July and the twenty-fifth of July, 1993, during the Muslim-Croat conflict, three hundred Croatian soldiers and six hundred civilians were detained in Bugojno. They were taken to the football stadium and they, our dearest relatives, were taken away in groups of one or two, and it has been five years since then and we still are waiting to find out if they are dead or alive. The Muslim authorities in Bugojno know where they are. They know where the mass grave is, if there is one. The high-ups in the government of Bosnia and Herzegovina know it. But silence covers everything."

Sabra Mujic, Srebrenica: "Mr. Dole, I am a mother who saw with her own eyes her sons taken away. I lost two sons and my husband. I have not a single member of my family anymore, and there are thousands of mothers like myself. I beg you to do all you can for the mothers. You are the last hope. You must make Mr. Milosevic release our sons from the underground prisons to which he holds the keys. Please do something. Please tell him to release our husbands and sons. Please, Mr. Dole, we are looking for someone who is human enough to help us. Maybe it is you, Mr. Dole."

This despair and wild, doomed hope would have been difficult for the most eloquent and emotionally facile of politicians to adequately answer. Dole, whose access to the language of emotion is barely adequate to cope with the routine of life, could only say that he knew from his own long involvement with the issue of America's missing in Vietnam that "one missing is too many," and that he and the other commission members would "renew our efforts." He ended with a weak promise: "There are some funds. I will be seeing Mr. Milosevic tomorrow and I hope to impress upon him the importance of cooperating, and we'll be back again in late March, April."

As the commission members stood, there was for a moment or two a frozen quiet in the room, and then everyone got up at once and swarmed them. Old men, old women, some weeping, surrounded Dole. They pressed family snapshots on him. A woman came up on Dole's right and thrust at him a creased, dirty bit of newspaper. "Mr. Dole, my son, he is alive, it says so here in this paper. He was taken to a prison in Serbia on sixteen January 1993." Dole, trapped, miserable, took the paper from her. "I will give this to Mr. Milosevic tomorrow," he said.

More people surrounded the commissioners; the complaints were coming with open bitterness now. A furious young man maneuvered Max van der Stoel up against the table and upbraided him about an infamous event in the fall of Srebrenica, the handover to the Serbs of 239 Bosniacs who had come to a Dutch base for protection.

"Our soldiers were outnumbered, outgunned," van der Stoel said.

"Their camp was never attacked, sir; the Serbs never entered their camp, sir; I was there, sir," the young man said. "I was the UN interpreter in that camp and I saw the Dutch troops throw my entire family out in front of my eyes, sir, and I have never seen a member of my family again, sir."

Van der Stoel, in a small, fading voice, said, "We are still investigating."

◆　◆　◆

After the meeting, the commissioners, looking weary and somewhat battered, trudged upstairs to attend a cocktail reception for Sarajevo's diplomatic community. Dole made an amusingly self-deprecating speech—"When I first heard about this commission, in June of 1996, I had in mind that I would appoint Bill Clinton to chair it," he said, "but something happened in November to change my mind"—and promised to work hard.

One of the people listening was Dr. Laurie Vollen, a member of Physicians for Human Rights. Dr. Vollen is working on the business of what she calls "exhumation and identification." She explained, matter-of-factly over a glass of wine, some of the complexities of the job.

There are, she said, layers upon layers of both political and forensic complications. A basic political problem that ethnic cleansing produces is one of proportionality. All the governments involved—the Republic of Bosnia and Herzegovina, the Federal Republic of Yugoslavia, the Republic of Croatia—possess, as Vollen put it, "the trader's mentality: I'll tell you where your bodies are if you'll tell me where my bodies are." But trading doesn't work here, because the Bosnians are missing many more bodies than the Serbs and the Croats combined. "The Serbs say to the Bosnians: We won't give you back your bodies until you give us back ours. But there just aren't that many Serb bodies to give back."

In the relationship between each government and its own people, there is another difficulty. For governments dealing with problems such as Bosnia's massive unemployment and Serbia's bankrupt economy, finding and identifying the war dead is not a priority. "We have asked the Bosnian government many, many times to form a national forensic team, and have received no help at all," Vollen said. "The federal government gives money to the canton governments, which divvy it out to the police departments to hire local forensic pathologists, but these pathologists are paid according to what they exhume, whether they identify the bodies or not, so there is no motivation for them to do the work of identification."

After the political impediments come the forensic ones. "You must remem-

ber there are hundreds if not thousands of mass graves," Vollen said. "To start
with, you have to find the grave. In the best scenario, you have surviving eyewitnesses who take you to the site. Then you just go poking around in the earth
with a stick. You take the stick out and smell it, and if it smells like corpses you've
got a grave. Another way you can tell is that grave sites sometimes have different
vegetation than the surrounding area—you don't see trees or big bushes at a grave,
only new vegetation, and it is usually just weed cover. More commonly, you
don't know the precise location of the grave, but you know the general vicinity,
and searching an area like that requires technical resources we don't have, such as
ground-penetrating radar. Once we find a grave, we have to test it for mines and,
if it is mined, demine it. Then you begin the actual work of exhumation and
identification."

Forensic pathologists identify bodies with evidence ranging from the general
(age, height, clothes) to the particular (teeth, DNA samples). If you are looking
for only one person, and you find a body that matches that person's general physical characteristics and that body is garbed in the clothes the missing person was
last seen wearing, you can be reasonably sure you have found the person. But if
you are dealing with hundreds of missing you must turn to the more laborious,
more precise methods. If you are dealing with bodies in the thousands, even
those methods are not enough.

"Consider the difference between Vukovar and Srebrenica," Vollen said. "In
Vukovar, where we were dealing with just a couple of hundred bodies, we had a
lot of variety among the missing to help us. They were men, women; they were
young, old; there was a lot of variety in clothing; some people had received
much better dental care than others. Then we were able to take DNA samples
from the relatives of all the missing, and we just matched those samples with
forensic samples. In Srebrenica, where there are nearly eight thousand missing,
you had a population of missing that was first of all much more homogeneous,
and there was not much in the way of dental records, because the standard dental procedure in rural Bosnia is extraction. And DNA matching is especially difficult here, because Srebrenica was a place where people had been intermarrying
for a long time, and this produces what is called redundancy—such a high frequency of repeated patterns that you cannot easily distinguish large numbers of
relatives from one another. You can see it gets quite difficult."

To date, the Physicians for Human Rights team at Srebrenica has identified a
total of twelve bodies.

◆　◆　◆

The goals of Dole's trip were carefully modest. The commissioners had the same two principal chores to perform in each of the capital cities they visited—Sarajevo, Belgrade, and Zagreb. One was to meet with the representatives of the families of the missing and to hear their testimony. The other was to meet with political leaders and to press the causes of the families of the missing—to press the cause of the Bosnians with the Serbs, of the Serbs with the Croats, of the Croats with the Bosnians and the Serbs. These things were done, and done with sincerity. But it turned out that modesty was a wise course. What happened in the meeting in Sarajevo was typical of the entire trip. It wasn't that nothing was accomplished at all. But it was clear that there was a pretty large distance between what the commission for missing persons was doing—what little it was empowered to do—and what was required actually to resolve the issue of the missing.

In Belgrade, the meetings with the family associations took place in the Hyatt, a great hideous pile of marble and gilt in a great hideous suburb of leprous concrete. There were seventeen family association members around the table, but only eight of them were authorized to speak, for four minutes apiece. The first person who came forward, Dragan Medic, whose son, a pilot, has been missing since 1991, spoke of his dissatisfaction with the blatantly pro forma nature of the thing. "I have been through meetings like this so often before, Mr. Dole," Medic said. "Mr. Richard Holbrooke himself promised me he was personally going to obtain the release of pilot Medic from President Tudjman of Croatia—and until now we have heard nothing."

Medic's words were echoed throughout the meeting. Mirjana Bozin-Miodrag, whose father disappeared after being arrested by Croatian authorities in June 1990 in Vukovar, observed that "At every meeting, everyone has files, everyone takes notes, we submit lists. And there is never anything that comes of it. How many more times shall we have meetings and tell our sad stories, how many more times must we open our hearts? Mr. Dole, we have been telling our sad stories over and over again for six and a half years, and we never get anything in return but promises."

At the end of the allotted hour, Dole answered the accusations with a bleak candor that must have been unexpected, but that American political audiences have come to know well. "As someone said, you get together and tell your sad stories—and they are sad stories—and nothing happens," he said. "The politicians all have political agendas. They say, 'We won't do this unless they do that.' And what happens? Nothing happens. Well, I don't want to raise anyone's expectations, because I know they have been raised and dashed before, but I promise you . . ." And here, where another sort of politician (the sort, say, who beat

Dole in 1996) would have said something grand and grandiose, Dole simply said, "I can only promise you that our only interest is in helping families and that we will do our very, very best." One of the women at the table let out what was nearly a shout: "That's it? Shall we have another meeting today? Nothing? That's all?"

◆ ◆ ◆

The meetings with the heads of state also had a feeling to them of slogging in place, of heavy going without really getting anywhere. In Sarajevo, the commission met separately with two of the three members of the tripartite Bosnian presidency in a grand building, a drafty relic of Austro-Hungarian days. The first meeting, with Kresimir Zubak, the Croatian member, ended with vague promises of cooperation and a request by Zubak that Dole be so kind as to carry a message to Alija Izetbegovic, the Bosnian member of the presidency, with whom Zubak was not at the moment speaking. Izetbegovic thanked Dole for the message from Zubak and asked him to carry a message back.

In the third presidential meeting in Sarajevo, Dole was scheduled to meet with Momcilo Krajisnik, the Serbian member of the presidency, on Sunday morning, on the neutral turf of the Swiss ambassador's home. On Saturday, Krajisnik demanded that Dole and the other commissioners meet him in Pale, the ski town outside Sarajevo, which the Serbs say is the capital of the state of Republika Srpska. Dole recognized this as a ploy. By journeying to Pale, the commission would impute a legitimacy to the idea that the Serb-held area of Bosnia constitutes a state. Dole told the Serbs that they had until seven P.M. to show up in Sarajevo. The Serbs showed, but the meeting produced nothing beyond polite chat.

The meeting in Belgrade with Slobodan Milosevic, the president of what was Serbia and is now the Federal Republic of Yugoslavia, was the only one of the presidential meetings to produce a concrete result. Dole and Milosevic talked for more than an hour and got along well. (Milosevic can be charming when he wants to be.) The meeting ended with Milosevic pledging that his government would hand over the files on some 393 Croatians who have been missing from the border city of Vukovar since the 1991 Serbo-Croat War. Erwin Böhi sniffed that Milosevic's government had made this promise before, a year ago, and had not delivered on it. But Dole, who trusts his dealmaker's instincts, was sure that Milosevic wanted to do business, and he left Belgrade deeply pleased.

The final meeting, and the final event of Dole's trip, was on Monday evening, with the Croatian president, Franjo Tudjman, in Tudjman's vast and rather ugly presidential palace in Zagreb. During the meeting, Dole attempted to fulfill the promise he had made in Belgrade to Dragan Medic, the father of the missing pilot, and he pressed Tudjman to release information. But this infuriated the Croats, and the meeting degenerated into bickering from which it never recovered. After it was over, the Croatian deputy prime minister continued to berate the commissioners in the corridor. "For seven years, we have not had a single request for information answered," he nearly yelled at Dole, waving his index finger in Dole's face. "Not a single request answered, not one body returned! That is the reality! Why should we answer their requests?" Dole listened, stonily. Later, he said that he told Tudjman, as the two men were making their farewells, that the meeting had been a "waste of time."

◆ ◆ ◆

On the flight back to Washington, Dole, perhaps affected by the Tudjman unpleasantness, seemed to be brooding about the limits of what the commission could accomplish. "You know, listening to those mothers and wives and sisters in those meetings," he said, "I hope I didn't raise their expectations. You try to make it clear every time that we can't promise anything, but we will work at it. But unless these people cooperate I don't see how we can do anything."

This depressing thought led Dole to another depressing thought. In Sarajevo, he had spoken privately with the Bosnian prime minister, Haris Silajdzic, whom he has known for ten years, and he had asked Silajdzic for his prognosis of Bosnia's future. "He was pretty unhappy, you know, just down, depressed," Dole rambled darkly on. "He says we're gonna end up with Bosnia partitioned, says it's gonna happen, says they're down to about twenty-eight percent of the territory now. Yeah, he was a little discouraged." Dole trailed off, and his face for a moment took on that bleak, to-hell-with-it look that was the bane of his image managers in 1996.

The Balkans are discouraging. They have discouraged people who are more naturally sunny than Bob Dole. And it is hard to imagine that much good can come out of an ex-senator and three other old men flying around there a couple of times a year to listen to laments from widows and lectures from despots. But sometimes you get surprised. This time, Milosevic kept his promise. On February 3, the Federal Republic of Yugoslavia handed over the 393 files on the missing of Vukovar. It was a pittance, but it was something, and the old dealmaker had gotten it.

The Visionaries of
the Irish Agreement

◆ ◆ ◆

In February 1994, President Clinton rejected both the pleas of the British government and the advice of his own State Department and allowed Gerry Adams, the president of the Provisional Irish Republican Army's political wing, to visit the United States. This seemed to me then profoundly wrong, in terms both moral and practical.

Morally, I did not see how anyone could justify conferring the privilege of a visit on Adams and Sinn Fein, thereby legitimizing the IRA's policy of murdering civilians as a political tool—with 1,600 deaths credited to the Provos since they began their bloody business in 1969. Practically, it seemed foolish to take a step that would, in one fell stumble, alienate America's principal ally and infuriate one side of the Belfast equation.

In June 1996, when former senator George J. Mitchell was appointed to chair the Northern Ireland peace talks, I was similarly pessimistic. Mitchell, I had written earlier in the year, was a man whose political career exemplified the Peter Principle, having "gently floated ever higher, borne on the uplifting vapors of mediocrity rising to its natural level."

Well, at least I was consistent: wrong in every regard. The Irish troubles, which have persisted for three hundred years and which have cost more than 3,200 lives in the last tenth of that time alone, are not going to end tomorrow. But the Good Friday agreement, which was signed on April 10 by eight of Northern Ireland's ten political parties, and which goes to the voters on May 22, may be the beginning of the end. And this is in real measure due to the vision and dedication of Clinton and Mitchell.

In December 1993, after a period of exceptional bloodiness, the British prime minister, John Major, and his counterpart from the Republic of Ireland, Albert Reynolds, began the long process that was to lead to the peace agreement, offering Sinn Fein for the first time a place in the negotiations—if the IRA would forswear violence. This exchange—a seat at the table for a farewell to arms—would become the motivating dynamic of the peace process, but it at first went nowhere: The IRA could not bring itself to contemplate a peaceful life.

Then in February that year, Clinton let Adams come to America, and in return, Adams promised to produce a cease-fire. On August 31, 1994, the IRA announced the "complete cessation of military operations," for the first time since 1969. This step allowed the British and Irish governments to open, in December, exploratory talks with Sinn Fein and the two major Protestant paramilitary groups of Northern Ireland, the Ulster Defense Association and the Ulster Volunteer Force.

These talks, and the talks that grew out of them, nearly broke down many times during four exceedingly difficult years. One reason they didn't is that Clinton never stopped pushing them forward. In 1994 he tied peace progress to jobs in Northern Ireland, increasing U.S. aid and urging American companies to invest in Belfast. In 1995 he visited Belfast, and his passionate exhortations for peace there are credited by many in Ireland with imparting a new hope and energy to the cause. And also in 1995, most important, he finally persuaded the British to accept American involvement in the negotiations. On November 28, George Mitchell was appointed to chair the critical, and deadlocked, side talks on the disarmament of the IRA.

It was Mitchell's skillful and patient handling of this wretched assignment that led Britain and Ireland to appoint him in 1996 to chair the comprehensive peace negotiations. For twenty-two months, Mitchell commuted three days a week to Belfast, leaving his new Washington law practice and his new wife, to preside over talks so contentious that some participants refused to even speak to others. After the agreement was signed on Friday, everyone involved said the same thing: It couldn't have happened without Mitchell, and without Mitchell's immense patience in dealing with what must have been one of the more exasperating sets of negotiators ever assembled. Saying good-bye, one participant said to Mitchell, "I don't know how you stood us all that time." But he did, and so did his president, and the result, no matter what happens next, is a stunning achievement. For the first time, the Protestant and Catholic political leaders of Northern Ireland have committed themselves to the idea of coexistence and compromise within the structure of democratic rule. The Protestant majority has accepted the idea of sharing power with the Catholic minority; the minority has accepted the idea of majority rule, even if this means that Northern Ireland remains in the near term part of the United Kingdom. What was done on Good Friday may be undone by fresh violence or may be rejected by the rank and file of Sinn Fein. But the great conceptual breakthrough will remain, and history will credit Bill Clinton and George Mitchell for their part in this.

Ignoring Nuclear Threats

◆ ◆ ◆

The end of the American Century is a hungry time, filled with small nations aching with desire to be larger than they are. Inside every skinny power there is a fat one screaming to be let out, and from Beijing to Moscow to Baghdad to Tehran to Istanbul to New Delhi, ambitious souls dream tin-pot dreams of a new world order that is not the American Century II.

And the ambitious do more than dream. They build and they buy. For a commendably long time, the United States more or less kept the wraps on the weapons of mass destruction that it invented to win the great fight between democracy and totalitarianism. Five nations—the United States, Russia, China, Britain, and France—declaredly possessed the bomb. Three others—India, Pakistan, and Israel—possessed it but did not formally admit so. They did not because the United States applied immense pressure to anyone exhibiting nuclear ambition. But when the great fight ended, that pressure began to ease.

Now, the wraps are nearly completely off. The historians who chronicle the next century's wars will look back on the Clinton era as the age of proliferation, a sort of Great Awakening of nuclear ambition, when the power to deliver mass death (whether by means nuclear, chemical, or biological) was allowed to spread from the few to the many.

A case can be made that there is not much that could have stopped this. The territorial and even imperial ambitions that the Cold War froze were bound to thaw, and as they thawed, they were bound to expand. But if something could have been done, this administration certainly didn't do it. The business community wouldn't have approved, and the new Democratic Party fashioned by Ron Brown and Bill Clinton is not anymore in the business of irritating business. Commerce rules, and nowhere has this been more clear, and with more disastrous results, than in the area of nuclear proliferation.

For years, the administration has looked the other way from increasingly blatant violations of proliferation restrictions by China, Russia, and various European companies. It has done so, as the president recently hinted in unusually candid remarks, because it does not wish to admit truths that would trigger anti-proliferation sanctions that might get in the way of trade.

But the problem with proliferation is that it proliferates. Just because the United States chooses to look the other way doesn't mean that everyone else is blind, and nations that find themselves directly threatened by the expansiveness of others tend to be very watchful indeed. While the administration was busy assuring itself, and Congress, that the new, good-neighborly People's Republic of China was nothing to worry about, India noticed a few things. It noticed that Tibet was next door; and it noticed that China continued to occupy Tibet; and it noticed that China had deployed nuclear missiles in Tibet; and it noticed that China had recently improved its missile capacities, thanks to Clinton administration assistance; and it noticed that China had never renounced its claim to a swath of eastern India.

On May 3, India's defense minister, George Fernandes, appeared on television. He said that "China has its nuclear weapons stockpiled in Tibet right along India's borders," and that "China is potential threat number one." Recalling India's brief and humiliating 1962 border war with China, he said that his country had in the past made the mistake of failing to recognize China's territorial intentions, and that it was not going to make the mistake again. Of India's long-standing low-profile nuclear policy, he said, pointedly: "We believe we need to make a review of the defense policy." The review didn't take long. On Monday, India, which had not exploded a nuclear weapon since May 1974, detonated three devices under the desert ground about seventy miles from the Pakistan border. The White House said that it was surprised, which is doubtless true. Pakistan, which fears India as India fears China, said it was deeply concerned. But not to worry. Pakistan has its nuclear program, too, a program that has received lots of assistance in recent years from China, assistance that the White House did not notice—officially.

Now, three nuclear bomb blasts later, the president is suddenly "deeply disturbed," and he says he will punish India by enforcing the sanctions called for under the Nuclear Proliferation Prevention Act of 1994, which mandates that the United States stop aid and credit to a nation that behaves as India has. Only a few weeks ago the president was grousing about how sanctions laws force him to "fudge" reality and issue waivers. But there will be no fudging and waivering this time. Of course that may be because this particular law does not allow waivers.

Arafat Bombs
on Opening Night

♦ ♦ ♦

The main entrance to the Gaza Strip is an ugly thing, raw as a sore, bleak as an illness. The Erez checkpoint, as it is called, has been for twenty-seven years the main gate of one of humanity's larger holding pens, and its form has followed its function to a brutal conclusion. It is a clutter of small, shabby buildings set in a landscape of dirt, old asphalt, razor wire, and, especially, concrete. Concrete is the checkpoint's *grossmotif,* in the form of the rough cubes that are, literally, its building blocks. The massive squares are staggered in a slalom course in the strip of road that leads to the stopping point, and are stacked atop each other to form the crude watchtowers and machine-gun nests from which the soldiers of the Israeli Defense Force stare down: hard, brown young men, opaquely impassive behind their sunglasses, M-16s at the casual ready. The blocks are painted in bright regimental colors, but concrete grimed by diesel exhaust and gouged by would-be border runners and bullets is hard to prettify.

Gaza's checkpoints (Erez is only the first among many) are a physical manifestation of the reality of the Palestinian experience, which is nowhere expressed in a more pure or concentrated form. The Gaza Strip is a small, misshapen rectangle of generally barren land tucked into the corner formed by the meeting of Egypt, Israel, and the Mediterranean Sea. For most of its history, it has been sparsely populated, and its people always have been poor and powerless. They have lived under the control of armed outsiders for hundreds of years: first the Turks of the Ottoman Empire, then the British, the Egyptians, the Israelis. On September 13, 1993, on the White House lawn, Yitzhak Rabin of Israel and Yasir Arafat of the Palestine Liberation Organization signed an agreement that made this place the heart of something called the Palestinian Autonomous Region—an odd, ambivalent entity that is no longer a ward of the Jewish state but not a state of its own either. The pact also made Arafat the head of the Palestinian National Authority, a government that doesn't entirely exist or entirely not exist, but, in Cheshire cat fashion, fades in and out of reality depending on the angle and the time at which it is viewed.

The handshake on the South Lawn brought a new group of men with guns to Gaza—the PLO, un-diasporizing from Iraq, Jordan, Libya, Yemen, Egypt, Algeria, and the Sudan. It is to the more sardonic Gazans a perverse and amusing fact that the new Palestinian regime not only failed to remove many of the hated checkpoints but actually added new ones. The Israeli checkpoints remain, but for every Israeli post there is now a Palestinian one. The Palestinian checkpoints are poor cousins to the Israeli ones, smaller and shabbier. The guards, reedy boys and old men in vaguely matching uniforms, sit in the dirt drinking tea and wave amiably at passersby; they lack the hard efficiency of real soldiers. The most obvious difference is in the paint job; the Palestinian blocks are painted in the green, black, red, and white of their revolutionary flag.

On July 1, 1994, the day Yasir Arafat arrived in the Gaza Strip to establish the Palestinian National Authority as a fact on the ground, the Palestinian blocks at Erez were decorated with posters of his face. Arafat never saw the historic sight. The president of Palestine, as he prefers to be called, was not allowed by the Israelis to enter through the front door of his new home. Barred from setting foot on Israeli soil, he was obliged to arrive by the tradesman's entrance, coming to the promised land over the Sinai desert from Egypt, to arrive at the somnolent border town of Rafah in the midafternoon of a hot, still day.

The procession from the border to Gaza City was meant to suggest triumph, and instead achieved chaos. It was a multicultural motorcade, a rolling illustration of the bromide that beggars can't be choosers, composed of the borrowed cars of many nations: from America, the big camouflage green Chevrolet Blazers driven by the Palestinian National Authority's National Security Forces. From Italy, the blue Fiats of the police force. From various Arab states, the white and red ambulances of the Red Crescent Society, the Islamic answer to the Red Cross. From Israel, the (stolen) BMWs and Volvos of the local Fatah Hawks, the terror wing of Arafat's Fatah Party. There must have been seventy or eighty vehicles, snaked out over a couple of miles along the narrow road, all of them whipping along in a honking hysteria—the fat generals of the PLO and the slim boy gunsels of the Hawks leaning half out of windows, perching on roofs, standing on bumpers, waving their Kalashnikovs, shouting and screaming and firing in the air. In the middle were a dozen or so cars and trucks bristling with rifles, surrounding a royal blue Mercedes-Benz limousine, from a square hole in the roof of which appeared a flash of the man himself, a small gray face under the trademark black and white kaffiyeh, his pendulous lips set in a wide, fixed smile, waving his right hand as steadily as a metronome.

Gaza City is at its core old beyond history, and like most such places has grown in idiosyncratic ways far beyond the point of rationality. It is the city as chaos theory, a warren of dark alleys and twisting trails that are more potholes than pavement; of sheds and shacks and lean-tos, apartment blocks and concrete refugee shelters and mosques and sweatshops; of men and women and endless children and donkeys and roosters and skinny orange cats; and over it all, an endless drift of trash.

In this closed and wretched place, the end of the Israeli military curfew and of the intifada has occasioned a sort of population explosion; free to move safely for the first time in seven years, Gazans now go outside almost all the time. Even on a day of no particular moment, the streets of Gaza City are thick with people at nearly all hours, and for the occasion of Arafat's arrival they were jammed nearly to impassibility. The security forces and the police were ignored and overwhelmed. At one intersection, I counted twenty-six uniformed men, shouting and screaming and waving their hands in motions variously commanding and beseeching. They had no more effect than cartoons. The mob was so thick and strong that the motorcade could only move with it, proceeding in a crawl that eddied around the immovable—a stalled taxi and a pair of red-haired goats eating something in the road.

The procession led eventually to what was to be the great event of the day: Yasir Arafat's homecoming speech, to be delivered before the grateful masses at the central sports stadium. When the event actually occurred, at about four-thirty in the afternoon, it fell oddly and embarrassingly flat. The crowd was a great deal smaller than anticipated—probably somewhere between fifteen thousand and twenty thousand people, pressed sweating together under a baking sun in a dirt field—and from the beginning they did not seem much impressed with the speaker. Arafat, a small man with narrow shoulders and a little potbelly, was dwarfed by larger men on a crowded stage, and he spoke briefly and baldly. He must have known what the people wanted to hear: the good, old, rich stuff of blood and struggle and victory, of pushing the Jews into the sea and taking Jerusalem. But he couldn't deliver the goods.

The awkward truth was, he was now in political business with the Jews. They were his partners in the peace process, and his future depended entirely on the success of that process. He was no longer working in the blood-and-victory line; he was a diplomat and a bureaucrat. He was no longer the romantic leader of an outlaw army in undying opposition to authority; he *was* authority. He spoke accordingly—sober, rational, and practical. He barely touched upon the subject of the Jews. He talked of work to be done, of heavy burdens to be shouldered, of shared responsibilities. The audience listened politely, but people began wandering away well before he finished.

◆ ◆ ◆

I wonder, now that the deep flaws that were built into the experiment of Arafat and the city-state of Gaza (and into the larger experiment of peace between Israel and the PLO) are so obvious, whether Arafat understood the hints of disaster that were present that first day. Probably. He is smart enough. But perhaps not. At the core of what would go wrong in Gaza and in the Israel-PLO peace process are Arafat's own flaws, and they are the sort of flaws—incompetence and vanity and prideful delusion and impotence—that most people would naturally shrink from seeing in themselves. All the same, the hints were not subtle. Beginning about the time the president of Palestine entered his autonomous region by the back door, I spent five weeks or so in Gaza. I went there thinking I would see something along the lines of the birth of a nation, but what happened was more of a protracted stillbirth. Three months later—six months after the Israelis left Gaza to the Palestinian National Authority, a little more than a year after the signing on the White House lawn—the contradictory pressures incorporated within the structure of the arrangement threaten its continued existence.

Faced with conflicting demands from the Israelis, the West, and his own people, and also from within himself, Arafat is losing control of a situation he never grasped firmly. Having rejected, as contrary to the spirit of self-rule and his own pride, the requests of foreign nations for an accounting system that clearly shows how money donated to the Palestinian National Authority is spent, he has attracted only a tiny piece of the nearly $1 billion pledged for Palestinian support this year. The authority, consequently, is broke, unable to finance basic functions of government. The Israel-PLO peace process has been repeatedly stalled by events within and without Arafat's control, and each breakdown has further set back the possibility of a larger Palestinian entity under Arafat's leadership. Increasingly, the Israelis and even some West Bank Palestinians are showing a preference for dealing instead with Arafat's old enemy, King Hussein of Jordan. Indeed, many Palestinians suspect that the Israelis made peace with Arafat only to remove him to the isolation of Gaza, while they pursued a separate and more promising peace with Hussein. Meanwhile, in Gaza, support for Arafat and for the peace process has in recent weeks approached the vanishing point.

The great sign of disintegration, and the great force for further disintegration, is the killing, which has picked up smartly in recent weeks. The promise of an end to the slaying and counterslaying that had become the central, awful means of political dialogue between Palestinians and Israelis was the essential point and hope of the deal between Arafat and Rabin. To this end, Arafat had promised to disarm Gaza's terror factions—the Islamic Resistance Movement, popularly known by its Arabic acronym, Hamas, the Islamic Holy War and his own Fatah Hawks—and to this end also, he had filled Gaza's streets with his own armed men.

Within a month of Arafat's arrival in Gaza, however, Hamas and the Islamic Holy War had resumed terrorist operations. In August, Hamas operatives disguised as settlers picked up two Israeli Defense Force soldiers hitchhiking and killed them; members of the same group were, a few days later, involved in a shoot-out with police in Jerusalem. A few days after that, Hamas gunmen killed one Israeli citizen and wounded another six in two drive-by attacks on the road outside Gush Katif, a Jewish settlement in the southern Gaza Strip. The pace quickened in September, and again in October. Last month—just as Arafat and Rabin were receiving the Nobel Peace Prize—Hamas killed two and wounded thirteen in a Jerusalem street attack; kidnapped, exhibited, and killed an Israeli soldier, Nahshon Waxman, and exploded a bomb on a bus in downtown Tel Aviv, killing twenty-two and wounding forty-six. All told, ninety Israelis have been murdered by Palestinian terrorists since Arafat and Rabin signed the deal that won the prize.

The work of Gaza's gunmen is returning the relationship between the Israelis and the Palestinians to its accustomed base of kill and be killed. On November 2, Hani Abed, a leader of the Holy War, was blown apart in a car bomb explosion in the Gaza city of Khan Yunis; Rabin hinted broadly that the assassination was an act of revenge by Israeli security forces. Nine days later, a twenty-one-year-old Gazan named Hisham Ismael Hamad wrapped several pounds of plastic explosive around his chest and pedaled his bicycle into a group of Israeli soldiers, killing himself and three of them. In a letter he left behind, Hamad wrote, "There is no peace with the sons of monkeys and pigs, the enemies of peace, and no peace with Zionists who killed prophets."

In the face of all this, Arafat is isolated and bitter. He sits, in a small room in a half-finished building on the only decently paved street in Gaza City, surrounded by aides and sycophants, talking in querulous tones late at night about the injustice of it all: "And the money from the donors—where is the money? We have many promises from the donors, but only a few promises have been implemented. I am speaking of the pledges made at the time of the meeting with President Clinton. You remember, the meeting took place last October, which means approximately ten months have passed—and nothing. Not a thing. Nothing!" Around the table, the advisers' heads nod up and down, as the president of Palestine harangues on into the night.

TRASHING PUBLIC SPACES

In the opinion of Iyad Sarraj, any understanding of the problems at the heart of the Gaza experiment must begin with an admission of Gaza's pathology. Dr. Sarraj, a psychiatrist and director of the Gaza Community Mental Health Project, is one of those unfortunate people who are cursed with a clear vision of the place where they live. He sat one morning, drinking Turkish coffee and smoking Marlboros, at a white plastic table in the sand on the Gaza beach and delivered a diagnosis.

Earlier that morning, Dr. Sarraj had opened the 1994 summer beach cleanup program. The Gaza Strip's forty-six kilometers of fine Mediterranean shoreline is dirty on a heroic scale, the trash varying from bottles and plastic cups and the grimy translucent skins of trash bags, to bread husks and chicken bones and cobs from the charcoal-roasted ears of corn the beach vendors sell, to hunks of concrete, scraps of wood, shards of glass and twisted metal skeletons of washing machines and cars. One day I saw a dead donkey in the sand. Every year for the past four, Dr. Sarraj has organized an admittedly symbolic effort to clean the beach; the idea is that the sight of children and decent people doing something positive will inspire others towards a more sustained effort at cleanliness.

This year's cleanup began at 8:30 A.M., with 105 children of the Gaza Sports Club lined up in rows, the little boys and girls turned out in new T-shirts imprinted with the face of Donald Duck. The adults gave the children new wooden rakes with red plastic heads and black plastic trash sacks and organized them into squads, one trash-bag holder to every four or five rakers. The children managed by 9:30 to collect forty bags of trash but by then they were tired and bored. The girls wandered off hand in hand to play in the surf, the boys to chase and punch and kick each other. By 9:40, when Suha Arafat arrived for a photo op of the president's wife cleaning the beach, the only people still working were a group of pale Swedish peace missionaries.

Mrs. Arafat, wearing blue jeans and a silk blouse and little pink sneakers embroidered with tiny blue and yellow flowers, accepted the rake handed to her with a giggle and a slightly quizzical look, as if she had never held such a thing in her hands. But she worked enthusiastically, even after the photographers got

their pictures and left, and filled three bags by herself. It was shortly after she departed that Dr. Sarraj offered his diagnosis, starting, in keeping with the theme of
the morning, with a few reflections on the relationship between Gazans and
garbage and the state.

"For hundreds of years, public spaces here have been in the control of occupiers—the Turks, the British, the Egyptians, the Israelis—so people developed an
attitude of: 'So what if they are destroyed, so what if they do not function? It
doesn't matter,'" he began. "Moreover, during our centuries of occupation, we
learned to excel, as all occupied people do, at subverting authority—at stealing,
at evading authority, at thwarting the wishes of authority. Corruption has long
been regarded as a way of striking against the occupiers, and so, curiously
enough, has polluting. People think that if they put garbage in the streets, it is an
act of defiance. And so, traditionally, the identity of the Palestinian is very much
restricted to the private world—to the family, the house—and there is no real
identity with the public sphere, or with any authority. To change this will take a
long time.

"Consider just the matter of health care," he went on. "After the Israelis
withdrew, the health services began trying to organize themselves, but still, as
with everything else in Gaza, it is very chaotic. We have very good surgeons, very
good nurses, people who function very well independently. But no one functions
as part of a cohesive whole, part of an organized system. Most of the doctors are
very concerned with their private practices. Hospitals are used as reservoirs for
private practices. If you go to a hospital, and seek a diagnosis from a doctor there,
he will see you for one minute if you are lucky, and you will get the message that
you are not going to get decent treatment unless you go to his private practice
and pay him his fee.

"And the chaos and corruption is not limited to health care; it is universal.
Since the Israelis left, it is staggering. You cannot send a letter from Gaza anymore, because there are no stamps. There have been stamps printed, we are told,
in Germany, but they have never been made available here so, effectively, there is
no functioning postal system. And telephones—we've been waiting for a new
telephone line for my clinic for four months.

"And listen, we are still in the honeymoon. The worst is yet to come. The
worst is that we will be a complete police state: corruption, dictatorship, chronic
pockets of violence. Oh yes, I think this is inevitable. The PLO as a machine is
not ready for government, and definitely it is not ready for democracy. Democracy means accepting that the people in the street are allowed to pose a threat to
the people in power, and the PLO cannot even contemplate that idea.

"If the PLO is going to function as another form of dictatorship, people will continue to refuse to identify with anything in the public sphere, which means, of course, that they cannot really identify with the concept of a state or a nation. They suffer en masse here from the psychology of the victim, alternating between sustained periods of dependence and outbursts of defiance. They will remain as they have long been, alienated from the state."

The doctor's pessimism may sound exaggerated, but it is actually a model of reason and restraint. In coming to Gaza, Yasir Arafat took on responsibility for a deeply sick society. Of the strip's 850,000 residents, approximately 643,000 are refugees, more than half of whom live in extreme poverty in camps built decades ago as temporary housing. The population density in the camps is among the highest in the world—in one camp the number rises to 100,000 per square kilometer—packed in crude one-story concrete and tin shelters.

The economy is chronically weak and dependent on Israel, which is virtually the sole support of Gaza's farming, fishing, and small manufacturing operations, and which provides Palestinian day workers with low-paying jobs inside Israel. Gazans with work permits leave their homes at four or five A.M. every workday to walk or hitchhike to Erez, where they queue up in a long shuffling line to be examined and passed through metal gates, like cattle chutes. During the Persian Gulf War, when the Palestinians openly cheered Iraqi missile attacks on Israeli homes, and in the years following, which saw a great increase in attacks on Israelis by Palestinian terrorists, Israel cut the number of Gazan entry permits from about sixty thousand to just under eleven thousand. Consequently, unemployment in Gaza now runs at more than 50 percent. The average man marries by twenty-five, and the average family size is 4.7 people, which means that most unemployed Gazan men are responsible for the care of at least several children.

Apart from a brief period in 1956 and 1957, Gaza has been under the control of either Egypt or Israel since 1948, and has never developed a functioning government. The departure of the Israelis—who stripped government buildings to the bare walls before they quit Gaza—left the United Nations Relief and Works Agency as the real provider of the services that government is supposed to supply. Most of the territory is poor, sandy, and rocky, and most of the land that has been developed for modern agriculture is still owned and occupied by Israelis (who, in fairness, are the ones who improved it in the first place).

Almost all the public land—streets, sidewalks, parks, and beaches—is fouled with trash and garbage, a layer of filth that covers the ground like an oil slick on the ocean, thickening here and thinning there, but never entirely disappearing. One evening, I came across a small mountain of burning cattle carcasses. The boys who had set it afire (it's the fat that burns) were playing on top of the heap, grimy cheeked and golden red in the sunset amid the flies. The Gaza Strip produces approximately 720 tons of solid waste every day, and there is no coherent system for handling it. (In the refugee camps, and in a few neighborhoods bordering the camps, the United Nations maintains a rough system of trash collection. In most neighborhoods, residents rely upon donkey-cart trash haulers.)

Water in Gaza is scarce and heavily polluted. In the camps, and in some of the poorer neighborhoods, sewage and waste water run in a thick, greenish brown porridge through shallow gutters cut into the concrete alleys, to collect in great open pools situated in low areas or to run into the sea where Gazans swim and fish. The storm drain and sewage treatment systems were long ago overwhelmed by a population that has more than doubled in thirty years. One clogged and broken main in Gaza City has been sending up a geyser of yellow-brown sewer water through an open manhole in the street for so many years that the locals refer to it as the Eternal Fountain, and drivers use it as a landmark.

Apart from rain, the sole source of sweet water is an underground reservoir. With Israeli settlements; Israeli and Palestinian farmers; eight refugee camps; and four major cities (Gaza City, Rafah, Deir el Balah, and Khan Yunis) all drawing from it, the aquifer is being depleted at more than three times its annual rate of replenishment. The result is a steadily dropping water table that is becoming increasingly contaminated by salt water. United Nations technicians believe that, barring drastic measures of water conservation and management, most of Gaza's water will be too brackish to drink within a matter of perhaps ten years or so.

TRASHING AUTHORITY

Of all the aspects of Gaza's pathology, none is more dangerous than its politics, which suffers from a simple condition that produces profound side effects: Politics in Gaza expresses itself through illegality. In a society under occupation, what inevitably becomes recognized as the legitimate expression of political will is always, in one way or another, illegal. That is, it is dedicated to the refutation or subversion of those in authority, and their laws. Gaza, for all practical purposes, has been occupied forever, and its politics have evolved to the point where antiauthority has become true authority. Almost anything a citizen might want that authority is theoretically in a position to control—an Israeli work permit, decent medical care, a telephone line, police protection, an electrical hookup, a civil service job—is mostly unavailable through official channels but may be obtained on the political black market through bribes or the bartering of favors and influence. A few rich, powerful families—the Shawas, the Middeins (Freih Abu Middein is Arafat's minister of justice), and the Samhadanas chief among them—dominate business, politics, and society, manipulating everything from construction to the practice of medicine.

One morning, after a night of dysentery, I visited a doctor to get some antibiotics. Gaza is desperately short of physicians, and in a properly constituted society, this doctor, smart and well educated and ambitious, would be regarded as a treasure. Instead, sixteen months after he returned to Gaza upon finishing his education in Czechoslovakia, he remained unlicensed and therefore unemployed. He worked a bit, illegally, out of a pharmacy owned by a cousin.

"Here, you have to have protection to get anything done," he said. "If you don't have protection, you never get work. There are people who do not have medical degrees who are working as doctors because they have protection. It works like this: If you come from the right family, a famous or rich family, everything is open to you. But if you do not come from such a family, you must pay money to the head of one of those families, or to someone at the appropriate ministry, if you want to get anywhere. In medicine, for example, you must work for one year as an intern before you can get a license to open a practice. But you have to get on a waiting list to get that job, and if you don't have money or come from the right sort of family, you can spend years on that list. It is a system of class perquisites such as might have been practiced in England in the eighteenth and nineteenth centuries, where the sons of the aristocracy automatically got all the good jobs in the military, or in the government, whether they were idiots or not.

"And there is rampant stealing of the money that does come in here. For instance, the UN supplies medicine, paid for by Western aid, and the amount of medicine that comes in should be enough. But so much is stolen for sale on the black market that medicine is very hard to come by after the first week of the month, when the shipments come in.

"Listen," he said. "There is no chance of building an economy on our own. That would take billions and billions of dollars, and well-qualified and honest people, and hard work. And those things do not exist here. The good people leave if they can. A smart, hard-working Palestinian can make $5,000 a month in Kuwait, where they will also provide his family with first-rate medical care and education. Here, he might make $300 a month. Why shouldn't he leave?"

The familial arrangement of power complements and overlaps the underground political structure formed by the factions of the intifada, which began in the Jabaliya camp in 1987. They were, by 1994, a contentious lot, including

Arafat's own Fatah, or Palestinian National Liberation Movement; Fatah's quasi independent terrorist offshoot, the Fatah Hawks; George Habash's Popular Front for the Liberation of Palestine (PFLP), and the Democratic Front for the Liberation of Palestine, a PFLP splinter group. All of these groups trace their foundation and their ideology to the Marxist secular liberation movements of the 1950s and 1960s. Much more recently, fundamentalist religious factions have risen to prominence. Chief among them is Hamas, which was founded in Gaza in 1987 by the quadriplegic cleric Sheikh Ahmed Yassin.

The combination of tribalism and factionalism defines life. Everything in Gaza—every neighborhood, every civic association, every block, every family— is identified by its factional and familial fealty; any child can tell you which neighborhood is Hamas and which is PFLP and which is Fatah, and which also is Shawa or Samhadana, and how all of this is related. (The Samhadanas, for instance, are a much feared Fatah Hawks family; the Nuseirat and Sheik Radwan neighborhoods of Gaza City are Hamas strongholds.) While in Gaza I came due for a haircut, and I asked a friend to recommend a barber. He asked me if I preferred a Fatah cut or a PFLP. I chose the latter—short sideburns, closely trimmed temples, a bit longer on the top—and we went to a barber who specialized in that.

By 1994, Hamas had become the dominant faction in Gaza, because of what might be called its big-tent approach. To those who sought purity and rigor in rebellion, it offered the only school of revolutionary doctrine more pure and more rigorous than that of Marx, that of God. To those who appreciated practical results, it offered a substitute for government that was second only to the United Nations, providing basic services through a network of clinics, schools, day care centers, mosques, and small factories, and through a welfare system that aided widows, orphans, and cripples of the intifada. And, of paramount importance in a system wherein the highest expression of political will is to kill, Hamas surpassed all other factions in killing power.

Hamas began its terror campaign in 1989, acting first against Israelis, but soon broadening its threats to include suspected collaborators and, later, those accused merely of violating Hamas edicts. In 1990, the group founded an underground military wing, the Izzedine al-Qassam Brigades (named for a revolution-minded Islamic cleric killed by the British in Palestine in 1935). The Qassam Brigades, while never rising in numerical strength to more than a few hundred men, soon achieved a deserved reputation for murderous fanaticism impressive even by local standards. Hamas fighters were famous for never surrendering to arrest; if cornered, they killed until killed.

Hamas is tireless in its efforts to build its bank of potential martyrs, as I found visiting a summer camp for boys run by its social work wing, the Islamic Society. The camp was a weeklong affair, with 450 boys from eight to fifteen attending day sessions at a mosque in the middle of Gaza City. When I arrived at the mosque in midmorning, the boys were all sitting in the dirt in the big central courtyard, having a snack of hard-boiled eggs, bread, and orange drink. Afterward, they marched inside for the work of the day, which was revolutionary indoctrination. They split up, by troop, to classrooms formed by sheets hung from ropes to serve as dividers.

In one room, several dozen boys watched a television set playing a long and tedious videotape celebrating the death of Usama Husaid, a relatively recent martyr, having gone to Paradise on December 14, 1993, as a result of a suicide car-bombing attempt. Husaid was shown going stagily through some training exercises, running and skulking and crawling about in an olive grove. He was brandishing a Kalashnikov, but he did not really look like a fighting man; he wore eyeglasses, sported a neat little accountant's mustache and was dressed in slacks and shirt with a cardigan sweater. He seemed slightly puzzled by his own activities, in the manner of a Peter Sellers character: Inspector Clouseau in disguise as a terrorist. And, in fact, he had been a Clouseau-ish sort of hero. His bombing run, my escort noted mournfully, had "succeeded in killing only himself." Still, he was a bona fide martyr, and the boys gazed upon his video image in evident worship.

KILLERS AS SUPERSTARS

It was delusion on a grand scale to think that a political culture defined by the idea that established authority is illegitimate would suddenly discover the virtues of cooperation merely because the nature of the authority changed. And it was a delusion that Hamas lost no time in dispelling. One day about a week into Arafat's theoretical rule of Gaza, and about two weeks before Hamas began its current killing spree, I went to a Hamas rally in the Jabaliya refugee camp, Gaza City's largest. The point of the rally was to express defiance of—even contempt for—Arafat and the peace process to which he was wed. The featured speakers were leaders of the outlaw Qassam Brigades.

"My brothers, the battle hasn't started yet!" shouted Muhsin Abu Ita, a Qassam street leader who was the featured orator. "As long as there are prisoners in Israeli jails, as long as the Israelis exist in our land, as long as there is a single settler on our land, the battle isn't finished!" Abu Ita then moved to directly challenge Arafat on the central issue, his pledge to disarm Hamas. "The Islamic movement will never hand over its weapons," he declared. "And the fighters of the Islamic movement ask your blessing to use those weapons in the fight for our freedom."

On cue, a car roared around the corner, scattering the people in front of the stage, as a young man leaning out a car window fired his Kalashnikov into the air. The shooter, I was told, was Qamel Katel, a fugitive wanted by the Palestinian National Authority police for the recent shooting of two suspected collaborators. For Katel to show up in the middle of the day, shooting off his rifle only a few miles from where Arafat sat in his office, was a neat bit of nose thumbing, and the crowd cheered in delight.

This sort of open defiance was more or less routine from the beginning of the Palestinian National Authority's arrival in Gaza. At a PFLP rally, also in Jabaliya, I heard Abu Ali Nassar, recently released from an Israeli prison, win applause with his jeering dismissal of the peace accord. "The martyrs didn't die for the self-rule of Gaza and Jericho," he said. "The men who were crippled, who were imprisoned, who were assassinated, they didn't struggle to achieve this goal." And at a large Hamas rally in the city's central Palestine Square, I heard speakers accuse the Palestinian Authority of violating its promises of democratic rule and acting instead as "a military authority," language that was, within the context of Gaza politics, a clear signal that Arafat's government was to be regarded as an occupying force. The Hamas leaders at that rally gave broad hints of the escalation to killing. "Although all of the factions are unhappy at this point, we are still agreed not to use violence," said a Hamas official, Khalid Hiadai. "But the people will not accept to live for long under an authority that satisfies no one with its policies." On the edges of the crowd, the police and plainclothes security officers only watched and listened.

The police did not act because they dared not. From the beginning of Arafat's rule in Gaza, there was an understanding that—despite their public protestations to the contrary—his authorities would not seriously attempt to deliver on Arafat's promise to disarm the intifada gunmen and establish real control over the street. Major General Nasr Yousef, the director general of the PNA's security forces, and the overall chief of the authority's seven thousand soldiers, intelligence officers, and policemen, made this clear in an interview. "The problem is that we are dealing with a generation that is very difficult to control," he said, leaning forward over his crowded desk in his office on the third floor of the old Israeli central prison building in Gaza City. "This generation has been bred in the habit of carrying weapons; they regard it as one of their legitimate rights, even though it is now illegal to carry weapons." He paused, so that his chief aide, a former television broadcaster named Farid Assalya, could light his cigarette.

"Therefore," the major general continued, "in this first stage, we are focusing on an awareness campaign, teaching people that it is no longer necessary to carry weapons. And now, we are beginning to move beyond that to confiscate some weapons. Yet we have also adopted a policy that we will not detain the men whose weapons we are confiscating, we will not arrest or prosecute them. This is a balance, a compromise, that we believe is necessary because of the crisis suffered by this generation."

What Nasr Yousef calls Gaza's generational crisis is what Dr. Sarraj calls its pathology; the romanticization of violent death runs deep throughout all levels of Gaza. The intifada's shooters and bomb throwers are Gaza's superstars, celebrated figures who swagger about like Texas football heroes, worshiped by younger boys and treated with deference even by their elders. Girls and foreign correspondents flock to them. Their lives have a Huck Finn quality; in a culture otherwise very serious about parental discipline, education, and hard work, they are exempted from the grind by their willingness to kill and be killed, and are allowed to stretch out for years in protracted adolescence, hanging out in the boy heaven of their safe houses and hidey-holes, playing with other boys and guns.

To end the killing, Arafat's government must defeat not just Hamas but this entire culture; must defeat, as Nasr Yousef acknowledges, a generation. I gained some understanding of how extremely difficult this task is in talking with Arafat's own young superstars, the Fatah Hawks. The Hawks were theoretically brought under control before Arafat arrived in Gaza, and many had been given jobs within the new National Security Forces, mostly as bodyguards. In truth, I found, their new loyalty was fragile, and their desire to return to the old days of potshotting Jews, palpable.

The Shabura Camp in Rafah is a stronghold of the Fatah Hawks; the local head is Arafat Abushabab, a slim nineteen-year-old who has yet to muster a decent beard. I visited him one day in his clubhouse, where he sat on the sofa, flanked by two buddies.

"If I had a choice, I would prefer to be the president myself, but I don't care if I am only a soldier," he said. "I don't mind being the little Arafat." But the tone of his voice was more mocking than reverential, and his friends greeted the remark with laughter. "We are afraid to offend Chairman Arafat," Arafat Abushabab said, to more giggles and grins.

I asked him if he could foresee a time when the Fatah Hawks might turn against the new authority, and he turned serious. "If the government treats the people in an unjust way, we will stand against the government. If they starve the people, if they stop people from marching in the streets, we will turn against them."

He reminisced about better times. "I miss the shooting of the Israelis," he said. "I hope the Israelis come back again, so we can shoot them again. I always dreamed of the day the Palestinian troops would come to Palestine. Now, I hope we go to war against the Israelis and take all of the West Bank and all of Palestine."

FALSE SECURITY

Even if Palestinian National Authority forces seriously tried to disarm Gaza's underground, it is doubtful they would succeed. The authority's armed forces are much weaker than Arafat pretends and a great deal weaker than the Israeli Defense Force, which failed to defeat the intifada in seven years of near war.

At first glance, in Gaza City, Arafat's strength looked impressive. The streets were filled with men in uniforms. The blue-shirted police, who were mostly Gazans (and, not accidentally, mostly unarmed) directed traffic and hung somewhat listlessly about street corners while the men Arafat had brought with him to Gaza, the olive-uniformed ex–Palestine Liberation Army soldiers and the plain-clothed spies and bodyguards of the secret police units, strutted through the city, racing their big Chevy Blazers up and down the streets, gunning their engines, and sending up air wakes of dirt and gravel.

But the impression of power was false, as was hinted one day when Arafat went to a ribbon-cutting ceremony at an orange juice factory. The procession was conducted with the usual elephantine display of strength: ten army trucks, two black Mercedes limousines, three ambulances, seven more army trucks, sixteen assorted cars carrying various officials and extra bodyguards. After it was over, as the motorcade moved slowly away, several of Arafat's senior bodyguards— middle-aged men of considerable heft—leaped upon the rear trunk of his Mercedes, holding on to the car with one hand while they brandished their Kalashnikovs with the other. The intention was to emulate the U.S. Secret Service. But Arafat's car lacked hand grips, which are essential for this sort of thing, and as the Mercedes gathered speed it hit a small bump, sending fat men flying through the air, their bulky forms describing jumbled parabolas of arms and legs and Kalashnikovs, to land with thuds and oaths on the road.

In several weeks of touring military and police facilities in Gaza and Jericho, I found that the military and police units of the Palestinian Authority had almost none of the equipment, supplies, and facilities of even the most basic security force. They worked in offices and barracks that had been denuded by the departing Israelis. They survived by begging—except for elite headquarters, intelligence, and presidential security units, no army or police command had an operating budget. For office furniture, the police were dependent on the gifts of citizens. In some areas, they depended on local charity even for their uniforms and their food; local tailors sewed outfits for them out of donated cloth, and housewives delivered daily rations of soup and rice to soldiers on duty at Palestinian checkpoints.

On paper, Gaza's policemen and soldiers were well paid—approximately $900 a month for an officer and $500 for a regular cop or soldier, compared with an average Gazan's salary of about $300 a month. But Arafat cut all wages in half in July, and even senior officers were obliged to live in barracks, sleeping on pallets or blankets on concrete floors.

The office of Lieutenant Farid al Akhra, commander of the police force of Rafah, was typical: a small, empty room, with a battered metal desk and two metal chairs, and an old filing cabinet. "We started at zero and we have stayed at zero," the lieutenant said. "We have sixty-three police officers here, for a population of 150,000. We have no radios. We have no police laboratory. We have one patrol car. We have no sidearms, no handcuffs, no batons, no flashlights. We have only one telephone line. The one telephone line must handle all outgoing calls, and of course it is the only line for incoming calls, too."

In Khan Yunis, a city of 80,000, the police force consisted of seventy-three men, most of whom lived in the barracks attached to the station house; one patrol car, no laboratory, no radios, one telephone line. In Deir al Balah, with its 65,000 residents, the same. In all of the Gaza Strip, I saw only one law-enforcement unit that was being trained professionally and with new equipment: an elite, 200-member antiriot squad whose primary job would be to quell the frequent violent challenges to authority that the Israeli authorities so hated and feared in Gaza, and that the Palestinian Authority always understood would be coming for them, too.

The members of the antiriot squad were chosen for loyalty and intelligence from the ranks of the Fatah Hawks and from the university, and all were young and fit. I went several times to Gaza City's Ansar prison camp—appropriately enough, the Israeli army's erstwhile central detention and interrogation center— to watch the training of the forty-four young men of the squad's first class. The trainees had been outfitted with the latest in riot gear: fire-resistant Kermel bodysuits, helmets and vests of Tetranike, a threat-level-two bulletproof material (it will stop a bullet from a handgun, but not a rifle), heavy-duty clear-plastic full-body shields and Arnold riot batons, made of dense, unbreakable black nylon.

The gear had been donated by the United Kingdom, and two English trainers came with it; an older, Colonel Mustardy sort named Alan Skelton, and a tough-looking younger man named Tony Houldsworth, who was the chief instructor in public order for the shire of Nottingham.

Houldsworth, briskly commanding in blue jumpsuit and brass whistle, did the real work. By the end of the second day, he had the class sharply marching in goose-stepping unison; stiff-booted legs kicking high in counterpoise to swinging, clench-fisted arms; and he had taught them the basics of defensive posture: how to make a double line of men appear to be stronger than it is, how to advance and retreat in lockstep, how to reform the line after repelling a rush. On the third day, he taught them how to stand up to Molotov cocktails, a common means of expressing political displeasure in Gaza. The final lesson that day was in the proper use of the baton. The forty-four men lined up in full fig, with shields up, helmet masks down, and batons at port arms. Houldsworth selected one to serve as a model, and proceeded to demonstrate how to hit a person with a stick. ("One, ankle; two, knee; three, hand; four, elbow; five, collarbone," he intoned.)

"Now, men, this is very important. You must not strike"—he pronounced it "stroike"—"the head." The troops looked blankly at him. "You must not stroike the head," Houldsworth repeated. "You must not stroike the head. You must not stroike the head. You must not stroike the head." They looked blankly still. "Major," he said to the Palestinian army officer in charge. "Tell them in Arabic, please, that they must not stroike the head." The major obliged, and the men nodded, somewhat dubiously it seemed to me, and the trainer led them in the chant again. "You must not stroike the head!" By the time I left, he had them repeating it, like a mantra, the forty-four of them mumbling weirdly in the bright sunshine, "You must not stroike the head."

WRONG MAN, WRONG PLACE, WRONG TIME

A good argument can be made that Yasir Arafat was the worst possible choice to lead Gaza in its perilous experiment with independence. He is sixty-four, and he has spent most of his adult life as a leader of armed, revolutionary forces, an occupation that does not encourage democratic inclinations. He has run the PLO as a dictatorship of disorganization, largely by his own word and whims, and maintained power by maneuvering his rivals against each other. He is expert in the manipulation of the international press, and also in the uses of terror, but he has never run a government, participated in any traditional electoral process, or paid even minimal attention to the conventions of bureaucracy. He has always made his decisions in secret, with the concurrence of a few aides, and has never been accountable to anyone outside his own organization. In every place where the PLO has tried to establish a stable and permanent home—Jordan, Lebanon, Syria—it has failed, disastrously.

Moreover, Arafat arrived in Gaza in a weak and desperate condition. He took the deal Rabin offered because it was the last, best one he could hope to get. The collapse of Soviet support for Arab states that in turn supported the PLO, and the rupture of pan-Arab goodwill caused by the PLO's decision to back Saddam Hussein in the Persian Gulf War, had combined to lethal effect. By 1993, Arafat's organization was nearly out of money and in imminent danger of extinction.

Still, there was a momentary opportunity, after the departure of the Israelis in May, to rescue Gaza from pathology; to build a new order, based on democracy and the rule of law, that would establish the idea of authority as legitimate. The failure to do so was ultimately the result of Arafat's failings.

From the beginning of the Gaza experiment, Arafat set out, with conspicuous and purposeful intent, to subvert democracy and the rule of law. His first and most profound step was to announce, ten days after the White House signing, that Gaza and Jericho would no longer be governed according to the code of military law left behind by the departing Israelis. Without Israeli law, there was, as far as the behavior of government was concerned, no law in Gaza. There was only a criminal code, derived essentially from the old British colonial law. "What this means," said a United Nations official, "is that no matter what action the Palestinian Authority takes, its foundation in law is dubious and open to challenge. The Israeli code covered all the basic laws on banking, insurance, business. Without them, foreign businesses and nations are very reluctant to come in and do business here, because they don't know what law will apply to them."

Having dismissed law, Arafat dismissed order. The Israelis left behind a semi-functioning civil bureacracy of about seven thousand civil servants. Arafat's Palestinian National Authority imposed on top of that a second military and civilian bureaucracy of about eight thousand people. But the PNA failed to provide the chain of command necessary to join the two bureaucracies. Instead, as he had always done, Arafat insisted on making all the decisions himself, late at night and largely in secret. Suha Arafat acknowledged as much in an interview in which she defended her husband's antidemocratic rule.

"Now, it is one month since my husband got here, and already they are speaking about democracy, and he is supporting democracy, but at the same time, he cannot go too fast, too deep into democracy, because sometimes too much democracy isn't right, and there is a narrow line between democracy and the misunderstanding of democracy," she said. "Democracy is not terrorism, democracy is not violence. It will take some time, because, don't forget, the people here have never had a leader, a real leader, with them, so everybody wants to go to Yasir Arafat to get their problems resolved. People say that he is a megalomaniac, but that is not it," she said. "It is that people don't want to see any other person. They only want to see him."

The result was a kind of semicontrolled chaos. "There is no unifying structure of command that directs all the pieces, so everything is haphazard," the United Nations official said. "It is all really just in the mind of Arafat."

And the mind of Arafat, it became increasingly clear, was not well suited to the task. On the one hand, it was chillingly arbitrary. Arafat was free to invent law as the moment required, and did so. In late July, for example, he ordered the effective closure of the East Jerusalem newspaper *An-Nahar,* which had offended him with its pro-Jordanian editorial stance. In defending his actions, Arafat told reporters that he had closed the newspaper for its failure to obtain the proper license from the Palestinian authorities. It was a moment Orwell would have cherished: Until Arafat spoke those words, there had never been any such thing as a Palestinian Authority newspaper license.

The signal given by the closure of *An-Nahar* was reinforced by two other early missteps: the decision to delay the popular elections Arafat had promised, and his unexpected refusal to seat a municipal council that represented all the political factions of Gaza. (Instead he handpicked a puppet council of wealthy businessmen.) The council Arafat rejected would have been the first effort at representative democracy in Gaza's history. Its loss was widely and bitterly felt.

There were other, obvious danger signs. One of the first was the establishment of a "national" radio news program, to be followed at a later date by the television equivalent. One afternoon at the Palestinian Broadcast Center, I sat in on an editorial meeting run by Farid Assalya, chief aide to Nasr Yousef, commander of the National Security Forces.

"You see, the news must be guided," Farid Assalya explained. "Hamas and these groups, they only want to oppose the process, and they are not helpful, so items about them must be ignored. Right? Because they only want the publicity for themselves, even if it is negative, so it is better not to report about them at all."

Farid Assalya and the editors and writers of the seven-thirty broadcast sat around a table on the lawn, going over the news copy typed on carbon paper. It was just after lunch, and the remains of the meal, half-eaten platters of rice and chicken, lay on the ground nearby. The head writer, an old man with the smudged eyeglasses and dirty hands of someone who messes with carbon all day, sat at Farid Assalya's side, taking notes at his direction.

"Now, it is my job to go over each item proposed here for the newscast and approve it or not," Farid Assalya explained. "So, the first item is that the president met with the American and British consuls today to discuss matters of state. The second item is that Major General Nasr Yousef officiated at the graduation of a new police class at Raffah. Okay, that is approved. Hmm. Now, we come to a decision. Here, we have an item about a Turkish delegation visiting the president to pay their respects. But there is another item about a delegation from the Palestinian Contractors Association visiting the president; we have to decide which item is more important. Hmm. I think the contractors lead; they are more important than the Turks." There was agreement around the table. "Oh, but here we have an item that says an important member of the PLO Central Committee from Amman says that he fully supports the new Palestinian democracy in Gaza and Jericho. I think that must go before the Turkish delegation, too. And here is another item that the Fatah Committee in Tunis announced their full and absolute support for President Arafat. Okay, that is very important, that goes up very high."

He studied one story for a full minute before firmly crossing it out. "Now, here is an item that is a good example of what I will reject. It is an item about King Hussein of Jordan and the question of Jerusalem. That is of course a very delicate issue, so I reject this item completely."

On the other hand, and of equal damage to Arafat's reputation in Gaza, it soon became clear that there was something weirdly meaningless about the new president's dictatorial ways, an unpleasant contrast between his public posturing and private impotence. I saw this most embarrassingly exhibited on the day Arafat presided over a ceremony marking the construction of a hospital in the southern part of the strip. The hospital had nothing to do with Arafat, was not financed by his government or in any way under his control, but was, like nearly everything else in Gaza, a United Nations project. It was still in the early stages of construction, and there was no reason for any ceremony, except that Arafat's advisers had asked for one, so the president might pose for the press.

We all—a hundred or so bureaucrats, reporters, and hangers-on—followed Arafat up to the open second story of the main building where the construction supervisor, an Englishman, was waiting with a tabletop mock-up of the finished complex. Arafat stood behind the table, facing the cameras, and asked questions in a stern voice. When will the hospital be finished? December 1995, he was told. That was too slow, said Arafat, it must be built sooner. "We will be doing our best, Mr. Arafat," the supervisor said. "Hospitals are complicated buildings, you know." Arafat said, sharply, that he was himself an engineer, and that he had in fact once built a hospital himself, but nevertheless the construction period must be shortened. "Yes, yes," said the supervisor, soothingly, "We are fully committed to shortening the period."

"Maybe you can work some more shifts," Arafat said.

"Perhaps that will be possible," said the supervisor.

"Please," said Arafat.

As we were leaving, the United Nations official watched Arafat strutting out in front of the cameras, as the Englishmen and Irishmen of the construction crews watched with amusement, and he said: "Sad, isn't it? He's just a figurehead, of course. None of this is under his control. Nobody wants to put anything under his control. Nobody trusts him with the money."

"When will he be trusted with the money?" I asked.

The man smiled a small smile. "We'll give it to him when he's ready for it," he said.

WHINES AND SYCOPHANTS

It is axiomatic that the less power a politician has the longer he will make you wait for an audience. I spent most of my last week in Gaza hanging about the Palestinian Broadcast Center, watching the guards fondle their guns; the sleekly suited West Bank bankers come and go; and the delegations of well-wishers and favor curriers file in and out for their few minutes in the president's company. When at midnight on my fourth night of waiting my call came, I was led into a small room in the back, where Yasir Arafat sat at the end of a long table, flanked by his senior military and police officers. He spoke for about half an hour, and I think he intended to use the interview to register his strong protest at the treatment he was getting from an ungrateful, uncooperative world, but strength was not what he conveyed. It wasn't so much an interview as a protracted whine, as Arafat ticked off, point by point, all the ways he had been done wrong, all the things that had gone wrong, all the mistakes that others—not he—had made.

"I am sorry to say that the whole implementation is going very slowly," he began. "We were not expecting that the other side—I mean the Israelis—would continue backing far away from what had been agreed upon. As an example, the free passage between Jericho and Gaza is still closed. Did you know that? The entrances from Sinai and Jordan are still under their complete control without any Palestinian participation."

So on and on: "And the tax payments we are supposed to receive from Israel. We didn't receive anything yet, except 7.5 million shekels [\$2.5 million], which is peanuts. That's all! Unbelievable. Listen, I will give you one figure. We are importing from Israel around \$1.5 to \$2 billion in goods annually. The VAT taxes on that, which we should get, are 17 percent, which means approximately \$300 million per year, which means \$25 million per month. Where is it? Three months is now past and nothing. Hah! 7.5 million shekels!"

I interrupted. I had heard it frequently remarked in the streets, I said, that the arrangement he had made with Rabin had accomplished little to change Gaza's status as a huge prison, except to add Yasir Arafat to the population of the prisoners.

"Who told you this? Who?"

"Well, it's just something you hear all over the place."

"Where?"

"On the street."

"I challenge you. I challenge you that this has been mentioned on the street. I am challenging you. No! This has not been mentioned. Perhaps the opposition is saying that, but the opposition's view is not what the masses are saying. No, you do not hear this! Not in the streets. It is not so. This is not the opinion of the masses. This is not the opinion of the masses.

"Oh yes, we are facing troubles. We know this is not a picnic, because the other side is not implementing accurately what has been agreed upon. Not to forget, that in West Bank and Gaza, there is deep economic trouble. We have suffered a lot from the Israeli occupation. All our infrastructure has been destroyed. Everything. Even the railways here in Gaza have been removed, yes, even the railways. You know that? Even the railways have been destroyed. So all our infrastructure has been completely destroyed."

He was by now in full rant, his face puffed up in anger. All the aides around the table had careful, agreeing looks on their faces, and were, as always, nodding.

"The whole world has to bear responsibility for this. Because peace in the Middle East is not only a Palestinian need. It is an international need, an American need, a European need, an Israeli need. And they have to bear their responsibility. If they do not, the whole peace process will collapse. And they will have to bear the responsibility for that, and to face it. As I told you, peace is not a Palestinian need only. It is an international need. It is not a joke. This is not Rwanda. You know, peace in the Middle East affects directly the whole international peace."

He paused to take a breath, and I asked a few questions, which he answered briefly and unremarkably. Then I asked about Hamas. I tried to be polite about it. I said that it must be difficult trying to control a group like Hamas, but why hadn't he ordered his army to at least try to disarm the Qassam Brigades? He sighed.

"I haven't Moses's stick, you know. We are doing our best. And even the Israelis with their huge force, the biggest and strongest army in the Middle East, haven't been able to stop them. We are doing our best." A thought came to him: Blame the Israelis. "You know, before we arrived here, the Israelis had open markets—not black markets, open markets—in armaments here. Within months, 26,000 arms had been sold. I told Mr. Rabin how this had been done openly. Was it by chance? No, it wasn't by chance. It was because some of the security leaders in Israel were hoping there would be a civil war here."

Perhaps, I said, with the interviewer's practiced sympathy, it was impossible for him ever to disarm Hamas. After all, Hamas was strong, and the Palestinian National Authority was, by his own account, weak. Yasir Arafat rose from his chair to signal the end of the talk. He was coldly angry as he said his final words. "I have my plan, but I am not going to unmask it. I am not going to unmask it."

◆　◆　◆

That was three months ago. The secret plan to disarm Hamas, if there was one, never materialized. Instead, a dismal pattern has emerged, one that is familiar to veterans of insurrectionist movements and fans of *Casablanca*. First, a Palestinian kills a Jew, or Jews, eliciting protests and threats from the government of Yitzhak Rabin. Then the officers of Yasir Arafat go out in the night, or at dawn, and round up twenty or thirty or fifty of the usual suspects, with the understanding that the arrestees are not very likely to be the guilty parties. It is, as a matter of practical politics, nearly impossible for the Palestinian Authority to contemplate arresting the real hit men of the Izzedine al-Qassam brigades; they tend to go down shooting, which could easily turn into the sort of thing that starts a civil war. A few days or so after the arrests, the suspects are quietly released.

The arrangement satisfies no one—naturally, the Israelis object to the meaninglessness of the exercise and, naturally, the Palestinians object to even the appearance of Palestinian authorities' acting on Israel's behalf against men who are, after all, only doing what Arafat himself had long deemed right and good. Every new repetition of the cycle erodes a little more of Arafat's credibility with Israel and a little more of his authority over his own people.

My last day in Gaza, I visited a small town near Khan Yunis to collect reports about the local Palestinian Authority military commander, a man named Nabil Abu Batta. With no functioning command structure to keep him in check, the commander had set himself up as a tin-pot sheikh of sorts, and had casually shot and wounded a boy who had irritated him in the street. The boy's family included a local journalist, a stringer for the Reuters news agency; he went to the police station to confront the commander. The officer was rude and dismissive; the stringer responded with a threat to bring the case to the highest authority. "I said to him: 'You cannot do this. What about democracy? What about free press? I will bring this to the attention of Abu Amar,'" the stringer said, invoking Arafat's nom de guerre.

"Do not talk to me about democracy," the stringer remembered the commander as responding. "Do not talk to me about Abu Amar. I am Batta. I do what I want. Even if Abu Amar comes here, he cannot tell me what to do."

On November 4, just four months after Arafat entered Gaza, there occurred a small scene of mob violence that suggested that Yasir Arafat was, finally, losing the only real power he ever had, the power of the street. On that day in Gaza City, thousands of Gazans took to the streets to mourn the death of Hani Abed, the Islamic Holy War leader killed by a car bomb. The grieving throng was, by all accounts, closer in spirit to rioters than mourners; they advanced on the Omari mosque, where the funeral was held, shouting the chants of the old days: "Death to Israel" and "Death to America." Arafat entered the mosque surrounded by bodyguards, but they were not enough. The mourners, eyewitnesses told reporters, shouted: "Arafat is a collaborator! Get out of here, Arafat! Get out! You are not our leader!" They called him a traitor. They shoved by the bodyguards and manhandled the president of Palestine so roughly that they knocked his kaffiyeh off his head. They pushed him out the mosque's back door, into the rain.

Arafat now finds himself in a position of desperate weakness. With his performance increasingly questioned even within the PLO, he recently summoned the organization's executive committee to Gaza for a show of support; only eight of the eighteen members showed up. On November 18, the power struggle between Palestinian Authority and Hamas finally broke into open street fighting. Hamas militants in a crowd of several thousand worshipers at Gaza City's Palestinian mosque responded to urgings from the pulpit to throw stones at the Palestinian Authority police, who had positioned themselves around the building. The police, members of Arafat's crack new antiriot squad, responded with gunfire. As this article went to press, 13 people had been killed and at least 150 had been wounded as the riot escalated into running battles throughout Gaza.

Despite these ominous portents, it is probably too soon to count Yasir Arafat out entirely. While it is true, to paraphrase the former Israeli Foreign Minister Abba Eban's famous remark, that Arafat has never missed an opportunity to miss an opportunity, he also has an extraordinary ability to survive the messes he makes. He has risen from the ashes of self-immolation in Jordan and Lebanon, and he could do so again in Gaza.

But rise to what? When Arafat came to Gaza, he had a chance to transform himself and it, to become the leader not merely of a Palestinian nation of some sort but to rescue Gaza from pathology and himself from decline. His failure has left him on what amounts to a political life-support system. It is vastly in the interest of Israel and the United States that Yasir Arafat remain alive and reasonably well in Gaza. With Arafat in Gaza, Gaza is Arafat's problem, which must be a source of great satisfaction and amusement to many in Jerusalem and Washington. And, to both Israel and the United States, Arafat remains infinitely preferable to the alternative of Hamas. So, no matter how poorly he runs the government, or how unpopular he becomes in the street, he is likely to hang on for at least a while, with the backing of his powerful friends. They will go to great lengths to keep him in his place—the mayor of Gaza, sitting in a small room in a half-finished building on the only decently paved street in the city, worrying about garbage and municipal budgets, and whether someone will shoot him.

Mideast Myths Exploded

◆ ◆ ◆

The events of the past eleven months in Israel have been remarkably clarifying. When the Palestinians, on the pretext of a visit by Ariel Sharon to Jerusalem's Temple Mount, began the second intifada last fall, it was still possible for the aggressively delusional to pretend that the Israelis and the Palestinians equally desired a workable peace. That belief shattered under repeated, murderous attacks on Israelis that clearly occurred with at least the tacit blessing of the Palestinian leadership.

Now the other great founding myth of the peace process is also dead. This is the great falsehood of relative morality. For decades, the European Left has maintained that the Palestinians held a morally superior position to the Israelis: They were an illegally subjugated people who were striking back in what may have been violent but were also appropriate ways. The claim of Palestinian moral superiority ended when the world saw Palestinians cheer in the street a young man holding up hands red with the blood of an Israeli soldier beaten to death, or perhaps it was when Palestinians stomped two boys, one a U.S. citizen, to death in a cave, or perhaps it was some other moment of gross and gleeful murder.

What remained—the Left's final feeble resort—was a claim of moral equivalency: The Palestinians might be engaged in terrible acts but so, too, were the Israelis. Both sides were killing; indeed, the Israelis, with their better arms and soldiers, had killed far more than had the Palestinians.

Now this, too, has gasped its last breath. It is not possible to pretend any more that there is anything like a moral equivalency at work in this conflict. The facts are indisputable.

(1) The Palestinians are the aggressor; they started the conflict, and they purposely drive it forward with fresh killing on almost a daily basis.

(2) The Palestinians regard this second intifada not as a sporadically violent protest movement but as a war, with the clear strategic aim of forcing a scared and emotionally exhausted Israel to surrender on terms that would threaten Israel's viability.

(3) As a tactic in this strategy, the Palestinians will not fight Israeli forces directly but instead have concentrated their efforts on murdering Israeli civilians. The greater the number, the more pathetically vulnerable the victims—disco goers, women and children in a pizza restaurant—the better.

(4) Israel has acted defensively in this conflict; and while Israeli forces accidentally killed Palestinian civilians, their planned lethal attacks have all been aimed only at Palestinian military and terror-group leaders.

Since the Oslo accords were signed in 1993, Palestinian terrorists have killed more than four hundred Israelis. In June a bomber killed twenty-one teenagers at a Tel Aviv disco; last week, a bomber killed fifteen and maimed as many as a hundred in a Sbarro pizzeria in Jerusalem; three days later, another suicide-bomber wounded twenty persons at another restaurant.

After the Sbarro bombing, Secretary of State Colin Powell, astonishingly, lectured the Israelis in the language of the literally exploded idea of moral equivalency. "I hope that both sides will act with restraint," Powell said. "They both have to do everything they can to restrain the violence, restrain the provocation and the counterresponse to the provocation."

This official U.S. policy statement is beyond stupid. It is immoral, hypocritical, obscene. It is indefensible. Israel is at war with an enemy that declines, in its shrewdness and its cowardice, to fight Israel's soldiers but is instead murdering its civilians, its women and children.

This enemy promises, credibly, more murders. In the face of this, in the aftermath of an attack expressly and successfully designed to blow children to bits, how dare a smug, safe-in-his-bed American secretary of state urge "restraint" by "both sides"? How does the secretary imagine his own country would respond to such a "provocation" as the Sbarro mass murder? (His own country bombed Serbia to its knees for killing ethnic Albanians in distant Kosovo, let alone Americans on American soil.)

And when you get down to it, why, exactly, should Israel continue to exercise restraint? Why shouldn't it go right ahead and escalate the violence? The only point to waging war is to win. Israel is at war, and losing. It can win only by fighting the war on its terms, unleashing an overwhelming force (gosh, just what is called for in the Powell Doctrine) to destroy, kill, capture, and expel the armed Palestinian forces that have declared war on Israel.

So far, Israel has indeed chosen to practice restraint. But, at this point, it has every moral right to abandon that policy and to engage in the war on terms more advantageous to military victory. This is a matter for Israel, at war, to decide one way or the other. Whether Secretary Powell purses his lips or not.

· THE LAST WAR ·

When Innocents
Are the Enemy

· · ·

This is the end logic of terror. The long age of imperialism bequeathed to this century a world full of questions of who wronged whom, and who stole whose land, and what should be done. Those questions, far from finding resolution in the half peace of the Cold War's aftermath, roil ever more. Absent the relative stability imposed by the war of the giants, the grievances of those upon whom the giants acted out their territorial ambitions have much more room to grow.

In theory, this is not a bad thing. But there are two great problems. The first is that, in the end, the whole world was stolen from somebody, most of it repeatedly; there are claims and counterclaims and counter-counterclaims for every inch of the planet that is desirable and for much that is not. The second is that people (and the governments they form) do not like to give back what they have acquired, whether that acquisition is of dubious morality or not.

So, those with territorial claims turn to force. But here arises a third problem: By and large, the aggrieved do not possess the force necessary to win their way in open battle. Given this, a common response has been the use of terror: attacks by the aggrieved not on the soldiers of the enemy, but on the people of the enemy—on innocent victims, chosen at random, the more innocent and the more random, the better, tactically speaking.

Given that this is murder, you would think that terrorism would have a hard time finding adherents. But tribalism is a powerful corrupting force, and so is ideology, and an awful quality of modern times has been the degree to which terror by various movements has been accepted as legitimate by those who support the goals of those movements. Communism found no difficulty persuading generations on the Left that terror on the most massive scale was justified by the need to free the world from the yoke of capitalistic imperialism. Irish Americans have almost monolithically supported the IRA in its decades of bombings and killings aimed at scaring the British out of Northern Ireland. And so it goes, case by tribal or ideological case, around the world.

Of all the uses of terror, none in the past several decades has been more faddishly popular (at least on the Left), and none has been accorded more respectful media coverage, than that of the Palestinians. Yes, Palestinian terrorists and terrorists on behalf of the Palestinian cause murdered innocents—but that was understandable, the argument went. The Palestinians had been wronged. They were oppressed. They were weak. What else could they do?

Here is where we end up, with murder on a mass scale of people whose sole sin was, apparently, that they were Americans. Immediate suspicion focused on anti-Israeli (and therefore anti-American) terrorist groups. Yasir Arafat, who has championed the legitimacy of anti-Israeli terror his entire career, nonetheless was quick to express himself "completely shocked," at an attack he said he condemned, and he offered the American people condolences on behalf "of the Palestinian people."

I don't doubt Arafat's shock. And I don't think he had anything directly to do with the monstrous evil of September 11. Indeed, it is possible that what happened yesterday had nothing to do with the Middle East. But this evil rose, with hideous logic, directly from the philosophy that the leaders and supporters of the Palestinian cause have long embraced and still embrace—a philosophy that accepts the murder of innocents as a legitimate expression of a legitimate struggle.

If it is morally acceptable to murder, in the name of a necessary blow for freedom, a woman on a Tel Aviv street, or to blow up a disco full of teenagers, or to bomb a family restaurant—then it must be morally acceptable to drive two jetliners into a place where fifty thousand people work. In moral logic, what is the difference? If the murder of innocent people is for whatever reason excusable, it is excusable; if it is legitimate, it is legitimate. If acceptable on a small scale, so, too, on a grand.

In the West Bank city of Nablus yesterday afternoon, the Associated Press reported, thousands of Palestinians greeted news of the slaughter in New York and Washington with an impromptu street party, cheering "God is great" and distributing candy in a traditional form of celebration.

The revelers must have greeted their leader's words with some puzzlement. Was this not the ultimate expression of President Arafat's very own philosophy? Was this not a great blow—the greatest ever—against oppression? Was this not a necessary and good thing, as they had been taught, as they had been taught to teach their children? Is not a great good better than a small good?

Who We Are

◆ ◆ ◆

The idea that everything changed, utterly, on September 11 is, in a vitally important way, false. Rudy Giuliani demonstrated this perfectly, as he has done everything perfectly, when he chose to keep a commitment to stand in at the wedding of a fatherless bride whose brother had died in a recent New York fire. People still get married, the mayor reminded us; life goes on and life is good.

For this most basic truth, this latest war against America must fail. Terror always fails; those who believe in terror's strength to destroy the will of a people to persist in life are always proved wrong by the simple refusal of the people to permit this to happen.

But if the change is not utter, it is profound. What happened on September 11 recalled to us who we are and what our values are. We remember that we are not who those who hate our nation say we are, and our values are not what they say they are.

On the morning of September 11, as it happened, the *New York Times* ran a story that was typical of the *Times* in recent years. The story warmly profiled the life—and plugged the memoirs—of a former 1970s radical and terrorist bomber named Bill Ayers. "I don't regret setting bombs," Ayers was quoted in the lead. "I feel we didn't do enough." Ayers boasts in his book that he took part in the 1970s bombings of the New York City police headquarters, the U.S. Capitol, and the Pentagon. The *Times* called these "daring acts in his youth." The *Times* found Ayers to be possessed of an "ebullient, ingratiating manner," and accorded him the respect of two thousand words in the paper plus a generally fawning and deeply stupid interview in the September 16 *New York Times Magazine,* which was printed before the events of September 11.

Ayers's contention, uncritically accepted by the *Times,* that "this society is not a just and fair and decent place" has been for decades a foundation lie and essential tool of justification for those who would destroy that society. This has not been limited to the radicals of the Left but has been of equal service to the radical Right.

On the September 13 edition of *The 700 Club,* Jerry Falwell and Pat Robertson had a little chat. Falwell mused that "what we saw on Tuesday . . . could be minuscule if in fact God continues to lift the curtain and allow the enemies of America to give us probably what we deserve." To give us probably what we deserve. Robertson enthusiastically agreed with this blasphemy. Falwell went on to note that "the abortionists have got to bear some burden for this because God will not be mocked," and he and Robertson agreed that feminists, "the gays and the lesbians who are actively trying to make that an alternative lifestyle," and the ACLU also "helped this happen."

I don't think the *Times* will ever print another story celebrating political bombings as "daring acts." I don't think Robertson and Falwell will ever again be regarded by most Americans with anything other than the deepest contempt. I think that the perverted values of those on the Left and the Right who hate this country for being what it is—a liberal democracy—are now seen for what they are, in the terrible light of September 11. We have recovered who we are.

On September 17, David Letterman returned to the air. Approaching open tears, he swore to his audience and to himself that he would never forget that police officers and firefighters were heroes—men and women who put themselves in harm's way to protect us.

Yes, we remember that now. We remember that it is not creatures like Bill Ayers that we treasure but those who protect us from creatures like Bill Ayers. We remember that love of country is a wonderful thing; that it is not incompatible with a liberal society but rather the great force that binds together that society. We are reminded that our values are not the values that the civilization trashers of Hollywood join the civilization haters of the Taliban in ascribing to us, the values of *Fear Factor.* We remind ourselves, as David Letterman did, that our real values are the ones that led hundreds of firefighters and police officers to risk and lose their lives. We are, we learn again, brave and compassionate and strong. We are good people and we have built what is in fact "a just and fair and decent place," and we will preserve this place from those who would destroy it.

With a Serious
and Large Intent

◆ ◆ ◆

Sunday was a day of clarification on various levels. The first was the most basic. We have been under attack by Osama bin Laden and his Al Qaeda network for some years now, but we did not fully admit to that until September 11. On October 7 we answered September 11. There was a feeling to the day of something like relief. Well, that's that; war is joined, and we must win it.

What we must win was also made clear. Incredibly, in the light of six thousand dead, some (mostly on the Left) have persisted in the delusion that we are involved here in something that can be put into some sort of context of normality—a crisis that can be resolved through legal or diplomatic efforts, or handled with United Nations resolutions, or addressed by limited military "reprisals." We have been warned not to see this in too-large terms—as a holy war, or a crusade or a clash of civilizations.

Osama bin Laden himself put the lie to all that with a videotaped message that apparently had been recorded after September 11 but in anticipation of October 7. In this statement, released to the Al-Jazeera television network, bin Laden abandoned the shred of pretense that he was not responsible for the attacks of September 11. He crowed his joy: "Here is America struck by God Almighty in one of its vital organs, so that its greatest buildings are destroyed. Grace and gratitude to God. America has been filled with horror from North to South and East to West, and thanks be to God."

He described the conflict repeatedly in the terms of holy war. "These events have divided the world into two camps, the camp of the faithful and the camp of infidels," he said. And: "Every Muslim must rise to defend his religion." He ended with a promise: "I swear to God that America will not live in peace before peace reigns in Palestine, and before all the army of infidels depart the land of Mohammad, peace be upon him."

Is that clear now?

The way in which our government views this war was also made clear. In his address to the nation on Sunday, Bush dropped any suggestion that what we are about is merely a manhunt on a massive scale. He made plain that America is, in fact, at war not only with bin Laden's Al Qaeda but also with the Taliban forces of Afghanistan. Bush used language—"sustained, comprehensive, and relentless operations"—intended to signal that, while this may be an unconventional war, it will be a war in full, not a Clintonian exercise in a spot of bombing, a bit of missile rattling. He went further even, warning in hard language that the war could spread to other nations that sponsor terror against America: "If any government sponsors the outlaws and killers of innocents, they have become outlaws and murderers themselves. And they will take that lonely path at their own peril."

So there it is, out on the table. We are in a war, and we will be in it for some time, and this war is being undertaken toward a great and daunting end. With Sunday's speech, no one can doubt that President Bush and his advisers see the war on the same scale of magnitude as bin Laden sees it. It is us against them, and "them" has been defined broadly enough to encompass any state that harbors or sponsors anti-American terrorism. The goal here is not to knock off a few of terrorism's foot soldiers. It is to put out of business terrorism's masters, its networks, and its protectors—even if those protectors enjoy status as sovereign regimes.

That this is a goal worth fighting for may be judged by the extraordinary international support for the American effort. The world's leaders know, as Britain's Tony Blair said Sunday, that the atrocity of September 11 was "an attack on us all," by fanatics who threaten "any nation throughout the world that does not share their fanatical views."

No one can know how what began on Sunday will proceed. It is certainly possible that it will proceed badly, at least at times. It may appear, at times, that it will end badly. But we start out with a serious and large intent, facing an enemy that is likewise serious and likewise ambitious. If we remember this, if we stay serious and remember that the enemy, too, is serious, we will win. And it should not be hard to remember this. We have six thousand reasons to never forget.

Chicken Little Media

◆ ◆ ◆

Yesterday, the day after an aide to Senate Majority Leader Tom Daschle opened an envelope containing anthrax spores, the first-edition front page of the *New York Post* featured a trick photo of the statue of Lincoln in the Lincoln Memorial wearing a gas mask, above the headline: ANTHRAX HITS THE CAPITAL. The paper's gossip page reported, under the headline SCARED STARS CAVE TO TERROR, that Drew Barrymore had canceled a Manhattan movie premiere and fled the city, that Christy Turlington had postponed her wedding, and that Rosie O'Donnell had canceled her shows this week.

The *New York Times* led its October 16 paper with a story subheaded "Baby Falls Ill as Scare Widens Across the U.S." Note: baby, not babies. On *Today,* Tom Brokaw, whose assistant has tested positive for the generally nonfatal and easily treatable form of anthrax infection caused by skin contact, reported Monday that he believed that he, Tom Brokaw, "actually saw" the letter that contained the anthrax spores and that, indeed, he may have even "picked it up" (or may not have)—and that, while he had exhibited no symptoms of anthrax, he was taking the antibiotic Cipro anyway.

Ten years ago, during the anteceding days to what can now be seen as the first phase of a long war, President George H. W. Bush suffered a small crisis of confidence. Bush's great Gulf War ally, Margaret Thatcher, took the president aside. George, she famously said, this is no time to go wobbly.

This is still no time to go wobbly. Also, it is no time for the American media to revert to the hysterical, silly, fear-mongering, self-centered, juvenile, and ninnyish form that has made them so widely mistrusted and so cordially detested.

A *New York Times* article on Tuesday quoted a bioterrorism expert named Amy Smithson: "Welcome to our generation's Blitz. We are going to have to get hardened up here." Yes, and a good way to start getting hardened up would be not to compare a scare that, as of Ms. Smithson's utterance, had claimed precisely one life to the Nazi air war against Britain. Between September 1940 and May 1941, the bombing of Britain took more than forty thousand lives.

A campaign to spread fear by sending anthrax spores to media and political targets is not the same as two years of air raids and forty thousand dead. It is not the same as five thousand dead either. To confuse mass fear with mass murder is an embarrassment—and, worse, an insult to the dead and the destroyed of September 11. On that day, it is reported, something on the order of ten thousand children lost a parent. All over the country, people face each day numb with horror and despair because of September 11. It is not fair to them that the rest of us, who did not lose a husband or a wife or a child that day, should succumb to the vapors over a few threats to a few people in the media and politics. It is not decent.

Neither is it wise. What lies ahead really may be a test on the order of the Blitz. There are a great many targets in America, a great many office buildings, public spaces, landmarks. It is not possible to guard them all from attack, and, as we learned in Oklahoma City, such targets are vulnerable to devastating assaults of a nature far easier to arrange than the relatively sophisticated airliner attacks of September. We need to get hardened up not to deal with fantasies of fear over the mail but with the real possibility of more deaths, in large numbers.

The war so far seems to be going very well and it may end reasonably soon and in a reasonably clean victory, at least in terms of initial goals. But who knows? The conflict could spread, and Middle Eastern governments more or less friendly to the United States could be toppled and replaced with revolutionary regimes bent on jihad. It is possible (not likely, I think) that this will develop into a long, terrible fight, with a great cost in American lives.

It is certain, given the military realities, that we will win even this, if we keep our resolve, but our resolve will be tried. It is really not a good idea to begin chipping away at it now, each with our own little attack of the swoons.

Go to work. Don't ask your doctor for Cipro. Don't buy a gas mask. Take the kids to the park; take your wife to a restaurant. Open your mail. Boycott Drew Barrymore's movie (you know it's no good anyway).

Return of the
"Chicken Hawks"

◆ ◆ ◆

The general trump-it-all insult that the antiwar crowd aims at the prowar crowd these days is a neat little portmanteau term that manages to impute, at once, cowardice, ignorance, selfishness, bloodlust (as long as the blood spills from others' veins), and hypocrisy: "chicken hawk."

The generally accepted definition of the term, which dates at least to 1988, describes "chicken hawks" as public persons, generally male, who advocate war but who declined a significant opportunity to serve in uniform during wartime.

Chicken hawk is interesting as an insult because it is such a pure example of reactionary thinking or, rather, the substitution of reaction for thinking. It is the sort of thing you say when you need to stop the argument in its tracks because you simply can't bear to address its realities. Other obvious examples of the type might include "my country right or wrong" and "I don't know much about art, but I know what I like."

As these suggest, the power of the reactionary argument stopper is in inverse correlation with any underlying truth. Nothing could seem more immediately unanswerable than "my country right or wrong." Of course: It is your country, and it remains your country no matter what, and at first blush this seems the morally admirable position. But nothing could be more disastrous, or less morally supportable, than the philosophy this tautology represents: "My country right or wrong," wrote G. K. Chesterton, is on a moral par with "my mother drunk or sober." This is an idea that ends you up with Napoleon's France, Hitler's Germany, and Mao's China.

So it is with chicken hawk. Its power lies in the simplicity that comes with being completely wrong. The central implication here is that only men who have professionally endured war have the moral standing and the experiential authority to advocate war. That is, in this country at least, a radical and ahistorical view. The Founders, who knew quite well the dangers of a military class supreme, were clear in their conviction that the judgment of professional war makers must be subordinated to the command of ignorant amateurs—civilian leaders who were in turn subordinated to the command of civilian voters. That has given us the leadership in war of such notable chicken hawks as Abraham Lincoln and Franklin Delano Roosevelt.

Further, the inescapable logic of chicken hawk calling is that only military men have standing to pronounce in any way on war—to advocate it or to advocate against it. The decision not to go to war involves exactly the same issues of experiential and moral authority as does the decision to go to war. If a past of soldiering is required for one, it is required for the other. Chicken doves have no more standing than chicken hawks. We must leave all the decisions to the generals and the veterans.

I am myself not technically a chicken hawk, as I was, thank God, a few years too young to serve during the Vietnam War and too old and too untrained to be of any military use during the next significant war, the Persian Gulf War of 1991. But I suppose I fit the spirit if not the letter of the slur. I am certainly now a hawk, and during the Vietnam years I was certainly a dove. What changed me was in fact experience of war—but not as a soldier.

I covered the Gulf War as a reporter, and it was this experience, later compounded by what I saw reporting in Bosnia, that convinced me of the moral imperative, sometimes, for war.

In liberated Kuwait City, one vast crime scene, I toured the morgue one day and inspected torture and murder victims left behind by the departing Iraqis. "The corpse in drawer 3 . . . belonged to a young man," I later wrote. "When he was alive, he had been beaten from the soles of the feet to the crown of the head, and every inch of his skin was covered with purple-and-black bruises. . . . The man in drawer 12 had been burned to death with some flammable liquid. . . . Corpses 18 and 19 . . . belonged to the brothers Abbas . . . the eyeballs of the elder of the Abbas brothers had been removed. The sockets were bloody holes."

That was the beginning of the making of me as at least an honorary chicken hawk. After that, I never again could stand the arguments of those who sat in the luxury of safety—"advocating nonresistance behind the guns of the American Fleet," as George Orwell wrote of World War II pacifists—and held that the moral course was, in crimes against humanity as in crimes on the street corner: Better not to get involved, dear.

In a Borrowed Tie

◆ ◆ ◆

One day in 1998, I was invited to have an off-the-record chat with an important staff person on the Clinton administration's National Security Council. We met, at the important person's suggestion, at the important person's important club, where the major domo was kind enough to lend me a tie. We sat in important old chairs and drank important old whiskey and had a made-for-TV version of an important old Washington conversation—the personage from the White House setting me right, one important man to another, on the real and complex forces at work behind our government's seemingly mindless, but actually deep and subtle and clever, actions. And me trying to nod in a way that suggested a fine blend of Kissingerian cunning and Lippmannesque wisdom, which is hard to do in a borrowed tie.

The whole experience was terrific fun, although I never could shake the feeling that it was all a mistake—that I was supposed to be someone else entirely, someone who actually mattered, Tom Friedman or Bob Woodward probably. Right up to the end, I half expected the important person to suddenly say, with a mildly puzzled smile, "You know, you're a damned sight better looking on television, Bob."

At any rate, the encounter ended in a perfect straight-to-video moment, the two of us men of import standing on the corner, in a drizzle, backlit by a street lamp, having that cinematically crucial last word. It seemed to be my line, so I said something about how things didn't seem to be working too well with the Iraq policy. I can't remember which point of collapse the Clinton approach was precisely at that week, whether Saddam Hussein had actually gotten around to throwing out the UN weapons inspectors or was still enjoying the long defiance and humiliation of an impotent America too much to bid that last good-bye—but it doesn't really matter.

The important person leaned forward, his eyes unusually ablaze with deep and subtle and clever thoughts, and he said, in a demi-whisper: No, you don't understand. As long as Hussein behaves like this, the UN sanctions will stay in effect, and as long as the sanctions stay in effect, Hussein will stay weak. If he obeys the UN mandates, then the sanctions will disappear, and he will become strong again. We've got him just where we want him.

This Thanksgiving, I am thankful that this person, and all the other deep and subtle and clever people of the Clinton White House, and all the thoughts they thought, and all the damage they wrought, are history.

I am thankful that we live in reality again. Or, to be more precise, I am thankful that we live in a reality defined by the actual consequences of policies, rather than what columnists and correspondents and editors can be gulled into thinking are consequences—gulled at least for long enough to skate through that day's news cycle and this season's electoral cycle.

Liberals, in the Democratic Party and in their media and academic institutional bases, persist in seeing the accruing foreign policy triumphs of the Bush administration as accidents of history occurring within an aberration of history. This could not be more wrong. The accidents, and the larger aberration, belonged to the years this administration has led us out of, the long years of suspension of disbelief that constituted Clinton foreign policy in practice.

This was a policy accidental at its core—essentially, ad hoc reaction to, and street-corner justification of, actions that simply happened as they happened, under the management (well, more like stage management) of a president whose only enduring belief was that nothing was true but poll ratings.

But some things are true. It is true that Iraq, during the Clinton years, waged a war of attrition against the United States, massively violated the cease-fire it agreed to in 1991 and a long series of UN resolutions, almost daily firing on warplanes assigned to patrol the peace, even going so far as to attempt the assassination of an American president. And it is true that Clinton pretty much let Iraq get away with all of this, and ultimately walked away. And it is true that men like Osama bin Laden saw in Clinton's great aberrational abdication of American responsibility a wonderful shining hope: With just a bit more of a push, just one really big murder, America the paper tiger could be induced to walk away from all of the Middle East.

But, as it turned out, this last bit wasn't true at all. There are some things that no amount of wishing, and no amount of deep and subtle and clever dreaming, can make true. For which I am thankful.

Exit Hussein

◆ ◆ ◆

Soon—almost certainly by the end of January—it will be clear where we are going in Iraq. To assess what lies immediately ahead, it helps to think clearly about where we have come from, and where we are now.

We have come from a position of nearly absolute failure. Over the course of a deleterious decade, the structure of containment erected by the United States and the United Nations at the end of the war against Iraq in 1991 had collapsed, utterly.

The postwar revolution in Iraq that the first Bush administration had fomented died at birth in a terrible betrayal by its Bush I architects. This was the first of a series of acts of American presidential mal-leadership that cumulatively came to produce a perfect perversity of policy: the accidental, sequential rebuilding of Saddam Hussein, and the accidental, sequential "loss" (in the eyes of America's watchful, hopeful Islamic enemies) of a war that had been most brilliantly won.

Next, the economic sanctions. The apparent theory here was that if you starved the grass roots long enough they would become strong enough to overthrow the gardener. The roots starved fine, but the gardener and his battalions of heavily armed assistant gardeners were able to stay perfectly fat—and with enough cash left over to support palace building and weapons building, and still afford brand-name Scotch. Meanwhile, the suffering of the people worked brilliantly to undermine support for civilization's case and to resurrect Hussein as an Islamic martyr and hero.

The third and most consequential act was the collapse of the United Nations weapons inspections regime. Bush I, in his tired and feckless last days, did nothing to stop this. Bill Clinton, from his hyper but feckless first days, did the same, but with the added, typical loud claims that much had been done.

In 1998, the whole wretched mess ended in a gross defeat for the United States and the United Nations—a defeat made only more gross, and more telling, in the calculations of those such as Osama bin Laden—with the passage of a resolution of Congress committing the United States to a "regime change" in Iraq even as the United States essentially capitulated to the existing regime in Iraq.

And where are we now? We are in a position of triumph, and potentially much greater triumph. A few months ago, all was still in tatters. Hussein still defied with impunity, still ruled unchallenged over his torture state, still schemed to advance his dreams of himself as the atomic Saladin. The United Nations still went to work every day, conspicuously (not to mention purposely) failing at its charter mission. Everything was still a disaster and still in train for greater disaster. The will of one man, George W. Bush, changed all this.

Now, for the first time since 1998, the inspectors are back in Iraq—and they are back in with a determination and a power they never had before. Now, Hussein backs down, and down, and plays for whatever time he can get. Now, he is so desperate that he is forced to empty his prisons and to begin to free his captive people. Now, the United States is backed in its actions by a United Nations that is beginning to see, as in a sort of miracle, that it actually can be a force for peace and law in the world.

And the United Nations is beginning to like this. When the Bush administration declared that Iraq's most recent great tissue of lies was just that, the institutional voices of the United Nations backed up the president. Hans Blix, the formally appeasement-minded chief of the UN inspection program, and his colleague Mohamed El Baradei were polite but clear: Bush is right, Iraq is still lying—and this will not stand. Here is the key statement, from El Baradei in an interview several days ago, noting what the Egyptian nuclear weapons expert cited as Iraq's failure, so far, to come up "with evidence to exonerate themselves": "The less clarification they provide, the less certainty with which we can report to the Security Council. Without a credible or high degree of certainty, I do not see the Security Council exonerating Iraq."

The Security Council will not, this time, exonerate Iraq. There will be regime change in Iraq. The United States will be the forcing agency for this, and the United States will generally be backed in this by most of the world.

The only real question for Saddam Hussein—the question that will be answered soon—is: with or without war? Or to put it another way: with defeat by arms, conviction in a war crimes trial and execution, or with capitulation, a quick deal and a night flight somewhere with neck and numbered bank account intact?

Immorality on the March

• • •

PARIS—Last weekend, across Europe and America, somewhere between 1 million and 2 million people marched against a war with Saddam Hussein's Iraq. All protests against war are ultimately ethical in nature, and Saturday's placard wavers did not break with tradition: GIVE PEACE A CHANCE; MAKE TEA, NOT WAR; BUSH AND BLAIR—THE REAL WAR CRIMINALS. These are statements of sentiment, not power politics, and the sentiment is, or is meant to be, a moral one.

Of course, not all the marchers can be counted as 99.9 percent pure moralists. Some—perhaps many—marched out of simple reactionary hatred: for the United States, for its power, for its paramount position in a hated world order. London's paleosocialist mayor, "Red Ken" Livingstone, a speaker at that city's massive demo, comes to mind. His enlightened argument against war consisted chiefly of calling George W. Bush "a lackey of the oil industry," "a coward," and "this creature."

But doubtless, hundreds of thousands of marchers—and many more millions who did not march—believe quite sincerely that theirs is a profoundly moral cause, and this is really all that motivates them. They believe, as French President Jacques Chirac recently pontificated, that "war is always the worst answer."

The people who believe what Chirac at least professes to believe are, in the matter of Iraq, as wrong as it is possible to be. Theirs is not the position of profound morality but one that stands in profound opposition to morality.

The situation with Iraq may be considered in three primary contexts, and in each, the true moral case is for war.

The first context considers the people of Iraq. There are 24 million of them, and they have been living (those who have not been slaughtered or forced into exile) for decades under one of the cruelest and bloodiest tyrannies on earth. It must be assumed that, being human, they would prefer to be rescued from a hell where more than a million lives have been sacrificed to the dreams of a megalomaniac, where rape is a sanctioned instrument of state policy, and where the removal of the tongue is the prescribed punishment for uttering an offense against the Great Leader.

These people could be liberated from this horror—relatively easily and quickly. There is every reason to think that a U.S. invasion would swiftly vanquish the few elite units that can be counted on to defend the detested Saddam Hussein; and that the victory would come at the cost of few—likely hundreds, not thousands—Iraqi and American lives. There is risk; and if things go terribly wrong it is a risk that could result in terrible suffering. But that is an equation that is present in any just war, and in this case any rational expectation has to consider the probable cost to humanity to be low and the probable benefit to be tremendous. To choose perpetuation of tyranny over rescue from tyranny, where rescue may be achieved, is immoral.

The second context considers the security of America, and indeed of the world, and here, too, morality is on the side of war. The great lesson of September 11, 2001, is not that terrorism must be stopped—an impossible dream—but that state-sanctioned terrorism must be stopped. The support of a state—even a weak and poor state—offers the otherwise vulnerable enemies of the established order the protection they need in their attempts to destroy that order—through the terrorists' only weapon, murder. To tolerate the perpetuation of state-sanctioned terror, such as Hussein's regime exemplifies, is to invite the next September 11, and the next, and the next. Again, immoral.

The third context concerns the idea of order itself. The United Nations is a mightily flawed construct, but it exists; and it exists on the side (more or less) of law and humanity. Directly and unavoidably arising from the crisis with Iraq, the United Nations today stands on the precipice of permanent irrelevancy. If Iraq is allowed to defy the law, the United Nations will never recover, and the oppressed and weak of the world will lose even the limited protection of the myth of collective security. Immoral.

To march against the war is not to give peace a chance. It is to give tyranny a chance. It is to give the Iraqi nuke a chance. It is to give the next terrorist mass murder a chance. It is to march for the furtherance of evil instead of the vanquishing of evil.

This cannot be the moral position.

Who Would Choose Tyranny?

♦ ♦ ♦

KUWAIT CITY—Today is Kuwait's Liberation Day, celebrating the anniversary of the day twelve years ago when U.S. and allied troops rescued this small, soft country from the pleasures of life as Iraq's nineteenth province. The promenade by the harbor was to be the scene of parading and flag-waving, and already in yesterday's waning midafternoon heat, a few boys and young men were out strutting with their Kuwaiti and American flags.

The last time I was here was on the occasion of the liberation, and on that day, and for several days thereafter, the whole city was a parade and a party. Everyone was in the streets, cheering and screaming, and driving around ten to a car, madly honking and shooting guns in the air.

You could easily find grief and wretchedness, though. To be part of a country that has been raped by an invading force is nearly incomprehensible—incomprehensible at least, to a modern-day American; it is a routine part of life's education in many places at many times. To begin with, Kuwait City itself had been savaged—shot up, blown up, torched and, of course, thoroughly looted. The major buildings of state and commerce had been used for artillery practice. The beaches had been salted with land mines and strung with concertina wire. Garbage and human filth were everywhere, and the place stank.

About four hundred Kuwaiti civilians had been killed during Iraq's seven-month occupation, and many more had been brutalized in one way or another—ritualistically humiliated (forced to urinate on the Kuwaiti flag or on a photograph of the Kuwaiti emir, for instance), robbed, beaten, raped, tortured. Some of the subjugation, rape, and torture had been professional: the work of Iraq's terrible special security units and aimed at specific individuals annoying to the regime. But more had been the work of enthusiastic amateurs—poor-boy soldiers let loose in a rich land suddenly realizing that if they wanted to make some well-fed banker watch his wife and daughters get raped, why, they could just go ahead and do it. Shattered people were everywhere: I watched one torture victim, a big, strong man, being interviewed in the place of his torture by a BBC television crew—weeping and weeping, but absolutely silently, as he told the story.

Twelve years later, Kuwait City is an utterly different place, and the great difference is the abundance of the mundane. You can still see bullet pockmarks here and there, but mostly everything has been patched and painted up. The country's pride, a 372-meter telecommunications tower that was half-built and badly damaged when the Iraqis invaded, was completed in 1996. It is popularly known as Liberation Tower. It has a revolving restaurant.

The Bank of Burgan is building a new office tower, a curvilinear slab of gray-green glass and gray-silver metal. On a drive around town, I counted fourteen other major commercial buildings under construction. There is a new Museum of Modern Art, a new kidney dialysis center, a new marina, a new fish market, and a new shopping mall by the seaside that stretches along for blocks of knock-off neoclassical arches and pillars and broken pediments, just as cheerily affronting to those of delicate sensibility as anything you could find in Palo Alto, or even Houston. The promenade has been refurbished with red brick sidewalks, marble edgings, and "old-fashioned" green metal streetlights. Everything, at least in the downtown and seaside areas, is spotless; foreign labor is cheap in Kuwait.

The fish market is full of fresh tuna, mullet, flounder, drum, bass, shark, sardines, and prawns; the meat market rich with bloody halves and quarters of lamb and mutton and goat; the bins of the fruits and vegetable market bulging over; and likewise, no shortages of herbs, spices, dates, nuts, olives, pots, pans, clothes, toys, perfumes, watches, jewelry, McDonald's burgers, and Mercedes-Benzes.

Tyranny truly is a horror: an immense, endlessly bloody, endlessly painful, endlessly varied, endless crime against not humanity in the abstract but a lot of humans in the flesh. It is, as Orwell wrote, a jackboot forever stomping on a human face.

I understand why some dislike the idea, and fear the ramifications of, America as a liberator. But I do not understand why they do not see that anything is better than life with your face under the boot. And that any rescue of a people under the boot (be they Afghan, Kuwaiti, or Iraqi) is something to be desired. Even if the rescue is less than perfectly realized. Even if the rescuer is a great, overmuscled, bossy, selfish oaf. Or would you, for yourself, choose the boot?

A Letter from Kuwait City

♦ ♦ ♦

One of the larger news features of mid-February was the arrival in Baghdad of some two hundred peace missionaries from around the world, who had come, they announced in appropriately grave tones, to serve as "human shields"—to put themselves between the targets in Iraq and the bombers of the mad George W. Bush. The British contingent of the mission, traveling photogenically in two old-fashioned red double-decker buses, got the lion's share of the press, thanks in part to the media talents of sixty-eight-year-old Godfrey Meynell, who has an interestingly counterintuitive résumé for this sort of thing (he is a former Foreign Office man and a former high sheriff of Derbyshire), an attractive stiff-upper-lip yet unassuming-bloke-of-the-people manner, and the natural hamminess of a well-aged Smithfield. For a week or so you could scarcely pick up a London paper without catching a breeze from Meynell's stiff upper lip in action. "I do think if we have a large number of people at the sites, it will be very difficult for them to bomb," he said in a typical utterance. "I really do think so."

On March 2 the *Sunday Telegraph* reported that almost all of Britain's eleven would-be shields were among those who had decided, on second thought, that sequestering themselves in buildings slated to receive high explosives was actually too dangerous, and had quietly slipped away to home. The fault, apparently, lay with the perhaps naive Iraqi government, which apparently took at face value the missionaries' pronouncements of their willingness to risk life for peace. As the *Telegraph* reported, after nearly two weeks had passed in which only about sixty-five of the shields "had so far agreed to take up positions at the oil refineries, power plants and water-purification sites" selected by the Iraqi regime as "strategic sites," the government group hosting the pacifists, the Organization of Friendship, Peace and Solidarity, had presented them with an ultimatum: Choose their spots or leave. Meynell, who was among the relative few to have bedded down at a potential crater (a Baghdad power station), was admirably forthright in admitting his new understanding of realities. "I am ashamed to be leaving you," he told the workers at the power station, "but I'm going out of pure, cold fear." It had come to him, he said, that "this power plant is right next to a bridge, surrounded by Republican Guards. It's obviously a prime target."

When the antiwarriors depart the theater of the coming war, you know you are nearing the end of that familiar thing we have come to know as the phony peace. What is oddly reassuring or entirely depressing about phony peaces is how they are always phony in exactly the same way. Twelve years ago, in the last weeks before the previous war with Saddam Hussein, I flew to Amman, en route to Baghdad, in a plane that was thickly settled with peace missionaries of one stripe or another. Daniel Ortega and Louis Farrakhan were up in first class, and back in economy was a party of some twenty or so mostly young people, led by a man named Stephen Zunes, who was an assistant professor of political science at Whitman College, in Walla Walla, Washington. Zunes explained the rationale of his mission to me. "You see," he said, "you can't really have war unless you de-humanize the enemy. And dialogue humanizes folks. We will meet with the Iraqis and when we go back we will share with Americans that they are human beings. We will be able to say, 'Look, we talked to these folks and they are human beings and they are going to be killed if we go forward with this war.'"

At least several hundred people of this sort passed through Baghdad in the last days of the phony peace, and they all made the evening news, and they all left be-fore the bombing began. Then as now, the pope was calling for peace and the Russians and the French and the Arab states were expressing dismay and outrage and offering elaborate diplomatic alternatives that were not intended to be acted upon. Then as now, Saddam and his minions passed the days alternating between puffer-fish blustering and ostentatious displays of "cooperation."

Now as then, the better sort of global citizens are concerned with explaining to the great oaf America that war is not the answer. "Is it the right time to close the door?" Hans Blix, the chief UN weapons inspector, asked plaintively. "A cri-sis of this kind should be solved by exclusively peaceful means," declared Russian President Vladimir Putin, whose handling of the crisis in Chechnya has been much remarked on for its restraint. "The military option should only be a last re-sort," lectured France—a consistent nation, if nothing else: "Frenchmen, do not attempt to commit any action which might bring terrible reprisals," Marshal Pé-tain said in an appeal to his countrymen for continued collaboration with the Nazis on the day after the Americans and the British arrived in Normandy to ex-ercise the military option.

It is all enough to give phony peaces a bad name. The original phony peace was at least, so to speak, real. France and England had desperately sound reasons for appeasing Hitler and avoiding war with Hitler's Reich: If there was a war,

France and England would need to fight it. And having seen a generation of their men, and their national power, destroyed in the Great War, and having in consequence all but disarmed themselves, they were in no position to fight. Neville Chamberlain is derided for his "peace for our time"; indeed, his Blixian self-delusion is cringe-making still: "In spite of the hardness and ruthlessness I thought I saw in his face," he wrote after meeting Hitler, "I got the impression that here was a man who could be relied upon." Today we remember Chamberlain as the consummate fool, and it seems obvious to us what seemed obvious to Chamberlain's political opponent and successor. Britain had faced a choice "between shame and war," Winston Churchill wrote. "We have chosen shame, and we will get war." But it wasn't obvious to many until forced and forced and forced again on them, and it was Chamberlain, not Churchill, who was cheered in the streets when he brought back the peace that the people so badly wanted.

Today's phony peaces really are phony. Now (I am writing this in early March), as in the winter months of 1990–91, no one has any real belief that peace is at hand, or may be brought to hand. War is expected by everyone, and it is this expectation that allows the luxury of the phony peace—an interim between the advent of expectation and the arrival of reality, during which concerned parties may enjoy protesting against a war they know their protests will not stop. The phony peace provides a period of global theater in which the natural order of things may be reasserted: France behaves like France, Russia behaves like Russia, the United Nations behaves like the United Nations, America behaves like America. It is comforting in its way.

I spent the last days of the first Gulf War's phony peace in Baghdad, and I am spending the last days of this one's in Kuwait, soon to take part in the experiment of "embedding," as the jargon has it, some five hundred journalists with the U.S. military for the duration of what is generally expected to be a short, exceedingly one-sided conflict. On the whole, I'd say, the phoniness quotient is down this time. We are spared, at least, much of the death-and-destruction-and-quagmire talk that preceded the last conflict here. The lessons of the campaign in Afghanistan, adding to the lessons of the campaigns in Kosovo and Bosnia, have sunk in. The U.S. armed forces enjoy a technological superiority like nothing the world has seen before; they are, in a real sense, not even fighting the same war as their opponents—or in the same century. No one argues much now about whether these forces are capable of crushing even very serious opposition, and almost no one argues that Iraq offers serious opposition. Rather, the argument concerns whether the employment of this almost unfathomable power will be largely for good, leading to the liberation of a tyrannized people and the spread of freedom, or largely for bad, leading to imperialism and colonialism, with a consequent corruption of America's own values and freedoms. This question is real enough and more: Probably the next hundred years hinges on the answer.

Battle Stations
of the Press

◆ ◆ ◆

KUWAIT CITY—In a few days the U.S. armed forces will attempt to discover if it is possible to successfully place about five hundred journalists in military units (down to the company level) going into war. This experiment in what the military calls "embedding" entails grafting what amounts to a presidential-campaign-sized press corps onto an army in combat. The question of whether this is going to work, or implode, is a matter of much conversation among the involved parties here.

On Monday, in the lobby area of the Hilton Resorts, where the U.S. and British militaries have established the Coalition Press Information Center, two such parties were discussing, over cigarettes, a particular aspect of concern. Both were veterans of military-media relations: Max Blumenfeld, a major in the Army Reserve who is the chief of plans and operations for public affairs in the V Corps, and Alisha Ryu, who is a Nairobi-based correspondent with Voice of America.

Blumenfeld and Ryu were talking about what was going to happen in a basic situation of war reporting: A firefight, say, occurs at Point A, and cameramen and photographers rush to Points B through Z to cover it. Under the rules of embedment, this is not supposed to happen. Each cameramen and photographer, just as each reporter, is to be assigned to a specific unit, and is supposed to stay with that unit unless permitted to leave—and, anyway, none of the embedded journalists is permitted a vehicle, so as to enable him or her to run off to Point A from B through Z. In embedment theory, the cameraman attached to the unit engaged in the firefight is supposed to get the picture, and everyone not attached to that unit is supposed to stay where he or she belongs and not get the picture.

Ryu was of the fairly firm view that this arrangement could not work. There was no way, she said, that people for whom the picture was the story (and for whom the picture of the war could be a career maker) were going to sit still and miss the picture, no matter what the rules said.

Blumenfeld did not argue the point. "Okay, it is a problem," he said. "But we don't have a fleet of taxis. . . . We are trying to deal with what we can, as we can. This embedment process is the best we can do to work out a compromise. . . . It is something we will have to talk about as we go on."

In the first Gulf War, in which Blumenfeld served as a public affairs officer, the U.S. military, in collaboration with the major American media companies, built a system that was designed to sharply limit direct observational reporting to relatively few journalists, overwhelmingly drawn from the ranks of big media. The permitted few were to file "pool" reports and pictures that would be made available to all media through a military clearing process. Unsurprisingly, the arrangement turned out to please no one. The coverage was spotty and shallow, with the majority of American reporters covering the war from hotels and briefing rooms; one reporter's inevitably subjective view of an event that only he had covered was of little use to colleagues trying to craft an "objective" account several hundred miles away. Much was lost to history. And, of course, reporters who wanted to report the war for themselves simply went off on their own.

The experiment—"the huge experiment," as Blumenfeld says—this time represents an admirable attempt to do much better. And it would seem that it must be better: A system that allows eyewitness reporting across the spectrum of conflict, no matter how constrained, has to produce a picture of war, and of the military that goes to war, more true and complete than a system that seeks to deny eyewitness reporting.

But Blumenfeld's honest response—"it is something we will have to talk about as we go on"—will, I think, turn out to be something of an understatement. There are problems of control and independence that are unresolved here, and these, as Ryu suggested, will come roaring up the first time they meet the first practical test.

The Department of Defense ground rules for embedding speak of the imperative "to tell the factual story, good or bad." For the sake of that great goal, I hope the Pentagon thinks more about loosening things up a bit. But also, I hope so for the sake of the military's media front line, public-affairs officers like Blumenfeld. As any White House press secretary can tell them, there is no hell quite so annoying as the hell of an infantilized media pack.

The Calm Before

◆ ◆ ◆

KUWAIT CITY—Monday morning, at breakfast in the Marriott Hotel here, a man at the table next to mine was talking on his cell phone in one of those brisk executive cell-phone voices. He was not in uniform, but from his neat, straight, clipped look he was military of some sort. He was saying that he was calling on behalf of Captain So-and-So, following up on a call from yesterday, trying to make clear exactly what the captain needed.

"We're looking for the whole thing as a package deal," he was saying, "the bunk beds and the pillows and the blankets all for one price." A pause, as he listened to a question. "No, nothing like that. Basic stuff. The blankets—not fancy. You know, durable, but economical. Just looking for, you know, one level above airline. Just looking for a place for a guy to put his head." Another pause, another question. "No, that's too much. Look, these would be for, if you get my drift, guests. They're not high-end guests. They're guests that would be trying to kill us at one time."

In Washington and New York and Paris and London, the idea of war with Iraq is still, theoretically, theoretical. Although no one believes that war (or regime change and a temporary U.S. military occupation of Iraq without war) will be avoided, it is still barely possible, for the purposes of news product and national posturing, to pretend that the last bit of jaw-jaw remaining has some connection with reality: that it matters what judgments pass so finely parsed from the thin lips of Dr. Blix, the Great Equivocator; or what the precise details are of the latest ploy by the French to save their great, greasy oil contracts with their client-tyrant Saddam Hussein.

But here, where the army's Third Infantry Division and the First Marine Division wait for the word to attack, the conversation has moved entirely beyond these fictions and confections, except as they concern issues of timing and tactics on the periphery of things. The talk here is much more pragmatic: beds and blankets and fuel and gas masks and so on, a million little things to get done before the beginning of the foregone conclusion.

Last week the Third Infantry Division packed up its big tan-white tents at

Camp New York, its desert base since November, loaded up its tanks and its other assault vehicles with ammunition, and moved to a forward position farther north in the sand. A few days later, Maj. Gen. Buford Blount, the commanding general of the Third Infantry Division, spoke to the journalists who will be traveling with and reporting on the division as the main heavy armored force in the invasion of Iraq. Blount was clear and matter-of-fact on the nature of the job: "Our goal is to have a regime change in Iraq, plus make sure the area is free from weapons of mass destruction."

The invasion of a nation, the defeat of its army in its own land and the ouster of its government represent the height of ambition, danger, and difficulty in war. But here, too, Blount is matter-of-fact—not blustering (he does not seem at all the sort) but quietly and apparently absolutely sure of a victory based on an overwhelming superiority of force.

A reporter asked him about what has been presumed the nightmare scenario— taking Baghdad by arms. "I feel confident that, with the mechanized forces we have, we'd be able to do that very successfully," Blount said, in his low, almost monotonal voice. A reporter asked him about the dangers of chemical or biological attack. He said that this was his "biggest concern," but "if it happens, we're very well prepared for it." A reporter asked him what worries keep him up at night these days. He said, "I sleep pretty good at night."

The historian Paul Kennedy wrote a while back that the immense disparity of power between the United States and the rest of the world, unique in degree in history, was remarkable enough, but that what was really extraordinary was that the United States was able to achieve this by spending less than 3 percent of gross domestic product annually. A similar sense strikes an observer here.

It is remarkable enough that the United States is setting out to undertake the invasion of a nation, the destruction of a regime, and the liberation of a people. But to do this with only one real military ally, with much of the world against it, with a war plan that is still, by necessity, in flux days before the advent, with an invasion force that contains only one fully deployed heavy armored division— and to have, under these circumstances, the division's commander sleeping pretty good at night: Well, that is extraordinary.

A victory on these terms will change the power dynamics of the world. And there will be a victory on these terms.

Warriors at Work

♦ ♦ ♦

MAIN HEADQUARTERS, THIRD INFANTRY DIVISION, KUWAIT—
When President Bush began the blunt, brief speech that set the last clock running for war against Saddam Hussein, at four A.M. Kuwait time, a couple dozen
officers and soldiers gathered around a television in the corner of a big double
tent in the middle of twenty thousand troops spread across ten square miles of
sand here. When Bush finished, there was no cheering, and everyone quietly
turned and went back to work.

The Third Division has been preparing for this war for nearly a year and a
half. Many of its troops have spent the better part of a year training for battle
here. As the president spoke, one young female soldier methodically cleaned her
M-16 spread out in pieces on paper towels on the map table. Reactions afterward
reflected variations of personal expressions. But the viewpoint was generally one
of welcome relief.

The division's chief of staff, John Sterling, who was just selected for promo-
tion from colonel to brigadier general, and who has an operations man's metic-
ulous nature, said: "It was an expected speech—a required speech. If you're
going to initiate war, you're required by international norms to inform the other
side of your clear intention and to allow them to react and avert war. In a long
series of benchmarks that have taken place over a long time here, this was one of
the last benchmarks to check off."

Maj. Gen. Buford Blount, the division commander, who was told to prepare
the division for war with Iraq when he took command a little more than a month
after September 11, said: "We are very ready." Brig. Gen. Lloyd Austin, the assistant division commander who will direct the assault, said: "This is war now. This
is not a game. There won't be a playoff next year."

Pfc. Colin Wilson, nineteen, of Colorado Springs, Colorado, said, "I'm
happy now. I'm going to war before my twentieth birthday. It's a beautiful thing.
It beats sitting here, and it's the fastest way home."

There were worries. A primary one was the widely expected use by Saddam
Hussein of chemical or biological weapons, which the Iraqi forces are believed

to have the capacity to deliver, at least randomly and sporadically, through a limited number of missiles, buried explosives, or their fairly considerable artillery.

"Put yourself in his shoes," said Austin. "He's facing the ultimate. This time it is not a matter of just quitting a country he invaded. This time we're going to kill that guy or imprison him for the rest of his life. He is a nut to begin with, so he may well attempt to strike at something he knows will give him fame. He wanted to achieve fame as a modern Saladin, a restorer of Arab empire, but he can't get that so he may think fame lies in at least killing some Americans."

The division's planning assumes some Iraqi use of chemical weapons. "As I watched the speech, I thought about Saddam," said Sterling. "His military forces have already faced us and lost to us, and they have not improved in the last twelve years. Chemical weapons are one of his few trumps."

Sterling worries that Hussein will order chemical attacks not in hopes of victory but rather to impress his own population and forces—which intelligence reports say have been deserting at a brisk pace—with the notion of his continued power.

The concerns, though, do not approach the idea that any use of chemicals might actually defeat or even seriously impede the American force. Blount says his concern is largely for "the psychological impact on our soldiers if it happens: I think they'll be nervous—but they are well trained and I am sure they will hold." Concern for the Iraqi population is also paramount for Capt. Andrew Sims, the division's medical planner. "We would be able to handle our own casualties," said Sims. "But if he used chemicals near a population center of his own people, I couldn't even guess what the casualties might be."

There are other issues. Blount mentioned the danger of accidents in a force of about nine thousand vehicles that would try to move faster than any invasion in history. Austin mentions fratricidal casualties in an environment characterized by massive and varied American firepower. But while no commander expects serious organized resistance from most Iraqi forces, Sterling predicts fighting from elite forces and Ba'ath Party apparatchiks "who are less worried about what Americans will do to them than what their fellow Iraqis will do."

All real worries, but in the terms of war, worries are luxuries. The overall view is expressed by Austin: "We can see them. And what we can see, we can hit, and what we can hit, we can kill, and the kill will be catastrophic." And by Sterling: "A thousand things can happen to make life absolutely miserable for us. There is not one thing that can happen to stop us."

A "Much Tougher" Fight

◆ ◆ ◆

WITH THE THIRD INFANTRY DIVISION, SOUTHERN IRAQ—
On Monday afternoon, in a stiflingly hot tent that had been rigged up as the tactical operations center for the Third Infantry's First Brigade, Maj. Benjamin Matthews sat half-slumped in a metal folding chair by a metal folding table in the sand. He looked very tired. Outside, a moderate sandstorm was beginning to kick up, and the air in the tent was hazy with brown dust.

Matthews had arrived hours earlier here at the center of the Third Infantry's forces in southern Iraq, after more than thirty hours of hard desert driving and—unexpectedly—fighting.

Matthews is the fire support officer for the First Brigade. He had traveled here in a small convoy of unarmored vehicles filled with fellow headquarters officers and staff. He had been following a route already covered by combat units, and by the time of his journey—three days after the invasion of Iraq began—this route was supposed to have been secured. It had not been.

"We made contact in Samawah," Matthews said. "We were going right through the city, twenty of us in eight vehicles. We saw about five to eight guys carrying AK-47s running into an alley. They started shooting at us with the AKs and then started with RPGs [rocket-propelled grenades]. They had a couple of tall buildings with good lines of sight looking down at us and that was where they shot the RPGs from. We got out of the vehicles and went into a firefight. It was not a feasible fight for us. We're not tanks and Bradleys. We had to get out of there and call in CAP [close air support]."

I asked Matthews what he thought of the way things were going.

"This is much tougher than anticipated," he said.

The planners of this war considered a range of scenarios. At the most optimistic, they hoped that the imminent threat of invasion would trigger the collapse of Saddam Hussein's regime. At the next rosiest level, they thought a regime collapse would follow an invasion in a matter of days. On the next rung was the idea that the American advance would be met by little armed resistance, which would allow for accelerated movement and a possibly hard but brief battle with the Republican Guard's Medina Division south of Baghdad.

What actually happened in the first five days was a surprise and made the American advance significantly more difficult and dangerous. In large terms the plan has worked and the attack to date is an overwhelming success. The Third Infantry, which leads the assault, advanced more than 185 miles into Iraq in three days. It defeated the Iraqi Eleventh Division in one day with no American casualties. It established a supply line over forbidding terrain back into Kuwait that is provisioning a fast-moving force of more than twenty thousand soldiers and ten thousand vehicles.

But something else transpired. While Hussein's regular army has scarcely fought at all, an irregular force, controlled by the Ba'ath Party and comprised of militia, elements of special units, and fedayeen guerrilla fighters, has conducted a campaign of small-arms hit-and-run warfare. These forces have essentially taken control of the southern cities of Samawah and Najaf, where they have established themselves in schools and hospitals and where they are reportedly forcing local men to arm and fight by executing the unwilling.

From these small urban bases, the forces loyal to Saddam Hussein have been able to harass U.S. forces with mortar and artillery fire and to send out a stream of small attack teams against the Third Infantry, forcing it to engage in repeated skirmishes.

Typically, these attacks involve small groups—sniper teams of two or three men, or larger teams of as many as twenty or more vehicles manned by fighters with AK-47s, mounted machine guns, and rocket-propelled grenades. And typically, the attackers have been swiftly defeated. Third Division combat units have killed at least three hundred to four hundred Iraqi soldiers and irregulars and have captured as many prisoners. Air Force support and counterbattery artillery routinely have been able to take out the Iraqi guns soon after they expose themselves by firing.

But in an important sense, the attacks have worked. As Col. William Grimsley, commander of the First Brigade, put it, "They are diffusing some of our attention, causing us to fight them instead of focusing all our attention on our larger objective."

The division commander, Maj. Gen. Buford Blount, is candid about the threat. "The Ba'ath Party is very well organized and very active with a lot of forces in Najaf and Samawah," he said in an interview Monday night. "And they are capable of responding fluidly to us."

It has always been the hope of the American war planners to avoid Iraq's cities, so as to minimize both American and Iraqi casualties. But there are doubts. "I think these guys are going to keep coming out and harassing us," Blount said. "I think eventually we're going to have to go in there and kill them. I think we will have to kill them unless we can get rid of the top guy in Baghdad."

Limited War, So Far

◆ ◆ ◆

WITH THE THIRD INFANTRY DIVISION, IRAQ—The war the United States is waging against the regime of Saddam Hussein is a critical test of several related and very ambitious concepts. First it is a test of an evolving military doctrine. This holds that the American armed forces' uniquely massive superiority in weaponry and in observation and communication allows it to conduct war, in a sense, on the cheap: to achieve even very large goals with relatively little force in little time at little cost in American lives.

It is, second, a test of systems—a hugely complex system of integrated battlefield command and control and a hugely laborious system of training officers and troops. These are intended to produce an armed force made up overwhelmingly of soldiers who will perform in their first real battles as they have been taught to perform in years of mock battles.

The third test is of the most radical notion: war as an oxymoron, total limited war. The idea is that, given its great and unique advantages, the American military can wage a victorious war that is at once brutally effective in its killing power while being miserly of American life and property and of the enemy.

The nature of the conflict so far has raised these tests to steep heights. The Third Infantry, leading the assault, has faced no serious conventional military opposition. Instead, in the south of Iraq, the division has been plagued by a continued series of skirmishes and battles with irregular small and lightly armed paramilitary units that have mounted suicidal attacks. The clear intent of this campaign has been not to achieve any conventional victory but to slow the American advance and to distract, disrupt, and demoralize the American forces. At the same time, the campaign seeks to draw the combat into high-civilian-casualty engagements in the cities.

To a very limited degree, the Iraqi regime's strategy has been a success. The American advance has been slower than planned, and the effort of fighting day and night battles has occupied much of the time and energies of everyone in the division. But none of this seems to have demoralized officers and troops or effected a distraction or delay sufficient to affect the ultimate outcome. Hussein's forces have lost every engagement, catastrophically. The Third Infantry and its accompanying forces had, as of Friday night, killed probably more than 1,000 of the enemy and taken more than 560 prisoners. The division's own casualty list stood at 1 killed in action, 1 killed in a vehicle accident, and 23 wounded seriously enough to require hospitalization.

As Col. William Grimsley, commander of the division's First Brigade, put it, the Iraqis have not so much attacked American positions as impaled themselves on them.

Maj. Mike Oliver, the operations officer of the First Brigade, directed the brigade's armored task force, the 3-69 Armor Battalion, in a fierce thirty-hour battle last week. Fighting nearly the entire time in a sandstorm, the battalion held a bridge across the Euphrates River at the town of al Kifl. Against four M1 Abrams tanks and ten Bradley fighting vehicles backed by artillery rockets and air force bombers dropping satellite-guided bombs, the Iraqis attacked in trucks and on foot, armed only with AK-47s and rocket-propelled grenades (RPGs) backed by mortars.

"The trucks would just drive pell-mell down the road at us, sixty miles an hour, until they would get shot, and then any guys that were left would jump out of the trucks and rush at us with RPGs, trying to get in their shots," Oliver recalled the day after the battle. "They would fire their RPGs at the Bradleys. And we would kill them." In its essence, this battle was typical of all those against the Iraqi irregulars.

Meanwhile, air force bombers and army artillery and rockets, the combined force of which has accounted for much of the Iraqi dead, have destroyed at least several hundred vehicles and all artillery and mortars that have exposed themselves to fire on the U.S. forces. They have leveled numerous Ba'ath Party and Iraqi army command facilities, barracks, and fuel and ammunition storehouses.

The only task that has proved genuinely trying to the division has been the third one, that of the oxymoronic war. As the first week of the conflict wore on, its human reality became clear. Some of the hopelessly attacking Iraqis were true Ba'ath and Republican Guard loyalists. More—it seems likely most in the first waves of attack—were just local men, forced into self-annihilation by threats of execution or the murder of their families. Judging from the talk, the knowledge that many of the Iraqi dead never even wanted to fight is depressing to at least some of the frontline officers and soldiers.

Walking back to his Humvee for a few hours' sleep on its hood, Lt. Col. Peter Bayer, the divisional operations officer said, "We are learning what happens when a principled nation goes up against an utterly unprincipled one."

So far, the third test is being met: The principles are holding. But it is hard.

Across the Euphrates

◆ ◆ ◆

EAST OF THE EUPHRATES RIVER, IRAQ—Near the crest of the bridge across the Euphrates that Task Force 3-69 Armor of the First Brigade of the Third Infantry Division seized yesterday afternoon was a body that lay twisted from its fall. He had been an old man—poor, not a regular soldier—judging from his clothes. He was lying on his back, not far from one of several burning skeletons of the small trucks that Saddam Hussein's willing and unwilling irregulars employed. The tanks and Bradleys and Humvees and bulldozers and rocket launchers, and all the rest of the massive stuff that makes up the U.S. Army on the march, rumbled past him, pushing on.

On the western side of the bridge, Lt. Col. Ernest "Rock" Marcone, commander of Task Force 3-69, stood in the sand by the side of the road, smoking a cigar and drinking a cup of coffee. Marcone's soldiers say he deeply likes to win, and he seemed quietly happy. At two A.M. yesterday, Marcone had led his battalion into the assault with two objectives, both critical to the Third Infantry's drive to Baghdad. The first was to seize the Karbala Gap, a narrow piece of flat land between a lake and a river that offers a direct and unpopulated passageway to this bridge. The second was the bridge itself, the foothold across the Euphrates, last natural obstacle between the division and Baghdad.

Marcone's tanks, infantry, and artillery, supported by air force bombers and the division's Apache and Blackhawk helicopters, had taken the Karbala Gap by 7 A.M. and the bridge by 4:20 P.M. "We now hold the critical ground through which the rest of the division can pass to engage and destroy the Republican Guard," Marcone said.

Saddam Hussein, of course, knew the Americans coming from Kuwait would have to cross the Euphrates. But he did not know where the crossing would be made. The American forces' plan, drafted and revised and revised again under intense pressure in the field, centered on keeping the regime in confusion on this one great question.

There were surprises. No one anticipated the degree to which the regime would be able, using guerrilla tactics, to harass and, for a brief while, stall the offensive in the south. But the basic structure of the plan never changed. It was to employ repeated feints to deceive the enemy as to the true direction of the assault north. This would force him to redeploy his key forces away from the Karbala Gap, while exposing his moving troops and his artillery to a devastating air campaign.

On Tuesday, after the division's Second Brigade conducted a successful two-day feint at the bridge across the Euphrates at the town of Hindiyah, and after days of increasingly intense targeted bombing and counterbattery artillery had reduced the Iraqi artillery in the area of the Gap to no more than two battalions, Maj. Gen. Buford Blount, the commander of the Third Infantry, approved the assault for the following morning. As the main brunt of the assault—two tank companies and an infantry company—began to move out toward the gap, the task force's 3-7 Infantry Company moved east in one last feint, threatening the city of Karbala, to fix any Ba'ath Party irregular forces in place there. The main assault, three columns of armored and soft-skinned vehicles, made its great, loud, dusty way across sand tracks through the gap.

Weeks before, the battle for the Karbala Gap had been expected to be fierce. But misdirection and bombing had done great work of attrition. The night before the assault, Marcone had said, he expected to find little resistance left at the Gap. And he found little—a small and lightly armed force.

The task force took twenty-two prisoners at the Gap, killed no one, suffered no casualties, and pushed on as fast as three columns of armor can move, which is not fast at all, toward the bridge. There they found the first organized, coherent, and serious military opposition in the war to date: what Marcone judged to be two battalions' worth of infantry, one of irregulars on the western side and one that he thinks might have been Republican Guard. The troops had rigged the bridge to explode and had established what Marcone said were excellent defensive positions on the eastern side.

But none of this affected the outcome, or even much slowed the advance. "First we destroyed all the near-side forces," Marcone said. "Then with artillery and aviation we destroyed much of the far side. The 3-7 crossed the river in boats, six of them, with engineers, to deal with the demo [explosives]. That was followed by an armored assault by three companies, two tanks and one infantry."

The fight lasted only several hours but was intense, Marcone said. "We took no prisoners," he said. "They fought until they died."

There were no American fatalities. By full dusk, the sporadic mortar fire had ceased, and everything was quiet except for an occasional bit of light arms fire in the farm fields beyond the bridgehead.

V

· · ·

Family Wealth

Family Wealth

◆ ◆ ◆

This year, as every year, my family will spend Christmas together, at my parents' house. Actually, this year will be a little different. My mother and my sisters are iron traditionalists, and they have always insisted that we all spend Christmas Eve in the house where we grew up, sleeping in our old and now slightly uncomfortable beds, and that we wake up early Christmas morning and go downstairs together, and that we open the stockings first, and then the gifts, and then more gifts and more gifts. But with everybody getting married and so on, the family now runs to platoon size, and in recent years the orgy around the tree has lasted from eight in the morning to two in the afternoon, ending with everyone nearly spavined with fatigue and staggering off under great loads of loot for restorative naps upon the lumpy mattresses of yesteryear.

So this year, we are all opening gifts in our own homes and then going to my parents in the late afternoon in an attempt to break the conspicuous excess into two, theoretically less taxing, parts. Other changes are promised, too: My mother is, heretically, considering goose instead of turkey, and we are going to do away with the plum pudding. But these are not very big changes in the overall scheme of things. We will still get together as a family, to celebrate being a family (the more important celebration of the birth of Jesus Christ is to me a separate and more private event); we will still adhere to our own peculiar customs of togetherness; we will still have, all in all, a loving time of it.

This is more or less the way most families in America spend Christmas. But this is not the way our popular culture describes the way most families spend Christmas—or Thanksgiving or Passover or whenever they gather together. If you were to take your view of reality from movies, television, theater, literature, and journalism, you would think that family life in the United States is one never-ending exercise in dysfunctionality. The typical story of the American family and its values (whether in a production of Hollywood or of ABC News) is either a mocking tale of a stereotypically normal family that turns out to be filled with horrors of abuse and adultery and other manifestations of perversity and hypocrisy; or it is about a self-consciously alternative, decidedly nonnuclear family (as in, say, *La Cage Aux Folles* or *Rent*), which turns out to be an exemplar of love and compassion.

This is odd. Popular culture is supposed to describe popular reality. The reality of American families is one of a mostly successful search for conventional happiness. Most men and women are quite boringly heterosexual and are not very promiscuous except for perhaps a relatively brief period in youth, and most of them find lasting love.

Most husbands and wives love one another. Most of them consider one another best friends; most of them are faithful, or at least mostly so (neglected housewives who startle house painters with indecent proposals are as rare in life as they are common in *Penthouse*). Most husbands never batter their wives, and most wives never remove parts of their husbands with household cutting implements, nor do they set their beds afire. Most parents would rather die than sexually abuse their own, or any, children. Most children grow up to honor their parents, and most parents grow old in the comfort that they have, in the raising of their children, created something of irreplaceable value. It's a wonderful life, and art used to imitate it.

Why doesn't it anymore? At bottom, the fault lies in the nature of modern intellectualism, which has at its core the adolescent notion that conventional lives of conventional values are somehow wrong: that they are not merely politically improper, but are, worse, uncool—not worth living, or at least not worth examining. Tolstoy wrote in *Anna Karenina* one of the great founding untruths of the intellectual age, "Happy families are all alike; every unhappy family is unhappy in its own way." This was exactly, entirely wrong. Happy families are all idiosyncratic, each with its own unduplicable history, each with its own cherished oddities. Very nearly every unhappy family is very much alike, the same tedious, awful story of selfishness and dead love and the destruction wrought by the fall of one or another family member into the grip of one or another vice.

Reject Tolstoy and all his minions. Look around the table on Christmas night, or as you light the menorah, and regard your doddering parents and your annoying siblings and your dotty aunt and your insufferable uncle and your cousin the schnorrer and your nephew the nose-ringed, and rejoice in your magnificent wealth.

The Lure of the Evil Weed

◆ ◆ ◆

One day in 2010 or thereabouts, if all goes as current indicators suggest, I will find tucked away in my boy Tom's sock drawer the great contraband of his adolescent life, a pack of cigarettes. And when I go, pack in hand, to confront my son, I will be muttering under my breath: God bless Bill Clinton and Al Gore and John McCain and all the other visionaries of 1998.

It is a small point that seems to have escaped the great thinkers of our statecraft, but teenagers have a certain affinity for bad behavior—for sin, for danger, for self-destruction, for outrageous acts and everyday rebellions. And an American teenager is blessed in this regard, for history's greatest consumer society offers as wonderful a variety in the fashion of being bad as it does in every other.

There is alcohol, of course, but also marijuana and hashish and heroin and cocaine and LSD; amphetamines and methamphetamines; barbiturates and airplane glue; and animal tranquilizer and Ecstasy. There are the aesthetic means of self-harm: tattooing, body piercing, scarification, anorexia, bulimia. There is the outlaw life: gangs, guns, crimes, prison. In the area of physical activity, there are many means of ensuring that one lives fast, dies young, and leaves a beautiful corpse, above all, the James Dean perennial of fast dumb driving. And finally there is that most traditional method of ruining one's young life, the love of someone much more bad than you.

Tom will have the choice of all of these horrifying options, and doubtless more. But thanks to the new Prohibitionists, I have hope he will have no need for any of them. I have hope that he will be able to satisfy his wish to be as bad as he can be not in the fashion of 1998 but of 1908, not in the manner of Snoop Doggy Dogg but of Penrod Schofield. He will instead sneak off in the alley to smoke the evil weed. Because the evil weed will be the greatest evil, and the cheapest, and the most available, and the easiest to master, with the least real short-term risk. The teen dream, fulfilled.

Already, the signs are profoundly promising. Between 1991 and 1997, during which time there was an unprecedented effort in America to both propagandize and legislate against cigarettes, the Centers for Disease Control found that smoking rates among high school students rose by nearly one-third, going from 27.5 percent to 36.4 percent. Among white male high schoolers, the smoking rate climbed to 51.5 percent; among white females, it rose to 40.8 percent. Among black students, who have traditionally smoked much less than their white counterparts, smoking increased by an astounding 80 percent, with the rate rising from 12.6 percent to 22.7 percent.

These figures confused Michael Eriksen, the director of the CDC's Office of Smoking and Health. "There's no way to take a good message out of this from the data," Eriksen recently informed the *Washington Post*. "There's been incredible rhetoric over the past few years, but very little has actually changed." No, that's not quite scientifically correct. What's correct is that there has been incredible rhetoric over the past few years and a great deal has changed: Across sex, race, and class lines, adolescents have chosen to respond to the cigarette's newly enhanced status by smoking more.

Most parents (me, too) would, of course, prefer that their children skip the whole teen badness business, including smoking. But I suspect most also, if they are honest about it, would admit that they would much rather their children act out by means of an occasional sneaked cigarette than by taking up drugs or booze or crime or by dropping out of school. For while most forms of adolescent self-destruction are genuinely and immediately threatening—with the capacity to cripple a young life, or snuff it out entirely—smoking is not.

It is true that smoking often kills in the long term, and it is true that 90 percent of smokers start as teens. But smoking doesn't end anybody's life at fifteen or eighteen or twenty-one. And it is also true that two-thirds of teen smokers will not go on to become long-term regular smokers. With tobacco the great taboo, most will be forced to smoke in secret, which means relatively rarely, and they will probably quit the vile habit fairly early in life. Cigarette smoking will not have done them any good, but it won't have killed them, or landed them in jail, or kept them out of college or otherwise ruined their young lives. Which is not a bad deal, from a parent's point of view. So keep it up, bluestockings, and here's a quiet hypocritical hurrah for the new smell of teen spirit that is wafting across the land.

Back to You, Tom

◆ ◆ ◆

I used to watch television news, but at some point between the time CBS married Westinghouse, NBC married General Electric, and ABC married Mickey Mouse, I sort of lost interest. More and more, I find the really interesting reports on the events of our times on National Tom Radio.

National Tom Radio is written, directed, produced, and aired by Tom, who is two and a half, and it is concerned solely with events and people of interest in the life of Tom. Generally speaking, it broadcasts daily and continuously from about six or seven in the morning to somewhere between eight and ten at night. NTR begins each day with an update on overnight events—sleeping conditions, snoring reports, dream coverage and analysis, followed by early-morning weather.

But it may be fairly said that NTR never really sleeps. When events warrant, NTR does not hesitate to fulfill its duty to inform its listeners, no matter what the hour. Just this week, NTR went on the air at three A.M. with a bulletin directed at Tom's friend Phoebe Lewis: "Phoebe, we have to change the lightbulbs now!" So dedicated is NTR to its duties that it actually sleeps with its two principal listeners (between its two principal listeners, to be precise).

I recently experimented with wearing one of those Breathe Right strips on my nose. At about three A.M., I woke in a moment of searing pain to catch an urgent NTR bulletin: "Mommy, Mommy, I pulled off Daddy's nose Band-Aid!" What could have been more concise, objective, informative, and factual? Timely, too. James Fallows, I suppose, would carp at the slightly sensationalist tone of the report, but NTR's devotion to the bulletin form and the exclamatory manner is an admired hallmark of its work, and its listeners enjoy this expressive style of delivery.

A core mission of NTR is to serve as a clearinghouse of interesting information about and between its listeners, reporting news of each to all and of all to each. Thus, NTR enlivens the day of Debbie, who cares for Tom on Tuesdays, with the tidbit that Mommy sleeps with her socks on but Daddy doesn't. And, at the end of the day, NTR reports that Debbie's apartment has no basement and that she doesn't cut the crusts off of peanut butter sandwiches.

One of the best features of NTR is that, unlike television news, it sticks with a story over time. One of Tom's friends at nursery school, Geordie, developed a deep personal interest in the classroom gerbils, and also in their food. NTR's reporting on this has been splendidly dedicated, covering every twist and turn in an eventful story over a period of weeks:

"Geordie climbed *onto* the gerbil cage and Mrs. Appella said, 'No, Geordie!' . . . Geordie *ate* the gerbils' food and Mrs. Appella said, 'No, Geordie!' . . . Geordie *climbed into* the gerbil cage . . . Mrs. Appella *took* the gerbil cage away and *put* it into the *other* room!"

There are a number of two- and three-year-old boys in our neighborhood and all have broadcast licenses, so the competition for scoops is fierce. A week or so ago, Tom and Ike were at the library, taking part in a circle game of pat-the-head, rub-the-tummy, scratch-the-back, when Ike delivered a bombshell later much quoted and discussed: "My mommy does that to my daddy every night." The general belief is that this report referred to back scratching, not tummy rubbing.

Tom's best friend Max is particularly devoted to the bulletin form, and encounters between the two often begin with a brief, escalating exchange of the headlines:

TOM: Maxie, I'm not wearing any underwear!
MAX: I have new pants!
TOM: *I'm* not wearing any *underwear!*
MAX: I have new *pants!*

Another difference between television news and NTR that I appreciate is the latter's insistence on reporting objectively only the news that, by direct observation, Tom knows to be factual. NTR never reports secondhand stuff, never speculates, never regurgitates leaks or spin.

An illustration of this approach can be found in NTR's reports of events last Sunday, when Tom went to a stable to observe horses and also (a truly newsworthy event) to fill up the trunk of the car with horse manure for the tomato beds. NTR reported the following: All horses have brown eyes. Horses eat with their *noses* (admittedly, not absolutely accurate). The black horse was kicking and kicking! Horses *love* apples. And this special bulletin, breaking into the program of manure hauling: "We are two men who pick up horse poop." All in all, a most entertaining and informative broadcast. And for NTR, just another day's work.

Some Closing Thoughts

◆ ◆ ◆

On Monday, I bought a house. Well, that's not right. On Monday, I agreed to allow the Mellon Bank NA to buy a house, which the Mellon Bank NA agreed to allow me to fix up, live in, pay taxes on and take care of, for the next thirty years, on the strength of my promise to (1) stay alive for the next thirty years and (2) give to the Mellon Bank NA a large check on the first of every month of those thirty years, until I have paid the Mellon Bank NA a sum of money totaling about 150 percent more than the sum of money I borrowed from the Mellon Bank NA in the first place, or, in other words, a sum of money that is clearly more than I or anyone else other than Pa Mellon NA is ever likely to get his hands on.

At some point in life, the secret of even a tenuous grasp on happiness is permanently not noticing almost everything. The true nature of the relationship between you, your house, and the Mellons is just one more thing to hustle into that corner of subconsciousness where you are also storing the news about your federal withholding taxes and your waist size. But before arriving at that long-term solution, you must survive the short term—the moment where you are forced to sit down and listen to the truth, acknowledge that you have heard the truth, understand the truth, and are legally bound by the truth. This is called the settlement, or the closing. It is called that because if it were called the indenturing, no one would show up.

Closings are two-person shows; the seller's lawyer and the buyer's lawyer get all the good lines. Everybody else gets to sit and try to look as if he has some say in, or grasp of, what is happening. The lawyers arrive in suits, armed with great sheaves of important paper and excellent pens. It is as both lawyers are performing the ceremonial uncappings of their Mont Blancs that you realize that you of course have forgotten to bring a pen and that you will have to open your bit role in the proceedings by asking in a small voice if someone can lend you an instrument with which to sign away the remainder of what it now occurs to you has been a life filled with small failures of exactly this sort. It is at this point also that it occurs to you that you really should have put on a tie and that it may not have been wise to bring to the settlement a four-year-old and an eleven-month-old, both of whom, in the presence of lawyers, appear suddenly quite remarkably dirty.

But wait—there is your check on the table. How comforting it is to look at that. Such a magnificent amount of money! Who would have thought that your name would ever appear on a check bearing a sum like that? Why, you must be rich to have your name on such a check! This cheering thought lasts until you recall that your name is on this check as the payer, not the payee. You are giving that money away, and it took you your life up to now to accumulate that money, and when it goes bye-bye, what you will be is not rich but poor.

After this, it all goes rapidly downhill. You sit there and your wife sits there, signing, signing, signing, while the lawyers say things like: "And here, you are agreeing to maintain payments of the promissory note on the first of every month, and to maintain home insurance at the appropriate value, and to maintain payments of the property taxes and to maintain the home in such a condition that it maintains a value at least equal to the amount of the loan, and if you fail to maintain these requirements, the bank maintains its right to foreclose, not that this would ever happen of course, ha, ha, ha, and at any rate you would receive ample warning."

The nadir arrives with the presentation of the federally mandated truth-in-lending mortgage disclosure statement. This tells you, in a little box, "the amount you will have paid after you have made all the payments as scheduled." Why the government thinks you want to know this is a national mystery. We are Americans. We want the Mellons to give us a truth-in-lending statement about as much as we want McDonald's to give us a truth-in-eating statement.

But there it is. You really should look at it. A grown-up would. So you look. Oh dear, oh dear, oh dear me. That was a mistake.

Sunshine on My Shoulders

◆ ◆ ◆

A walk in the woods with a four-year-old (more or less verbatim): "Carry me. Please, carry me. Please, carry me. I really need you to carry me. My legs are very tired. Just a little bit, okay? No, not that way. Shoulders, carry on shoulders. Okay, I'll hold your hair, and I'll pull it this way when you should go this way and that way when you should go that way. Right?

"It's very muddy. Why is it muddy? What makes mud? It's very slippery, right? Why is mud slippery? When sand gets wet it's not slippery, right? Why isn't sand slippery? If it rains some more, there will be more mud, right? Will there be a tornado? If there is a tornado, we will go in the basement, right? Because in a tornado, you go in the basement, right? Why aren't there tornadoes here? There are some tornadoes here, right? One or two, probably. If there is a tornado while we are walking, we'll go home and go in the basement, right?

"Can I walk in the mud? This mud is making my boots muddy. It's good that we're wearing boots, right? All men wear boots, right? Some ladies wear boots, too, right? If there is a tornado, you should always wear boots, right? You should wear boots and go in your basement. Can I walk in the water? Are there fish in this water? Where are the fish? Why can't you see the fish? Are there frogs in this water? Where are the frogs? Are the fish and the frogs hiding? We'll throw rocks in the water and that will make the fish and the frogs come up, right? Can I walk on this rock? Why are there rocks in this water? Why is this rock flat and the other rock not flat? I'm just going to put my feet in the water a little bit, okay? My boots fell off. Can you get my boots? Get my boots, please. See, one is over there and one is over there. Don't go in the water. Why did you go in the water? Your legs are wet, did you notice? It's good that you got my boots, right? Shoulders, please.

"This hill is very hard to go up, right? Why do people pick up dog poop and not horse poop? Why are horses bigger than dogs? Why is there a fence here? Why is there a tractor here? Why did somebody leave the tractor here? Why is the tractor broken? Why doesn't somebody fix the tractor? Somebody should fix the tractor, right? Probably somebody will come and fix the tractor tomorrow, right? Why don't we have a tractor? Probably we used to have a tractor, right? When we move to Boston we will get a tractor, right? Why won't we get a tractor? We should get a tractor. I really need a tractor.

"Why is it raining now? I need my umbrella. Will you go back to the house and get my umbrella? I'll wait here. You bring my umbrella here. Please. I said please. Why won't you go back to the house and get my umbrella? I really need my umbrella. Is this a tornado? Probably this is a tornado, right? We better go back to the house and get in the basement. You should run. Why can't you run with me on your shoulders? I'm very heavy, right?

"It stopped. The rain stopped. Why does it rain and then it stops? Now, it's even more slippery, right? It's very hot now, isn't it? I don't want to go back anymore. Let's go this way. I said, go this way, horsey. Why does it hurt when I pull your hair? Okay, I'll only pull it a little bit, okay? This hill is very hard to go down, right? Don't fall. Why did you fall? Where are your glasses? Why are they broken? Why did you step on them? You should not have stepped on them, right? It's okay. Probably we can get some glue and fix them, right? You have a hole in your pants, did you notice that? Probably you made a hole in your pants when you fell down, right? You should not have fallen down, right?

"I don't want to go home. Why do you want to go home? It's not raining anymore, so we don't have to go home. Anyway, they don't have tornadoes here, right? No, I don't want to go home. I really need to walk some more. Let's go just a little more. Okay?"

Growing Up with Mr. Fixit

◆ ◆ ◆

The Russians last week released John E. Tobin Jr., a twenty-four-year-old Fulbright scholar whom they had accused of spying and had convicted and jailed on marijuana charges. The trumped-up case against Tobin was an obvious retaliation for the United States' expulsion of Russian spy-diplomats in retaliation for the recruitment of the traitor Robert Hanssen. Tobin spent six months in prison.

So, what does John E. Tobin Sr., the father of this wrongfully punished young man, have to say? In a news conference in Moscow this week, he said that, in a way, his son had "had a marvelous experience. . . . He's gotten to see Russia from the inside."

When I read Tobin's father's words, I could hear my own father. My father, Tom Kelly, is seventy-eight, and he has four grown children, and they have had their ups and downs. And over all the years, for every up, my father has been there to say how splendid (and how deserved) was this particular up; and for every down, he has been there to say how splendid (though not at all deserved) was this particular down.

An insane love, a failed grade, a lost job—there is nothing that befalls one of his children in which my father is not able to find "a marvelous experience." This is not to say that he is irresponsible. If you (assuming you were one of his children) were to tell him that you had always felt yourself to be a duck trapped in the body of a human, and that you were determined to rectify the situation through trans-species surgery, he would argue (gently) against the idea. What about your mother's feelings? he might say. And what about duck season, what about duck à l'orange?

But he would not say that no Kelly had ever been a duck and by God none was ever going to be one, or that he had not fought the Nazis and worked two jobs for ten years to send you to college to have you spend the rest of your life sitting around on your tail bobbing for duckweed.

And if you went ahead and had yourself duckified anyway? Oh, he would proclaim it through the neighborhood: What a wonderful, what a brilliant, what a brave and clever and good thing this was to do—and what a duck you were! Was there ever such a duck?

What you might call the duck, or the Tobin, response is not peculiar to a few men, and it is not, despite all appearances, irrational. It is the necessary reaction to the quality by which most men define what it is, in the long run, to be a good husband and a good father. For what by now amounts to most of his life, my father has thought of himself, and judged himself a success or failure, in primarily these terms. And in these terms, at a minimum, what a good father is supposed to do for the people he loves is fix whatever goes wrong with them.

But life presents much—wars, famines, depressions, sicknesses, broken hearts, and broken lives—that is beyond fixing. So, the good father endures by denying. This, admittedly, can be annoying, especially to women, who generally regard as a mysterious lunacy the male view that a problem expressed is a problem that must be addressed. My mother has often marveled, with exasperation, that it is impossible to engage my father in a simple complaint about the weather. If he admitted that 99 in the shade was intolerable, or that four days of rain was enough, then he would have to fix it, for the sake of the children. And, in fact (although this has never been acknowledged in my family), my father has no control whatever over the forces of nature.

Yet there is something to be said for the compulsions of the fathers. Men, as has been frequently noted, have their failings. The urge to make things right is their counterfailing, their allegory to women's urge to nurture. The male urge is of course ridiculous. Who can fix the world, even for one child? But its ridiculousness makes it great. In every life, there should be someone who believes that whatever goes wrong must be fixed, and if not fixed, must at least be made to go away.

So, happily, it was for me. In the house where I was lucky enough to grow, the weather was always balmy, rain or shine. And life was always good, good or bad, and the children were always successes, succeed or fail. And the experiences were always marvelous.

The Nine Days
of Tom and Jack

◆ ◆ ◆

I am Catholic and my wife is Jewish, so in our house we celebrate both Hanukkah and Christmas, which our sons, Tom and Jack, regard as an excellent thing. People sometimes ask me if it is hard to raise children in respect and love for two great faiths that have a slight doctrinal disagreement between them, and I say: not if you give them presents every day for eight days of Hanukkah and for Christmas. The more Gods the merrier, is Tom and Jack's strong belief.

Like other parents, we try not to let the materialism get out of hand, and to keep the focus on the sacred. This year, on the first day of Hanukkah, we gave Tom, five, a realistic, detachable, revolving red police cruiser roof light, so that he may follow the ancient Jewish holy practice of impersonating a state trooper. He received the gift with appropriate reverence. We gave Jack, two, some Silly Putty. He received the gift in his hair, and now he is in a fine shape to play the role in the Christmas pageant of the Wondering Child with a Bald Spot.

Actually, Jack has not been cast in a pageant. Tom has, though. He has a walk-on in the pageant staged by our local Unitarian church. There was a rehearsal the other Sunday after the service, which featured the lighting of a menorah (during which apologies were offered to anyone who might take offense at a lighting before sundown), followed by the traditional singing of the great Christian hymn "Oh, Mitten Tree" (during which the faithful paraded around a tree that was decked, in fact, with mittens). A Unitarian pageant turns out to be different from a Roman Catholic one. In Tom's pageant, Jesus Christ is celebrated as "a very special person" and "a great rabbi" and an all-around asset to the community. The Son-of-God debate, which has proved so regrettably contentious over the years, is not mentioned.

No doubt this is all to the good. There is too much disputation around Christmas anyway. One growing issue is the white versus colored lights debate. Like all matters of taste, this is also a matter of class. White lights are high-class; colored lights are somewhat less so. White lights make the statement that one is a refined sort who appreciates that less is more and who celebrates Christmas (and life in general) in such a fashion that one would not be absolutely mortified if Martha Stewart dropped by unexpectedly for tea. Colored lights make the statement that one is the sort of person who believes that Christmas is not Christmas without an electric sled and reindeer on the lawn, an electric Santa on the roof, an electric Frosty by the front gate, and an electric Very Special Person in a manger on the porch.

Most of the houses in my neighborhood are white-light houses, and I have to admit they are lovely, but I was raised in a colored-light family, and I am raising Tom and Jack to be colored-light men, too. They do not take a lot of convincing on this. Boys are naturally colored lighters.

We got up the first three strings of our lights the weekend before last, and another two last weekend, at which time we threw away the rotted Halloween pumpkin. I might have gotten more lights up by now except that the remaining three strings are not working. To fix them you have to go through and find the burned-out bulb and replace it, and there are a lot of bulbs in a string, and the whole enterprise is one of those things that leads Daddy to point out that this is really the sort of job Mommy does better, and Mommy claims that she doesn't know how to do it because she wasn't raised in a colored-light family. This is a cop-out, and unworthy of her.

Still, I am confident we will get all the lights up by New Year's, and all down by Easter. In my family, it was considered poor form to leave the lights up past Easter; it suggested shiftlessness. One elderly woman in our neighborhood did leave her lights up, and also her tree, and her electric Santa, all year around. But she was considered a special case and no one held it against her. This may have been because everyone back then was a colored-light person. Colored-lighters are more relaxed about this sort of thing than white-lighters.

But that was judgmental, wasn't it? I should not be judgmental. I learned that from the Unitarians. Colored-lighters aren't any better than white-lighters; we are all special persons. Very.

EPILOGUE

• • •

E-mails from the Front

❖ ❖ ❖

In late February and early March 2003, as he prepared to embed with the army's Third Infantry Division to cover the Iraq War for the *Atlantic Monthly* and the *Washington Post,* Michael Kelly sent a series of e-mail messages to his wife, Madelyn, whom he called Max; to their young sons, Tom and Jack; to his parents, Marguerite and Tom; and to his friend and boss, David Bradley, the owner of the *Atlantic Monthly,* and David's wife, Katherine.

—— Original Message ——
From: Michael Kelly
Sent: Sunday, February 23, 2003 5:49 AM
To: Bradley, David
Subject: Re: Late to the News but Nonetheless Pleased

Dear David and Katherine,

I am taking quick advantage of this note to thank you a million times for the terrific time we had at Valfond. We were overwhelmed by Sara's hospitality and, of course, by the house and place itself. We could not have had a better time, and the fact that it was off-season was a huge plus, not a minus. We were able to go to some of the big attractions—Vaucluse, Les Baux, the pope's castle at Avignon, and really enjoy them, which, as you know is not easily done in the high tourist season. We ate like champs, slept blissfully in the cool evenings—and the days were lovely too. It was in the 50s and 60s and even 70s every day, mostly sweater weather.

We have been in Paris the past several days, also doing tourist things much better done in February (Mona Lisa, Eiffel—an immense hit—bateaux mouches, etc.) and loving the kind attention in restaurants from tip-starved waiters actually pleased to see a loud, un-chic party of eight Americans, four of them les enfants. I am pleased to say I have not insulted a single Frenchman on issues such as surrender, appeasement, etc. There is something about being in France that makes you just feel like having another bowl of soupe de poisson and just being les amis after all.

Well, off to Kuwait—where, David, you have heard, we got the coveted slot with the Third Infantry Division—final approval came in several days ago.

You guys are the nicest. Thank you again so much for all your generosity.

Best as always,
Michael

PS: Ever since Valfond, wherever we go (hotel, restaurant), Jack says: "This place is too small for me. I want to go back to Mr. Bradley's."

—— Original Message ——
From: Michael Kelly
To: Madelyn Kelly
Sent: Tuesday, February 25, 2003 3:21 PM
Subject: from me

Sweetie,
Don't know if you'll get this or if I have to send to a new Verizon address. If you do get it, you will see I am functioning computerially. Wrote and sent and edited *Post* column zippo zippo, by 11:30 *Post* time; *Post* delighted, amazed. Went for a good tour around the city today for quick material for column; will explore more tomorrow. Talked with Major Mike [Birmingham] on the phone, all good. He says I need to check in/register tomorrow but actual "deep embedding" is a week or so off. Told him not to use language like that on possibly tapped phone. He seems easy to get along with; serious about working with me. Which is very good, as I will def. need special treatment to get a special piece, as

there are/are going to be 300 journalists here, 85 with 3ID alone. He reaffirmed that my slot was by the side of "the big guy" (there he goes again) and said that he figured they wd have to put me in earlier than the others, as I needed to know, learn more, and that he hoped I understood if they did that I couldn't be going and using still-classified info for *Post* columns. All of which v. encouraging.

I hope and trust you all are back well and sound. Missing you all.

IMPORTANT: Tell Tom that the Kuwaitis, like the French, also name their toilets—AND IT IS THE SAME NAME!!!! The toilet in my hotel bathroom is named JACOB DELAFONE too!! . . .

Love,
M

—— Original Message ——
From: Michael Kelly
To: Marguerite Kelly
Sent: Wednesday, February 26, 2003 4:52 AM
Subject: Re: you!

Dear Mom and Dad,

I am indeed here in Kuwait City, which is much cleaned up from 1991. We had a great time in France, both in Paris and at the Bradleys' pretty spectacular house in Provence. For several days after we left the house, wherever we went, Jack would say "Dis place is too small for me. I need to go back to Mr. Bradley's house." Followed by "OK. Certainly, we're going back to Mr. Bradley's house, sure, OK, C'mon. . . ." I would like to say that boy was born to lead, but I think born to rule is more like it.

The boys were mighty impressed with France in general, Tom especially with Paris. We did quite a lot of touristing, which I have never liked, but I find you really have to with kids, and it was more or less fun.

I did have one insight into French arrogance while I was there. Going through the motions of life day to day there, in Paris or in a small country village, being constantly amazed at the perfections of so many things that make up daily living (the food, the buildings, the furnishings, the style and shape of the towns and cities, the entire civilized, deeply pleasure-giving rhythm of life) you realize that the French, too, are always aware of what they have built, as a culture, and are always thinking, with some real justification—Oui, oui, oui, you may have all the aircraft carriers, but look what WE made. You have never done this, you don't know how to do this, and this is a greater and more meaningful and more permanent contribution to civilization than you can dream of. When you think about it, when the French boast of themselves (frequently) it is rarely about accomplishments in war or politics or government, but about culture in its various forms—about making things that make life more civilized. Well, that is the effect of a week of French food. Also several pounds, I suspect. I should be able to take that off here.

I am going to register today as a journalist with the Third Infantry Division, but the word is that there won't be much to do in terms of actually living with the division for a couple of weeks. Which is fine. I can use the time to learn its structure, processes and mission. Missing everyone already. Being safe.

Love,
M

———— Original Message ————
From: Michael Kelly
Sent: Thursday, February 27, 2003 7:58 AM
To: Bradley, David
Subject: hello from kuwait

Dear David,

Some initial observations. . . . Registered with the army yesterday—signed various forms acknowledging that I knew combat was inherently life-threatening, that I understood nobody in this man's army was obliged to protect me in any way, that if I bought the farm it was my own damned fault, and (this last part is key) that I waived all rights to sue. Ok-doke.

You would not believe how polite the army is these days. Registering was like checking into a four-star hotel—or dealing with your Advisory Board young ones: "Michael! How good to see you! Now, you come over here and have a seat. . . . No, no, let US bring the forms to YOU." And so on: "Private First Class Harris, Michael is ready to be measured for his bio-chem suit, now!" Did you get some kind of contract to train these people you didn't tell me about? I suspect the sergeants in the field will be a little different.

It is all incredibly efficient, too. They think of a lot—including telling me how to send off to a navy ophthalmological lab for special lens inserts for my gas mask that will be made to my prescription—because glasses don't fit under the mask. Cool. I will be the only guy in Swampscott with my own prescription gas mask. The other soccer dads will be sick with envy.

Even allowing for the rather huge difference between seeing a city just after it has been raped and pillaged and 12 years later, Kuwait City is astonishing. Half of it must be less than ten years old now, and its heart is now its posh, sprawling, rich-people, landscaped suburbs. In another 20 years it will be nearly indistinguishable from a California seaside town, and I am not saying that to exaggerate. I had lunch in a sprawling mall by the shore today (had to choose among ten restaurants, mostly American chains) that you could have picked up and plopped down in Palo Alto, and once you changed the signs, no one would notice. There is probably nothing (except booze and porn) you can buy in Washington that you can't buy here. English is so much the second language that it is very nearly the first. You walk by groups of rich Kuwaiti teens, and they are chatting away in colloquial English to each other—and it's not for your benefit. The vast service class is all foreign—Indian, Jordanian, Filipino, Korean, etc.—and almost all of them speak English absolutely fluently. It occurs to me that the world is creating an immense new class of global service (not class in a strict sense; people in it range from gardeners to managers of great hotels), which increasingly lives transnationally and nation-hopping, and for which English is the lingua franca. This will change the world in meaningful ways, not the least of which (and this is obvious even in a traditional country like France) is in travel: my sons will hardly know the experience of travel I have known—where half your energies are spent simply in trying to dope your way through a day and a place where you can't make yourself understood or understand anyone else. They will be able to wander from Argentina to Lebanon to Tahiti to Korea speaking English to get whatever they want.

Is Tony Blair a hero or what? Can't believe the pounding he is taking. We shd do something on him. Something smart. I'll think about it.

Well, off to errands.

Salem Alaikhem.
Michael

—— Original Message ——
From: Michael Kelly
To: Madelyn Kelly
Sent: Friday, February 28, 2003 2:09 PM
Subject: hi from qwait

Sweetie and Boys,

Hello, how are you? Is it snowing there or only in Washington? What a lot of snow this winter. Today I met a bunch of the other reporters who are going with the Third Infantry Division. They seemed nice.

I am running all around the place every day getting errands done to get ready. It seems like every ten minutes someone tells me something new I need to get. The latest, today, is something you need to draw power from the Humvee battery. (Tom: I will get to ride in a Humvee with a gun, I bet.) It is called a 12-to-24 volt power inverter. Of course, when the briefer mentioned we shd get one of these, all of the print reporters were frankly baffled and showed it, and, of course, all the cameramen knew exactly what it was, and already had one, and lectured us in a superior way about the whole thing, and were openly scornful. It appears the press pack has not changed.

Max: GUESS who is the CBS cameraman attached to the 3ID? Mario [De Carvalho]! I am delighted. Now I know there will be at least one person there I get a kick out of talking to.

Tom and Jack: they have some very nice fishing boats here. Very big, wooden, really cool. If I can, I will buy one and mail it back to you. Of course, they ARE about 40 feet long and they weigh about 4000 pounds, so I might not be able to find enough stamps. Also it might not fit in the mailbox.

I am getting my helmet and my vest and my lenses for my mask on Monday, inshallah [Allah willing], and will be embedded some time between Sunday and Friday. They can't tell us more than that—not because of security; they are just a little overwhelmed, I gather. This is, basically, getting a 20,000-person division ready for war and then having to put together a presidential-campaign-level press operation on top of it. And of course, they have never done anything like this.

All good clean fun.

(Just talked to you all on the phone.)

Much love. Love you all. Miss you. Love you.
Waldo Waldiferous Walrus (yr. dad)

—— Original Message ——
From: Michael Kelly
Sent: Saturday, March 01, 2003 4:41 AM
To: Bradley, David
Subject: A Quick Report

Dear David,

Well, I am nearly in the army for real, or getting closer. We embeds had a briefing by various officers yesterday. They are waiting for gas masks for us, but say we shd be actually in with our units by the end of next week—me, maybe sooner. The briefing was interesting. For reasons I have never entirely fathomed, but probably come down to (a) routine group dynamics and (b) the fact that a very high percentage of reporters were in their school years Class A Weenies, who, confronted with anything like a classroom situation, revert to form and start jumping up and down and yelling "Me! Me! I know!" and asking questions to show the teach how smart they are, any press pack en groupe cannot shut up for wondering and worrying and nagging and hypothesizing and so on. They take a lot—A LOT—of care. This is why campaign press secretaries always get that haunted look and take to drink by mid-primary season.

The U.S. military is maybe just grasping this. They have never done anything like this. They have never had a real, big, combat-covering press corps that was their responsiblity since Korea (in Vietnam, an anomaly, reporters were accredited but on their own, basically)—and in those old days, the odds were that 80 percent of the all-male press corps would have served in the military themselves. And so now, these guys are trying to get ready for a war two weeks away, and, at the same time, build and manage a press operation that is the size (500 embedded journalists, another 300 or so just hanging around feeding points such as DC, London, Kuwait) of a presidential campaign. The result is something of a confusion and a culture clash.

Here are some illustrative exchanges from yesterday's briefing:

Q: So, the Third Division—it's a division, right?

A: Right.

Q: What is a division—I mean, I know it is a unit of troops, but what is, you know, IN a division?

A: Battalions, eight of them, in our case.

Q: What is in a battallion?

◆ ◆ ◆

Q: If we are embedded in a few days, and then, after we get settled in, and it looks like we are just going to be sitting around in the desert for a few weeks, can we, you know, leave? And come back to Kuwait City or go somewhere else and come back later?

A: No.

Q: (After the briefer had explained carefully that no reporter should bring more stuff than he could carry on his back, as each soldier already has a hundred pounds or more to carry and will look with disfavor on requests for luggage help, the questioner being a Japanese woman who cannot weigh more than 95 pounds): My luggage is the kind with wheels that you drag—will I be able to drag it?

A: You mean like in an airport?

Q: Yes.

A: Uh, ma'am, we'll be in the desert, which is, uh, sand, so I don't know about that. But you'll have to be the judge yourself if you can drag it under those circumstances.

Q: After the briefing, could you come look at it and tell me?

A: (Pause.) Yes.

My colleagues. What a crew.
More soon, all best, hi to all.
Michael

—— Original Message ——
From: Michael Kelly
To: Madelyn Kelly
Sent: Saturday, March 01, 2003 8:19 AM
Subject: Re: boy mania

I am type O positive, as it turns out. This is official, too: certified with a stamp by the Government of Kuwait. And only cost one dinar! Best bargain in town.

It is about 6 o'clock now, and I am on my way to the store to buy some dust-colored khakis (to my surprise, dark winter-weight corduroys are not what the best-dressed men are wearing this season in the Iraq desert) and ditto shirt, as Major M. strongly advises blending in with the sand whenever possible. Walked another four hours today. Dogs barking. Bought some sunscreen and some very nice medical gauze tape. No word from Major M on early embed, which is fine by me, as I have to write *Atlantic* column tomorrow and Monday and *Post* column by end of Tuesday. I do love this time difference for writing tho; it is like getting an extra day.

Tom and Jack: I have looked all over town for a camel and cannot find one anywhere. I don't know what's wrong with these people. All they have is cars. I keep telling them, we have cars back in Swampscott. Where are the CAMELS? Oh, man. Tom, did you tell Grammie and Poppa that excellent camel joke I told you? They wd love it. Jack, why are you telling Mommy you want to live in Washington? Did you know they don't have a beach in Washington? Or boats with propellers? Also, they don't have Lincoln's Landing or the Buttermilk Cafe. Or the Red Rock Bistro.

I am trying to teach the Kuwaiti people how to speak English. I am telling them that when we want to say hello to each other in the morning, the first person says "Swiper, no swiping," and the second person says "Oh, man." I am also telling them that the president of the United States is a baboon named Bad and that his wife is an elephant named Ellie. Also I am telling them that, in English, if you sneeze, the polite thing to say is "Excuse me, I gassed." It is a lot of fun teaching people English.

I love you, Tom. I love you, Jack. I love you, Max. And love to Grammie and Poppa, too.

Bye for now.

Love,

Dad

—— Original Message ——

From: Michael Kelly

To: Madelyn Kelly

Sent: Monday, March 03, 2003 5:24 PM

Subject: Re: PS

I can't believe it is freezing. It is already climbing into the 70s here and will be in 80s soon. I miss the howling wind. And you and the young walruses.

Here is something for them:

Tom and Jack:

Here is a list of everything I will be carrying with me on my back when I go join up with the army—but I have added some FAKE things, too. See if you can guess which ones are not real:

two pairs of socks (plus wearing one)

two pairs of boxer briefs (plus wearing one)

one pair of pants (plus wearing one)

one half-shirt

one regular shirt

one long-sleeved undershirt (plus wearing one)

one bathtub

one toothbrush

one tooth

one tooth fairy

one bottle of camping soap

vitamins

aspirin

medicine

a little bit of sugar to help the medicine go down in the most
    delightful way

Band-aids and bandages

razor blades

sun screen

a large pillow filled with cat whiskers and hippopotamus toenail
    clippings

14 notebooks

one laptop computer

two computer batteries

one power inverter, which is a thingie for getting electricity from car
    batteries to the computer

one car, with battery

eight pens

one sleeping bag

one bandanna

one banana

one satellite phone

one telephone pole

one rain parka

one rain forest

one sweatshirt

one sweater

one picture of Tom, one picture of Jack, one picture of Mommy

one picture of Waldo Waldiferous Walrus
one compass
one map
one secret pirate's buried treasure map
one pocket knife
one flashlight
batteries
one pair of binoculars
one pair of ladies' dancing shoes, extra large

I bet you didn't guess the fake ones.
I love you
Daddy

—— Original Message ——
From: Michael Kelly
Sent: Thursday, March 06, 2003 4:31 PM
To: Bradley, David
Subject: Re: Friends in Kuwait

Dear David,

I am sorry not to write sooner; I have been running around like a nut getting ready to get into the 3ID, as we old veterans call the Third Infantry Division. Re your last note, no, there is nothing really I need from you, except not to worry. I am not going to be in one iota of danger. I am going to be one step behind the commanding general, and the army does not lose commanding generals. Anyway, the Iraqis are all going to surrender or be wiped out from the air before ground troops even see them. I bet a four-to-seven-day war, in liberated Baghdad the following week. I've got everything I need, so really don't worry. But thank you.

All best,
Michael

PS: To finally put yr mind at rest, Ted Koppel is embedding with the 3ID too— going all the way to Baghdad (the division is THE key to Baghdad force, very much right bet, it turns out). And ABC feels much the same way about losing Ted as the Pentagon does about losing generals.

—— Original Message ——
From: Michael Kelly
To: Madelyn Kelly
Sent: Saturday, March 08, 2003 10:32 AM
Subject: Re: new email

Sweetie,

I'm sorry I missed you guys yesterday twice. I will get you today. Think I'll try sat [satellite] phone to see how it works. Latest news is embed Tuesday. I am trying to at least get a day trip in Sunday or Monday. I am running out of things to buy here. It's beautiful weather today, sunny in the high 70s; I took a four-hour walk. Lost about five pounds so far and am feeling very good.

There is not much news to report because there is not much happening. I think after we embed we will sit in the desert for a week or more, which is actually great for me. I really need days and days of observing and interviewing time before the action starts. But it will be very much roughing it. It is basically camping at its worst: living in a tent, no hot food, etc.—and fairly frequent 50 mph sand storms. But that's ok, sweetie, as Jack wd say (if he was speaking to me).

Speaking of the boys:

Dear Tom and Jack,

How are you? I am getting ready to go off to camp to join the army's Third Infantry Division in a few days. I have been out there once for a day. I thought you would want to know what it is like.

Well, it is like camping, except that it is in the middle of the desert instead of in the woods. There is nothing out there but sand and more sand. And more sand. The sand is very fine and gets into everything, especially when there is a sandstorm, which is when the wind blows hard enough to blow up all the sand in the air. There was one last week that lasted for TWO DAYS and the wind blew 50 miles per hour. I was glad I wasn't out there yet. I bet the soldiers were picking sand out of their noses for days afterward.

Speaking of soldiers, guess how many I will be camping with and traveling with? 20,000. That is twice as many people as live in Swampscott. And none of them ever take showers because there is no water for showers. Also no bathrooms. Jack, we will all have to pee and poop in the sand.

Tom, you would not believe how many amazing tanks and helicopters and trucks and stuff there are out there. When I was out there I saw twenty tanks in a row, all racing as fast as they could across the desert, practicing.

Here is a list of some of the stuff that this division has, besides 20,000 soldiers:

203 tanks

18 rocket launchers

18 big Apache Longbow attack helicopters (these have guns on them, like tanks, but not as big)

54 Paladin armored fighting vehicles (like tanks, with guns, but can carry more soldiers)

267 Bradley armored fighting vehicles (also sort of like tanks, but carry even more men; these carry all of the infantry soldiers)

36 Avenger spy helicopters

178 very very big flat-bed trucks for getting tanks when they break

232 fuel tankers (the division's machines drink up half a million gallons of diesel fuel every day that they are moving)

another 900 other kinds of trucks

1,731 Humvees, many with machine guns on them (each Humvee carries two or three soldiers, and they get to put their names on the outside of them and also sometimes write nicknames on them)

another 400 or so other kind of vehicles of different sorts

all in all: 4,346 vehicles

Plus one roll of toilet paper. (I think they should buy another roll; I don't think one is enough for 20,000 soldiers.) No, seriously—really—you know what a lot of the soldiers keep tucked in a pocket? A little container of baby wipes! They are very handy in the desert; you can use them, of course, when you poop, but also just to clean the sand off your face.

What is going to happen is that all of these people (mostly men but there are some ladies, too) are going to wait out in the desert for a week maybe, and then when the war starts, they will all—all at once, when the commanding general says GO—start driving north as fast as they can. You cannot move 20,000 soldiers and 4,346 vehicles as fast as you can move a family car (although you can move it as fast as you can move a family car if you are trying to get Tom and Jack to put on their shoes and coats and get in the family car). Even if the enemy soldiers do not try to stop us (which they probably will not even try very much, because their tanks and stuff are very old and broken down and not very good), the fastest we will be able to go is maybe 150 miles in a day (that is a little farther than [Aunt] Cheryl and [Uncle] Dan's house is from us, I think). That is considered moving very fast for an army. One reason they can move this fast, is that this army trains all the time to travel at night, and the soldiers have special night-vision glasses and binoculars, which allow them to see at night without lights even if it is pitch dark. In fact, they like to travel at night better than during the day, because the enemy soldiers do not have night-vision glasses and can't see us. Pretty cool.

I will give you more reports when I go out there to live and know more about it. I love you guys. Be good. Swiper, no swiping. Tom and Jack, I heard about how great, great, great you have been about going to bed, and I am very proud of you. Of course, I am always very proud of both of you.

I love you.

And I love you too, sweetie,

Love,
Dad

SOURCE NOTES

The following citations are the original publication information for the pieces in this collection.

"King of Cool," *Washington Post,* May 20, 1998.

"Girth of a Nation," *Washington Post,* August 1, 2001.

"Three Things I've Learned Since Kindergarten," *Men's Health,* June 1993.

"Faux Commotion," *Washington Post,* January 3, 2001.

"Good Riddance to the 'New Man,'" *Men's Life,* Fall 1990.

"The Road to Paranoia," *New Yorker,* June 16, 1995.

"Imitation Activism," *Washington Post,* April 19, 2000.

"Oh, Those Heartwarming Communists," *Washington Post,* April 8, 1998.

"The Systematic Corruption of the Catholic Church," *Washington Post,*
    March 20, 2002.

"Getting Hip to Squareness," *Atlantic Monthly,* February 2002.

"The Nice Column," *Washington Post,* July 24, 2002.

"Master of the Game," originally as "David Gergen: Master of the Game,"
    New York Times Magazine, October 31, 1993.

"Wonk New World," *New Republic,* May 26, 1997.

"A Plea for Diversity," *New Republic,* December 16, 1996.

"The Midlife Crisis of Jesse Jackson," *GQ,* December 1990.

"Banality and Evil," *New Republic,* May 5, 1997.

"A National Calamity," *Washington Post,* June 16, 1999.

"Mass Sentimentality," *Washington Post,* July 21, 1999.

"Richard Daley Jr. Gets the Last Laugh," *GQ,* August 1990.

"Texas-Size Failure," *New York Times,* July 18, 1992.

"But What About Dad?," *Washington Post,* July 26, 2000.

"Ted Kennedy on the Rocks," *GQ,* February 1990.

"Truth Be Told," *Washington Post,* August 7, 2002.

"A Man Who Wants to Be Liked, and Is," *New York Times,* November 4, 1992.

"The Making of a First Family: A Blueprint," *New York Times,*
    November 14, 1992.

"Saint Hillary," *New York Times Magazine,* May 23, 1993.

"The President's Past," *New York Times Magazine,* July 31, 1994.

"Clinton's Escape Clause," *New Yorker,* October 24, 1994.

"Bob Dole's Last Hurrah," originally as "Ire in the Belly," *New Yorker,*
    November 11, 1996.

"Class," *New Republic,* June 16, 1997.

"The Reich Stuff," *New Republic,* June 30, 1997.

"The Artful Dodger and the Good Son," *Washington Post,* December 17, 1997.

"I Believe," *Washington Post,* February 4, 1998.

"I Still Believe," *Washington Post,* March 18, 1998.

"A Pathetic Speech—and Untrue," *Washington Post,* August 19, 1998.

"'Hairsplitting,'" *Washington Post,* September 16, 1998.

"Farmer Al," *Washington Post,* March 24, 1999.

"Starr Wars: The Twenty-first Century," *Washington Post,* July 8, 1998.

"That's Entertainment," originally as "Beatty and Buchanan: That's Entertain-
    ment," *Washington Post,* September 15, 1999.

"Conan the VP," *Washington Post,* October 5, 2000.

"Clinton Versus Bush," *Washington Post,* March 7, 2001.

"Before the Storm," *New Republic,* February 4, 1991.

"Blitzed," *New Republic,* February 11, 1991.

"Desert Rat," *New Republic,* February 18, 1991.

"Souk Kook," originally as "Amman Diarist: Souk Kook," *New Republic,*
    February 25, 1991.

"Speech Defect," *New Republic,* March 4, 1991.

"Kiss of Victory," *New Republic,* March 11, 1991.

"The Rape and Rescue of Kuwait City," *New Republic,* March 25, 1991.

"Highway to Hell," *New Republic,* April 1, 1991.

"Rolls-Royce Revolutionaries, *New Republic,* April 8, 1991.

"The Other Hell," *New Republic,* May 13, 1991.

"Back to the Hills," *New Republic,* June 3, 1991.

"The Fear of Death," *Washington Post,* November 19, 1997.

"Where Are the Dead?," *New Yorker,* February 16, 1998.

"Visionaries of the Irish Agreement," *Washington Post,* April 15, 1998.

"Ignoring Nuclear Threats," originally as ". . . To Be Ignored," *Washington Post,* May 13, 1998.

"Arafat Bombs on Opening Night," originally as "In Gaza, Peace Meets Pathology," *New York Times Magazine,* November 27, 1994.

"Mideast Myths Exploded," *Washington Post,* August 15, 2001.

"When Innocents Are the Enemy," *Washington Post,* September 12, 2001.

"Who We Are," originally as "We Know Who We Are," *Washington Post,* September 20, 2001.

"With a Serious and Large Intent," *Washington Post,* October 10, 2001.

"Chicken Little Media," *Washington Post,* October 17, 2001.

"Return of the 'Chicken Hawks,'" *Washington Post,* October 30, 2002.

"In a Borrowed Tie," originally as "Deep, Subtle, Clever—and (Thank Goodness) History," *Washington Post,* November 27, 2002.

"Exit Hussein," *Washington Post,* December 25, 2002.

"Immortality on the March," *Washington Post,* February 19, 2003.

"Who Would Choose Tyranny?," *Washington Post,* February 26, 2003.

"Letter from Kuwait City," *Atlantic Monthly,* May 2003.

"Battle Stations of the Press," *Washington Post,* March 5, 2003.

"The Calm Before," *Washington Post,* March 12, 2003.

"Warriors at Work," *Washington Post,* March 19, 2003.

"A Much Tougher Fight," *Washington Post,* March 26, 2003.

"Limited War, So Far," *Washington Post,* March 30, 2003.

"Across the Euphrates," *Washington Post,* April 3, 2003.

"Family Wealth," *Washington Post,* December 24, 1997.

"The Lure of the Evil Weed," originally as "Reviving the Lure of the Evil Weed," *Washington Post,* April 22, 1998.

"Back to You, Tom," *Washington Post,* January 20, 1999.

"Some Closing Thoughts," *Washington Post,* May 3, 2000.

"Sunshine on My Shoulders," *Washington Post,* May 31, 2000.

"Growing Up with Mr. Fixit," *Washington Post,* August 8, 2001.

"The Nine Days of Tom and Jack," *Washington Post,* December 12, 2001.

INDEX

ACKNOWLEDGMENTS

In putting this book together, I am profoundly indebted to Robert Vare of the *Atlantic Monthly,* for taking on the enormous task of selecting and organizing the best of my husband's work, and for putting up with a long-distance editorial partner who did her reading and e-mailing in the middle of the night, after the kids had gone to bed. Robert brought the same passion, creativity, and patience to this project as he did to Mike's pieces in the years they worked together.

David Bradley and Cullen Murphy, Mike's great friends and colleagues at the *Atlantic,* gave wise counsel and enthusiastic support. Mike's longtime agent, Kathy Robbins, stood behind this collection, as she did with all of Mike's projects. Ann Godoff at The Penguin Press steered this book from the table of contents through the index, and through at least fifteen conversations about jacket photos.

Finally, I would like to express my deepest gratitude and love to our families: our children, of course, Tom and Jack; Mike's parents, Tom and Marguerite Kelly; his sisters, Katy Kelly, Meg Rizzoli, and Nell Conroy, and his brothers-in-law, Steve Bottorff, Tony Rizzoli, and Dennis Conroy; my parents, Anita and Irwin Greenberg; my sister, Cheryl Greenberg; and brother-in-law, Dan Lloyd.

In the midst of our great sorrow, this book has brought us solace, and a connection to what we have lost.

MADELYN KELLY

ABOUT THE AUTHOR

Michael Kelly's remarkably varied career ranged from war correspondent to presidential campaign reporter to syndicated columnist to editor of three magazines (most recently the award-winning *Atlantic Monthly*). Publications he wrote for included the *New York Times,* the *New Yorker,* *GQ,* and the *New Republic.* His coverage of the Gulf War won him a National Magazine Award and an Overseas Press Award, and his 1992 book, *Martyrs' Day: Chronicle of a Small War,* won the PEN/Martha Albrand Award. While covering the Iraq War as editor at large of the *Atlantic* and a columnist for the *Washington Post,* he was killed on April 3, 2003, when the Humvee he was riding in came under fire. He was forty-six years old. He is survived by his wife and two sons.